PREFACE

ONE HEARS much of the simplicity of colonial civilization as contrasted with the complexity of modern society. In the good old days before the invention of railways, the telegraph, the radio, the automobile, before the introduction of the tractor and reaper on the farms and mass production in factories, our ancestors, so we are made to believe, cast their lives in a homely, uniform pattern, dealt only with simple, uniform problems. But if we could project ourselves back into colonial days to live even for a week or two the life of the farmer, the artisan, or the merchant, could discuss with them their personal and their public problems, we would quickly change our views. It is true that society as a whole was not so intimately interrelated as today, but it was far more variegated. Each section, each colony, each group had its own character, its differences of blood, language, religion, architecture, customs, agriculture. We may define the great principles governing the founding of American civilization, but the application of those principles is as complex as colonial society was varied.

Obviously, it would be impossible, even in the restricted field of the Middle Colonies, to treat of every phase of colonial civilization within the limits of one volume. The writer must select certain topics, which he considers especially well suited to illustrate the principles of transit and development, and concentrate his attention upon them. In the preparation of this volume chapters on the religious history of the Pennsylvania Germans, the artistic crafts of Philadelphia, the Swedes on the lower Delaware, on education, superstitions and other phases of colonial life had to be omitted because of the limitations of space. Political history has been purposely neglected, not because its rôle in early American civilization is unimportant, but because so much emphasis has already been placed upon it. The founding of civilization in the South and in New England has been deferred to future volumes.

The author has been handicapped in his work by the paucity

of scholarly monographs in the field of colonial culture, and over and over has had to dig out the facts from primary sources. He has been fortunate, however, in having the aid for limited periods of time of three research assistants, Dr. C. P. Stacey of Princeton University, Dr. C. L. Lundin of Indiana University, and Dr. N. R. Burr, Assistant State Director of the Historical Records Survey in Connecticut. He wishes to acknowledge his debt to these able young scholars, each of whom has accompanied him in many excursions into the fascinating realm of early American culture. He also extends his thanks to Mr. R. T. H. Halsey, of New Haven, for many helpful suggestions, to Mr. P. H. Waddell Smith, of Princeton, for assistance in the chapter on the Puritan in East Jersey, to Mr. Joseph S. Sickler, of Salem, N. J., for placing at his disposal photographs of colonial Salem houses, to Professor H. D. Learned, of Temple University, for the use of his father's manuscripts on the Swiss barns of Pennsylvania, to Mr. Malcolm O. Young, Reference Librarian of Princeton University, and to Miss Joan Taylor, Princeton, N. J. Grateful acknowledgment is made to the Rockefeller Foundation for generous financial aid, extended through the Council of the Humanities of Princeton University.

T. J. W.

CONTENTS

TEXT ILLUSTRATIONS

TEXT ILLUSTRATIONS

PLATES

PLATES

PLATES

THE FOUNDING OF AMERICAN CIVILIZATION

The Middle Colonies

Chapter I

THE OLD WORLD IN A NEW MOLD

THE most stupendous phenomenon of all history is the transit of European civilizations to the two American continents. For four and a half centuries Europeans have been crossing the Atlantic to establish in a new world their blood, languages, religions, political institutions, agriculture, commerce, industries, literatures, arts, customs. This movement, involving many nations and millions of men and women, has been termed the expansion of Europe, or the creation of a new Europe in America. The Indian civilizations have been overwhelmed or subordinated, and in their place have arisen great nations speaking English, Spanish, Portuguese or French, whose peoples profess the Christian religion, are partly or entirely European in blood, accept Shakespeare or Cervantes or Molière or even Tolstoy as their own.

Yet the civilizations of these nations have not duplicated those of Europe. Mexico is far from being an American Spain, Brazil is not another Portugal, French Canada has grown very far apart from France, no one would call the United States a chip of the English block.

In fact each American nation, or racial group within a nation, has its own individuality. The United States today has a closer kinship with parts of Canada than with any other part of the world, but one has only to cross the Great Lakes or the Forty-ninth parallel to note important differences. With some of our neighbors on the south, where Spanish or Portuguese culture has been superimposed upon a people still largely Indian in blood, there is a decided contrast.

So early as the American Revolution European visitors have recognized the existence of a distinctive American civilization and have tried to describe it in their memoirs. Most of them were impressed by the prevailing spirit of democracy. The boarding-house keeper, instead of bowing and scraping with European servility, treated her guests with an indifference which bordered on rudeness; there was a shocking familiarity between servant and master; the field hand, the tailor, the ferryman, the bricklayer looked you steadily in the eye, exchanged comments on the weather or on politics, and perhaps offered you a drink. It is a thing difficult for Europeans to understand, this lack of class consciousness which has done so much to mold American life and the American character. The story is told of an American lady living in England who nursed back to health through personal attention her maid who had become seriously ill. Thereupon the maid resigned her position with the remark: "No lady would do such a thing." It is the possibility of rising above one's present condition, of being recognized for what one is rather than by the class in which one was born, which has gripped millions in America and spurred them on to achievement. Not that there are no class distinctions. The American lady in England would never have invited her maid to sit at the table with her, an American minister would not invite the janitor of his church to have tea with his family. Yet the janitor might some day become a millionaire and, without resentment for the past, condescend to invite the minister to his home.

The vital phenomenon in American history has been the lifting of millions of people from the lower class into the middle class. The destitute, the unfortunate, the oppressed trooped across the Atlantic in an ever-increasing stream, and America has turned them into prosperous farmers, tradesmen, manufacturers, lawyers, doctors, skilled artisans. In certain countries society has tended to level itself down to the lower class, in the United States the process has been reversed, and the levelling has been upwards. This movement began with the founding of Jamestown, and it is still in progress. In colonial Virginia Sir William Berkeley declared in an address to the Assembly that hundreds of examples testified to the fact that no man was denied the opportunity to rise and acquire both property and honor. In New England Edward Johnson stated, two decades after the founding of Boston, that "there are many hundreds of laboring men who had not enough to bring them over, yet now worth scores, and some hundreds of pounds." As it was in the seventeenth century, so it was in the eighteenth and nineteenth. The immigrant ditch digger of yesterday is the boss today; the farm hand becomes a large land holder; the German butler sends his sons to college and makes a doctor of one, a banker of another.

It is this spectacle of continuous rise, this fermenting within the social body, this lack of class bonds which account for another American characteristic—optimism. From the earliest days the colonists sent back to their friends in the Old World glowing accounts of America—the richness of the soil, the high wages paid workers, the opportunities for trade, fishing or shipbuilding. To the German peasant his farm in the rich limestone region of southeastern Pennsylvania, his comfortable home, his great barn, his horses and cattle seemed wealth beyond one's wildest dreams. The tobacco planter of Virginia or Maryland, the ship-builder of New Hampshire or Maine, the merchant of Boston or Philadelphia, or the wheat grower of the Ohio valley considered the world a bright place indeed. To the man who had tripled his income within a few years, or doubled his land holdings, or progressed from a clerk to a rich merchant owning a fine residence, a great warehouse by the wharf and a ship and a brig or two, nothing seemed impossible.

Out of optimism grew the American nervous energy which so amazes foreigners and sometimes is so irritating. "In the streets all is hurry and bustle," said a visitor to New York about 1840, "the very carts, instead of being drawn by horses at a walking pace, are often met at a gallop, and always in a brisk trot. The whole population seen in the streets seem to enjoy this bustle, and add to it by their own rapid pace, as if . . . under the apprehension of being too late." The story is told of a New Yorker, who while taking a Japanese guest uptown by subway, rushed him from a local train into an express and from the express back to the local. "You see," he explained, after reaching the destination, "those changes saved us three minutes." "Now that we have saved them, what are we going to do with them?" was the laconic query. The American idea is to make haste while the sun shines.

In lands where the sun of opportunity is hidden under the clouds of class prejudice and restricted opportunity one may as well take his time, but here the rewards of energy, ability, hard work are boundless.

One can understand why foreigners accuse Americans of being money-mad, of having bartered off their souls to Mammon. "Big profits overshadow liberty in all its forms," says one observer, "and the exercise of intelligence is encouraged only if it fits in with the common aim." Yet no people in the world are more generous. The man who amasses millions often gives away millions. The United States is filled with colleges, libraries, hospitals, museums, scientific foundations endowed in part or wholly by private gifts. The habit of giving, even among families of moderate means, has become so established that private income is regarded in part as a trust for public use.

Nor has the pursuit of material gain prevented the American from becoming an idealist. It was idealism as well as the desire to better their condition which brought many of the early settlers to our shores. When Cotton and Winthrop led the Puritan hosts to New England it was the ideal of a Wilderness Zion which sustained them; William Penn founded his province on the ideal of religious liberty, equality and peace; the colonists in the Revolution were battling for the ideal of a government based on the consent of the governed; for a century and more the nation has held before its eyes the ideal of Jeffersonian democracy; in the World War Americans fought for the ideal of a better, a more democratic, a juster world.

The American, throughout the three centuries of his history, has been characterized by initiative, self-reliance and individualism. It is said that in the World War the American soldiers, while inferior to the Germans in discipline, were far superior in meeting sudden or unforeseen crises. The German was reared in a society where freedom of action was narrowly limited, all his life he had encountered *verboten* signs; the American still carried with him something of the spirit of the frontier. Stories were fresh in his mind of how his grandfather had built his cabin with his own hands, cleared the forest, planted his crop, played the doctor for his family, led in worship at the log church, acted as local judge, served as captain of militia. In those days the government had seemed a very remote thing, either in bringing aid and protection, or in interfering with the daily rounds of life.

It is this which engendered that spirit of lawlessness which has been the object of so much criticism both at home and abroad. Philip Fithian relates the story of two travellers who apprehended a murderer in the wilderness, and being unable to find either police officer or jail, assumed the rôle of jury, judge and executioner, in trying, condemning and hanging him.[1] From taking the law into one's hands when the law could not operate, it was but a step to taking the law into one's hands when it did not operate as one judged it should. The colonists often thought it quite proper to break the Navigation Acts if one could keep out of the Admiralty courts, millions in the North openly avowed their defiance of the Fugitive Slave Law of 1850, the Volstead Act became a kind of bad joke.

The American's struggle to win the continent for civilization and secure material prosperity for himself has made him resourceful, adaptable and practical. The early colonist often fashioned his own utensils—buckets, firkins, spoons, trays—whittling them out laboriously with his knife; he converted gourd shells into dippers, crooked saplings into sled runners, oak logs into salt mortars.[2] The frontiersman adapted to his own uses the Indian methods of trapping and hunting, of signalling with smoke columns, of cooking food, of dressing skins; he took over the Indian canoe, snow-shoe, and moccasin. The resourcefulness which conquered the wilderness proved invaluable in building up the vast industrial and agricultural systems of the United States. The Americans became a nation of inventors. "Americans invented the steamboat, the cotton-gin, the sewing-machine, the telephone, the typewriter, the talking-machine, the incandescent lamp, the linotype, and the single-type composing machine, the motion-picture machine, the airplane, vulcanization of rubber, modern agricultural machinery, modern boot-making machinery."[3]

[1]Albion and Dodson, *Philip Vickers Fithian: Journal*, p. 28.
[2]H. E. Nourse, *History of Harvard, Mass.*, p. 27.
[3]J. Ellis Barker, *America's Secret.*

Americans have been reproached for their failure to create a great national literature, or a national art, or national music. "Even the humblest European sees in art an aristocratic symbol of his own personality," says André Siegfried, "and modern America has no national art and does not even feel the need of one." America has produced no Beethoven, no Raphael, no Rodin, no Shakespeare, he thinks, because the genius of the people has been diverted wholly to making profits.

One wonders, however, whether this is the real explanation. It is true that Americans have been busy conquering a vast continent for civilization, clearing away the forest, making homes, planting crops, laying down railways and highways, building great cities, endowing schools, colleges, hospitals, museums. The task before them has been material rather than spiritual, and that task they have done well. But a nation cannot give voice to its soul until the nation itself has attained spiritual independence and unity. For over a century and a half America was part of the British Empire and looked to London for direction in cultural as well as governmental and economic matters. And though she declared her political independence in 1776 and at least partial economic independence at the time of the War of 1812, cultural independence has not yet been fully attained.

Moreover, the American people are a very young people indeed. In colonial times the only bond between province and province, or section and section, was the common allegiance to England, and when this was dissolved the somewhat closer tie of the national government. But a true sense of nationalism came only in the nineteenth century, and even then it was weakened by the contrasting interests and life of North and South, or East and West. Today the marvels of communication—the railway, the automobile, the radio, the telephone, the airplane—together with standardized industry, farming and education are working fast to unite the people, but they have still to overcome the vast differences in national origin, in traditions, in economic interest. When the American people have been a people as long as have the French or the English they will no doubt have produced their Molière or their Shakespeare.

We need not be disconcerted at Sydney Smith's sneering remark that "others claim honor because of things done by a long line of ancestors; an American glories in the achievements of a distant posterity." In the years since this statement was made many of the prophecies which he derided have been fulfilled. "Who in the four quarters of the globe reads an American book?" he asked. "What new substances have their chemists discovered? Who eats from American plates? . . . or sleeps on American blankets?" Today this brings a smile. Before the passing of many decades the reproach that America has no national art, music or literature may seem equally amusing.

In fact, few will deny today that there is an American literature. It is true that the New England group—Bryant, Longfellow, Whittier, Holmes—who once seemed the harbingers of a great literary epoch, whose books flooded the country and whose portraits adorned the walls of many an humble home, are receding into the background. They were too much under the influence of the Old World to become the interpreters of American life. Abroad Cooper and Sinclair Lewis are widely read, one as the portrayer of life on the early frontier, the other as the critic of the America of today, but in the United States the former has become archaic, the latter has yet to stand the test of time. Yet a country which has produced Emerson, Whitman, Mark Twain cannot be said to lack interpreters.

The case for music is not so clear. Foreign composers, attracted to this country by the opera or the concert stage, have sought to find in the songs of Stephen C. Foster, or in the Negro spirituals the national music of America, but their efforts have not been very convincing. Until the melting-pot has fused more closely the diverse racial units of the population, it is probable that the soul of the nation will not find its expression in song. Some of the nations which have contributed heavily to the American stock themselves have produced no great musical literature, it could not be expected that the emigrants they have sent to this country should do so; other groups cling to the music of their homelands, the Italians continuing to sing Italian songs, the Germans German songs.

In architecture individuality asserted itself so early as the seventeenth century, not in a uniform colonial style, but in regional styles—the New England style, the Dutch colonial, the Chesapeake Bay style. These in turn gave way to the Georgian styles of New England, of Philadelphia, of Maryland, of Virginia, of Charleston, each different from the other and different from the English Georgian. In the nineteenth century the attempt was made several times to create a uniform American architecture, based on European precedents but modified to meet the needs and the spirit of America, but the results were far from satisfactory. So late as the early years of the twentieth century many were so discouraged at the ugliness of the structures of the preceding decades that they abandoned hope of a real American architecture and began to borrow again from Europe. Princeton University, turning its back upon charming old Nassau Hall with its simple Georgian dignity, began to model all her new buildings upon the English Gothic style.

Then came the sky-scraper. As the huge structures of steel and stone reared their heads in the business sections of New York and Chicago the architects looked on in horror, for in all history they found no precedent for them. When the Woolworth Building was erected, that famous temple of nickels and dimes, the attempt was made to conceal its proportions under a Gothic façade. But the effect is not pleasing, for no amount of exterior decoration can transform a sky-scraper into a medieval cathedral. Then the city of New York, in 1916, by pure accident gave to business architecture a new direction by requiring builders to "step back" their structures in the interest of light and air. The resulting "pyramidal" architecture, with its vast proportions, its glittering turrets, its use of straight lines, is truly expressive of the power, the energy, the hugeness of modern America. It is something born of America, breathing the very spirit of America. In 1665 New York was merely a little Amsterdam, in 1785 it was a miniature London, today it is itself, unique among the cities of the world. And not only has it thrown off its architectural dependence, but it is in turn affecting the architecture of European cities. An American several years ago stood with a distinguished English architect gazing at the noble dome of St. Paul's. "I suppose Sir Christopher Wren's work has a profound influence on modern British architecture?" he remarked. "Listen," replied the Englishman, "do you really want to know the greatest influence in British architecture today? Well, it's the United States of America."

The spirit of America is well depicted by the lives of its leaders in different periods. Benjamin Franklin has been described as the first typical American. Born and reared in New England, but an adopted son of Pennsylvania, he avoided the sectionalism in which most colonials were steeped. Franklin was entirely a self-made man, rising in the world by his industry, shrewdness, business ability and thrift, yet possessing an intellectual curiosity which led him into philosophy, science and invention, and won for him a place among the savants of the world. His versatility was typical. Now we find him inventing a stove, now organizing the militia, now founding a college, now drawing up a plan of union for the colonies, now investigating the nature of lightning. In France, when pictured by the intelligentsia as the simple, rustic representative of the American Utopia, he played the part admirably to the great advantage of his diplomatic mission. The combination that was Franklin could have been produced by no other country.

It was Thomas Jefferson who typified the spirit of American democracy. His father a middle-class Virginia farmer, his mother of an aristocratic family, Jefferson combined the polish of the Southern gentleman with a passionate love of democracy. He not only wrote into the Declaration of Independence the statement that all men are born free and equal, but all his life he strove to make them free and equal. Privilege in any form found him an implacable enemy, and in his old age he expressed the wish that posterity should remember him for his work for political freedom, religious freedom and educational freedom. Not less versatile than Franklin, he found diversion from the cares of public life in botany, archæology, mathematics, scientific agriculture. He was one of the nation's greatest architects. Jefferson glorified the individual, argued for his ability to manage his own affairs, and defended him against those who would dictate to him in the matters of government and religion. Not only was he the typical American democrat, he made American democracy Jeffersonian.

Andrew Jackson was the representative of the new nationalism which swept the country in the decade or two following the War of 1812 and of the new democracy of the West. Born of poor parents, a man of limited education, prosperous through speculation and horse-trading, fond of wrestling and fighting, a deadly hater and a loyal friend, a lifelong enemy of the Indian, honest, open-hearted, patriotic, at times wearing soiled clothes, his mouth usually full of chewing-tobacco, a student of the Bible and conversant with Watts's hymns, he was typical of the vast new America west of the Appalachians. As President he fought for the rights of the common man with a directness and naïveness, a disregard of consequences which amazed and confounded his enemies. So long as he lived Old Hickory was the idol of the people, who looked upon him as the plain, honest, patriotic man they liked to think typical of themselves.

The civilization of the United States has been formed by the interplay of four great forces—the transit of European civilizations to North America, the effect of American conditions upon those civilizations, the continued intercourse of America with Europe, and the mingling of racial, religious and regional groups, the so-called melting-pot.

The history of the United States leads back first of all to England—to Westminster Hall, Westminster Abbey, Oxford and Cambridge, to the East Anglican village, to the fishing towns of Devon and Somerset, to the ports of London and Bristol. We have inherited the English language, English political institutions, English common law, English literature, English respect for individual rights; millions of Americans pride themselves on their English ancestry, English traditions constitute still a force to be reckoned with.

Yet the United States is by no means entirely English in inheritance. Even in the period when they were part of the British Empire the people were of mixed origin, the English of New England touching elbows on the west with the Dutch of the Hudson valley, Long Island and New Jersey; the Pennsylvania Quakers facing a group of Swedes, Finns and Dutch on one side and Welsh, Germans and Swiss on the other; the great frontier region from the forks of the Susquehanna to Georgia being predominantly Scotch-Irish, with groups of English, Germans and Scotch Highlanders among them; here and there little bands of Huguenots struggling to maintain their identity and their French culture. With the nineteenth century came new waves of migration of such vast proportions as to threaten seriously English supremacy in American civilization—Irishmen, driven from their native land by poverty and famine, frugal Germans seeking to win new homes in the vast agricultural reaches of the West, Scandinavians, Italians, Poles, Greeks, Russians.

If we are to understand the American inheritance it will not suffice to study the London Company, or the Puritan movement in England which resulted in the Great Exodus, to know the religious, cultural and economic background of the English who came to America. We must go back also to bustling Amsterdam, with its quaint, narrow houses, its canals, its warehouses, its prosperous merchants and bankers, its skilled artisans; we must become acquainted with the Rhine Palatinate, its rich soil, its climate, its peaceful, hard-working people, the tragic story of its hardships and woes; we must delve into the history of the Huguenots, their religion and their culture, so that we may evaluate aright their contributions to America; we must take our studies to Belfast, to Dublin, to Moscow, to Naples, to Warsaw.

Historians have been too prone to neglect the factor of inheritance in interpreting the United States, especially the multiple inheritance which makes it the child, not of England, but of Europe. It is true that much has been done in recent years to follow the threads which lead back to England. George L. Beer has depicted the American colonies as parts of the great British Empire, Herbert L. Osgood and Charles M. Andrews have given many years of study to their political English background, the religious inheritance of Puritans and Quakers has been investigated, in M. S. Briggs's *The Homes of the Pilgrim Fathers in England and America* we have at least a beginning of investigation of the transit of architecture.

But for other races the work has been neglected or is pathetically inadequate. Books on the Scotch-Irish, Germans, Irish, the Huguenots seem concerned chiefly with making extravagant claims, with enumerating the great men their groups have produced and pointing out how important have been their contributions to government, education, science, etc. The story is told of the Irishman who was found indulging in melancholy reflection on an October 12, and when questioned as to his sadness replied: "I was just thinking what a pity it is that a fine country like America was discovered by an Italian Dago." Some of our racial historians have not let this consideration disturb them; they simply try to prove that America was not discovered by Columbus. The things we should like to know are only too often omitted. What was life like in the German agricultural village? In what kind of homes did the Swiss peasants live? What was the character of the peasant art of the Rhine Palatinate? What were the cultural influences in Ulster? Whence came the octagonal churches of Long Island and northern New Jersey? What have been the inheritances in religion, education, art, government, of the vast numbers of Swedes, or Russians, or Italians who for decades poured through Ellis Island to become bone of our bone, flesh of our flesh?

The transit of civilization is made more complex by the religious, social or economic differences of the migrating groups, or within the migrating groups. Could a complete cross-section of English life—nobility, squirearchy, yeomen, artisans, laborers, fishermen, sailors; Anglicans, Congregationalists, Presbyterians, Independents, Roman Catholics, Quakers—have been transplanted in New England or in Virginia, colonial society would have followed more closely the English pattern. But the migrations were never of this character. In some cases one finds the gathering of persons of one religious faith—perhaps Puritans, perhaps Quakers, perhaps Roman Catholics—to form Puritan, or Quaker, or Roman Catholic colonies in America. Colonial Massachusetts was almost entirely English, but it was far from reproducing England in its entirety. Pennsylvania in the first decades of its history was hardly less English than Virginia, yet in spirit, religion, and life it presented a decided contrast to the Old Dominion. Quakerism, though born in and of England, was but a minor factor in English society; in Pennsylvania it was a pervading and powerful force.

In all of the major national groups it was the poor man rather than the rich who migrated, the day laborer, the peasant, the artisan and his apprentice, not the nobleman, the great merchant, the bishop or the squire. Why should one in the higher walks of life turn his back on his manor house with its gardens, lake and hunting park, or his home in the Strand or Drury Lane, or the joys of Court life for the isolation of a Virginia plantation or the simplicity of a mercantile town in the colonies? It was the chance to get ahead, to exchange poverty, rags and hunger for comfort and plenty which uprooted millions from their fatherlands to make the great adventure in the New World. Even to Virginia, despite the so-called Cavalier migration at the time of the English Civil War, there came practically no titled immigrants save the British governors. From time to time religious persecution or political upheavals or exceptional opportunities for acquiring wealth brought over persons of the middle class, or in rare cases of the aristocracy, but all in all the structure of America was reared by the poor and the downtrodden of Europe.

Each of the immigrant groups brought its distinctive culture and clung to it stubbornly, often desperately. The Englishman who came to Maryland or to Connecticut expected to remain an Englishman, expected his grandsons and great-grandsons to be Englishmen. The German peasant fleeing to Pennsylvania, although he realized that he must transfer his allegiance to the English government, had no intention of surrendering his tongue, religion, art, customs, costume, even his superstitions. The Dutch made New Amsterdam a miniature replica of old Amsterdam; the little handful of Swedes and Finns on the lower Delaware clung to the Swedish language for a century and a half; the Virginia planters spoke English "without idiom or tone" a century after the founding of Jamestown.

In the American civilization of today inheritance is still a factor of major importance. Despite the great gulf which separates Carter Glass from Captain Newport or Captain John Smith, or President Conant from John Harvard, our roots go down deep into the soil of the England of Shakespeare's day. We speak Shakespeare's language, although with many changes of words, spelling and intonation which would have perplexed and perhaps offended the great dramatist. Time works many changes with language. As a young man I once had a conversation with an old gentleman of over ninety, a friend of Thomas Jefferson, and though we had been born and reared within a few miles of each other I had some difficulty in understanding what he said. If his pronunciation and intonation were like those of Jefferson, and Jefferson were here today to give us a "fire-side chat" over the radio, we might need the services of an interpreter.

The English of America and the English of England, despite many differences, are more like each other than either is like the English of Elizabethan times. London was for centuries, perhaps still is, the cultural center of the English-speaking world, and her dictates in the matter of language long had almost the force of law. American writers looked to Addison or Steele or Johnson for their models, the Philadelphia merchant or the Maryland planter boasted that his language was free of provincialisms. In recent years America has been less sensitive to the dictates of London, and in turn is exerting a noticeable influence upon England. More and more the English employ "Americanisms" in their daily conversation. I was rather surprised to have a young master of a famous English school turn to me with the query: "Have you ever seen any one bumped off?" But the English are quicker to take up American slang than to accept words for which they have their own equivalent—drug store, street car, flashlight, cooky, etc. Whether the speech of the two nations will drift farther and farther apart until they become entirely different time alone can tell.

One could ask no better illustration of the power of inheritance than the survival of German in Pennsylvania. Pennsylvania German, a medley of south German and Swiss dialects, has had to battle for over two centuries against the prevailing English of America. Even in colonial times when a German settler purchased a tract of land the deed was made out in English; when he was forced into court with a lawsuit the complaint was in English; when his son went to school he might have to read English books; if he were elected to the Assembly he would have to debate in English. English words and expressions began to creep into his dialect so that he found himself talking about a fens, a zapling, fram haus, seyder press, mortgatsche, bille-sal.

By 1783 his speech had become so corrupted as to excite the scorn of the traveller Schoepf. "The language which our German people make use of is a miserable, broken, fustian salmagundi of English and German. . . . People come over from Germany forget their mother tongue in part while seeking in vain to learn the new speech. . . . The children . . . grow accustomed to English in the streets, their parents speak to them in one language and they answer in another. . . . If the necessary word does not occur to the memory the next best English one is at once substituted. . . . Even among themselves the Germans speak at times bad German, at times worse English."

But the Germans had already rallied under the leadership of Christopher Saur to the defense of their language. Banding together in the Deutsche Gesellschaft and the Mosheimische Gesellschaft, they vowed to read it, think it, speak it; books were imported from Germany and others printed in German by local presses; German newspapers were published at Philadelphia, Germantown, Lancaster and Reading; parents insisted that instruction in the schools be in German. These efforts were so successful that Pennsylvania German has persisted to the present day, and is still often used in conversation, in business and the pulpit.

Yet the stubbornness with which the various groups battled to maintain the culture of their fatherlands could not prevent local conditions, the second of our four great forces in the shaping of American civilization, from effecting far-reaching changes. The moment Englishmen set foot on the Jamestown peninsula or the sandy shores of Cape Cod Bay, they were subjected to forces which were to convert them or their children into Americans. The soil under their feet, the rivers which bore their ships, the interminable forests, the many safe harbors, the heat of summer and the cold of winter, all were to influence their life and leave a deep imprint on their character. Just when the planter on the James or the York ceased to be an Englishman and became a Virginian, or the Berks County farmer ceased to be a German and became a Pennsylvanian it is impossible to say. The process was a matter of decades, perhaps of centuries, but it was nonetheless irresistible.

The influence of soil in shaping the life of the immigrants can hardly be exaggerated. In Virginia and Maryland it was the all-important factor. The leaders of the Virginia Company of London had a very clear conception of what the industrial life of their colony was to be. Since England was at that time dependent upon foreign countries for most of its ship-stores, timber, potash, iron and glass, Virginia was to devote itself to the production of these commodities. The forests were not to be sacrificed to make way for fields of grain or tobacco, but were to constitute the main natural resource of the colony, upon which her economic life was to be based. As for the people, they were to be tar-burners, potash-makers, glass-makers, iron smelters, with perhaps a few farmers and a few traders.

But though the London Company planned, it was the soil of Virginia which actually decided. West Indian tobacco had found its way into England and won devotees among the upper classes, so that a market was at hand could the plant be cultivated in Virginia. It was John Rolfe, the man who later won the heart and the hand of the Indian princess Pocahontas, who discovered that the Virginia leaf could be so cured as to make it palatable to the English taste. After a shipload had been sent to England and sold at a huge profit, the people abandoned all idea of producing forest commodities and devoted themselves with enthusiasm to the Indian weed. Tobacco became the very foundation of the economic and social structure of the colony, making the Virginians planters instead of merchants or artisans, determining the system of labor, shaping the character of immigration, preventing the development of towns and cities, influencing architecture, altering the structure of the Church.

In New England, where most of the soil is not very fertile,

agriculture was very different. The Puritan farmer had to make up by hard work and intelligence for nature's niggardliness, clearing the glacial boulders from his fields and tilling them with his own hands or the hands of his sons, raising his own fruit and vegetables, tending his own cattle, working on the long winter evenings to repair plow or utensils or table or perhaps to spin and weave. He had no great staple comparable to tobacco which he could send to England in exchange for clothing, farm implements and other manufactured goods, and so was forced to rely chiefly upon his own resources.

Rivers have been hardly less important than soil in shaping the character of American civilization. The first century of our history may very aptly be termed the deep-water period, for during that time the settlements never advanced more than a few miles from water navigable for ocean-going vessels. The frontier line might ascend far inland to embrace the lower reaches of the Hudson, the Delaware or the James, but it always came back to hug the coast where such natural highways were lacking. The colonists were so dependent upon the Europe whence they had come and of which they considered themselves a distant outpost, that they dared not cut themselves off from ready communication. The vast American continent stretching away to the west remained for them a land of mystery, and the first decade of the eighteenth century had passed when Governor Alexander Spotswood, of Virginia, led his Knights of the Golden Horseshoe on their expedition of discovery to the summits of the Blue Ridge.

For Virginia and Maryland the Chesapeake Bay was a great highway, with the Potomac, Rappahannock, York, and James intersecting roads, and the innumerable creeks the lanes and alleys. The great English fleets which came over each year, after passing through the capes, lost themselves in this network of waterways to visit the private wharves of the planters, where they discharged their English goods and took on cargoes of tobacco. In New Netherland the Dutch master could load up his vessel with furs at Albany and sail with them direct for the wharves of the West India Company at Amsterdam. The Charleston rice planter might import his coach from London, the New Amsterdam merchant might decorate his mantel with tiles from Holland, William Penn furnished his country home near Philadelphia with English Turkey-work chairs.

With the dawn of the eighteenth century there came a new period which we may call the shallow-water period. The colonists, like an infant learning to walk alone, now cautiously, timorously began to move away from deep water and so to relinquish in part direct touch with the outer world. Settlements pushed up the James above the site of Richmond, up the shallow reaches of the Susquehanna, up the Delaware above the Trenton rapids, up the Raritan, the Passaic, the Mohawk. The rivers and creeks remained the chief highways of commerce, but the character of navigation was greatly changed. Goods were brought down to deep water on rafts, or in canoes lashed together, or on flat-bottomed boats of the Durham type, and propelled sometimes by oars, sometimes by poles, occasionally by sails. At the fall line inland ports developed—Petersburg, Richmond, Fredericksburg, Trenton, New Brunswick—where goods were transferred to ocean-going vessels. In this way the frontier line was pushed back to the foot of the Appalachian Mountains, and in places beyond, before the end of the colonial period, and territory occupied far greater than the fringe held during the deep-water period. It was the beginning of the western advance which was to stop only at the Pacific.

Life in the shallow-water or Piedmont sections differed from life in the tidewater region because of the greater isolation. Since it was a matter of such great difficulty to bring a chest of drawers, or a plow, or a box of hardware up the Delaware to Easton, the people of the Lehigh valley were forced to rely in large part on their own resources. The Piedmont settler was more isolated, more self-reliant, more independent. The colonist at Jamestown, however great his hardships, might always hope to see an English vessel coming up the James with supplies; the settler under the shadow of the Blue Ridge knew that he must rely almost entirely on his own industry, skill, resourcefulness, bravery. And in proportion as he was cut off from England he became less an Englishman, more an American.

The high cost of labor in America has from the very beginning had a profound influence on the life of the people. George Alsop, in urging the impoverished English laborers to come to Maryland, declared that after working out their passage money they could live there "plenteously well." The immigrants of later times, as soon as they set foot on American soil, expressed wonder at the ease with which one could earn a good living. "We see no misery, no disgusting army of paupers, not even beggars," says Welby, while Henry B. Fearson, who came over in 1819, testified that the American laborers were "more erect in their posture, less care-worn," than those of Europe. An Irish machine-worker, after three weeks in this country, managed to save enough to buy a cow. "How long would you have had to labor in Ireland to buy a cow?" his employer asked. "My wife and I have been calculating that and find that it would have taken exactly one year and ten weeks."

In the South the high cost of labor played an important part in shaping the structure of society. It was soon discovered that for the production of tobacco many hands were needed. So the planters turned to the poor of England, bringing in under terms of indenture many thousands of men and women. When the indentured worker had completed his four or five years of service he became free and often acquired land of his own. It was this which covered Virginia and Maryland with small plantations and built up a prosperous, self-respecting, intelligent middle class.

Instead of recognizing high labor costs as a Heaven-sent blessing, the planters, abetted by England, sought to bring them down by importing swarms of Negro slaves. The farmer who did his own work, having now to compete with cheap slave labor, received very little for his crop and so was faced with ruin. Those who had the means to purchase a slave or two saved themselves, the others had the alternative of migrating to one of the other colonies or of sinking into poverty. The South fell largely under the control of an aristocracy of large slave-holders, backed by a far more numerous group of small slave-holders, while the "poor white trash" who owned no slaves were kept in a condition of economic and political dependence. There is evidence of a class of skilled mechanics—gunsmiths, shipwrights, saddlers, cabinet-makers, silversmiths—but they constituted a very small fraction of the white population.

North of Mason and Dixon's Line conditions were very different. Slave labor was not suited to the comparatively intensive agriculture of the North, its fishing industry, its shipbuilding or its commerce. The Northern worker, be he small farmer, sailor, cooper, blacksmith, because of his substantial income occupied an enviable position in society. The selectmen of a New England town were often made up of a medley of husbandmen, seamen, artisans and fishermen. It was men of this stamp who constituted the backbone of society, a real democracy of labor.

Perhaps the most serious threat to equal rights in the American colonies was the attempt to establish institutions based on the feudal system. The Maryland manor and the New York patroonship, with their leet courts and vexatious dues ran directly counter to the American spirit of self-reliance and independence. But there was no place for such a system in a land where the rewards of free labor were so great. Why should one remain a tenant when it was easy to earn a living as a freeman? As for John Locke's vision of a nobility on the one hand, and a peasantry on the other, expressed in the Fundamental Constitutions, it faded before the fact that the people could not be kept in economic bondage when they could sell their labor almost at their own figure.

The high cost of labor was the result originally of a superabundance of natural resources and a paucity of hands to develop them. It was cheap land most of all which in the colonial and early national periods brought hundreds of thousands to our shores. But the effect upon industry has been equally far-reaching. In the second half of the nineteenth century the factory absorbed its full share of immigrant workers. And the American industrial system, which has excited the wonder of the world, is based upon labor-saving machinery, which in turn grew out of the high cost of labor. Since the day when Samuel Slater came to America to teach us how to duplicate the machinery of the English cotton mills, we have clutched at any device which would save a day's wages.

Today standardization has been carried so far that the American factory has been likened to a great robot, which performs astonishing tasks with marvelous speed and with a minimum of direction from the workers. In the crude iron and steel industry the average output per man was 23.1 tons in 1860, in 1925 it mounted to 286 tons; in 1849 the average industrial worker turned out annually goods worth $1066, the men on the job today turn out goods worth $7500. The use of labor-saving machinery, instead of reducing the demand for labor and lowering wages as might have been expected, has had an opposite effect. By cheapening the cost of production and making low prices possible, it has so stimulated buying that both wages and jobs have multiplied. In 1849 when the average worker received $247 a year there were 957,000 jobs; in 1927 when his wages were $1310 there were more than 8,000,000 jobs.

There is every reason to hope that the people's chief asset, the labor of their two hands, will continue in the future to become more and more valuable. The invention and adoption of labor-saving machinery is proceeding today at an ever-quickening pace, but unless organized labor, or organized business, or the government interfere to prevent the passing on of lower production costs to the public in lower prices, increased demand will offset any immediate diminution in the number of jobs. And with new inventions—the so-called electric eye, television, air-conditioning, synthetic rubber, prefabricated houses, steep-flight airplanes, and many others—promising to revolutionize old industries or to create new ones, the outlook for labor seems as bright as ever. It was America which first brought a new dignity to labor, a new standard of living for laborers; it will be America which leads the way to still higher things in the future.

The influence of the New World in transforming Europeans into Americans would have been even stronger had the colonies been cut off from communication with the mother countries. But the colonists and their descendants have by no means been completely isolated. As we have seen, in their first century the settlers had their eyes turned, not on the vast continent stretching away to the west, but eastward toward Europe. The Atlantic ocean was not only a barrier between them and their old life, it was also a convenient means of communication, a highway of commerce. The colonists looked to Europe, especially to England, for their cultural inspiration, for leadership in literature, art, science, the artistic crafts, architecture. As English civilization developed, the colonies endeavored to keep step.

The influence of the mother country upon the life and thought of the colonies was determined in part by the direction and extent of commerce. The staple crop colony which sent over to England its tobacco or rice or sugar, received in return, not only farm implements, cloth, furniture, but books, gazettes, letters. The colony which had little or nothing to send the mother country, had a larger degree of cultural as well as economic independence. Thus the foreign groups, the Dutch of New York and New Jersey, the Swedes and Finns of the lower Delaware, the Germans and Swiss of Pennsylvania found it difficult to keep step with cultural changes in Holland, Sweden, Germany or Switzerland because of the restrictions on colonial commerce with foreign nations.

In New England the influence of the mother country was weakened by the failure of the colonists to find any great staple commodity which England needed and could import in large quantities. New England industry paralleled rather than complemented the industry of the mother country. With both offering farm products, fish and ships for sale, there was little reason for exchange. In the eighteenth century England began taking naval stores from the forests of New England in considerable quantities, but this export never assumed major proportions. It was to the West Indian ports not to Great Britain that the Yankee master usually headed his vessel. Thus New England economic life, since it was so similar to that of the mother country, tended to preserve the original English inheritance, while it weakened the tie between the two peoples, made it more difficult for the Bostonian to keep step with developments in England.

The situation in the tobacco colonies was in direct contrast. As the life on the plantation weakened the tie with England, so the constant intercourse with London renewed and strengthened it. Despite the three thousand miles of water between the planter and the old country, he was reminded of it at every turn—by the clothes on his back, the furniture in his home, the pewter utensils of his kitchen and the silver of his dining room, the books in his library, the saddle on his horse, the hinges on his doors, the very wig on his head. He hailed with joy the arrival of the English merchant ship at his wharf, brought the master to his table and listened eagerly to the latest gossip of the coffee houses or of the quarrels of King and Commons. "Our lives are uniform . . . till the seasons bring in the ships," wrote William Byrd II, "then we tear open the letters they bring us from our friends as eagerly as a greedy heir tears open a rich father's will." It is this which explains why visitors could find "men leading secluded lives in the woods of Virginia perfectly *au fait* as to the literary, dramatic and personal gossip of London."

Hardly less important than commerce in binding the colonies to the mother countries was immigration. The newcomers were carriers of new European ideas, were instructors in the latest developments in every line of endeavor. The builder brought the current styles in residences and churches, the cabinet-maker the latest word from Chippendale or the Adam brothers, the minister, fresh from the theological school, kept the church in touch with the old organization and did much to prevent the development of independent tenets or practices. When a Virginia planter wished to build a house, he sometimes sent to England for his carpenters and bricklayers or even his architect. The drying up of the tide of migration from England to Virginia and Maryland in the early years of the eighteenth century as a result of the large importations of Negro slaves, was an important factor in the development of an independent culture. The planters could no longer benefit from the information formerly brought them by the indentured workers, some of whom were men of wide practical knowledge and technical skill.

For the Germans and Swiss of Pennsylvania and Virginia the stream of immigration which poured in during the eighteenth century was vital in the struggle to keep in touch with the fatherlands, and in renewing their cultural inheritances. There were fresh impulses to architecture, to cabinet-making, to the mechanical arts, to religion, to education. "Baron" Stiegel, the celebrated glass and stove maker, was a late comer. On the other hand, the falling off of migration from Holland to New York after the English conquest made the struggle of the Dutch population to maintain their national culture almost hopeless.

The severing of the ties which bound America to Europe has been a matter of centuries, indeed is still far from complete. The movement for independence in religion came early. Not only did thousands migrate to America for the sake of religious freedom, but the conditions they encountered tended to widen the breach with the mother countries. The Puritans of New England gradually drew away from the Puritans of England. The life of the Virginia Anglicans made it impossible for them to conform fully to the regulations and tenets of the English Church and before the end of the colonial period they had become a distinct religious group. The Dutch Reformed Church in New York and New Jersey desired ardently to remain under the direction of the Classis of Amsterdam, but the necessity of making changes to meet distinctly American conditions made the tie weaker and weaker.

Political independence also began early and culminated early. The first step towards independence was taken at Jamestown with the establishing of the Assembly in 1619, the last by the Declaration of July 4, 1776. Had the colonies been merely an extended England, had the Londoner who settled in Philadelphia remained as much an Englishman as though he had gone only to Cornwall or Devon, had the interests of Virginia and Massachusetts been identical with those of the mother country, there would have been no desire for independence. But as each colony developed its own individuality and separate interests, the people through the Assembly wrung from the English governors an ever-increasing autonomy, until at the accession of George III they were in local affairs almost independent. "The last cause of this disobedient spirit in the colonies . . . is deep in the natural constitution of things," said Edmund Burke. "Three thousand miles of water lie between you and them. . . . Nothing more happens to you than does to all nations who have extended empire; and it happens in all the forms in which empire can be thrown."

It was in economic matters that America exerted the most immediate and powerful influence, and that England insisted upon the most rigorous control. The Navigation Acts were designed to make the British Empire a compact economic unit in which England should be the sun and the colonies the planets bound to it and dependent on it for life. The colonies were to produce the goods needed by England and in return receive English manufactured goods, and so contribute to the prosperity and strength of the empire and of themselves as parts of the empire. But the colonies, because of conditions of soil, or labor, or location from the first could not be fitted into this system. Virginia and Maryland insisted on raising tobacco which England did not want; New England was even more of a disappointment, competing with rather than assisting English industry. The Middle Colonies, finding their soil suited to the production of wheat, which England did not need, found their best customers in the West Indies.

Yet the influence of the Navigation Acts on American economic life was profound. Trading with foreign nations was largely prohibited, England became the distributing center for the great Chesapeake Bay tobacco crop, large quantities of English manufactured goods found their way into the American market. Nor did political independence effect any important change save the exclusion of American vessels from the trade of the British West Indies. A degree of economic independence came only with the Embargo, the War of 1812, and the protective tariffs which followed. Even then the United States was far from supplying all her own needs, and for several more decades continued to look to England for vast quantities of manufactured goods. Today perhaps no country is more self-contained, less dependent upon the outside world for food, coal, iron, oil and other resources vital to modern life.

However important to American civilization have been its European inheritances, the effect of American conditions upon those inheritances and the contact of America with Europe, the story is incomplete until we shall have considered the melting-pot. Even in the colonial period the process of fusing different races, different languages, different religions, different architectures, different arts was in full swing. A Dutchman living on the Hudson might move to the Raritan and there marry a Scotch girl; their son might wed a New Englander from nearby Morristown, their daughter a German from Hunterdon County. In the Shenandoah valley Scotch-Irish, Germans and settlers from eastern Virginia, living side by side, began the slow process of merging into a homogeneous population.

The smaller groups had to struggle desperately and usually hopelessly to save themselves from being completely swallowed by the surrounding populations. The Swedes and Finns of the lower Delaware have disappeared, leaving only a few family names, a few traditions and perhaps the frontier log cabin. The Huguenots, scattered in small congregations or as individuals in various colonies, merged with the English and other groups after contributing many distinguished men out of proportion to their numbers, and adding a leaven of French polish to colonial life. The Dutch on the Hudson held out stubbornly during the colonial period, but were finally submerged by the influx of other peoples following the opening of the Erie Canal and the vast growth of New York commerce. But we are reminded of our debt to Holland by such names as Roosevelt, Van Dyke and Van Buren, of our debt to France by the memorials left us by Latrobe and L'Enfant.

The Germans and Swiss of Pennsylvania, constituting a large group concentrated in a restricted area, have had a fair degree of success in resisting the melting-pot. Despite many marriages with other nationalities, despite the gradual relinquishing of German architecture, art and customs, they still constitute a distinct group, with their own religious denominations, traditions, and language. When one enters Pennsylvania German land he is conscious of a foreign flavor, a reminder of Europe in the great barns, the strange dialect, sometimes in the costumes of the people. Two centuries and more have not sufficed to melt the Germans of this region into the American population, and one is inclined to predict that after the lapse of another two centuries the Teuton atmosphere will still linger around the old farms of Berks and Lancaster.

At the end of the colonial period the country was still overwhelmingly English, but a change came with the nineteenth century. With the improvements in navigation—the advent of the clipper and the steamer—together with the opening of new agricultural areas by the canal and the railway, and the increased demand for workers in the factories, millions of foreigners flocked in. In 1930 the number of residents in the United States of foreign birth or with one or both parents foreign born was 38,727,593; nearly seven millions from Germany, four and a half millions from Italy, three and a third millions from Poland, three millions from the Irish Free State, two and a half millions from England, three and a third millions from Canada, two millions seven hundred thousand from Russia, three millions from the Scandinavian countries.

The task before the melting-pot is indeed tremendous. America is busily at work turning these foreign millions into Americans. They learn the English language, go to American schools, become acquainted with American political institutions, catch the spirit of the United States. But experience teaches us that they will give as well as receive, will contribute their share to the American civilization of the future. Already they have exerted a powerful influence upon our political thinking, our foreign relations, our literature and art. And who can tell what the ultimate result will be, just what bit of Russian tradition will weave itself into our life, just what German music, or Irish wit, or Italian art, or Scandinavian dialect will become a column in the American temple?

It is obvious that the process of assimilation will be more rapid in the future than in the past. With the automobile, the railway, the airplane, the radio the vast distances of the United States are fast vanishing, and isolation for any group becomes more difficult. The Swede of Minnesota is closer today to New York City than was the eighteenth-century German of Bethlehem; the French-Canadian of Maine or the Polish worker in a Pennsylvania coal mine may listen to the voice of the President over the radio. The United States is becoming rapidly centralized in government and economic life, the tendency is towards standardization, whether in factory, education, social life, or even in thought. The foreign citizen is more readily caught up by the vast social machine and made over and standardized. The fire under the melting-pot is hotter than in former days, perhaps even the vast and heterogeneous mass of humanity in the American cauldron cannot for many generations withstand its operation.

In the interplay of forces which has created American civilization it is not possible to say which has been the most important. European inheritance, local conditions, continued intercourse with Europe and the melting-pot all have contributed their share. The founders of the nation, the settlers at Jamestown, Plymouth, Boston, St. Mary's, Charleston, laid down an English substructure upon which our civilization still rests. On the other hand, the forces of climate, waterways, soil, labor conditions, working for three centuries have produced great changes. American civilization today is not less a product of America than of Europe. At the same time we cannot minimize the importance of our contact with Europe, the willingness, even the eagerness with which we have imitated European literature, music, art. American civilization has continually changed to keep pace with changing civilization in Europe.

But American civilization differs from others in that it is international rather than national. The United States has reversed the age-old European process of dividing men into nations with different governments, different tongues, different cultures, different psychologies. Here we are casting Englishmen, Irish, Poles, Italians into the same furnace, and out of the whole has come the American. The United States is largely a cross-section of Europe, fused in the American melting-pot and molded by life in America.

Chapter II

NETHERLANDS, OLD AND NEW

THE Dutch created their country from the sea, and the sea created the Dutch. In ancient days a large part of the present kingdom of Holland was an enormous swamp. "The ocean pours in its flood twice every day," wrote the elder Pliny. "The wretched inhabitants take refuge on the sand-hills, or in little huts which they construct on the summit of lofty poles. . . . The Batavians subsist on the fish left by the receding waters, and they catch these in nets made of rushes or seaweed. Neither tree nor shrub is visible on these shores."[1]

Even in Pliny's day the people had begun to protect themselves from the sea by means of dykes. A stupendous task it was, for no materials were at hand save mud, and the fierce gales of the North Sea proved a relentless enemy. Moreover the Rhine, the Meuse, and the Scheldt were slowly lifting themselves by depositing sand and mud in the riverbeds, so that additional dykes had to be built to keep them from flooding the country. Yet through the centuries the work of rescuing land went on,[2] until a very large part of all Holland lies sixteen feet or more beneath the sea-level.

At first sight one might wonder whether the rescued land was worth the vast expenditure of time and labor entailed. It yielded no timber so necessary for fuel and for houses and ships; no stone for fortifications and churches; no coal, no iron, no copper; it was so infertile that grain and vegetables could be grown only after a costly process of enrichment with manure and other soil. If the farmer, despite these handicaps, succeeded in starting a crop, it was apt to be killed by the sharp, cold winds of spring; if he turned to the raising of stock, he had to import timber for costly barns to protect his cattle and sheep from the cold.

[1]Pliny, *Historia Naturalis,* XVI, p. 1.

[2]It is still continuing. Within the past ten years 550,000 square miles have been added to the land.

It is amazing that this barren spot, little more than a fourth the size of England, should have become at one time the richest country in the world. If the poverty of the Batavians aroused the compassion of Pliny, the opulence of the Dutch seventeen hundred years later provoked the envy and hostility of all Europe. Perhaps with nations as with individuals the school of bitter experience is the best preparation for success; perhaps the age-old struggle of the Dutch against barren soil, threatening sea and the biting northern winds developed the qualities which made of Holland the great center of finance, commerce and industry.

The Dutch early learned to make use of their one great resource, the sea. For centuries they cast their nets in the shallow stretches of the Zuyder Zee or sent their little vessels out into the uncertain waters of the North Sea. When the immense schools of herring which had long frequented the Swedish coast moved south to the North Sea, the drag-nets of Hoorn and the Enkhuizen "buizen"[3] began to make enormous hauls. This, together with the discovery by an obscure fisherman of a method of curing and barrelling fish which preserved them indefinitely, made Holland the great fish-market of the world.

For their fishing the Netherlanders found it necessary to construct boats, and from this beginning grew up a prosperous industry in shipbuilding. Purchasing the necessary timber, metal, hemp, pitch and tar from neighboring countries, they began to turn out great numbers of shallow, wide-bellied vessels. The Dutch ships were slow, but what they lacked in speed they made up in cargo-space and the small number of men needed to handle them. Before the end of the sixteenth century the country was building no less than 2000 ships a year.[4]

As fishing led to shipbuilding so the possession of boats led to commerce. Situated between the British Isles and the Baltic nations, and at the terminus of the vast stream of traffic which flowed up from Italy and down the Rhine valley, possessed of many harbors, favored by inland waterways, the Netherlands were admirably suited for trade. To establish relations in the Baltic the

[3]Roomy fishing boats, easily handled by a few men.
[4]Grotius, *Annales*.

Dutch had to wage war on the Hanseatic League, while they spread their commerce across the seas to America and the East only after their heroic struggle against Spain. With the advent of the seventeenth century, however, they had become the most successful merchants in Europe, and their vessels swarmed in the ports not only of England, Scotland, Ireland, France, Spain, Italy, Russia and Sweden, but of Africa, Brazil, the East Indies and the West Indies. In 1634 the Dutch boasted of a fleet of 35,000 vessels.[5]

Commerce brought to the doors of the Dutch the raw materials of which there was such a dearth in their own country, and so stimulated manufactures. When the ruthless Spanish invaders in the closing decades of the sixteenth century crushed the flourishing cities of Flanders and Brabant, thousands of skilled artisans fled to Amsterdam and other Dutch cities. It was largely their knowledge of the art of weaving and other mechanical arts which converted Holland into a vast workshop.

Even in agriculture the Dutch made remarkable progress. Building up their soil with turf and manure, and applying all the devices known to farming science of the day, they made every available acre bloom. To the visitor who viewed the Dutch countryside from a river boat or canal barge it seemed in places but a succession of gardens—truck farms, dairies, orchards, wheat fields, flower gardens—stretching out below in checkerboard fashion. The Dutch made a study of the diseases of domestic animals, they early adopted the system of crop rotation, they learned how to cross fruits and grains or cattle so as to secure the species best suited to their country.[6]

For the produce of the farms there was a ready market, for Holland was chiefly an urban country. The teeming populations of Amsterdam, Leyden, Delft, Rotterdam, and Utrecht took everything the farmers could supply and still had to import from abroad. Amsterdam, with its 260,000 people,[7] its busy streets and still busier canals, its great warehouses, its rows of ships, its crowded wharves, its exchanges, was for years the business and financial center of the world.

[5]J. Ellis Barker, *The Rise and Decline of the Netherlands,* p. 199.
[6]Melvin M. Knight, *Economic History of Europe at the End of the Middle Ages,* p. 183.
[7]In 1620.

The people had great difficulty in constructing roads, because of the nature of the soil, but this was more than offset by the best system of waterways in Europe. The merchant of Rotterdam could send a boat up the Lek to Arnheim and thence into the Waal all the way down to Gorinchem, then into the back country on the Meuse or the Scheldt. Or he could dispatch it north by canal to Amsterdam and out into the Zuyder Zee, thence up the Lissel and back by canal to the Lek and to Rotterdam. The whole country might properly be called the Venice of the North.[8]

The growth of commerce developed a wealthy burgher class, powerful enough to shape the character of Dutch civilization and to control the economic and political destiny of the country. These men were the most far-seeing traders of Europe, the ablest financiers, the most skilled manufacturers. Their great warehouses lined the harbors and canals of every city, their quaintly ornamented homes the residential streets. They moulded the structure of the State to conform to the needs of their business, dictated the foreign policy, and built up a great colonial empire. Less powerful but more numerous was the group of skilled artisans—weavers, coopers, cabinet-makers, silversmiths, tanners, etc. These men, many of them foreigners, refugees from crushing taxes or religious persecution, made the Dutch wares the cheapest and best on the market. One found their draperies, their furniture, their silverware in the home of the English squire, or the French count, or the far-off Virginia tobacco planter, or the sugar-lord of the West Indies.

The Dutch boer or peasant differed greatly in different parts of the country, in race, dialect, customs, education. The rugged features of the North Holland farmer bespoke his long and bitter struggle with winds and tides, and the soggy infertile soil. But he was well-to-do, independent, intelligent; his cattle[9] were well fed, his barn was large, his home comfortable.[10] The farther south one went the poorer and dirtier the peasants became, though there

[8]"Dans les villes, hors des villes, des canaux se croisent en tous sens; hommes, bêtes, denrées, tout est transporté par la voie de l'eau." R. Murris, *La Hollande et les Hollandais,* p. 27.

[9]"Oh, ces vaches hollandaises. Comme elles excitent d'admiration." *Ibid.,* p. 24.

[10]Often the barn and residence were under one roof.

were many fine fields of tobacco in Utrecht and Brabant and from Wateringen to the Hoek van Holland the country abounded in smiling orchards. And everywhere the masses were prosperous, and beggars, the bane of other countries, were almost unknown. All in all the population was the most industrious, most prosperous, the best educated, the most liberal of Europe.

After many centuries of battling with the forces of nature the Dutch were forced to wage a heroic war for the preservation of their liberties and their religion. The story of the defense of Holland from the encroachments of Philip II of Spain is an epic of heroism. Undaunted by repeated defeats, by bloodthirsty reprisals, by the discipline, size and equipment of the armies sent against them, by the vast resources of Spain in men, money and ships, they fought on year after year until their independence was established. Despite their tremendous losses and the ruthless destruction of property the Dutch emerged from the war richer and more prosperous than ever.

Unfortunately hardships and wars did not suffice to make the Dutch a united nation. Like the British American colonists they had learned that independence was necessary to preserve liberty, but unlike them they did not learn that union was necessary to promote and preserve national greatness. So they sacrificed the interests of the whole to those of the province, of the province to those of the city, of the city to those of a group. Foreign policy, dictated by the needs of the mercantile class,[11] was short-sighted and only too often faithless. The heroic age of Holland was followed by an age of disintegration and humiliation, in which her greatness fell beneath successive blows delivered first by England and then by France.

The organization of the East India Company in 1602 marked the beginning of the Dutch colonial empire. This great corporation, with a capital of six and a half million florins, became a state within a state, for it had power to conclude treaties, to keep an army and navy, to build forts, to acquire and govern colonies. In a few years not only had it secured a virtual monopoly of the East

[11] "The mercantile spirit prevails in the Netherlands to such an extent that all affairs of state are reduced to a question of profit and loss, and as if they were mere transactions of commerce." Ambassador Brasset to Mazarin, April, 1650.

India spice trade but had established its authority over Java, the Moluccas, Celebes and large parts of Sumatra, Borneo and New Guinea, a colonial empire many times larger than the Netherlands themselves. Despite frequent clashes with the English and other European rivals the Company made enormous profits and added greatly to the prosperity of Holland.

In the earlier stages of the war with Spain the Dutch had had to fight for their very existence, but in time, as they grew stronger and more confident, they took the offensive and struck back with telling blows. It was the rich commerce with her American colonies which made Spain especially vulnerable to attack. The stream of gold and silver from Mexico and Peru was the life blood in the veins of her economic system which Holland had only to interrupt to bring weakness and decay. "The question of whether the Dutch would succeed or fail in capturing the silver fleet . . . had become one of life or death for Spain."[12]

The better to prosecute this phase of the war the States-General chartered the West India Company, in 1621, with privileges similar to those of the East India Company. With a capital of 7,200,000 florins and monopoly of trade on the west coast of Africa and in American waters, the new organization was expected to add enormously to the wealth of the Netherlands and to break the power of Spain and Portugal in the New World. Nor were these hopes entirely disappointed. Within a few years the new Company had captured 545 ships with their cargoes valued at ninety million florins and had conquered a large part of Brazil. The most spectacular achievement was the destruction by a few small ships under Piet Hein of a large Spanish fleet; but the richest haul was Hein's capture of the silver fleet a few years later with precious metals, pearls, spices and drugs valued at twenty million florins.[13]

It was unfortunate that the Dutch settlements in North America should have fallen under the authority of this great Company. To the Directors sitting around the council table at Amsterdam counting their profits, the little posts at Fort Orange and on Manhattan were of very minor importance. Had they spent on New

[12]J. Ellis Barker, *The Rise and Decline of the Netherlands,* p. 148.
[13]*Ibid.,* p. 187.

Netherland a fraction of the money they distributed in dividends, they could have planted Dutch civilization in the Hudson valley so firmly that the English might have found it impossible to conquer the region. Had they poured in settlers, erected forts, built up a trade in foodstuffs and naval stores to supplement that in furs, strengthened their hold on the Delaware on the south and the Connecticut on the east, a large part of North America might today be Dutch. But they neglected the colony, failed to give it adequate financial support and actually hampered its growth to squeeze out of it a few florins in profit, while their eyes were fixed on their fleets and armies in Latin America and the stream of gold that came pouring into their treasury.

The very prosperity of the Netherlands was an impediment to the growth of Dutch America. Why should Dutchmen migrate to the New World when there were so many opportunities at home? The founders of British America envisaged their colonies as a place of refuge for the thousands of sturdy beggars who infested England, but there were no sturdy beggars in Holland. The man who wanted a good job at high wages had no need to migrate to New Amsterdam, he could easily secure it at home. Even the religious motive for migration was lacking, for the Dutch government was tolerant to all sects save those whose doctrines were subversive to the state. So, while New England received thousands of Puritan settlers bent on establishing in America their distinctive political and religious structure, while Maryland and Virginia were flooded with poor workers seeking to better themselves in a place where labor was dear and land cheap, only a tiny stream of settlers trickled over from the Old to the New Netherland. When the English took possession of the province in 1664 the total population did not exceed 8000,[14] and of these a large proportion were not Dutch at all but French, Flemings, Walloons and English.[15]

Yet New Netherland was predominantly Dutch, not only in its political institutions, but in blood, language, customs, industry, agriculture, education, architecture, religion. At any time in the

[14]Helen W. Reynolds, *Dutch Houses in the Hudson Valley*, p. 12.

[15]Records of marriages in the Dutch Reformed church in New Amsterdam from 1639 to 1659 show about 59 per cent Dutch. There were many English and Germans with a sprinkling of French and Scandinavians.

seventeenth century a stranger in New Amsterdam who visited the town to wander along the wharves or through the streets, or loitered beside the canal, or worshipped in the old church in the fort, or made purchases in the shops of Pearl Street might have imagined himself in a town of old Holland. There were the same houses with stepped gable ends, the same mercantile spirit, the same atmosphere of mingled pettiness and broad tolerance. For a century after the English conquest New Amsterdam remained largely Dutch and Albany almost entirely so.

To the Dutchman who sailed into the mouth of the Hudson to trade or to make his home, the region seemed in many ways similar to his native land. "As to the climate and the seasons of the year," says Johannes de Laet, "they nearly agree with ours. . . . There is also the same variety of winds. . . . In short, it is a country well adapted for our people to inhabit."[16] The network of great waterways—the Hudson, Long Island Sound, East River, the Hackensack, the Passaic, the Raritan—must have brought to his mind the rivers and canals of Holland. For commerce New Netherland was almost as advantageously situated as the Old, for it too was the natural outlet for a great continent, it too was a halfway station for what some day must become a great coastal trade. And though the wooded highlands of the Hudson presented a strange contrast to the low-lying stretches of Holland,[17] the Dutchman had no difficulty in finding fertile spots where he could produce his accustomed wheat, rye and vegetables.

The West India Company, like the Virginia Company, tried to foster in America the production of forest products needed for the industry of the mother country. They spent considerable sums in "tar-burning" and "ash-burning," and erected mills for lumber and staves.[18] These ventures "came to naught" not only because of "bad management and calculation," but because the high cost of labor made it difficult for the colonists to compete with the forest products of the Baltic. Unless New Netherland could base its pros-

[16]J. F. Jameson, *Narratives of New Netherland,* p. 50.

[17]"The lands in New Netherland are not all level and flat and adapted to raising grain," one Hollander warned those expecting to migrate. *New York Colonial Documents, Holland Documents,* Vol. I, p. 356.

[18]J. F. Jameson, *Narratives of New Netherland,* p. 321.

perity on something for which it had greater natural advantages, something corresponding to tobacco in the Chesapeake Bay colonies and sugar in the West Indies, its growth would be slow indeed.

The fur trade proved the key to prosperity for Dutch America. Whereas the mountains interposed a barrier between the English colonies and the fur-producing regions, the Dutch found in the Hudson and Mohawk valleys a natural pathway to the Great Lakes. So Fort Orange became an important trading post where the Iroquois or the Miamis met the keen Dutchmen to exchange their beaver or fox skins for guns, knives, blankets, or perhaps for whiskey and gin. From Fort Orange the precious peltries were sent down to New Amsterdam on river sloops, where they were transferred to ships bound for Holland. "Nothing comes from New Netherland but beaver skins, mincks and other furs," declared a report to the States General.[19] In time, as the population increased, other articles were added to the exports—grain, tobacco, hemp, flax, pork, tar, timber, masts, wainscoting, salt and potash[20]—but the fur trade continued to overshadow all else. In return for their exports the New Netherlanders took the manufactured goods of the mother country—cloth, clothes, firearms, household utensils, farm implements.

Trade was not exclusively with Holland, for the merchants of New Amsterdam sent their vessels to New England on the one hand and all the way to the Chesapeake on the other.[21] Nicolas Boot traded extensively in Virginia tobacco, while Cornelis Steenwyck, Frederick Gijsbertsen and others also included tobacco in their transactions. So many English ship-masters on their voyage between New England and the Chesapeake put in at New Amsterdam that it became necessary to erect the City Tavern[22] for their accommodation. It must have been a case of Greek meeting Greek when the close-bargaining Yankee met the canny Dutch

[19]Alexander C. Flick, *History of the State of New York*, Vol. I, p. 334.

[20]*Ibid.*, Vol. I, p. 334.

[21]"One trades upwards, southwards and northwards," said Wassenaer. I. N. Phelps Stokes, *Iconography of New York*, Vol. I, p. 12.

[22]T. A. Janvier, *The Dutch Founding of New York*, p. 95. J. F. Jameson, *Narratives of New Netherland*, p. 212.

to haggle over the price of a cask of rum, or sugar, or tobacco, or a crate of beaver skins.

Despite the efforts of the West India Company New Netherland never became important as an agricultural region. The fertile spots were not extensive enough, the winters were too long and severe, the soil was unsuited for any staple crop for which there was a strong demand in Europe. However, bouweries or farms crept up Manhattan and over into Long Island and Staten Island. Here the sturdy boer built his house and his great barn, laid out his fields of wheat and rye, kept his cows and hogs and planted his vegetable garden and his orchard. It was his custom to load his little sloop with beef, pork, butter, cheese, turnips, carrots, cabbage, etc. and set out for the canal in Broad Street, there to dispose of them to the shopkeepers on either side. In time it was discovered that there was much arable land on the Hudson highlands at a considerable distance back from the river, and prosperous agricultural communities came into being along Kinderhook creek and Claverack creek and at Bonte Koe and Wagen Dal.[23] The farmers at these places brought their wares down narrow roads through the woods to river landings, where they were shipped to some near-by village or perhaps to New Amsterdam.

In order to stimulate migration to the colony the West India Company made extensive grants on the Hudson to several of its stockholders, each of whom promised in return to transport and settle fifty families at his own expense. On his huge estate the patroon, as he was called, was in fact a feudal lord, exacting dues from his tenants and organizing courts which had jurisdiction over their property and even their lives.[24] It required long experience to convince European colonizers, whether English, French or Dutch, that America was not the proper place for the revival of dying medieval institutions. On the Hudson the able and energetic management of Kiliaen van Rensselaer brought a measure of success to his patroonship, but before the end of the seventeenth century the others were almost deserted. Governor Bellemont wrote: "Mr. Livingston has on his grant of sixteen miles long and

[23]H. W. Reynolds, *Dutch Houses in the Hudson Valley,* p. 12.
[24]J. F. Jameson, *Narratives of New Netherland,* pp. 90–96.

twenty-four broad but four or five cottagers, as I am told, men that live in vassalage under him. . . . Colonel Cortland has also on his grants four or five of those poor families."[25] Obviously there was no reason why one should remain a feudal vassal in the wilds of America when fertile land could be had almost for the asking. So the tenants of the patroons moved over into New Jersey or Pennsylvania, leaving the patroons to the contemplation of their empty privileges and their equally empty estates. The system explains in part the slowness with which the region filled up.

The backbone of the province was not these sham lords, but the merchants of Fort Orange and New Amsterdam—Hendrick Philipsen, Cornelis Steenwyck, Nicolas de Meyer, Oloff van Cortlandt, Johannes de Peyster, Jeronimus Ebbing and others like them. These men built their warehouses on the Strand overlooking the East River, where they stored the furs which came down the river, or the finished goods from Holland, or the tobacco of Virginia. Cornelis Steenwyck traded in his own ships which he sent each year to the West Indies and the Chesapeake for cargoes of salt, slaves and tobacco. His residence, with its stepped gable-end looking out over the fort, was the envy of his neighbors.[26] Augustine Herrman, who came to New Amsterdam as agent for the great commercial firm of Peter Gabry and Sons, a man of wide culture who could speak Dutch, German, English and French, became one of the most prosperous merchants in the colony, trading in his own ships in tobacco, furs, wines, slaves and drygoods.[27] It was such men as these who built substantial homes, almost exact replicas of those of Amsterdam or Delft, filled them with cumbrous Dutch furniture and with treasures of silver and pewter, laid out their back yards in vegetables or fruit trees or tulip beds,[28] quarrelled violently with each governor in turn and sent in their protests to the Directors of the West India Company.[29] They constituted a burgher aristocracy comparable to the merchant aris-

[25]H. W. Reynolds, *Dutch Houses in the Hudson Valley,* p. 15.

[26]The New York Historical Society has a portrait of Steenwyck.

[27]J. F. Jameson, *Narratives of New Netherland,* pp. 289, 375; New Jersey Historical Society, *Proceedings,* 1890–91, pp. 23–34.

[28]See the Castello Plan of 1660, reproduced in I. N. Phelps Stokes, *Iconography,* Vol. II.

[29]J. F. Jameson, *Narratives of New Netherland,* pp. 287–386.

tocracy of New England or the planter aristocracy of Virginia and Maryland.

Living side by side with these wealthy men on Pearl Street or the Strand or Beaver were the middle-class burghers—small traders up the Hudson, tavern-keepers, sea-captains, soldiers in the service of the West India Company, professional men—doctors, notaries, surveyors, accountants; glaziers, smiths, masons, carpenters, coopers, shoemakers, painters, sailmakers, cabinet-makers; shop-keepers, their wares displayed in the open stalls of their stores overlooking the Broad Street "graft."[30] This was the group which intrudes itself most upon the musty pages of the records of New Amsterdam, with their petty jealousies, their "small town gossip," their quarrels over a boundary line or a broken promise of marriage, their tap-room fights, their love of gardens and flowers, their close bargaining. Mingled with them were the humbler workers —wood sawyers, porters, carmen, day laborers, domestic servants, a few African slaves.

As the people of New Amsterdam were much the same as the people of the average Dutch trading town, so was the place in outward aspect a replica in miniature of Amsterdam or Middelburg, or Leiden or Hoorn. There were the same curving streets lined with quaint houses, the same use of every open space for gardens or orchards, the same canals running through the heart of the town, the same sky-line with its tiled roofs, church tower and picturesque windmill, the same water-front with its wharves and slips, and protecting batteries.[31]

It was the close similarity between the economic and social systems of New Netherland and the Old which in large part accounts for the similarity in architecture. Had Dutch America become a great agricultural region, covered with tobacco or sugar or wheat plantations, the houses of the people would have changed to conform to changed conditions. But the merchant or shop-keeper or artisan of New Amsterdam or Albany saw no reason why he should not build in the same manner as his father or his grandfather. And if architecture in the farm regions overlooking the

[30]Compare C. H. Peters, *De Nederlandsche Stedenbouw,* Plate 108.
[31]*Ibid.,* Plates 104, 118, 121, 126.

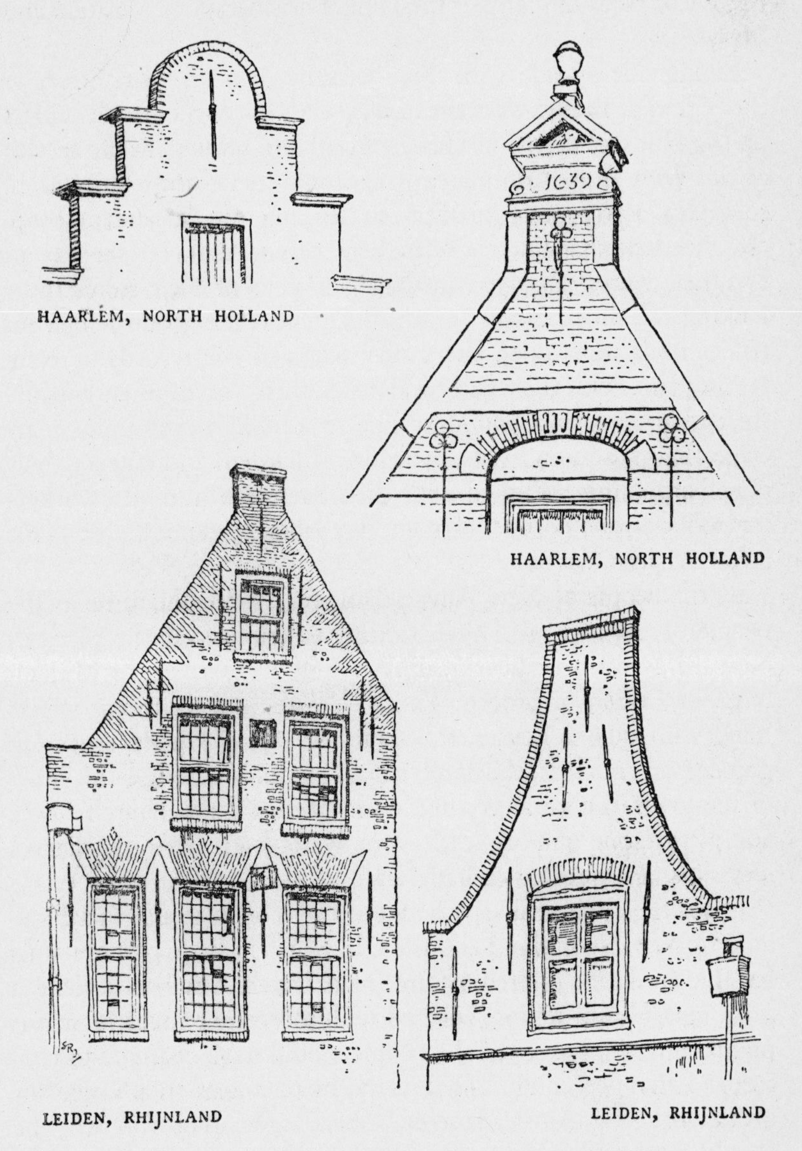

FIGURE I. GABLE TYPES OF HOLLAND AND BELGIUM

Hudson tended to wander from the old models, the reason is to be sought in the very large admixture of Flemings and Walloons. In the districts where the Dutch were the dominating group Dutch architecture prevailed in a very pure form.

At the time of the settlement of New Netherland Dutch architecture was still medieval. Jacob van Campen was then but a lad, the works of Palladio had little influence on the Dutch builders. The cities at the beginning of the seventeenth century were much the same as in the fifteenth century. There were the same Gothic churches, the same fortifications with their round towers, conical roofs and battlements, the same jumble of steep gable-ends set off here and there by picturesque windmills or by the masts and spars of the ships which crowded the many canals.

The character of the urban architecture was shaped in part by the costliness of building lots. The narrow limits within the walls and the fact that the land often had to be built up over boggy lowlands, gave to even the narrowest frontage on the Vismerckt at Groningen or the Hout Wallen at Hoorn an extremely high valuation. So the thrifty burgher built his warehouse or his shop or his residence with a very narrow front, securing needed space by raising his building to three or four stories, and by stretching it out behind. If one could have flown over a typical Dutch city three centuries ago the houses would have given the appearance of little Noah's arks packed closely side by side with the bows to the streets (Plate 1). But upon descending to walk along the canal banks or through the streets, he would have seen, instead of ship-bows, unending rows of narrow houses each with its steep roof set off by a quaintly decorated gable.

Since the gable-end was the only part of the city house visible to the public it became the distinguishing feature of Dutch architecture. There were four types—the stepped gable, the *klokgevel* with concave curves, the *tuitgevel* or Flemish gable with convex curves, and the straight-lined gable with square elbows[32] (Fig. 1). All of these types appear in every part of Holland, but the first might be predominant in one city, the second in another, the third in still another. The stepped gable was almost universal in Delft,

[32]Sydney R. Jones, *Old Houses in Holland,* p. 108.

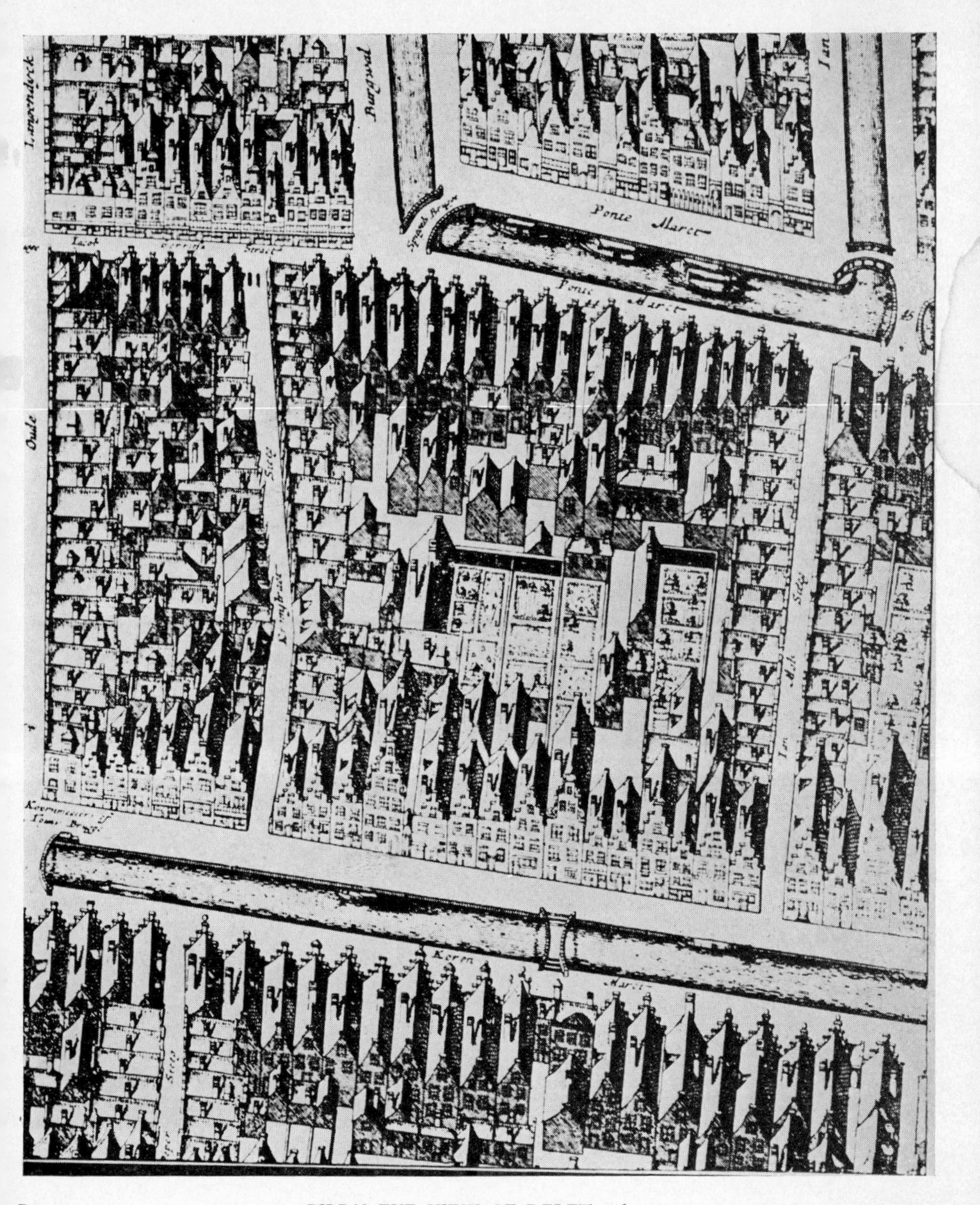

Plate I. BIRD'S EYE VIEW OF DELFT, 1675

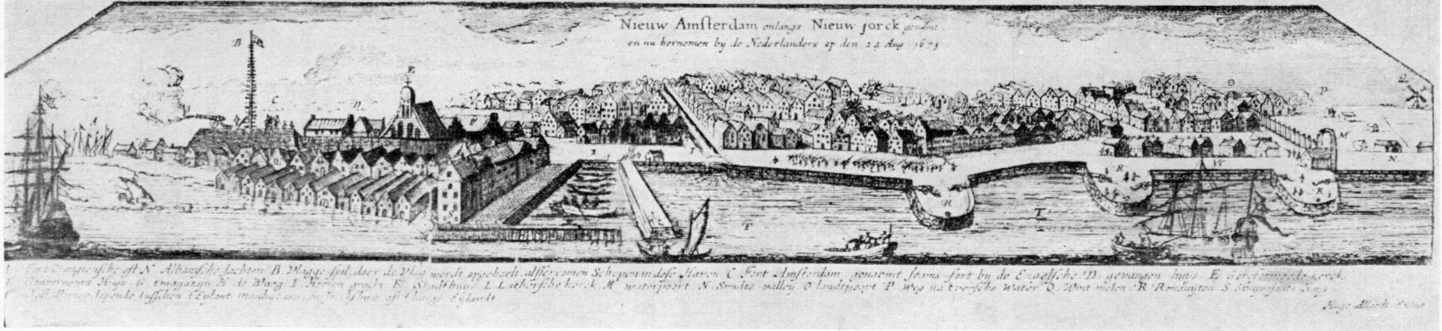

PLATE 2. EARLY VIEWS OF NEW AMSTERDAM

Montfoort, and Rotterdam, the straight line gable was frequent in Groningen and the *klokgevel* in Devanter, while in Utrecht and Middelburg the stepped gable and the *klokgevel* were equally common.[33] The gable invariably terminated in a finial, which might resemble an ordinary chimney or might assume the form of a ball, or perhaps a lion holding a shield. The severe plainness of the straight line gable was often relieved by the mouse-tooth finish, made up of small triangles of bricks set diagonally and looking much like the teeth of a saw.

The scarcity of timber and stone made it necessary for the builders to use these materials sparingly. It was a costly matter to float stone down the Rhine or to import beams and planks from the Baltic. In large structures, where strength and endurance were vital—city walls, great warehouses,[34] cathedrals, town halls—stone was not unusual, but the burghers could seldom afford it in building their homes. On the other hand, frame residences were fairly common, especially in north Holland. Strangely enough the Dutch seem rarely to have used half-timber construction, with its great saving of wood, which was so common elsewhere, preferring to cover the frame with planks laid vertically.[35]

Since clay was abundant and lime for mortar cheap, brick was the material commonly used in all kinds of structures, and the Dutch brickmakers and bricklayers were the most skilled of Europe. The bricks were long and narrow, and were made in various colors—red, purple, yellow, salmon pink. This gave the workmen an opportunity to break the monotony of the walls by parti-colored bands laid horizontally, or mouldings set off from the wall by differences in color, or by arched spaces over the window heads filled with mosaic brick decorations.[36] The Dutch bricklayers made use of the English bond,[37] not the Flemish bond as is so frequently supposed.[38]

[33]C. H. Peters, *De Nederlandsche Stedenbouw*, Plates 80, 100, 102.

[34]M. Révész-Alexander, *Die Alten Lagerhäuser Amsterdam*, pp. 63, 124.

[35]*Noord-Hollandsche Oudheden*, Tweede Stuk, p. 47, Derde Stuk, p. 49; C. H. Peters, *De Nederlandsche Stedenbouw*, Plate 108.

[36]Compare the use of glazed headers in pattern work in French and English brick houses. See Nath. Lloyd, *History of English Brickwork*, pp. 68, 69.

[37]Alternate layers of headers and stretchers.

[38]Sydney R. Jones, *Old Houses in Holland*, pp. 21, 22, 26, 27.

A charming feature of these old Dutch houses were the windows. It was usual to divide each window into four parts, the two upper sections being fitted into the masonry on the outside, the lower sections hinged inward. The bars between the sections were often painted milk white to harmonize with window frames of cream and contrast with the heavy red of the brick façade. A note of richness was added by the little panes of glass, which from the outside assumed a violet tint, and by the dark green of the doors and ironwork. Perhaps it was the drear emptiness of the level stretches of his landscape which made the Dutchman so insistent upon a touch of color in his home. Certainly the houses of old Amsterdam or Delft or Utrecht, with their varied gable-ends, their arched windows, their brick patterns, their distinctive finials, their harmonious color schemes, their richly carved corbels and stone panels, their stone and brick mosaics, their wrought-iron weather vanes must have presented a vivid and charming scene.[39]

Many of the houses, especially those used in part or in whole as warehouses or shops, had doors in the upper stories, to which goods could be lifted by means of a rope and pulley attached to a beam projecting from the gable just under the finial. This device, the forerunner of the modern elevator, saved precious space and time and energy in lugging heavy wares upstairs. Almost universal, also, were the ornamental beam anchors or metal strips which tied the walls to the floor beams and so strengthened the structure. One finds them in infinite variety, sometimes in the form of the fleur-de-lis, sometimes as a cross, sometimes as the letter X, sometimes as a heart[40] (Fig. 2).

The Dutch turned to good account their abundant supply of clay not only in making brick, but for the pantiles with which they covered their roofs. Holland would lose much of its charm were it not for the bright red or the gray of the tiles, their curved surfaces glittering in the sunlight or reflecting the somberness of the leaden sky. In the rural districts thatch was frequently used for roofing barns and residences, but the danger of fire made it impracticable for the cities.

[39]Francis R. Yerbury, *Old Domestic Architecture of Holland.*
[40]Sydney R. Jones, *Old Houses in Holland,* p. 121.

FIGURE 2. ALKMAAR, NORTH HOLLAND (DATED 1609)

The interior of the Dutch houses as we see them in the paintings of Pieter de Hoock, Johannes Vermeer, J. A. Hendrik Leys, and in restorations in various museums, was as picturesque and colorful as the exterior. Stepping through the street door, one found himself usually in a long, narrow hallway, with rooms on one side and the staircase in the rear. The kitchen, which served also as the dining room, with its quaintly moulded doors, heavy mantel, blue-figured wall tiles, casement windows, great ceiling-beams, large fireplace with brass crane or fire irons, delft plates in long rows around the walls, a table which seemed too light for its bulbous turned legs, stiff Turkey-work chairs, wall cupboard with ponderous lock and intricately wrought hinges, gave an impression of comfort, warmth and cleanliness. The bedrooms above in contrast seemed rather bare and cold, for the tile floors were unrelieved by rugs, the alcove bed was hidden behind heavy curtains, and the furniture was stiff.

When the Dutch first rowed ashore from their round-bellied ships, bought "the Island of Manhattes from the Indians for the value of 60 guilders" and founded the town of New Amsterdam, they were forced to improvise the crudest kinds of shelter.[41] Some of them probably dug square pits in the ground, "cellar fashion," lined them with timber and erected overhead crude structures of sticks and bark.[42] When Nicolaes van Wassenaer visited the colony in 1626 he found the people living in houses made "of the bark of trees,"[43] and it was only two years later that Jonas Michaelius stated that they were beginning to build new houses in place of the hovels and holes in which they heretofore huddled rather than dwelt.[44] There seems to be no evidence that the Dutch built log cabins in the Hudson valley. In Holland trees were too scarce and the cost of importing logs too great to permit of this type of construction. No doubt some of the settlers had seen log houses during voyages to the Baltic or trips up the Rhine, but the West India Company carpenters could hardly have known anything about

[41]James G. Wilson, *Memorial History of New York*, Vol. I, pp. 159, 160.

[42]The first shelters by the Dutch on the Delaware were made in this way. *Penna. Archives*, Series II, Vol. V, pp. 182, 183.

[43]J. F. Jameson, *Narratives of New Netherland*, p. 83.

[44]I. N. Phelps Stokes, *Iconography of New York*, Vol. I, p. 14.

them. The inspiration for the log watch-house at New Amstel undoubtedly came from the neighboring Swedish colonists.[45]

But with timber houses they were thoroughly familiar, and we may imagine them, broad axe in hand, felling trees, squaring the great beams, setting up the framework, covering it with crude boards, erecting wooden chimneys. When the West India Company, wishing to develop an export trade in timber and clapboards, set up great windmills for sawing timber,[46] planks and perhaps even small beams became abundant. Most of the quaint little houses stretched out along the bank of the East River in the Prototype View of New Amsterdam of about 1650, are obviously of wood. One has only to glance at their steep roof-lines, the curved gable-ends, the boarding in some cases vertical in others horizontal, to pronounce them almost identical with the frame houses of Edam, Alkmaar, Eiland or Durgerdam.[47] Even in later years when the little metropolis had assumed an air of well-being, frame houses were to be seen sandwiched in between structures of stone and brick.[48] At tiny New Amstel on the lower Delaware the Dutch carpenters, scorning the log construction of the Swedish cabins nearby, went out into the woods axe in hand to trim the beams for frame houses. Though Vice-Director Alrichs described them as of "country fashion and make," and covered with clapboards or shingles, we recognize the typical Dutch house in the proportions, in the "planked closets" for bedsteads,[49] and even in the circular window (Plate 2).

From the very first, however, the burghers must have looked forward to the day when they could build, as they had been accustomed to build in Holland, of brick. Suitable clay was at hand, the great heaps of oyster shells left by the Indians or near-by quarries of limestone, afforded abundant lime for mortar, they had with them skilled brickmakers and bricklayers. So early as 1628 kilns were in operation at New Amsterdam,[50] and as the colony

[45] *Penna. Archives,* Series II, Vol. V, pp. 319ff.
[46] J. F. Jameson, *Narratives of New Netherland,* p. 131.
[47] J. G. Veldheer, *Alte Holländische Stadte und Dorfer,* Plates 26, 29, 30.
[48] Alexander Hamilton, *Itinerarium,* p. 51.
[49] *Penna. Archives,* Series II, Vol. V, pp. 469, 470.
[50] J. F. Jameson, *Narratives of New Netherland,* p. 131.

emerged from the pioneer stage more and more brick houses arose along the crooked streets of the little town. Before the end of the century New Amsterdam was almost as solidly built of brick as the cities of Holland itself.

The colonial masons must have been quite as skilful as those of the mother country, and the red, yellow, black and blue bricks turned out by the local makers gave them an opportunity to indulge in their favorite designs. One can only wish that colored photography had been known in those days, so that the vivid tints of the shops and houses along the Strand or Broad Street could have been preserved for us. But the old Vechte-Cortelyou house at Gowanus, with its mouth-tooth gable, its diamond diaper work and date in black headers, must have been typical.[51] And we have the testimony of visitors like Madam Knight, who noted with interest that the "bricks in some of the houses are of divers colors and laid in checkers,"[52] or like Samuel Chandler who found the Albany houses "curiously flowered" and dated with black brick, the "Governor's house having two black hearts."[53]

Though the Dutch masons were less accustomed to working in stone than in brick, they could not afford to neglect entirely the "much beautiful quarry stone of all kinds" noted by the travellers Dankers and Sluyter.[54] In New Amsterdam the counting house,[55] the church in the fort,[56] the Company's five houses in Winchel Street, Peter Stuyvesant's house,[57] the City Tavern;[58] in Albany and its vicinity the old square church, the Barent Staats house, the Van Loon house, the Van Vechten house; at New Castle on the Delaware the celebrated tile house were all of stone. If the builders found uncut stone a rather somber medium in which to work they could add a touch of color by brick gable-ends or by mosaics in

[51]Henry R. Stiles, *History of the City of Brooklyn,* Frontispiece; H. D. Eberlein, *Manor Houses and Historic Homes,* etc., pp. 217, 218.

[52]*Journal of Madam Knight* (N. Y., 1825), pp. 52–54.

[53]Alice M. Earle, *Colonial Days in Old New York,* p. 100.

[54]Dankers and Sluyter, "Journal of a Voyage to N. Y.," Long Island Hist. Soc. *Memoirs,* Vol. I, p. 333.

[55]J. F. Jameson, *Narratives of New Netherland,* p. 83.

[56]R. G. Thwaites, *Jogues', The Jesuit Relations,* XVIII, pp. 105–7.

[57]Burgis View of New York, New York Hist. Soc.

[58]J. F. Jameson, *Narratives of New Netherland,* p. 212.

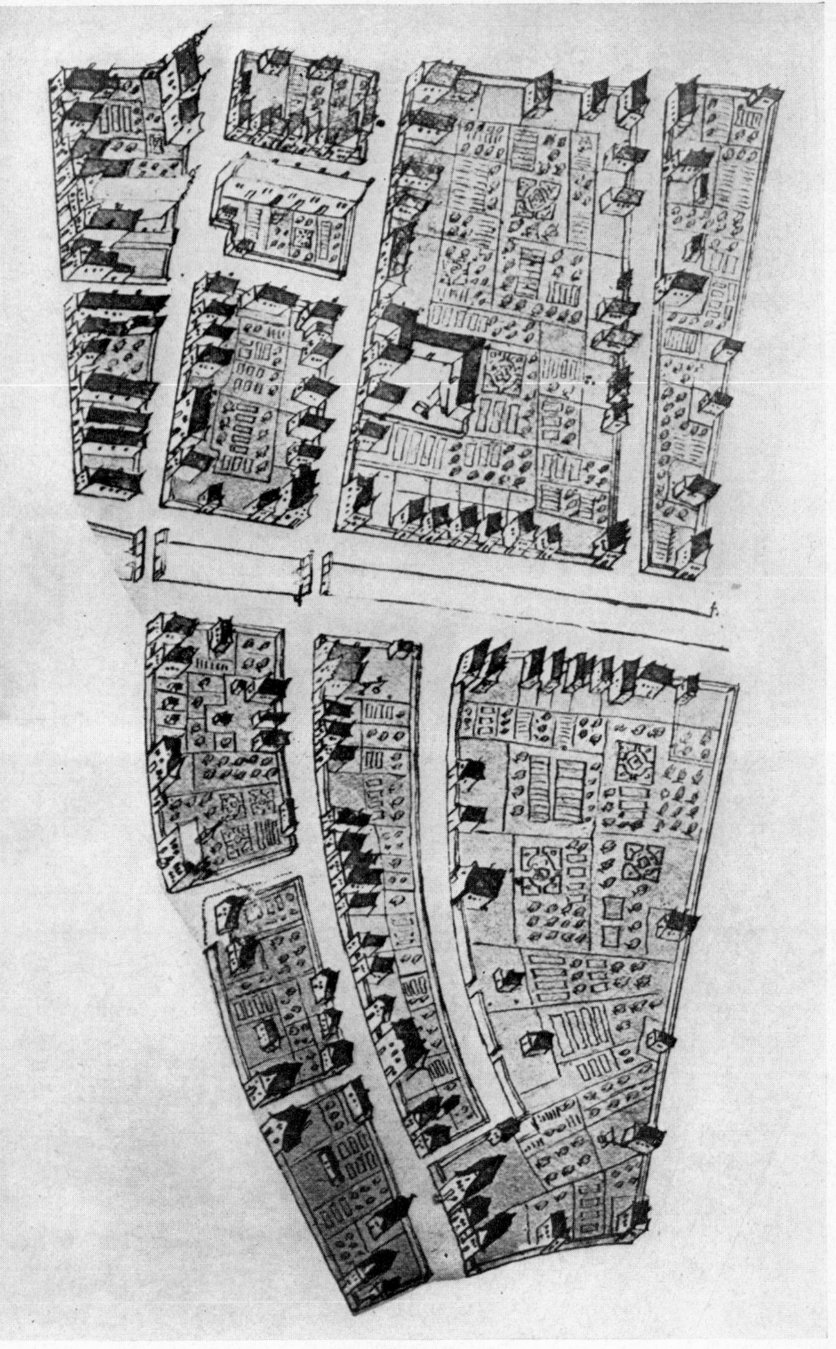

PLATE 3. SECTION OF CASTELLO VIEW OF NEW AMSTERDAM, SHOWING CANAL

the recesses of the window arches. After all there was not so much need for color in the villages or farmhouses of the settlers so long as they were framed in the vivid green of the American forest.

In roofing their houses the first settlers would have liked to use the pantiles to which they were accustomed, but since they were so costly and difficult to make they resorted usually to thatch, and occasionally to planking or to wooden shingles. The counting house, probably the first substantial building in New Amsterdam, was "thatched with reed" as no doubt were most of the picturesque little cottages which sprang up around the fort.[59] Even so late as 1647, with many substantial houses of two or three stories going up, thatch was still the usual roof covering, and not until the town authorities, fearing that a spark of fire might send their little city up in flames, strictly banned the use of straw roofs, did the custom begin to die out.[60]

Then those who could afford it turned to the red and black pantiles which the brickyards were now turning out, so that before the end of the seventeenth century the roofs of Albany and New York were almost as vivid with color as those of Amsterdam or Delft. "New York is built most of brick and stone and covered with red and black tile," giving from "a distance a pleasing aspect," Daniel Denton tells us.[61] In time, however, the cheapness of wooden shingles brought tiles into disuse. In 1749 an article in the *Post Boy* deplored this change, pointing out the danger of a great conflagration. "As there is plenty of clay in this province," it said, in the space of six years a sufficient quantity of tile might be procured. . . . Several houses in this town have been tiled with very good pantiles made at Albany, as cheap as they could be had from Holland."[62]

In New Netherland as in Holland not only was the gable end the most conspicuous feature of every house, but one finds all four of the gable types—the stepped, the straight line and the Flemish gable and the *klokgevel*. As we gaze down upon the roofs of New Amsterdam as shown in the remarkable Castello view

[59] J. F. Jameson, *Narratives of New Netherland,* p. 83.
[60] I. N. Phelps Stokes, *Iconography,* Vol. I, p. 65.
[61] Daniel Denton, *Brief Description of New York* (1902 reprint), pp. 40, 41.
[62] New York *Post Boy,* September, 1749.

of 1660, the graceful lines of the *klokgevel* seem to predominate, with the stepped gable a close second[63] (Plate 3). A half century later the sky-line was somewhat different. Looking across East River toward the old fort we see that the house of the rebel Jacob Leisler, the Daniel Veenvos house, the Paul Richard house, the house on the Great Dock which Cornelius de Peyster built "to be the ornament of the said city," were all of the stepped gable type; the unique house of the joiner John Ellison of the Flemish gable type; while sandwiched in between, the Abraham de Peyster warehouse and the Thomas Roberts house and the William Boyle house on Queen Street were of the straight line type[64] (Plate 4).

Although we have for Albany nothing comparable to the remarkable series of drawings of New Amsterdam and colonial New York, the descriptions left by travellers and views of individual houses and streets give us an accurate idea of what this outpost of Dutch civilization looked like. The houses are chiefly of one story with the gable-end "notched like steps" and surmounted by vanes in the form of horses, lions, geese, sloops, wrote Samuel Chandler in 1755.[65] Most of the houses are built in the old way, with the gable-end towards the street, says Peter Kalm, the gable-end of bricks and all the other walls of planks.[66] As for the type of gable which prevailed in the Albany region outside the town, we know from numerous old houses still standing that the straight line was almost universal.[67]

Time has not been kind to the houses of Dutch America. There is not as much left of the New Amsterdam of Peter Stuyvesant as of the Athens of Pericles; Dutch Albany has been obliterated; the older people of New Castle recall the pulling down of the last true Dutch house on the Delaware; it was within recent years that the Vechte-Cortelyou house at Gowanus was almost buried

[63]The small scale upon which the houses were drawn makes it difficult in some cases to determine the type of the gable.

[64]Compare Burgis View, New York Historical Society and I. N. Phelps Stokes, *Iconography.*

[65]Alice M. Earle, *Colonial Days in Old New York,* p. 100.

[66]Peter Kalm, *Travels into North America* (edition of 1772), pp. 96, 97.

[67]H. W. Reynolds, *Dutch Houses in the Hudson Valley,* pp. 129–174.

by the grading of new streets and left to go to ruin.[68] And since the views which have come down to us are usually made at a considerable distance we are often left in the dark concerning many architectural details—finials, cornices, windows, doors, beam anchors, mosaic work. Yet we know enough to be certain

FIGURE 3. DUTCH HOUSE IN WILLIAM STREET, 1648

that in these features the builders followed the prevailing styles in Holland just as closely as in the gable types or in building material or in structural proportions (Fig. 3).

One wonders what has become of the thousands of ornate beam anchors which undoubtedly contributed their share to the charm of the houses of Dutch America. Fortunately a few still

[68]H. D. Eberlein, *Manor Houses and Historic Homes, etc.*, pp. 217, 218.

grace the sides of old houses in the Albany region, while others have been preserved by collectors interested in decorative wrought-iron. From these we may conclude that the fleur-de-lis was the most popular motif, used alike in letters and beam anchors, but among the hundreds ruined in the great New York fire of 1776 or melted down as scrap iron there must have been many examples of the trefoil, the heart and other forms common in Holland. The date numbers from the Tile house in New Castle,[69] together with the beam anchors of the Yates house, Schenectady, and "Watervliet" near Albany bear striking evi-

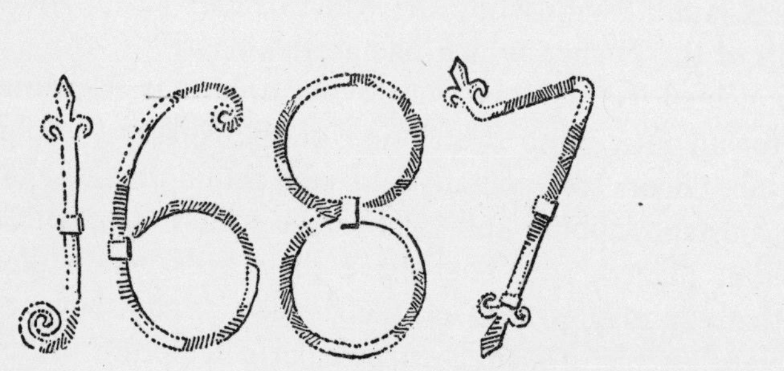

FIGURE 4. DATE NUMBERS FROM TILE HOUSE, NEW CASTLE, DELAWARE. TYPICAL BEAM ANCHOR

dence of the skill and artistry of the iron-workers of New Netherland[70] (Fig. 4).

As one views the most perfect remaining specimens of the urban type of colonial Dutch house, such as the Van Allen house or the Hendrick Bries house he is disappointed to find that the windows have been modernized.[71] Ugly two-pane sashes have replaced the old casements with their tiny diamond panes, the arched recesses over the windows have been bricked up, the quaint wooden shutters have given way to blinds. True, some of the old prints show the arched window recesses clearly, but they too leave us in the dark as to whether the windows were topped by brick mosaics and if so what were the colors and the patterns.

[69]Albert H. Sonn, *Early American Wrought Iron,* III, Plates 254, 256.
[70]H. W. Reynolds, *Dutch Houses in the Hudson Valley,* Plate 173.
[71]*Ibid.,* Plates 15, 56.

Visitors to New Amsterdam and Albany found the interiors of the houses just as typically Dutch as the exteriors. There were the same wainscoted or whitewashed walls, the same heavy mantels, the same tiled hearths, the same built-in beds, the same heavy ceiling timbers, the same rows of Delft plates, the same framed pictures. "The inside is neat to admiration," says Madam Knight, "the wooden work, for only the walls are plastered . . . kept very white scoured. The fireplaces have no jambs, but the backs run flush with the walls. The house had chimney corners, and they and the hearths were laid with the finest tile I ever see, and the stair-cases laid all with white tile which is ever clean, and so are the walls of the kitchen which had a brick floor."[72]

We are indebted to the Maryland physician, Doctor Alexander Hamilton for an interesting description of the Albany interiors. "Their chamber floors are generally laid with rough plank, which in time by constant rubbing and scrubbing becomes as smooth as if it had been planed. . . . They have their beds generally in alcoves so that you may go thro' all the rooms . . . and never see a bed. They affect pictures much, particularly Scripture history, with which they adorn their rooms. They set out their cabinets and buffets much with china. Their kitchens are likewise very clean, and there they hang earthen or Delft plates and dishes all around the walls."[73]

While the carpenters and masons of New Netherland were building in the style of old Holland, in Holland itself architecture was slowly yielding to the influence of the Renaissance. Even in the closing years of the sixteenth century Lievan de Kay in Haarlem, and Hendrik de Keyser and Cornelius Danckerts in Amsterdam, while clinging to the old forms, had added a few touches suggestive of the new Italy—classical finials, quoins, marble steps, winged heads.[74] However, it was only with Jacob van Campen that the Netherlands were won over for the new architecture. Originally a painter, van Campen became enamored of the work of Palladio while travelling in Italy, and returned to Holland to demonstrate to his countrymen the beauties of the

[72] *Journal of Madam Knight*, pp. 52–54.
[73] Doctor Alexander Hamilton, *Itinerarium*, p. 87.
[74] S. R. Jones, *Old Houses in Holland*, pp. 12, 14, 55.

classical revival. His rathaus in Amsterdam, with its balanced façade, pilasters, classical pediment, cupola, and hipped roof, broke in form as well as in detail with Dutch tradition and marked the beginning of a new architectural era.[75]

The work thus begun was carried forward by Philip and Justus Vingbooms, and by Pieter Post. Their public buildings and coun-

FIGURE 5. DUTCH RENAISSANCE BUILDING

try residences, characterized by regular spacing of windows and doors, high hipped roof with chimneys rising out of the ridge, classical dormers, pilasters, pediments, quoins, urns and balconies, gave to Dutch architecture a flavor which smacked partly of Italy, partly of France, partly of ancient Greece and Rome[76]

[75]H. von Jan Lauweriks, *Alt-Holland,* p. 40.

[76]The close affinity of French and Dutch Renaissance architecture may be noted by a comparison of the work of the Vingbooms and Post with the plates shown in Louis C. Newhall's *The Minor Chateaux and Manor Houses of France.*

(Fig. 5). But the ablest of architects could not change the form and proportions of the shops and homes along the crowded streets of the Dutch cities. The gable-end remained now as before the only part visible to the passer-by, and upon it the Renaissance architects like their predecessors were compelled to focus their attention. Under the skilful touch of the two Vingbooms the mouse-tooth, the stepped gable, the arched window recesses, the corbels, the mosaics gave way to classic details in which pilasters, consoles, urns, quoins, garlands of flowers and fruit carved in stone, pedimented windows, doors and finials were prominent (Fig. 6). The new style at its best was dignified and charming, as shown by many existing examples, but it was very susceptible of abuse, and before the end of the seventeenth century when whales, dolphins, wild men and similar motifs appeared in the decorations, the effect was artificial and bizarre.[77]

FIGURE 6. URBAN DUTCH RENAISSANCE BUILDING

The Renaissance movement in Holland was in full swing when New Netherland passed into the hands of the English. Thereafter the colony was subjected to two conflicting cultural influences, the one from England, the other from Holland. For decades the latter was the more important. Colonel Nicolls could take possession of New Amsterdam, put English officials in control, run up the English flag over the old fort and change the name of the

[77]H. von Jan Lauweriks, *Alt-Holland*, p. xv.

town to New York, but he could not transform the Dutch inhabitants into Englishmen. Yet the future lay with the English. Gradually the stream of ideas from England became more important in the life of the colony, the number of English settlers increased, the commercial ties grew stronger. It is impossible to set the exact date when English influence became predominant, but a full hundred years had elapsed before the cultural conquest of the province had supplemented Nicolls's military and naval conquest.

The Burgis View of New York in 1717 shows with remarkable clearness the development of architecture in the half century following the English occupation. In the lower section of the town from the fort to Wall Street the quaint stepped or straight line gable-ends, the steep roofs, the finials indicate clearly enough that here the architecture is almost as definitely medieval Dutch as it had been in the days of Peter Stuyvesant (Plate 4). When we proceed north of Wall Street, however, we see a marked change, most of the buildings being either Dutch Renaissance or English Renaissance in character, with here and there a house in the medieval style (Plate 6).

Even in the southern quarter, however, there are ample evidences of Dutch Renaissance influence. The pedimented finial so characteristic of the two Vingbooms is clearly discernible on the Thomas Roberts house, the Jacob Leisler house, and many others. The handsome de Peyster house shows on the elbows of its Flemish gable dormer two small figures obviously the characteristic Renaissance urns or pineapples. Of especial interest is the towering roof, the low dormers, and the four high chimney stacks of the Robert Livingston house on Pearl Street, so suggestive of the contemporaneous Dutch influence.

North of Wall Street the medieval gable-ends have almost disappeared, and in many cases the roof slopes toward the street in true English fashion (Plate 6). On the other hand the height of the roofs, which seem to rise from fifteen to twenty-five feet above the eaves, is suggestive of Holland. In the Burgis view one sees in the distance, rising high over the houses on the river front on King Street, a towering roof crowned by a balcony, with

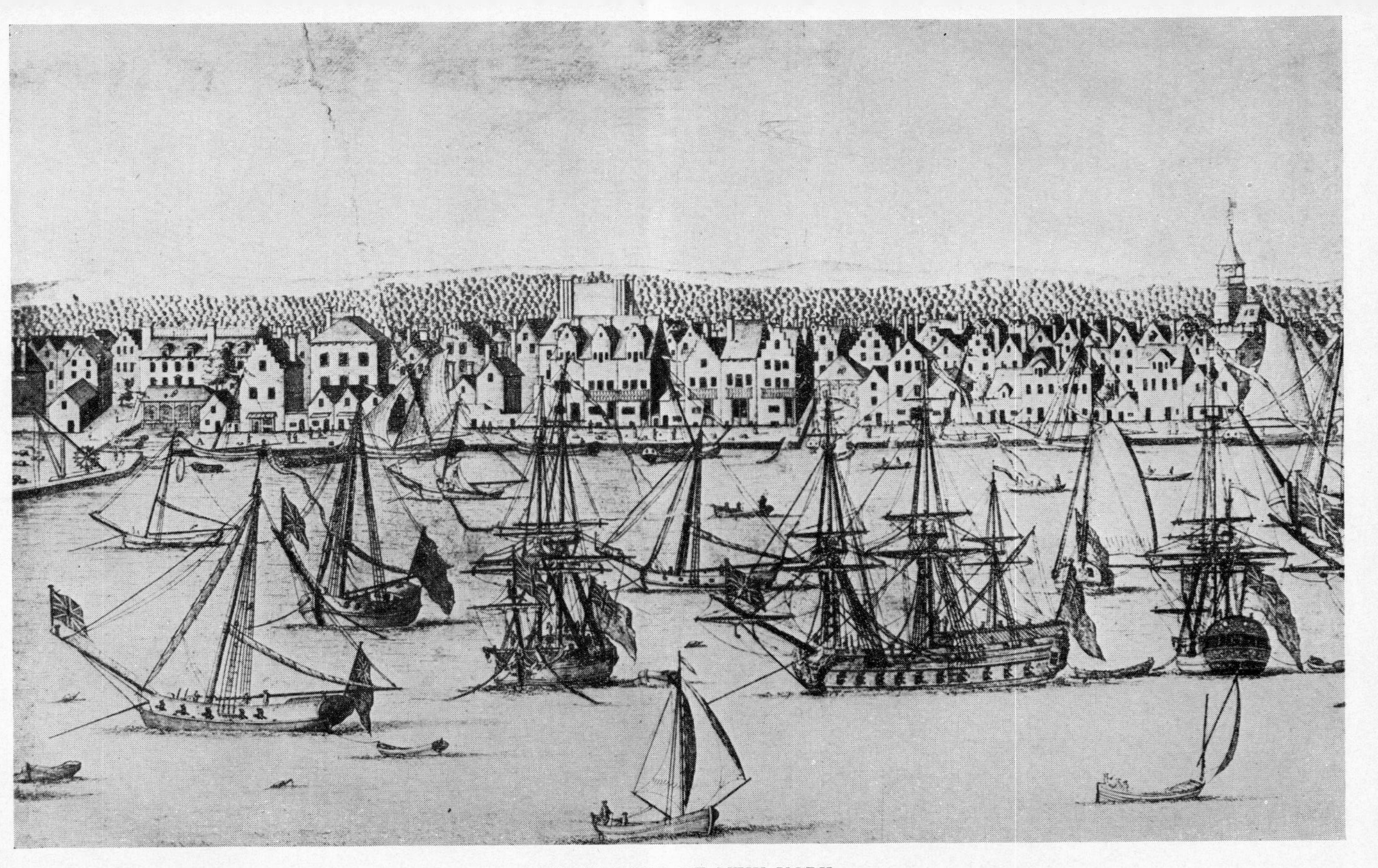

PLATE 5.

BURGIS VIEW OF NEW YORK
Coenties Slip to the Dutch Church

PLATE 6.

BURGIS VIEW OF NEW YORK
Wall Street to Fulton Street

gable-end dormers and pierced by triple chimney stacks, which might well have been designed by Pieter Post himself.[78]

One must be cautious, however, in explaining Dutch features of New York architecture at this time by direct contact with Holland, since Holland itself was exerting so powerful an influence upon England. One has only to glance at Eaton Hall, or other English manor houses of the late seventeenth century, to appreciate how much William Winn, William Talman, Sir John Vanbrugh and other Dutch born architects had done to shape English architecture. An English builder, newly arrived in New York, might design a house strictly in accord with the latest styles in the mother country, yet Dutch in atmosphere and in many details. Thus the town in the first half of the eighteenth century witnessed a strange conflict of architectural ideas, a mingling of direct and indirect influences. Eventually, of course, the English victory was complete. More and more English books on architecture found their way into the local libraries, more and more English-trained architects came to New York to hang out their shingles. "Dobie and Clow, builders in Division Street," who inserted an advertisement in *The Mercury,* announcing that they were ready "to build after the London taste," must have been typical of an increasingly large group.[79] On the new streets which gradually encroached upon the boweries north of the old town the houses nearly all showed the familiar Georgian features—the cornice, quoins, regularly spaced windows and doors. Here and there one would see a gambrel roof with gently sloping lines, surmounted by a balustrade, where the New Yorker sat on hot summer evenings to catch any breath of air coming in from the harbor or the river.[80]

The city south of Wall Street retained its Dutch flavor until the Revolution, and the British soldiers as they entered the place in September 1776 noted with interest the stepped gables and finials of the old houses. But the end was at hand. "We were up

[78]Compare the Mauritshuis at the Hague, H. von Jan Lauweriks, *Alt-Holland,* p. 58.

[79]*New York Mercury,* April 8, 1765.

[80]"Many of the houses had a balcony on the roof on which the people used to sit in the evenings in the summer season," Peter Kalm tells us. *Travels in North America,* Vol. I, p. 194.

by three this morning to view a great fire down the river towards New York," Philip Fithian from his post in the American camp at Harlem wrote down in his journal. "Many suppose it must be New York set on fire by some of our zealous Whigs."[81] This surmise proved only too correct. The conflagration, sweeping away almost all the buildings between Broad Street, the Hudson and Wall Street, turned north in the section west of Broadway to

FIGURE 7. CROSS SECTION OF LOWER SAXON PEASANT HOUSE

leave a swath of desolation as far as King's college. What English influence had not been able to do in a century, the flames accomplished in a few hours, and the New Amsterdam of Minuit, Stuyvesant and Leisler had vanished.[82]

Turning from urban to rural architecture in Dutch America, we find that the barns afford just as interesting and clear an illustration of the transit and survival of European ideas as the farmhouses. If one wanders through some of the more secluded regions, down the Millstone and Raritan valleys, or in Dutchess and Albany counties, he will find here and there still standing the barns of the early settlers (Plate 8). In many cases new shingles on roof and sides, perhaps also a fresh coat of paint, give a modern appearance, but the wide gable end with its large central

[81] R. G. Albion and L. Dodson, *Philip Vickers Fithian: Journal,* pp. 240, 241.
[82] I. N. Phelps Stokes, *Iconography,* Vol. V, p. 1021.

door and the smaller side doors, the broad sweep of the roof and the low eaves betray its antiquity. When one enters he finds the massive timbers, hewn from heart oak, as sound as on the day two centuries ago when they were lifted into place. Even then he would probably not suspect that these old buildings, both in their structural details and in the arrangement of their floor plans, are almost identical with the Lower Saxon peasant houses of northern Germany.

The Niedersächsisches Bauernhaus originated in the lower valleys of the Elbe and the Weser, but spread over the region from Rügenwalde in Pomerania to the banks of the Rhine, and from the Baltic and the North Sea to Hanover.[83] Like the peasant houses of many other parts of Europe it comprises not only a residence but a workshop in which are centered almost all the activities of the family. Here are the peasant's sitting room and chambers, with oven, *koffers,* bed alcoves, fireplace, spinning wheels and tables; here the great threshing floor, the hay-loft, the stalls for horses and cattle.[84]

As one approaches the building he is struck by the great sweep of the roof, which rises sharply from low eaves to a lofty ridge running perhaps ninety or a hundred feet from one gable-end to the other. The roof covering is of tiles or shingles or thatch, and there are no dormers. The residence is at one end, occupying a third or a fourth of the building, with the barn stretching out behind like a Noah's Ark. In the center of the rear gable-end is a door large enough to admit loaded wagons, and smaller doors under the eaves for horses and cows (Fig. 7).

Upon entering we find ourselves in a large room, sixty feet by twenty, whose great supporting beams and ceiling timbers give the impression of the interior of one of Lord Nelson's ships of the line[85] (Fig. 8). On one side are small compartments for storing wood or hay, a long stall for cows, and perhaps the farm-hand's room; on the other the horse stalls; and above, the hay loft. The great room or *diele* is separated in some cases by a

[83]Klaus Thiede, *Deutsche Bauernhäuser,* p. viii.
[84]*Das Bauernhaus in Deutschland,* Plate 101.
[85]*Ibid.,* Plate 21.

partition from the residence, in others it merely continues into the household workroom, which in turn leads into the sitting room and bedrooms.[86]

The combining of residence, barn, stable and hay loft under

FIGURE 8. INTERIOR OF LOWER SAXON PEASANT HOUSE

one roof, which to Americans seems so strange, has many advantages. It effects a great saving in building and repair costs, for one roof and one set of walls do the duty of four or five, while it saves valuable time in going from one task to another. In fact, the Lower Saxon peasant house is a model of convenience. The busy *frau* from her seat by the fire in the household workroom where she cooks and spins, has under her eye children and servants, horses and cattle, the entrance to the cellar, and through the various doors the activities in the yard. Without moving from her place she can direct the feeding of the cattle, the cleaning of the stalls, the drawing of water, the storing of hay, the milking of the cows.[87]

[86]Klaus Thiede, *Deutsche Bauernhäuser,* pp. 21, 30.
[87]Konrad Hahn, *Deutsche Volkskunst,* pp. 68, 69.

From Germany the Lower Saxon peasant house found its way across the Dutch border, spreading over Drenthe and parts of Overyssel and in a modified form over all central and southern Holland.[88] Whereas the lofty hipped roof and mouse-tooth gable-ends of the peasant houses in Groningen bespeak Frisian origin and the long farmhouses of the Zuyder Zee region are mixed Frisian, the so-called Halle-Typus harks back to the Weser and

FIGURE 9. DUTCH PEASANT HOUSE

the Elbe.[89] There is no mistaking the Lower Saxon house even amid its new surroundings. "The back part is for the cattle which stand in rows on either side, with a large open space in the center, called the deel where the carts are kept," says P. M. Hough, in his *Dutch Life in Town and Country*. "A large arched double door leads into it, while the thatched roof comes down low on either side. Leading from the *deel,* or stable, into the living room is a small door, with a window to enable the inhabitants to see what is going on among their friends of the fields."[90] (Fig. 9). Although the Lower Saxon peasant house in its original form was confined to a restricted area in the north-

[88]H. Van der Kloot Meijburg, *Onze Oude Boerenhuizen,* p. 16.
[89]J. H. Gallée, *Das Niederländische Bauernhaus und seine Bewohner,* Vol. I, pp. 18–45.
[90]P. M. Hough, *Dutch Life in Town and Country,* p. 89; H. Van der Kloot Meijburg, *Onze Oude Boerenhuizen,* pp. 53, 84, 85.

east, in the shape of a T-house, in which the roof beam of the residence is at right angles with that of the barn, it spread over parts of Gelderland, North Brabant, Utrecht and South Holland whence came so many of the emigrants to America.[91]

We are not surprised, then, that they brought it with them to their new homes on the Hudson, and the Raritan. From the first, however, they seem to have separated the residence from the barn. It is true that in 1643 Jacob van Curler wrote Killiaen van Rensselaer that he had contracted with the carpenter Jan Cornelissen for a farmhouse "120 feet long by 28 feet wide," forty feet of the length being used for the dwelling and the rest to house the laborers, cattle and horses. The whole was to be thatched with reed.[92] But this typical combination dwelling and barn seems to have been exceptional. In 1646 we find Thomas Chamber receiving directions to build a farmhouse in Rensselaerwyck sixty feet long and twenty feet wide, "in all its parts and members similar to the barn of Poentje," and the dwelling house to be "apart and separate."[93] Why the old combination farm building was abandoned in America we can only conjecture. Perhaps the labor of hewing out the huge beams for the framework was too great, perhaps the heat from the cattle and horses was uncomfortable in the scorching American summers, perhaps it was deemed unwise to have the thatched roof of the barn too near the roaring fire in the residence necessitated by the bitter cold of winter.

The barn, none-the-less, remained as nearly as conditions in America permitted a reproduction of the rear section of the Halle-Typus combination farmhouse. The barn "was very great, so as to almost equal a small church," says Peter Kalm, "the roof was pretty high, covered with wooden shingles, declining on both sides but not steep. The walls which support it were not much higher than a full grown man, but, on the other hand, the breadth of the building was more considerable. In the middle was the threshing floor, and above it or in the loft or garret they put the corn which was not yet threshed, the straw, or anything else according to the season; on one side were the stables for the

[91] *Ibid.*, pp. 60–62.
[92] E. B. O'Callaghan, *History of New Netherland*, p. 458.
[93] *Ibid.*, p. 473.

horses, on the other for the cows. . . . On both ends of the building were great doors, so that one could come in with a cart and horses through one of them and go out at the other. Here, therefore, under one roof were the threshing floor, the barn, the stables, the hay loft, the coach house, etc."[94]

But we are not dependent upon Kalm's interesting descriptions to know what the early Dutch barns were like, since many of them are still standing. Even where the original residence has made way for a more modern structure, the barn often remains, no doubt because the soundness of the great beams of the framework made its destruction unnecessary. One may recognize them by the broad expanse of the roof, coming down on either side to low-lying side walls, by the large door in the center of each gable-end flanked with smaller doors under the eaves, and in some cases by the gable overhang (Plate 8). Inside we find the familiar arrangement of central threshing floor, stalls on one side for horses and on the other for cattle, and hay loft above. Even the framework is almost identical with that of the Lower Saxon peasant house, the roof resting not only on the wall beams but on sturdy hewn posts set in eight to ten feet and connected twelve or more feet above the floor with stout cross beams.

There is no possibility of confusing the Dutch barn with the German barn or the English barn. As one motors westward from New Brunswick, when he sees an old barn with the wagon entrance on the long side, he may be fairly certain that it is of English or New England antecedents; if the entrance is in the gable-end it is Dutch; and when, after crossing the Delaware, he finds barns with the stalls on the ground level and the threshing floor above he knows it is a Pennsylvania Swiss or German

[94]Peter Kalm, *Travels in North America* (London, 1772), pp. 174, 175; compare Thos. Anbury, *Travels Through the Interior Parts of America,* Vol. II, p. 250.

The great barn at the Philip Schuyler farm in Albany County was "at least a hundred feet long and sixty wide," the roof rising to a "great height" and sloping down to within ten feet of the ground. The cattle stood on one side and the horses on the other, "their hinder parts to the wall and their heads towards the threshing floor." At harvest time the wagons were driven in through the great central door of one gable end, and after the hay or corn had been tossed up into the loft, passed out through the other. Colonel Schuyler's barn was perhaps the largest in Albany County, "but all . . . were constructed on the same plan."—Mrs. Anne Grant, *Memoirs of an American Lady* (Albany, 1876), pp. 116–117.

barn. Even in many localities where the Dutch were so outnumbered by Flemings and other foreign groups that their residences have lost all of the Dutch flavor, the barns are almost as Dutch as though they had been built in Holland. From the medieval peasant house of the lower Elbe and Weser to the barn of the Raritan valley is a long cry indeed, but the descent of the one from the other is clear.

In the fields adjacent to some of the old Dutch barns one is interested to see a unique type of haystack, consisting of four or five heavy poles planted in the ground at equal intervals, and covered by a roof which can be raised or lowered according to the amount of hay (Plate 8). This device was brought over by the early settlers from Holland, where its origin is lost in antiquity, but where it is still in active use.[95] We are told in the Van Rensselaer-Bowier manuscripts of "two hay barrocks each of five poles fifty feet high" in Rensselaerwyck, and another of "four poles fifty feet above the ground."[96] It is a remarkable illustration of the persistence of inheritance that the decendants of the Dutch should have clung to the adjustable-roof haystack for three centuries, even in localities where Dutch architecture and customs have long since vanished. It is even more surprising, however, that in all that time their neighbors, whether English, Scotch-Irish or Germans have turned their backs upon it. In searching through the Raritan and Passaic valleys I have never seen a sliding-roof haystack outside of the regions of original Dutch settlement. Apparently it has been a tough bit of inheritance for the melting-pot.

Having determined to turn their backs on the old combination peasant house, and to separate the residence from the barn and stable, the settlers were somewhat at a loss as to the type of house best suited for their needs. In the north, in Rensselaer, Albany and Columbia counties, the farmers built in the traditional Dutch urban style (Plate 8). Their homesteads, many of them still standing, differed little from those of the merchants of Albany and New York. We find the same sharply rising roof lines, the

[95] J. H. Gallée, *Das Niederlandische Bauernhaus*, p. 37.
[96] A. J. F. van Laer, *Van Rensselaer Bowier Manuscripts*, pp. 308, 604.

use of finials, beam anchors, the mouse-tooth finish, painted shutters, the stoop, even the same crane for hoisting goods to the loft. Although the American Dutch barn is merely the barn and stable end of the old combination house, the residence end was discarded in favor of the urban type of house. One sometimes finds in Holland attached to the great barns but under a separate roof residences whose steep roof or stepped gables betray their close affinity to the city residence, and it is possible that this influenced the farm architecture of the upper Hudson valley.[97]

The farmers, as soon as they had passed out of the pioneer stage, built solidly of brick and stone. Since transportation was difficult and labor dear they used the materials at hand, stones cleared from the fields or brick if suitable clay could be found. In the earlier stone houses the stones were seldom tooled, so that the appearance of the walls, although by no means displeasing, was in marked contrast to the sophisticated façades of the Dutch cities. Since rough stones did not lend themselves to ornamentation the familiar mouse-tooth finish, the elbow, the gable steps, and the finial all are lacking; in their place appears a single gable with projecting raking cornices. But the sharp lines of the roof, the beam-anchors, casement windows in arched recesses, the round ventilators under the ridge show their affinity to the houses of Albany and New Amsterdam.[98]

The brick farmhouses of the Albany region are merely Dutch urban houses in the country, save that the main entrance is invariably on the long side and not in the gable-end. The gable is always of the straight-line elbowed type; one never sees the stepped gable or the convex gable. But we recognize instantly other features of the urban house, the mouse-tooth finish, the simple finial, the beam-anchors, the quaint casement windows and wooden shutters now only too often replaced by ugly sashes and blinds. The charming Hendrick Bries house, Rensselaer County, the Leendert Bronck house, Albany County, the Adam Van Alen house, Columbia County, are among the most perfect surviving samples of true Dutch architecture in America.

[97] S. R. Jones, *Old Houses in Holland,* pp. 70, 77.
[98] Helen W. Reynolds, *Dutch Houses in the Hudson Valley,* Plates 16, 42.

Entirely unlike the houses of the Albany region are the so-called Dutch farmhouses of southern New York and northeastern New Jersey. One finds today, lost in the maze of suburban Brooklyn, or overlooking the upper Hackensack, or tucked away in some little valley of Rockland County, these charming relics of the time of Rip Van Winkle and Ichabod Crane. Long, low structures, usually of stone, but sometimes of brick or timber, in some cases their low roofs curving out over the front and back walls like the visor of a cap, their individuality is striking. There is no possibility of confusing a Bergen County farmhouse with a Columbia County or Albany County farmhouse (Plate 9).

Historians have long been puzzled by the farmhouses of the southern and central regions of New Netherland. Assuming that their origin was to be sought in the area embraced by the modern kingdom of Holland they have searched for the prototype through the pages of Peters, Sydney R. Jones, Gerburg, Veldheer, Gallée, Lauweriks and other writers on Dutch architecture. Failing in this, they have jumped to the conclusion that the settlers in erecting their homes turned their backs upon the habits and traditions of centuries and invented a new and unique type of architecture. "It is a distinctive architecture and our only indigenous form until the coming of the modern sky-scraper," says a recent writer.[99]

This explanation is so contrary to the principles of inheritance exhibited by innumerable examples in early American history that one could safely dismiss it even though every other explanation should fail. Settlers in a new country cling tenaciously to the practices and traditions of the old; relinquishing them in part only because different conditions make it necessary or highly advantageous. We may assume then that the pioneers on the lower Hudson and the Hackensack built their homes so far as building materials, climate, etc., permitted, in the style of their fathers and their grandfathers.

This was made the more obvious by the consideration that houses duplicating in almost every detail the "colonial Dutch"

[99]Rosalie F. Bailey, *Pre-Revolutionary Dutch Houses and Families,* etc. (N. Y., 1936), p. 20.

farmhouse, even to the bell-shaped roof and projecting eaves, are to be found in Canada. It is absurd to assume that pioneers on the Hackensack and the St. Lawrence chanced to "invent" simultaneously the same highly distinctive type of architecture. Canadian historians, after searching fruitlessly in France for the prototype, fell back on the explanation that the cottage originated in Quebec and was brought thence to New York and New Jersey by Dutch traders who came north in search of cheap furs. But this also may be dismissed as too improbable for serious consideration. Even though the farmers of Tappan or Blauvelt or New Utrecht happened to come in contact with an occasional trader to Canada, they certainly would not turn to him for ideas as to the construction of their homes. It would seem then that the origin of the "Dutch colonial" farmhouse must be sought in some part of Europe which sent emigrants to both Quebec and to southern New York and northern New Jersey. This leads us directly to the maritime sections of Flanders, the region embracing the extreme northern tip of France, western Belgium and parts of Zeeland, in Holland.

The Flemings are a Germanic people, tall, blond, with long skulls, contrasting strongly with their fellow Belgians, the Walloons, who are short and dark, with round skulls. In their origin, racial characteristics and tongue the Flemings are almost identical with the Dutch, although long separated in part or in whole by the accidents of history. "The language spoken by the Flemings differs only in dialectical variations from that spoken by the Dutch."[100] Although the Belgian Flemings today are bound to their fellow countrymen the Walloons by the ties of patriotism and religion, they constitute a distinct racial group having more in common with their neighbors across the Dutch border.

The political boundaries of old Flanders, with shiftings from time to time, included what is now southern Zeeland in Holland, all Belgium west of the Scheldt, and the extreme northern tip of France. The linguistic boundaries, however, extend over all northern Belgium, including the province of Antwerp and most of Brabant and Limburg. The line between Flemish on the one hand

[100] S. B. Clough, *A History of the Flemish Movement* (N. Y., 1930), p. 30.

and French and the Walloon dialect of French on the other, runs from a point on the North Sea just west of Dunkirk southward to include Hazebrouck, and then turns due east to the Dutch border north of Liège.

Political oppression, war and religious persecution, that dread triumvirate which drove so many thousands from their homes in Europe to seek protection in foreign lands, laid a heavy hand on the Flemish provinces. During the war with Spain the region was so devastated that it seemed at one time that it might become a wilderness. The cities had "been abandoned by a large part of their inhabitants, agriculture hardly in a less degree than commerce and industry had been ruined." The Flemish loss was in one respect the Dutch gain, for a constant stream of exiles poured over the border to join the famous Sea Beggars or the armies of the Prince of Orange, or to set up their looms in Amsterdam or Utrecht. With them mingled so many Walloons, who had been reared on Guido de Bray's *The Belgic Confession,* or were inspired by the teaching of Peregréne la Grange, that at one time they had established no less than twenty-one congregations in the United Provinces.

The artisans among these exiles soon made for themselves an enviable place in their new homes, for the great commercial cities of Holland needed skilled workers. But the Flemish and Walloon farmers were not so fortunate. The agricultural areas in Holland are restricted, and the *boers* were not inclined to sell a part of their farm-lands to the newcomers even in the rare cases when the newcomers had the wherewithal to purchase. Crowded into the Dutch cities, seeking to earn a living by unaccustomed vocations, the exiled Flemings and Walloons were easily tempted to make the great adventure of migration to America. It is this which explains why the proportion of Flemings and Walloons in the rural districts of New York and New Jersey was so much greater than in the towns.

It is a matter of great difficulty to determine how many Flemings came to the Hudson valley. Sailing from Holland, speaking Dutch, of the same religious faith as the other settlers, they were easily lost amid the mass of Holland Dutch. More attention has been paid to the Walloons, whose French speech at once betrays their origin. Even though we should be cautious in accepting the statement of one writer that "probably two-thirds of the inhabitants of New Netherland called 'Dutch,' were from the southern or Belgic part of the seventeen provinces,"[101] there is every reason to believe that certain counties were predominantly Flemish in blood, while the Flemish, Walloon, and French element was

FIGURE 10. FLEMISH COTTAGE, SHOWING FLYING GUTTER

numerous throughout the farm regions of southern New Netherland.

We have additional evidence of the predominance of the south Netherlanders in northern New Jersey in the fact that the old families spoke the Flemish dialect. "The Jersey Dutch was originally the South Holland or Flemish language," says Professor J. Dyneley Prince.[102] When a group of north Dutch came to Paterson in recent years, the descendants of the original settlers kept strictly aloof from them, pointing out that "our language is low Dutch and theirs is Holland Dutch."[103]

The visitor to West Flanders, as he approaches the coast in the vicinity of Furnes, finds himself in the *Houtland,* or wooded Veurne-Ambachtsch region. It has been described as a forest which at a distance seems somber and impenetrable, but on closer sight dissolves into great trees widely spaced around cultivated fields and farmhouses. The farm buildings present a striking con-

[101]William E. Griffis, *The Story of the Walloons* (N. Y., 1923), p. 8.
[102]"The Jersey Dutch Dialect," *Dialect Notes,* Vol. III, Part VI, p. 459.
[103]Onze tâl äz lêx däuts en hoelliz äz hôl-läns.

trast to those of Holland. In place of the great peasant house, with residence, barn and stables under one roof, one sees a series of low buildings grouped around three sides of a court, seldom touching elbows but connected by wooden fences.

One glimpse at the residence convinces us that here we have the source of the "Dutch colonial" houses of southern New York and northeastern New Jersey (Fig. 10). Before us is a long, low cottage, one story in height with loft, with additions to right or left in similar style, the chimneys sometimes in the middle, sometimes at the gable ends. But what interests us most is the discovery that in many cases the low lines of the roof curve out for two feet or more over the front and rear walls. When the roof is thatched, the projection is usually formed by several rows of red tiles to constitute what the Flemings call a "flying gutter"; if tiles are used, the sweep of the curved roof is uninterrupted. Upon closer examination one discovers other similarities to the American "Dutch" farmhouses—the recessed windows, the rear lean-to with roof descending to within a few feet of the ground, the paucity of dormers. Were it not for the difference in building materials, these cottages would fit perfectly into the landscape of Tappan or Blauvelt.

The mystery of the projecting eaves now ceases to be a mystery, for we find that many of the Flemish farm buildings, residences as well as barns and stables, are built of clay mixed with lime and straw.[104] "In the Lys plain three-fourths of the farms are thus built; moreover, the proportion of clay walls is still nearly two-thirds in the Alost region, a good third around Lille and in the woodlands of Cassel."[105] It is imperative that there should be some protection for walls of such perishable material from the driving rains common in this region, else the farmer would soon find his house crumbling about him. In fact, many seem pathetically decrepit, "bent over, warped, sinking under the weight of the roof,"[106] and without the *auvent,* or pent-roof, they would not last a generation.

104Raoul Blanchard, *La Flandre* (Lille, 1906), pp. 416, 417.

105*Ibid.*, p. 417; Jos. Viérin, *L'Architecture Régionale de la Flandre Maritime* (Brussels, 1921), p. 25.

106R. Blanchard, *La Flandre,* p. 417.

On the gable-ends the problem is met in a different way. Here the walls are constructed with an outer and an inner section separated by a space of an inch or two and tied together by iron anchors, vitrified brick or sometimes by bottles.[107] In this way the outer section protects the inner from the rain, while any water seeping through is drained off through the aperture. Should the outer wall begin to crumble, the roof is supported by the inner

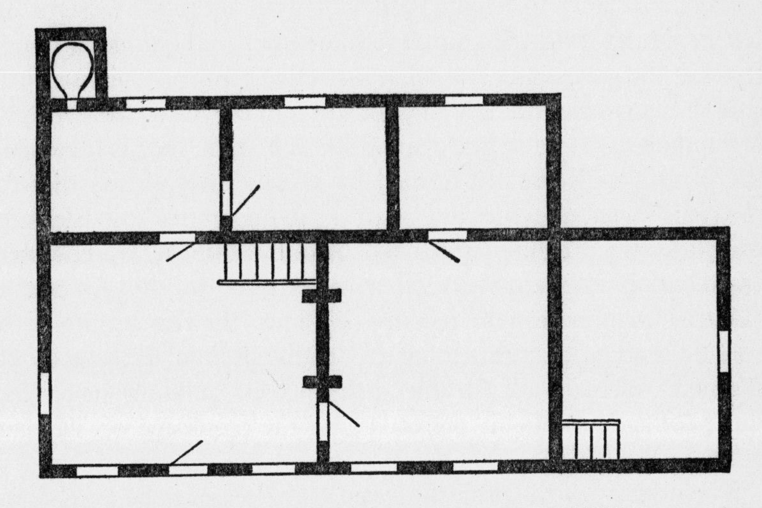

FIGURE 11. TYPICAL PLAN OF FLEMISH COTTAGE

section until repairs can be made, and no serious damage to the house results.

There is an air both of gaiety and repose about these little cottages, heightened by the row of dahlias and hydrangeas under the front wall, the white or green shutters, the little square panes of the windows which permit a glimpse of the curtains and the flowers blooming on the inside. One enters the living-room, or *het huis,* with its great stove, table, clock, cupboard and objects of devotion (Fig. 11). To the right is the *beste kammer* or parlor, reserved for great occasions—marriages, baptisms, funerals—beyond it, elevated several feet, to make room for the shallow cellar beneath, is the "vaute," and behind, under the low-lying

[107] J. Viérin, *L'Architecture Régionale de la Flandre Maritime,* p. 74.

roof, a shed, wash-room, or a bedroom or two.[108] Flanking the court on one side is the stable, on the other the barn, both often constructed of the same materials as the residence and having the same proportions. The barn, with its low roof lines and its doors in the long side has nothing in common with either the Lower Saxon peasant house or the great barns of Zeeland.

When the Flemish emigrants reached their new homes in America, like other settlers they must have sought to build as they and their fathers had built in the plains or the *Houtlands* of Belgium, Zeeland or France. But they were confronted by differences in climate and available building materials. Those who came to the wooded hills and narrow valleys of Bergen and Rockland counties, from very early days made use of the brown sandstone which they found in abundance on their own property. If any built of clay and straw after the manner of Flanders, the houses have long since succumbed to time and the weather. But tradition asserted itself in their substitute for mortar, which "was mud or clay, strengthened by straw or hogs' hair."[109] The stones used during the earlier period were irregular in size and laid in random bond, while for later houses they were cut into oblong blocks usually about eight inches high and varying in length from six inches to two and a half feet.[110] Sometimes the owner, perhaps thinking of the old homestead in far-away Flanders, and dissatisfied with the rich brown of his walls, gave them a coat of sand and lime, or of paint or whitewash. On Long Island and in other regions where stone was rare, the Flemings often fell back upon their accustomed clay and straw, fitting it in as filler to a timber framework, however, and protecting it with long hand-hewn shingles. Occasionally the construction was of brick.[111]

Though the Fleming yielded to necessity in the selection of his building material, he clung rigidly to tradition in the outward

[108] L'abbé J. Lemire, "L'Habitat dans la Flandre Française," *Annales du Comité Flamand de France,* Vol. XX, 1892, pp. 1–18; Jos. Viérin, *L'Architecture Régionale de la Flandre Maritime,* p. 25.

[109] Rosalie F. Bailey, *Pre-Revolutionary Dutch Houses,* etc., p. 23.

[110] *The White Pine Series,* XI, No. 3, p. 3.

[111] The Washington headquarters at Tappan is partly of stone, partly of brick.

form of his house, in the interior arrangement of rooms, and even in minor architectural details. The quaint cottages of Tappan or Paramus or New Utrecht are merely Flemish cottages built in America (Plate 9). There is the same original central unit, the same extensions to right or left, the same low roof flaring at the eaves and projecting over the front and rear walls, the same interior chimneys, the same bake-oven built at the back of the kitchen fire-place and protruding beyond the outer wall, the same simple transom over the front door. Upon entering, we find the same arrangement of rooms, "the kitchen, which was also the dining room and living room" adjoining "the parlor," which was also the "best bedroom," while behind are "narrow bedrooms" varying in size and opening directly into the front main rooms.[112] The interior finish and the furnishings also follow closely the Flemish model. The massive hand-hewn beams of the ceiling, the great fire-place set against the wall without jambs[113] and decorated with glazed blue Delftware tiles,[114] a panelled and painted *kasten,* a table, a chair or two, perhaps a grandfather clock.

The feature of the American Flemish cottage which has attracted most attention is the sweep of the eaves and the pronounced overhang. Although unaware of its origin architects have guessed its real purpose. "It was the means by which water was diverted from the walls of the building and prevented the washing out of the clay joints in the masonry,"[115] says one writer. It must be emphasized, however, that the overhang, so far from being indigenous to America, is an excellent example of the survival of European inheritance under changed conditions. The Flemish builders of Bergen or Rockland would probably not have used clay and straw mortar in their new homes had they not been accustomed to this material in Europe, they would certainly not have protected it with the overhang, had not the "flying gutter" been indispensable to the *Houtland* farm buildings.

112R. F. Bailey, *Pre-Revolutionary Dutch Houses,* p. 25.

113See interior view of Hasbrouck house, B. J. Lossing, *The Hudson* (N. Y., 1876), p. 200.

114Note George Washington headquarters at Tappan.

115C. C. Wendehack, in *White Pine Series,* Vol. XI, No. 3.

The "flying gutter" seems at first to have been unchanged in the American cottages, occasionally even taking the form of several rows of tiles or shingles, at the base of a thatched roof. The Lossing view of the famous Nicasius de Sille house, New Utrecht, where General Nathaniel Woodhull died, shows it as a pent roof separate from and projecting from under the main roof.[116] But in time, with the discarding of thatch in favor of tiles or shingles, it became a mere overhang of the roof, frequently sheathed on the under side with boards. With the gradual substitution of very hard mortar for the clay and straw filler, one might suppose that the overhang would become less pronounced and eventually disappear. Actually it was extended farther and farther out over the wall, especially the front wall, until wooden columns were added to form a narrow front porch. "There is a peculiar neatness in the appearance of their dwellings," said James Thacher in 1778, "having an airy piazza supported by pillars in front."[117]

But it must be emphasized that the bell-shaped roof and "flying gutter" are by no means universal among the Flemish and Walloon cottages of New Netherland (Plate 9). In Ulster the straight line roof is the accepted form, while there are numerous examples in Dutchess, Richmond, and even in Rockland. Although many of the old houses have been so altered that some of the original features have been lost, if one sees a cottage with the roof lines curving out over the front and rear walls, he may assume that the original owner came from the clay house region of Flanders; if the roof lines are straight and the projection is lacking, that it belonged to a settler from the sandy plains or some other district where the farmers built solidly of brick.

In the houses which have "flying gutters" in front and rear, the fact that the walls of the gable-ends are entirely unprotected from rain has long puzzled historians. Assuming that the overhanging eaves were designed to protect the clay mortar of the walls, "it is not easily explained why the gable walls were made so extremely flat," says one writer. It is true that the upper part,

[116]B. J. Lossing, *Field Book of the Revolution,* II, p. 605.
[117]R. F. Bailey, *Pre-Revolutionary Dutch Houses,* Appenda.

TE 7. CHURCH AND MARKET STREETS, ALBANY, 1805

TE 8. *Left:* Adam Van Alen House, Kinderhook. *Upper Right:* Dutch haystack. *Lower Right:* Dutch barn, Pluckamin–Somerville road

PLATE 9. *Upper Left:* Ackerman house, Paramus. *Upper Right:* Abraham Hasbrouck house, New Paltz

under the gable itself was almost invariably sheathed with shingles or clapboard, but below it was exposed to the full sweep of rain or snow. Perhaps it was the force of custom alone which made the Flemish settlers build these unprotected walls. Their gable-ends in the old country seldom had pent roofs, so they could not accustom themselves to them in the new.[118] But one wonders whether a close examination of the gable-end masonry in some of the Bergen or Rockland houses would not reveal some means of inner draining similar to that in vogue in Flanders. The occasional rows of stone chips which one finds in some of the old walls may be the binding for an inner and an outer section.

As time passed the Flemish cottage in America was gradually reshaped by local conditions, until it developed into a distinct and charming architecture, clearly Flemish in origin, but having its own individuality. Climate, building materials, and especially increasing prosperity brought about this change. As the farmer's cattle doubled and tripled in number, as his loft became crowded with vegetables and fruits, and his barn with wheat and corn, the little cottage of his father or grandfather no longer seemed adequate to his needs. So he replaced it by, or more often added to it, a somewhat pretentious residence of perhaps forty-five feet by thirty, with low gambrel roof terminating in the characteristic pronounced projection both in front and behind, usually without dormers, the walls of neatly dressed stone (Plate 9). A number of these houses are still standing, on the Tenafly road or the Polifly road or on Saddle River in northern New Jersey, their beautiful proportions and quiet charm contrasting strangely with the ugly boxlike modern structures inspired by them and miscalled "Dutch colonial."

The gambrel which was introduced here as elsewhere in America in the eighteenth century assumed a unique and charming character. The builders of Queens or Bergen, retaining their traditional roof lines, merely cut back the top to form an obtuse angle at the ridge. The "Dutch" gambrel adds no additional space

[118] Yet we find the overhang in the Hendrick Brinckerhof house, Teaneck, extended around the gable end to form a pent roof between first story and loft. R. F. Bailey, *Pre-Revolutionary Dutch Houses,* Plate 79.

to the upper floors, but its lines are far more pleasing than those of the New England gambrel or the Virginia and Maryland gambrel. One has only to view the beautiful old Abraham Ackerman house, Hackensack, or the Cosyn Haring house, Old Tappan, to agree with the judgment that "the Dutch combination of slopes and curved overhanging eaves is the most beautiful gambrel known."[119]

In view of the supremacy of the Flemish and Walloon farmhouse throughout most of Dutch New York and New Jersey, it is not easy to explain the prevalence of the Dutch barn in the same regions. It is possible that the Flemings and Walloons at first built barns similar to those of the *Huitland* or of Hainaut, but later discarded them in favor of the convenient and simple type used by their Dutch neighbors. It is also possible that some, before migrating to America, had worked as laborers on farms in Holland and so had become acquainted with the Dutch peasant house. Yet the fact that Dutch barns were so widely diffused in the farm regions of New Netherland should warn us not to jump to the conclusion that few or no Dutch farmers settled there merely because the prevailing type of residence is Flemish and Walloon.[120]

In church architecture the colonial builders were clearly dominated by the ideas prevailing in the homeland. The distinctive feature of Dutch Gothic is the use made of gables, perhaps because the architects were so dominated by the influence of gable-ends in domestic buildings that they could not design their churches without assigning an important place to them. Whereas the usual Gothic church has one great roof over the nave and choir, with smaller roofs over the transepts, in Holland the churches often consist of two or perhaps three distinct sections lying side by side, each with its own roof. Were it not for the Gothic windows, the buttresses and the spire, these buildings would look much like a group of large houses. Of this type are St. Michaels, at Zolle, the church at Hasselt, St. Joriskerspel,

[119] R. F. Bailey, *Pre-Revolutionary Dutch Houses,* p. 21.

[120] I have twice scoured parts of Bergen and Rockland in search of old barns, to little purpose. The interesting Smith barn, Germonds, seems to have little in common with either the Dutch or the Flemish barn. The barns of the other houses I visited are gone.

Amersfoort, and many others.[121] Even more striking is the simple basilica dominated by several transverse gables as illustrated by St. Jakob's Church, the Hague,[122] St. Martens, at Groningen, etc.

When the colonists in New Amsterdam erected their first house of worship the design was faithful to Dutch traditions. The earliest views of the little town show the typical twin gables rising sharply over the walls of the fort, the whole dominated by a square tower capped with a low spire[123] (Plate 2). Before 1660 a large addition had been made in the rear having one large gable, and the whole linked by a cross gable. The building, in the days when Peter Stuyvesant worshipped in it, must have resembled many small churches of the Dutch cities.

However, the New Amsterdam church, so far as we know, was the only one in the colony to hark back to medieval traditions. In Holland itself profound changes were taking place. The Protestant Revolution had brought a revolt not only against the tenets of Rome, but against her art, especially against her ecclesiastical architecture. Calvin had warned against "seeking the church of God in the beauty of buildings," and his followers in the Netherlands took his words so deeply to heart that the churches they erected were simplicity itself.[124]

The emphasis placed upon preaching by the Calvinists made the pulpit rather than the altar the focal point in the church. This no doubt explains in part why the first Protestant church in Holland, built at Willemstad in 1595, accepted "the genuinely central building scheme, or a regularly octagonal ground plan," in which the preacher is in easy range of the entire congregation. It was Prince Maurice himself, acting perhaps under the advice of the versatile architect Simon Stevin, who directed that the church be in *"achtcantige forme."*[125] The building was supported at the corners with buttresses, the sides were pierced by large rounded windows, while the eight-sided roof receded to a belfry,

[121] C. H. Peters, *De Nederlandsche Stedenbouw*, Plates 14, 16, 43.
[122] Jan Lauweriks, *Alt-Holland*, pp. 6, 9.
[123] See Prototype View.
[124] F. A. J. Vermeulen, *Handbock tot de Geschiedenis der Nederlandsche Bouwkunst*, Vol. II, pp. 354–357.
[125] *Ibid.*, pp. 363–364.

the whole conveying rather the impression of a watch tower than a house of worship. Similar were the church at Jzendijke, the Noorderkerk at Amsterdam, the church at Maasluis and the Nooderkerk at Groningen.

Killiaen van Rensselaer seems to have been the first to introduce the octagonal church to Dutch America. "In the box is a

FIGURE 12. OCTAGONAL DUTCH CHURCH, BERGEN, NEW JERSEY. BUILT 1680

wooden model of a small church," he wrote to Arendt van Corlaer in 1641, "please use diligence in erecting it. It ought not to be a very complicated matter, the shape being mostly that of an eight-cornered mill."[126] Although it is doubtful whether this church was ever built, it is possible that the "wooden model" was used in constructing some of the octagonal churches which

126A. J. A. van Laer, *Van Rensselaer Bowier Manuscripts,* pp. 551, 561.

became so familiar in New York and the Dutch sections of New Jersey.

Typical were the Bushwick church, Brooklyn, the churches at New Utrecht, Jamaica, Bergen (Fig. 12), Hackensack, the Ponds, and elsewhere, all octagonal in form with peculiar candle-extinguisher roofs. Visitors to New York and New Jersey, struck by the strangeness of these little churches, have likened them to light-houses, "only occupying more ground at the base, and not extending to so great a height."[127] We have a distant but clear view of the roof of the Reformed Church in Philadelphia in the George Heap drawing of 1747, its cupola rising high above the surrounding buildings at Race and Fourth Streets. Like the church on Staten Island it differed from the others in being "six square" or hexagonal. Peter Kalm thought it looked like a church near Stockholm.[128]

The interiors of the churches were severely plain in keeping with the simplicity of the Reformed worship and of conditions in a new country. We catch a glimpse of the church at Claverack from the description of Reverend F. N. Zabriskie. "The tinkling of the bell has ceased its clatter in the little old belfry . . . the men were ranged around the walls and the women in orderly rows in the center. Above their heads is a wooden ceiling with prodigious rafters. The walls are plastered and meant to be white; the wood-work is painted blue. . . . The pulpit stands at the north end . . . shaped like a wineglass, and surmounted by a sounding board."[129] The pulpit in fact was the most conspicuous object in all the churches. The one at Albany was octagonal in form, as usual raised upon a pedestal and reached by a flight of narrow steps, the trimmings and mouldings were of oak, beside the minister's hand was a small bracket for the hour-glass.[130]

In time the octagonal churches gave way to square or approximately square buildings, with the roof receding as before to a central belfry, somewhat in the style of the seventeenth-century New England meeting house. In accordance with the centralized

[127] N. S. Prince, *History of Long Island*, p. 69.
[128] Peter Kalm, *Travels in North America*, Vol. I, p. 196.
[129] F. N. Zabriskie, *History of the Reformed Church of Claverack*, p. 12.
[130] Alice M. Earle, *Colonial Days in Old New York*, p. 267.

space idea the pulpit was placed against the rear wall, facing the door, within easy earshot of the entire congregation. The Albany church, built in 1715, was perhaps the most pretentious of this type (Plate 7). A drawing made in 1805 shows a stone building nearly square with slender Gothic windows and roof rising to a narrow ridge, straddling which is a closed cupola. A vestibule in

FIGURE 13. DUTCH REFORMED CHURCH, NEW BRUNSWICK, NEW JERSEY

the form of a typical urban Dutch house is obviously an afterthought. The windows were of stained glass decorated with the coats-of-arms of prominent Albany families, while painted escutcheons hung on the walls.[131]

The Dutch church at New Brunswick, built in 1767, was in the same mould (Fig. 13). "Two pillars supported the roof from the center, which went up on four sides, ending in a small steeple.

131 *Ibid.*, pp. 269–270.

A bell was put up about the year 1775, and the sexton, in ringing, stood in the middle aisle, winding the rope during service around one of the pillars."[132] The little building looked more like a pepper box than a church, and one might easily imagine a giant lifting the top by the cupola to get at the contents. But the gold of the weather-vane and ball, the blue of the dunce-cap spire, the red of the roof shingles and the white of the cornice and of window and door frames lent a typical touch of Dutch color.[133]

As the little square or octagonal churches crumbled with age, or proved too small for their growing congregations, they were replaced by buildings more in the English than the Dutch style. The charming old oblong church at Millstone, with its gleaming white weatherboarding, its little steeple set on the ridge over the gable, the three rounded front doors, the cornice extending across the front wall makes a picture which fits better into the New England village than the Dutch landscape. The church erected at Bergen in 1773 was in the same style as the Presbyterian churches of Newark and Elizabeth; the Paramus church, the Fishkill church, the Schraelenburgh church all resemble closely the English or New England churches around them. By the end of the colonial period there was even less of the ecclesiastical than the domestic architecture of Holland lingering in the Dutch parts of New York and New Jersey.

[132]Richard H. Steele, *Historical Discourse,* pp. 50, 51.
[133]Archibald Robertson drawing of New Brunswick, N. Y. Public Library.

Chapter III

FOR CHURCH AND MOTHER TONGUE

FOR the Netherlander religion and patriotism were almost synonymous. It had been his heroic resistance to the persecutions of Philip II of Spain which had brought him civil as well as religious freedom. So whenever his thoughts returned to the cruelties of the Duke of Alva and the Council of Blood, to the inspired leadership of William of Orange and the exploits of the Sea Beggars, religion and independence seemed inseparably united as one sacred cause. He could hardly conceive of a branch of the Dutch Reformed Church independent of Holland. This explains why the Church in America continued for many decades after the English conquest under the jurisdiction of the Classis of Amsterdam, why it found it difficult to adjust itself to American conditions and why it evinced so little interest in proselyting people of other nationalities.

The West India Company made the Dutch Reformed Church the established Church of New Netherland. It pledged itself to maintain the national religion "as it is at present preached and practised by public authority in the United Netherlands," and to send over and support "good and suitable preachers, schoolmasters and comforters of the sick."[1] But the Company was never over-zealous in religious affairs. For several years after the founding of New Amsterdam the only place of worship was a large room above the horse mill where two comforters of the sick held informal services,[2] and it was only with the arrival of the Reverend Jonas Michaelius in 1628 that a congregation was organized[3] and early in Van Twiller's administration that the picturesque little church reared its head above the walls of the fort.

[1]*Ecclesiastical Records, State of New York,* Vol. I, pp. 119–123.
[2]W. W. Sweet, *Story of Religions in America,* p. 124.
[3]J. F. Jameson, *Narratives of New Netherland,* p. 124.

During the entire Dutch period only thirteen ministers were sent over.[4]

The responsibility of maintaining religious services upon the patroonships fell to the lot of the patroons, their charters binding them to procure clergymen "in order that Divine Service and zeal for religion may be planted in that colony."[5] The contract made by Killiaen van Rensselaer with Reverend John Megapolensis, in 1642, shows the terms on which some of the ministers came to the colony. The domine and his family were to provide their own furniture, clothing, etc., but the patroon promised for the first three years meat, drink and lodging, together with a salary of one thousand guilders.[6]

It was to the Classis of Amsterdam, however, that the infant Church looked for guidance. Whenever a doubt arose as to this tenet or that, whenever the ministers engaged in unbrotherly disputes, whenever there was discouragement and dissatisfaction the matter was sure to go before the reverend brothers sitting in far-off Holland. If you "deem it necessary to administer to us any correction, instruction or good advice, it will be agreeable to us," wrote Domine Michaelius in 1628.[7] He did not realize how difficult it would prove for a body three thousand miles away to understand and solve all the problems of a pioneer clergy. His desire and the desire of his successors for decades was for the colonial Church to be as much a part of the national body as any congregation in Holland itself. As a matter of course the Dutch Reformed was made the established Church of the colony. Taxes were levied for the erection of church buildings and the support of the clergymen, and the Quaker or Anglican who demurred was sure to be hauled before the Governor and Council and forced to pay double.[8]

Yet the Quaker and the Anglican, having paid their dues, were permitted to worship according to their own views. The Netherlands was the most liberal country in the world, a refuge

[4]W. W. Sweet, *Story of Religions in America*, p. 133.
[5]*Ecclesiastical Records, State of New York*, Vol. I, pp. 45–48.
[6]*Ecclesiastical Records, State of New York*, Vol. I, pp. 119–123.
[7]J. F. Jameson, *Narratives of New Netherlands*, p. 125.
[8]*Ecclesiastical Records, State of New York*, Vol. I, p. 420.

for the persecuted of other lands, and the colony in its early days reflected the spirit of the mother country. When a number of New England families fled from the harshness of the Puritan tribunals to New Amsterdam, they were welcomed and promised "liberty of conscience according to the custom and manner of Holland."

This policy would probably have continued indefinitely had it not run afoul of the sturdy orthodoxy and nationalism of Peter Stuyvesant and aroused the fear of the ministers for the Church establishment. There were many dour looks and some open complaints as "singing Quakers, ranting Quakers, Sabbatarians, Antisabbatarians, some Anabaptists" rushed in. Matters came to a head when the Dutch Lutherans, who at first had worshipped at the Reformed Church, presented a request for a pastor of their own. Stuyvesant and the Council answered with a law forbidding preaching by unqualified persons and the holding of unauthorized religious meetings. This reversal of the traditional Dutch policy brought upon the colony many harsh criticisms in Holland and the remonstrances of the West India Company, but the stubborn Stuyvesant held to his guns to the last.[9]

But the day was at hand when the Reformed Church itself was to ask religious liberty. When, in 1664, the British fleet presented itself before New Amsterdam, and Colonel Nicolls demanded immediate surrender, the Dutch were forced to make the best terms they could. One of their chief concerns was for their religion, and in this, as in other things, the English were inclined to be lenient. The eighth article of surrender guaranteed that "the Dutch here shall enjoy the liberty of their consciences in divine worship and church discipline."[10] This article, which came to be regarded as the Magna Carta of the Reformed Church in New York and New Jersey, with a few execptions was honorably adhered to by the English government.

The Dutch Reformed Church now found itself in a peculiar and somewhat embarrassing position. A distinctly national body,

[9]Leonard W. Bacon, *A History of American Christianity*, p. 73—*The American Church History Series.*

[10]*Ecclesiastical Records, State of New York*, Vol. I, pp. 557–559.

it was cut off from the nation of its birth; subordinate to the Classis of Amsterdam in spiritual matters, it was at the same time under the temporal jurisdiction of England; developed as an established church, it now had to fall back on its own resources. The ministers themselves were at a loss to know whether they could swear allegiance to the King of England, and retain their status in the church of the Netherlands. The articles of surrender made it clear that they were not to be considered dissenters, yet they were not members of the Church of England.

The so-called Duke's Laws, published in 1665, as a kind of fundamental code for the colony, conceded to the Dutch Reformed Church even more than its clergy could have expected. In each community there was to be a church, ministered to by a Protestant clergyman selected by a vote of the freeholders. When once chosen, however, he was to be supported by taxes levied upon all alike. Since in all save a few places the Dutch Reformed Church counted a majority, the law meant in effect that other groups—Quakers, Lutherans, Congregationalists, Jews—must contribute to its support.[11] On the other hand, should one of these groups become numerous enough to form a congregation of their own, their minister, in turn, was to be supported from the public levies, or as one domine put it "by obligatory contributions by John Everybody." In other words, the law created not one established church, but an indefinite number of established congregations.[12]

The joy of the Dutch clergy over this favorable arrangement was tempered by the lukewarmness of the English governors in forcing Anglicans and others to pay taxes for their support. "People crowd into the church and apparently like the sermon," wrote Domine Megapolensis to the Classis of Amsterdam in 1669, "but most of the listeners are not inclined to contribute to the support of the church and salary of the preacher. They seem to desire that we should live on air. . . . We have several times spoken to the Governor but he answers that if the Dutch will

[11]Herbert L. Osgood, *The American Colonies in the 17th Century*, Vol. II, pp. 335-336.

[12]Schuyler van Rensselaer, *History of the City of New York*, Vol. II, p. 263.

have divine service their own way, then let them also take care of and support their own preachers."[13]

When this situation had existed long enough to threaten the ruin of religion in the colony, the government began to co-operate better. The governors realized that after all there was nothing to be gained by starving the Dutch ministers. In some places the courts confirmed the obligation of all the inhabitants to pay church dues, in others it gave authority to the church to collect taxes from its own congregation. In 1706 it was stated that it had long been the custom for "the respective congregations through subscriptions and voluntary contributions by members" to pay the ministers' salary.[14]

The Dutch clergy had hardly reconciled themselves to the changed conditions under the English government, when they were dealt a severe blow by Leisler's rebellion. The good ministers, like many others before and since their time, did not want to offend the great men of their congregations—the Van Cortlandts, Bayards, Phillipses and the like. So when Leisler seized the government, drove Governor Nicholson into exile, slapped some of the wealthy men into jail and seized the property of others, they denounced him roundly in their sermons, refusing to recognize his authority, ridiculing his claim to be the champion of Protestantism against the Roman Catholic peril and advising their congregations to be faithful to the old government.

Leisler was not the man to take this meekly. Advising his followers, who made up in some cases the majority of the congregations, to stay away from services and refuse to contribute to the ministers' salaries, he succeeded in dividing the Church into two hostile factions. When this did not bring the ministers to terms, he proceeded to more vigorous measures. "It has not been permitted to ministers here to write to other ministers," ran a complaint to the Classis of Amsterdam. "They have been cast under suspicion through slanders. . . . Choristers and schoolmasters have been encouraged to perform ministerial duties. . . . Domine Dellius escaped to Boston. Domine Varick followed his example

[13]*Ecclesiastical Records, State of New York,* Vol. I, pp. 601–602.
[14]*Ecclesiastical Records, State of New York,* Vol. III, pp. 1657–1662.

and fled southward to New Castle. No one remained to be troubled and plundered except Domine Selyns."[15]

When Colonel Henry Sloughter, the new governor, arrived at New York in 1691 and Leisler and his chief lieutenants were brought to trial, the clergy urged the court to show no mercy.[16] Domine Varick is said to have been "very zealous" for Leisler's execution, making "intolerable sermons," and even when himself facing death would have none of reconciliation.[17] The harsh treatment of Leisler and the collapse of the cause he supported merely aggravated the bitterness of his followers against the clergy. Nine years later we find the Classis of Amsterdam complaining that the old animosity "still lingers in the Church," and advising "that henceforth everybody should try to forget about it."[18]

In fact there was urgent need for harmony, for the governors for the first time were making a serious effort to establish the Church of England. Fletcher, who succeeded Sloughter in 1692, was as ardent an Anglican as he was vainglorious and avaricious. Telling the somewhat startled Assembly that "the same laws which established your privileges provided for the religion of the Church of England," he demanded immediate steps to "establish the ministry" on an Anglican footing.[19] In 1693 the Assembly yielded far enough to pass an act which applied only to New York, Westchester, Queens and Richmond, providing for the election of wardens and vestries, and the support of ministers by public taxation. But there is no mention in the act of either the Book of Common Prayer or the Church of England.[20] "The act is very loosely worded," wrote Colonel Lewis Morris. "The dissenters claim the benefit of it as well as we."[21] Fletcher understood this well enough and sought in vain to insert an amendment giving him the right to induct ministers.

When Lord Cornbury became governor in 1701, he made a

[15]*Ibid.*, Vol. II, pp. 1041–1043.
[16]*Ibid.*, pp. 1131–1132; *Colonial Documents*, Vol. IV, p. 219.
[17]*Ibid.* [18]*Ibid.*, 1428–1429.
[19]E. T. Corwin, *History of the Reformed Church*, pp. 96–106.
[20]*New York Legislative Journal*, pp. 47–48.
[21]Sanford H. Cobb, *Rise of Religious Liberty in America*, p. 339.

determined effort to foist the Church of England upon the reluctant congregations by claiming that his instructions gave him the right of induction. No church should make a call, he insisted, until they had secured his permission, and no minister sent over by the Classis of Amsterdam should begin to preach without his express license.[22]

But Cornbury met with a severe repulse in his dealings with the little church at Kingston. Upon the departure of their minister, Domine Nucella, the Governor sent them an Anglican named Hepburn. Apparently this gentleman found that the Dutch congregation would not pay taxes for his support, for he took his departure in August 1704. Thereupon the church sent to the Classis of Amsterdam for a minister, who in response sent Domine Henricus Beys, a student at the University of Leyden. Upon his arrival Cornbury told him that if he began preaching without his license, he would banish him from the province. Fortunately, Colonel Henry Beekman and other members of the Kingston consistory were present to defend the bewildered domine. Ignoring the Governor's "stinging words," hurled at them as though they "were the lowest negroes or heathen," they secured legal advice and took the matter up with the Council. Some of the councillors who were members of the Dutch Reformed Church forced the Governor to show his instructions, which revealed that his right to induction referred only to the Church of England.[23] The Governor no longer had a leg to stand on and Domine Beys remained undisturbed in his pastorate.[24]

In the meanwhile, Domines Beys, Antonides, and du Bois, together with eleven elders and deacons, appealed to the Classis of Amsterdam to request the Dutch government to protest to the British government against this breach of the articles of surrender. The Great Pensionary was to ask Queen Anne "to issue her command to her Governor" to allow the "Consistories to call their ministers from Holland, without asking the Governor's consent," and otherwise to leave them undisturbed in their former rights.[25]

[22]*Ecclesiastical Records, State of New York*, Vol. III, pp. 1657–1662.
[23]*Ecclesiastical Records, State of N. Y.*, Vol. III, pp. 1615–1619.
[24]*Tercentenary Studies, Reformed Church in America*, pp. 141–144.
[25]*Ecclesiastical Records, State of New York*, Vol. III, pp. 1657–1662.

Although this request seems never to have reached England, it doubtless chilled the zeal of Cornbury, since he must have realized that the Queen would not thank him should his attempts to establish the Anglican church in New York develop into an international incident.

After all it was not the English governors nor the Church of England which constituted the chief obstacles to the growth of the Dutch Reformed Church in America, but the frontier conditions inevitable in most newly settled countries. Nor did this obstacle disappear with the drying up of the streams of migration from the Netherlands after the surrender of 1664, for there was a constant shifting of the population as new and more fertile lands were opened. With the migrations from Long Island to the Raritan valley, the founding of new churches on the Delaware at Port Jervis, Minisink and elsewhere, the movements up the Passaic, the Hackensack, the Wallkill and the Mohawk, the frontier problem was constantly renewed. And the Dutch Church, like the Anglican Church in Virginia and elsewhere, found it very difficult indeed to maintain its organization, its form of worship, the high character of its clergy in the face of the physical difficulties presented by the vast American wilderness.

For a little community lost in the forests, numbering perhaps two or three hundred souls in all, to maintain a regular minister would have been an insupportable burden. So they were, many of them, forced to resort to lay readers, trusting to occasional visits from a regularly ordained minister to baptize their children and administer the Lord's Supper. "I have been requested to preach to the people of Bergen, a village lying across the river, three times a year," wrote Domine Selyns, of the New York church, in 1682. Reverend Rudolphus Varick journeyed from his home on Long Island twice a year to preach and administer the Sacraments at Hackensack and "two other neighboring places."[26] The Monmouth County church was for years dependent on occasional visits from the ministers on Long Island.

When two or more small congregations existed in comparative proximity, it was customary to secure a minister in common,

[26] *Tercentenary Studies, Reformed Church in America,* p. 261.

sharing his services and also the burden of his support. Thus Brooklyn, Flatbush, Flatlands, New Utrecht and Bushwick formed the collegiate churches of Kings County; Jamaica, Newtown, Oyster Bay and Success the collegiate churches of Queens; Reverend Theodorus Jacobus Frelinghuysen served the churches at Raritan, New Brunswick, Six Mile Run, and North Branch.[27] It was no easy matter for the clergy to minister to these scattered flocks, to ride back and forth through the woods, or to cross large bodies of water in little boats, to preach or baptize, or visit the sick, or catechize. My churches are "three good hours from each other," wrote Reverend Cornelius Van Schie of Poughkeepsie in 1732, "and every other Sunday I must ride that distance, thither and back, through the woods and along steep paths."[28]

Despite his hard labors the domine's remuneration was apt to be small. Even when the churches united for his support their utmost efforts produced only bare necessities, so that it was difficult to induce able ministers to come to the colony. And those who came complained bitterly that the high cost of living restricted still further their meager salaries. "This is not Holland by any means," wrote one. "Excepting food and drink, everything here is almost as dear again as in Holland." No wonder many churches long remained vacant. At the time of the surrender there were six Dutch ministers in the colony to serve thirteen churches;[29] in 1740 nineteen ministers for sixty-five churches;[30] in 1771 thirty-four ministers for over a hundred churches.[31]

Under such circumstances religion and education alike suffered. "Many people here were born and grew up in the woods," one minister testified, "and know little of anything except what belongs to farming. Indeed it can hardly be believed what trouble and toil a minister has to introduce any civility into these places where there never has been a minister before. For many people

[27]*Ibid.*, pp. 35–44; 51–63; 213–214.

[28]*Ecclesiastical Records, State of N. Y.*, Vol. IV, pp. 2589–2591.

[29]W. W. Sweet, *Story of Religions in America*, p. 133.

[30]Leonard W. Bacon, *A History of American Christianity, The American Church History Series*, Vol. XIII, p. 134.

[31]Edward T. Corwin, *A Manual of the Reformed Church*, p. 60. These figures differ slightly from those given in *Centennial Discourses, Reformed Church.*

here are like the wild horses of the woods which have never yet been broken.—Yet although most of these people can neither read nor write," they have respect for God and His Word.[32] When Domine Frelinghuysen came to Somerset County, the people there had been living under frontier conditions for nearly forty years. An entire generation had grown up without adequate schools, hearing the Gospel only a few times a year.[33]

The effect upon church solidarity and organization was equally bad. For a conference of ministers held, let us say, at the town of New York, the representative of the upper Delaware churches would have to make his way on horseback across New Jersey, probably along the Minisink trail; the ministers from Schoharie, the Mohawk region and Albany could come down the Hudson by boat; those serving the congregations on the Passaic, the Hackensack and the Raritan probably made the journey partly on horseback, partly by boat. For all save those in the town or close at hand, it was a tedious and dangerous trip. "The situation of our churches here is such that the mutual interchange of opinions cannot be well kept up otherwise than by letter," the clergy explained to the Classis of Amsterdam. "Personal conferences once a year would be very useful to us, although this is not yet quite possible. The expense involved also cannot yet be well met."[34]

In the Dutch Reformed Church, as in other churches, the age of heroism was succeeded by an age of security and, as a result, of comparative apathy. Men cannot remain indefinitely worked up to a high pitch of enthusiasm, where they willingly give their all for religion's sake. When once the danger is removed and they enjoy the security their sacrifices have won, religious zeal is apt to give way to mere formalism. Nor did the congregations in America escape this tendency, even though they embraced at first many zealots.[35] Their ministers, educated in Holland, and ordained by the Classis of Amsterdam, good and sincere men

[32]*Ecclesiastical Records, State of New York*, Vol. IV, pp. 2589–2591.

[33]Abraham Messler, *Forty Years at Raritan*, p. 164.

[34]*Ecclesiastical Records, State of N. Y.*, Vol. II, pp. 753–755.

[35]Note the Walloons and other groups of foreigners who had fled their native lands to escape persecution.

though most of them were, had little of the fire which is essential to the missionary and the reformer.

They were shocked and not a little alarmed, then, when a group of zealots came to the colony in 1684, and began catechizing, holding services in private houses, and denouncing the liturgy and public prayer. "They were only tailors or cobblers," wrote Domine Selyns, "yet they tried to be promoted in this place or in that to the office of precentor and schoolmaster."[36] One of these men, William Bertholf, established himself in Bergen County, and in a few years had won the hearts of the congregations there. "He is well known to me," wrote Reverend Rudolphus Varick, "of courageous but stubborn spirit.—They chose him for about one-fourth of our usual salary to be their teacher, and he is about to take ship to be ordained by some Classis."[37]

Bertholf was examined by the Classis of Middleburg, Holland, and ordained to the ministry in September, 1693. Returning to America, he took up his duties as pastor of Hackensack and Aquackenonk churches, and was reluctantly recognized by the other ministers. They had no reason to be ashamed of him, for he became the Reformed Dutch apostle of northern New Jersey. Casting aside all formalities, he went from one isolated community to another, preaching, teaching, praying, and organizing. We find him now on Staten Island, founding the church at Port Richmond, now he is on the east bank of the Hudson at Tarrytown, now he is deep in the New Jersey wilderness organizing the church at Ponds, now he is preaching at Harlem, now at Tappan. "Through the forests, over rugged hills and broad plains, up quiet valleys, wherever a group of Dutchmen had cleared for themselves homes in the wilderness, he went, comforting the sick and troubled, baptizing children, bringing into the hard and lonely lives of the settlers the cheer of his kindly presence and longed-for news of distant relatives and friends."[38] It mattered nothing to them that Bertholf's fellow ministers complained to the Classis of Amsterdam of his doubtful ordination, his disregard of the

[36]*Holland Society, Year Book, 1912*, p. 907.

[37]*Ibid.*, Vol. II, pp. 1051–1052.

[38]*Tercentenary Studies, Reformed Church in America*, p. 193.

liturgy, his "running around."[39] Not only did he become the real founder of the church in New Jersey, but he instilled into it an evangelical spirit lacking in many of the other congregations.

Perhaps, then, it was not a matter of chance that the congregations on the Raritan called as their first pastor Reverend Theodorus J. Frelinghuysen, a brilliant young minister tinged with the doctrines of the German Pietists. It was Philip Jacob Spener who founded the Pietist movement by starting devotional groups within the Lutheran Church for Bible study and promoting true piety. Out of the University of Halle, which became the center of Pietism, came Mühlenberg and other founders of the movement in America.[40] At the time when young Frelinghuysen was growing to manhood, Pietism, with its emphasis upon the religion of the heart, was sweeping over the Protestant parts of Germany, and had a profound influence upon his views and his future career.[41]

No sooner had he arrived in New Jersey than he began, in simple but forceful sermons, to arouse his congregations from their lethargy. Insisting upon regeneration, repentance, faith and holiness, he declared that most of his listeners, since they had had no profound religious experience, were unfit to participate in the Lord's Supper. On one occasion, when he was administering the communion in the church at Six Mile Run, he exclaimed: "See! See! even the people of the world and the impenitent are coming, that they may eat and drink judgment to themselves!" Thereupon several persons, thinking that he had singled them out as unregenerate, returned to their seats.[42]

Before long the young minister had aroused the bitter hostility of some of the most influential members of his congregations. "He sets himself up to be the judge of men's hearts," they complained. "How can he know if the heart is changed? What right has he to excommunicate any who have made a confession of faith in the Reformed religion?"[43] Pointing to several of his

[39] *Year Book of the Holland Society,* Vol. II, pp 1105–1106.
[40] W. W. Sweet, *Story of Religions in America,* pp. 201, 202.
[41] Abraham Messler, *Forty Years at Raritan,* pp. 165–166.
[42] Abraham Messler, *Forty Years at Raritan,* p. 170.
[43] *Ibid.,* p. 172.

sermons, they condemned them as visionary and contrary to the long-established doctrines of the church. Thereupon Frelinghuysen, in 1721, published a small volume, containing three of the sermons which had been most bitterly criticized.[44] In them he emphasized the difference between godliness and mere belief, and insisted upon a real change of heart. Domine Freeman and Domine Bertholf declared them "learned, well digested and thrilling,—highly sound and scriptural."[45]

His enemies, with the support of some of the more conservative ministers, came back with a pamphlet of 146 pages, in which they assailed Frelinghuysen's views and picked flaws in the three published sermons.[46] The domine replied in a third pamphlet, vindicating his conduct and explaining his doctrines.[47] In the meanwhile the whole matter had been referred to the Classis of Amsterdam. The decision of this body, if it could be called a decision, served only to show its inability to rule the distant American congregations. Explaining that they hesitated to act because they were under a foreign civil government and because a premature decision might increase the strife, they fell back on a policy of procrastination. It was eight or ten years after receiving the complaints before they gave anything like a final decision, which was little more than an exhortation to peace. Frelinghuysen was instructed not to exclude from communion any "who made a confession of faith in the Reformed Religion," but they gave him a loop-hole by adding, "and who also have the testimony of a pious deportment."[48] In the end it was the domine who triumphed, not because of the decision of the Classis, but because of the increasingly powerful support which his evangelical teaching drew around him. Unlike Jonathan Edwards, who also made the battle for the religion of the heart as opposed to formalism and was thrown out of his church, Frelinghuysen gained strength, until

[44]The sermons were on The Broken Heart and Contrite Spirit, The Lord's Supper, and Christian Discipline. *Ibid.*

[45]*Ecclesiastical Records, State of N. Y.*, Vol. III, pp. 2178–2181.

[46]*A Complaint against Rev. Theodore Jacobus Frelinghuysen and his Consistory*, etc. Printed in New York by Wm. Bradford and J. Peter Zenger.

[47]His refutation is lost.

[48]*Ecclesiastical Records, State of New York*, Vol. IV, pp. 2638–2640.

before he retired "even the hearts of his enemies were conquered."[49]

Identified with this struggle, and growing partly out of it, was a wider and even more bitter battle to determine whether the church was to become an American church, expanding and changing as America expanded and changed, or remain a restricted national sect. Was it to embrace only or chiefly people of Dutch descent, permit only services in Dutch, ordain only men born in the Netherlands or educated in the Netherlands, and refer every matter of importance to an ecclesiastical body residing in Amsterdam? With political ties long since severed with the parent country, with Dutch traditions gradually growing weaker, with the population yielding to the molding influences of local conditions, with New Englanders, Scotch-Irish, English, and other groups settling near and mingling with them, with the Dutch tongue giving ground to English, the Church had to determine whether it would perish with the old civilization or rise on the crest of the new.

This fact Frelinghuysen seems to have grasped clearly. We must not permit our loyalty to the Netherlands, our desire to adhere to the form of worship or of church organization prescribed by the mother church, to stand in the way of religious advancement, he insisted. If we cannot secure a sufficient supply of able, pious ministers from Holland, let us educate them here and ordain them here. Gradually there grew up a party, not only in his own congregations, but in every church, who took the same point of view—the American party, they might well have called themselves.

Opposed to them were those who looked with dread upon the changing forces of time. Led by a group of ministers born, educated and ordained in the Netherlands, they strove desperately to defend Dutch civilization in the colonies, especially the Dutch character of their church. To permit preaching in English seemed to them a desecration, to set up English schools a weak surrender of their dearest traditions, to create a colonial Synod or Classis a severing of their allegiance to the mother church. They were too

[49]Abraham Messler, *Forty Years at Raritan,* p. 26.

short-sighted to realize that the forces they were challenging were irresistible, and so tried to tie up the future of their church with a hopeless cause.

The storm, which had long been brewing, broke with the organizing of a Coetus, or provincial Church assembly.[50] When the liberal group at once made use of this body to ordain new ministers for some of the vacant pulpits, the more conservative drew back in alarm. If we permit this practice to go on unchecked, they said, "perhaps there will be a total defection from our dear Netherlandish Church." It needed only the proposal to convert the Coetus into a Classis with greatly expanded powers, to solidify the conservatives into an opposition party under the name of Conferentie.[51] Our desire is, they wrote, "to have the tie between us and the Church of the fatherland, instead of growing weak, to become stronger and stronger."[52]

Involved in the controversy was the question of the educating of young men for the ministry. Domine Theodore Frelinghuysen[53] had proposed the founding of a college "for the Low Dutch alone, by means of the free gifts of rich and bountiful Holland."[54] This plan met with wide approval, but the Conferentie group opposed it, at first on the ground that it would weaken the dependence upon Holland, and later because it conflicted with a scheme of their own to establish a chair of theology in King's College, New York.

As time passed the struggle became acrimonious. The little band of ministers, instead of presenting a united front to combat the difficulties of service on the frontier under a foreign jurisdiction, now turned upon each other with bitter invectives. "Their only aim is to undermine us here with lies and slanders," complained the Coetus of the Conferentie party,[55] while the latter in turn accused them of acting from passion and ambition.[56] The

[50] *Acts and Proceedings of the General Synod,* Vol. I, pp. vii–viii.

[51] *Ibid.,* pp. xciii, xciv. Domine Mutzelius' opposition to any kind of church independence in America had brought about his removal from the Tappan pulpit in 1749 (*Tercentenary Studies,* p. 186).

[52] *Ibid.,* p. xcvii.

[53] Son of Reverend T. J. Frelinghuysen.

[54] *Acts and Proceedings of General Synod,* p. xciv.

[55] *Ibid.,* pp l & li.

[56] *Ibid.,* p. cv.

quarrel spread to the people, so that many congregations were disrupted, friend turned against friend, child against parent, wife against husband. In some cases there were two ministers for the same church, occupying the pulpit on alternate Sundays.[57] At Poughkeepsie, when Domine Goetschius and others of the Coetus party met to ordain Henricus Schoonmaker, the Conferentie seized the church building and barred the doors, making it necessary to hold the ceremony in the open under a large tree.[58]

The schism became worse when the Conferentie group organized themselves into what they termed an Assembly subordinate to the reverend Classis.[59] The Church now had two bodies, each claiming to represent the American clergy, each pouring out its complaints to the Classis of Amsterdam. But the liberal group was gaining in power. The Coetus from year to year had examined and licensed ministers,[60] and these new clergymen, young and enthusiastic, were accepted joyously by various congregations. Their willingness to sanction sermons in English, so earnestly desired by many of the younger generation, counted heavily in their favor.

In the meanwhile, Domine Goetschius and others, pushing vigorously the project for the college in New Jersey, in 1766 succeeded in securing a charter.[61] The President of Queens College, or Rutgers, as it was later called, had to be a member of the Dutch Reformed Church, and the primary object of the college was to be the educating of ministers, so that young men need no longer go to a foreign country for their training. But it was expressly stated, also, that the college should "promote learning for the benefit of the community and the advancement of the Protestant religion of all denominations."[62]

It now became obvious that the Coetus party was carrying the day. Counting a majority of the ministers, churches and people, with their ranks growing, with the means of educating clergymen

[57] *Tercentenary Studies, Reformed Church in America,* p. 180.

[58] *Ibid.,* p. 315.

[59] *Ibid.,* p. cxv.

[60] E. T. Corwin, *Manuel of the Reformed Church in America,* pp. 41–42.

[61] Nelson R. Burr, *History of Education in New Jersey;* Part I, Book I, Chap. III, *Princeton History of New Jersey.*

[62] E. T. Corwin, *Manual of the Reformed Church in America,* p. 58.

at hand, and above all with the irresistible forces of Americanization working for them, the future was surely theirs. When the final settlement came, then, they were able to secure every essential point for which they had contended.

It was John H. Livingston, a young American minister, a graduate of Yale and a student at the University of Utrecht, who had just been ordained in Holland and called to the new Fulton Street Church in New York, who brought the final triumph. Livingston, deeply concerned at the discord in the Church, took it upon himself to bring the points in dispute before the Church in Holland. He then drew up a plan of union which conceded every essential contention of the Coetus party, and after securing for it the provisional endorsement of the Classis, set sail for America.[63]

He found the entire church weary of strife and anxious for peace. The Conferentie, disheartened by the desertion of the Classis, saw no alternative but to yield. It was in October, 1771, that twenty-two ministers and twenty-five elders, forgetful of former contests and bitter words and accusations, met in amicable conference and unanimously adopted the plan of union. By its terms a general body and five local bodies were created to govern the church, subordinate, of course, to the Classis of Amsterdam, to examine and license candidates for the ministry and to enforce discipline.[64] The agreement was ratified by the congregations and at last the ruinous schism in the Church was healed.

It was none too soon. Already the rumblings of the Revolution could be heard, and within a few years the Church was again shaken to its foundation. In the quarrel between the British government and the Colonies the Dutch Americans, both laity and clergy, aligned themselves with the patriots.[65] Resentful of the growth of the Anglican Church and the favors shown it by the government, and suspicious of the movement to establish an American bishopric, the Dutch clergy saw that the future of their church depended upon resistance to British encroachments, if not upon complete independence. The Dutch families, with no tra-

[63] *Ibid.*, p. 59.

[64] *Ibid.*, pp. 60, 61; *Acts and Proceedings of the General Synod*, pp. 8–16.

[65] Alexander C. Flick, *Loyalism in New York, Columbia University Studies*, Vol. 14.

dition of loyalty to England, in a sense still a foreign group in a British colony, lined up behind their ministers. With the exception of the Rensselaers, Van Cortlandts, and a few other of the landed gentry or great merchants, an occasional doctor or lawyer or royal official, few Dutch names are found in the lists of the loyalists.[66]

The Dutch paid dearly for their patriotism. Not only did the British occupation of New York City, Staten Island, western Long Island and other near-by points expose the Dutch inhabitants of these localities to severe repression, but innumerable raids up the Hackensack, Raritan, and Hudson brought fire and sword to the outlying settlements. So violent had the Dutch ministers been in their denunciations of the repressive measures of the British ministry, and so urgent in their advocacy of armed resistance, that they were hunted out as especial objects of revenge. Many were compelled to flee before the invaders, happy to escape the horrors of the prison ships, while their church buildings and their homes went up in flames.

After the battle of Long Island, the Jamaica church was used for a storage house, and its seats and floors as timber for huts and barracks; the Newtown church became a powder magazine; Domine Solomon Froeligh was forced to flee.[67] In Staten Island the Port Richmond church was burned.[68] With the occupation of New York City a floor was laid from gallery to gallery in the North Dutch Church and the building used as a prison. The pulpit was sent to England and set up in an Anglican church there. The Middle Dutch Church at first was also used as a prison, where hundreds of unhappy wretches were herded together, but later was converted into a riding school for dragoons.[69] In 1777 the British swept through the Raritan valley, burning and pillaging. The Raritan church, where Domine Hardenbergh had thundered against the reactionary government, was burned to the ground, the Millstone church was plundered and the interior burned, Hardenbergh was driven into hiding, sleeping always

[66] *Ibid.*, p. 36.

[67] *Tercentenary Studies, Reformed Church in America*, p. 62.

[68] *Ibid.*, p. 92. [69] Mary L. Booth, *History of the City of New York*, p. 316.

with his loaded musket at his side.[70] With the churches thus desecrated, the ministers in flight, the congregations scattered, the plight of the Church was sad indeed. No wonder that the Synod of 1778, meeting at New Paltz, regarded with sorrowful hearts the pitiable condition of land and church. "Some of our cities have been desolated, our villages and boroughs subverted," they wrote, "many of our houses of worship and their furniture burned, desecrated, plundered and cast to the ground; many . . . driven from their peaceful homes and compelled to roam through the land."[71]

But though the Dutch Reformed Church suffered much, its compensations were also great. With the winning of American independence its fear of English dictation was gone forever, the possibility of an established Anglican Church now seemed like a bad dream. Above all, the war had impressed upon clergy and laity alike the fact that they were no longer foreigners looking constantly across the Atlantic to Holland for guidance and direction, but full-fledged Americans, a part of a new and vigorous nation. Prior to the Revolution the Dutchman was made to realize that his rights, in a sense, rested upon sufferance, at least upon no better basis than the treaty of surrender; now he was upon an equal footing with every other citizen, whether of English birth or not. So the Dutch Church in a very real sense soon ceased to be a Dutch church, became an American church. After the lapse of a century and a half from the founding of New Netherland, and more than a century from its political separation from the mother country, local forces had done their work, had worn away the bonds uniting the Church in America with the Church in Holland, and launched it upon an independent career in the young republic.

There is no chapter in the history of the development of a distinct American civilization more instructive than the prolonged contest between the forces of European tradition and the forces of Americanization within the Dutch Reformed Church. These forces were in direct conflict decades before the open breach

[70]John A. Todd, *Centennial Discourses, Reformed Church, The Church in the Revolution*, pp. 27, 28.

[71]*Ibid.*, p. 21.

between Coetus and Conferentie, even before Frelinghuysen launched his war against formalism in his churches on the Raritan. From the earliest years, every time a minister rode through the wilderness to preach to some isolated congregation, every time a lay reader conducted services, every time a congregation found it difficult to secure a minister from Holland, every time an entry was made in the church book in English, or a sermon preached in English, every time an American-born youth took up his studies for the ministry, the Church drew nearer the day of independence.

It was in vain that so many, clergy and laity alike, tried to arrest the forces of change. The Conferentie might enlist in their cause all the weight of Church law, all the influence of Synod and Classis, all the force of tradition, all the love of mother country; their cause was hopeless. Their real opponents were not the Coetus group, but the forces which created the Coetus group, the three thousand miles of water between America and the Netherlands, the proximity to other races and other faiths, the difficulties of communication.

But the Conferentie and the principles for which they stood, despite their ultimate failure, succeeded in doing untold harm. Had the Dutch ministers, instead of turning their eyes eastward to Europe, fixed them on the vast region in the west which was opening to settlement, the history of their Church might have been very different. Their inspired preacher Freylinghuysen was the forerunner of the Great Awakening; had they rallied around him, throwing aside narrow nationalism and sending out preachers and teachers to the frontier, they might have built up a chain of congregations from New York to Georgia. When, after the Revolution, they awoke to their mistake the opportunity had passed.[72]

As the story of the Dutch Church illustrates the force of American conditions in overcoming European inheritance, so the history of the Dutch tongue in New York and New Jersey shows the operation of the melting-pot. The struggle of Dutch with other languages began even before the time of Peter Stuyvesant, its last

[72] *General Synod of the Reformed Church,* Vol. I, pp. 114, 115.

echoes have hardly died out yet. At first it was a victorious battle waged against French and German, but after the conquest it changed to a stubborn, long-drawn-out, hopeless resistance to English. Since a people will cling to their mother tongue so long as they are conscious of their distinct nationality, the story of Dutch in America parallels the story of the rise and the decline of Dutch culture in America.

The province of New Netherland, like New York of today, was a cosmopolitan place. In New Amsterdam the Dutch merchants and tradesmen rubbed elbows with English, Germans, French and Scandinavians; in Bergen and Rockland the Flemish element was very strong; New Paltz was settled largely by Walloons; New Rochelle was a Huguenot community, while on Long Island, in Westchester and Dutchess the New Englanders crowded in upon the original settlers. Hoffmans from Sweden, Schoonmakers from Hamburg, Ten Broecks from Westphalia, Kierstedes from Prussia all multiplied in Ulster.[73] The record of marriages in the Dutch Reformed Church of New Amsterdam from 1643 to 1647 shows fifty-two Dutch from Holland, six from New Netherland, sixteen English, nine Germans, two Scandinavians, three French, and twelve blacks.[74]

On Manhattan the battle of languages began at a very early date. In the spring of 1623 thirty families, mostly Walloons, arrived in New Netherland.[75] Domine Michaelius, the first minister, wrote in 1628 that he had administered the Lord's Supper to fifty communicants—"Walloons and Dutch." "The Walloons and French have no service on Sundays otherwise than in the Dutch language," he added. "Nevertheless the Lord's Supper was administered to them in the French language—with a preceding discourse, which I had before me in writing."[76] With the arrival of other French-speaking groups, the difficulties of the church increased. Finally Reverend Samuel Drisius, who was pro-

[73]H. W. Reynolds, *Dutch Houses,* etc., p. 13.

[74]Ruth Putnam, "Dutch Element in the U. S.," American Historical Association *Annual Report 1909,* pp. 205–218.

[75]*Ecclesiastical Records, State of New York,* I, pp. 36–37.

[76]Thomas De Witt, *Discourse in North Reformed Dutch Church,* 1857, pp. 15–16; J. F. Jameson, *Narratives of New Netherland,* pp. 124–125.

ficient in French and English, as well as in Dutch, was called to minister to them, and to preach in French in the quaint little church in the fort every Sunday after the conclusion of the Dutch service.[77] No doubt the French and Walloons would have relinquished their native tongue in favor of the prevailing Dutch had they not been strengthened by fresh migrations resulting from the revocation of the Edict of Nantes.[78] Eventually the French built a chapel of their own on Petticoat Lane, where Reverend Peter Daille ministered to their needs.[79] It is said that some of the zealous exiles at New Rochelle, after finishing their week's work on Saturday evening, would march the eighteen miles to Pine Street singing Marot's Hymns, and after spending the night with friends there and attending Sunday services, return in time for work on Monday morning.[80] In 1704 the Petticoat Lane church was superseded by a more imposing structure, *L'Église du Saint Esprit,* where Reverend James Laborie soon gathered a flourishing congregation.[81]

In many of the smaller towns surrounding New Amsterdam, in Harlem, in Jamaica, in Bushwick, in Brooklyn, on Staten Island, at Hackensack, the Walloons and French were gradually absorbed by the Dutch and Flemish population. But the process was always slow, the resistance stubborn. At Harlem the Huguenots were so disgruntled at the exclusive use of Dutch in the church services that when the French church in New York obtained a minister, they refused to support the local voorleser.[82] On Staten Island the Walloons and French long maintained a separate church and at one time Samuel Drisius went over to preach to them once a month.[83] At Jamaica the French tongue seems to have lingered far into the eighteenth century, for Reverend Abraham Kettletas preached there in French as well as in

77Chas. E. Corwin, *Manual of the Reformed Church in America,* p. 25. (Fifth edition. Revised, N. Y. 1922.)

78N. Y. Historical Society, *Collections,* I, p. 35.

79Gabriel P. Disosway, *Earliest Churches of New York,* p. 121.

80Mary L. Booth, *History of the City of N. Y.* (1866, N. Y.) p. 281. This could have been only for the first year or so of the settlement, as in 1692 or 1693 the people of New Rochelle erected a church of their own near the old Post Road, with Reverend David Bonrepos as the first minister. G. P. Disosway, *Earliest Churches of New York,* p. 260.

81*Ecclesiastical Records, State of New York,* p. 866.

82*Tercentenary Studies, Reformed Church in America,* p. 76.

83Gabriel P. Disosway, *Earliest Churches of New York,* p. 20.

Dutch and English so late as the time of the Revolution. But the final outcome was certain. In one community after another the Huguenots intermarried with the Dutch, sent their children to Dutch schools, listened to church services in Dutch, eventually began to consider themselves Dutch.[84]

The history of the little village of New Paltz, in Ulster County, illustrates well the process of assimilation which has played so vital a rôle in American history. The place was settled by Protestant Walloons. For several decades the language of general conversation was French, the records of *l'église de Nouveau Palatinat* were kept in French,[85] the sermons of the good père Daillie were delivered in French, the schoolmaster, Jean Tebenin, taught his pupils in French.[86] But this little pocket of Walloon civilization, lost in the forests of America, and surrounded by Dutch-speaking people, could not for more than a generation or two retain its identity. When the little stone church at New Paltz was without a minister, those of the people who understood Dutch worshipped at the church at Kingston.[87] Dutch settlers in increasing numbers moved in and when all efforts to secure a French minister failed, services were held from time to time in Dutch. It was found necessary to find a schoolmaster who understood Dutch, and many a child who at home heard nothing save French, picked up Dutch from the master and schoolmates. The church records, so long kept exclusively in French, now were written in Dutch.[88] No doubt the older people continued to speak the language of their fathers, no doubt many of the customs and traditions lingered long after the real transition had taken place, but by 1750 New Paltz had become a Dutch community.

The victory over the French tongue was still incomplete when it became necessary for Dutch in certain localities to enter into a conflict with German. It was in 1710 that the British govern-

[84]The assimilation of the Huguenots into the Dutch population was made easier by the fact that many of the French had lived in Holland before migration to America.

[85]Irving Elting, *Johns Hopkins Studies in History and Political Science,* "Dutch Village Communities on the Hudson River," p. 63.

[86]Ralph Le Fevre, *History of New Paltz* (1909, Albany), pp. 25–28.

[87]*Ecclesiastical Records, State of New York,* p. 3209.

[88]*Collections of Holland Society of New York,* III, p. v. Records of Reformed Dutch Church of New Paltz.

ment sent to New York a large group of Germans who had fled from the Palatinate to escape civil and religious oppression. Placed first on the upper Hudson, some moved on to the Schoharie valley, others settled at Germantown, Catskill, Rhinebeck and Kaatsbaan, still others made their way to New Jersey or Pennsylvania. At once the work of assimilation began. The Germans intermarried with the surrounding Dutch, worshipped at the same church, sent their children to the same school.[89] It was in vain that they appealed for preachers and teachers who could speak both German and Dutch.[90] Eventually they were absorbed into the Dutch population and so lost their identity.

Like most other groups of colonists the Dutch were more concerned with making homes in the wilderness than with literature or science. Many were unable to read or write, and few indeed were those who possessed more than a few books—the Bible, a Psalm-book, and an almanac or two. The huge Bible, with its quaint Dutch printing, its thick covers, and its brass or silver corner-pieces and clasps, was the pride of many an humble family.[91] If the old inventories and wills show other books, they almost invariably are religious in character—*The Adorable Ways of God,* by Petrus Van Driessen, or Frelinghuysen's *Sermons,* or *Chain of the Godly Truths,* by Gerard Haeghoort.[92]

In New Netherland, as in New England, the ministers, as the intellectual as well as spiritual leaders, were men of education and learning. Reverend Theodorus J. Frelinghuysen was proficient in both Latin and Greek, and familiar with classic literature;[93] Reverend Cornelis Van Santvoord, a graduate of the University of Leyden, spoke both French and English, as well as Dutch, was a man of wide culture, and a writer of some ability;[94]

89*Tercentenary Studies, Reformed Church in America,* pp. 300; 355–358; 419–426.

90Reverend John G. Gebhard was called to the Claverack church in 1776. "Notwithstanding the large German element in his congregation, the Hollandish element was still greater, so that . . . he undertook to master [Dutch] . . . and in three months was able to preach his first sermon." F. N. Zabriskie, *History of the Reformed Church of Claverack,* p. 25.

91Henry R. Stiles, *A History of the City of Brooklyn,* II, p. 230.

92The books of Cornelis Jacobs were valued at £6, a very small sum compared with the entire estate, worth £1954.19.3.

93Abraham Messler, *Forty Years at Raritan,* p. 174.

94*Two Hundredth Anniversary of Dutch Church at Schenectady,* p. 107.

Reverend Warmoldus Kuypers wrote in Latin and preached in Dutch;[95] Everardus Bogardus, Joannes Backerus, Joannes Megapolensis, Samuel Drisius, the Dutch ministers of New Amsterdam, "were all educated in the Universities of Holland."[96] Some of these men brought their libraries with them, adding volumes now and then by importations.

The dependence of the colonist upon the mother colony for books of all kinds is shown by a letter of Reverend John H. Goetschius to the Classis of Amsterdam, February 1, 1757: "Each of my children needs a big Bible with marginal references. Other Dutch books, (I have a few in Latin) a minister also needs, for the better and more efficient performance of his work. . . . In order that I may educate my six sons in the languages and the sciences, I beg [you to] send them over the necessary schoolbooks. . . . I would also like for some poor but pious church members, some other edifying books for their increase in truth and Godliness."[97]

As the preachers were the chief owners of books, so were they the chief, almost the only, writers. Of the fifty books printed in Dutch in the years from 1708 to 1794, thirty-seven were on religious subjects.[98] Beginning with Justus Falckner's *Fundamental Instruction of . . . Christly Teaching,* published in 1708, the list continues with Bernard Freeman's *The Mirror of Self-Knowledge,* 1720, Johannes H. Goetschius' *The Unknown God,* Jacob Hoornbeek's, *The True Virtue,* etc. Occasionally religious and political controversies found their way into print, while in 1741 began the publication of American almanacs in Dutch.[99] The first volumes were printed by W. Bradford, but in 1725 the work was taken up by J. Peter Zenger, and continued by W. Weyman, Hendricus de Foreest, and others. Some were printed in the "Koop in den Nieuw Druckery in de Bever-Straat." New Netherland was not without its poets. Jacob Steendam wrote at least one of his poems

[95]*Tercentenary Studies, Reformed Church in America,* p. 181.
[96]Gabriel P. Disosway, *Earliest Churches of New York,* p. 19.
[97]*Ecclesiastical Records, State of New York,* p. 3693.
[98]Charles Evans, *American Bibliography* (Chicago, 1903).
[99]Charles Evans, *American Bibliography* (Chicago, 1903), p. 186.

there—*Klagt van Nieuw Amsterdam,* printed in Holland in 1659, while of the same period were the occasional verses of Henricus Selyns, the first permanent minister of the Brooklyn church, and of Nicasius de Sille, councilor of state under Stuyvesant.[100]

The position of the Dutch would have been stronger had there been published a Dutch newspaper in New York. This would have tended to preserve race consciousness, practise the people in reading their own language and make them more independent of English.[101] But they contented themselves with thumbing over their Bibles and almanacs until the first appearance of the *Post Boy,* after which they were gradually won over to reading the gazettes printed in English.

The lack of vigorous literary activity to sustain the Dutch language placed it at a great disadvantage in the struggle which it had to wage with English. Even in the days of Minuit and Stuyvesant there had been a sprinkling of English-speaking people in New Netherland, and with the conquest the number steadily increased. English merchants moved to New York City to take advantage of the mercantile opportunities there; a class of English officials grew up; the New Englanders pushing out to the western tip of Long Island, crossed over to New Jersey and made a wedge of settlements between the Dutch towns on the Raritan and those on the Passaic. By 1695 the Dutch and Flemings still constituted a small majority in the province of New York,[102] but a few decades later they found themselves outnumbered. English not only became the official language of the government, but also of the courts, the newspapers, and eventually of the churches and schools.

The Dutch language, where it did not give way entirely to English, was greatly affected by it. So many English words and expressions were incorporated into everyday conversation that a visitor from Holland might have had difficulty in understanding it. When Doctor Alexander Hamilton was on the boat from New

[100]Wm. H. Carpenter, "Dutch Contributions," etc., *Modern Philology,* VI, No. I, p. 6.

[101]Note the importance of the newspapers in preserving German as a spoken language in Pennsylvania.

[102]Charles E. Corwin, *Manual of the Reformed Church in America,* pp. 45–47.

York to Albany, in 1744, he was surprised to find that the passengers spoke "such a medley of Dutch and English" as to be very apropos of the subject, which was the Tower of Babel.[103] When Reverend Herman L. Boelen arrived from Holland in 1776 to preach in the Queens County churches, his language was so pure that the parishioners, accustomed to corrupted Dutch mixed with English words, had difficulty in understanding him.[104]

The contact with English wore off the original inflections, while the definite and indefinite articles, *de* and *en,* became uniform for all genders. The case-endings nearly all disappeared, the person-endings in the conjugation of verbs fell off, and pronouns were simplified. Many English words were borrowed without change, such as bottle, town, cider, smoke, potato; in some cases English words were modified, as säns (since), belange (belong), boddere (brother), bääznas (business); in still others English modified Dutch words, as in blaubääse (blueberry), and njeuspampir (newspaper).[105] The ease with which these changes took place is explained in part by the similarity of Dutch and English. Professor Wiliam H. Carpenter points out that there "is scarcely a sound in the Dutch language that is not readily convertible into its English etymological correspondent. . . . Many words are positively the same in sound and sense."[106] Even the sturdiest defenders of Dutch, who themselves refused to speak English, and fought against its introduction in school and pulpit, could not escape the daily use of words borrowed wholly or partly from it.

At the same time, English did not come out from this battle of languages unscathed. There must have been a time when the population was divided between those speaking Anglicized Dutch and those speaking Dutch English. The first deed recorded at Poughkeepsie, dated December 20, 1718, grants a lot to Captain Barent Van Kleeck for the "behoof of the Inhabitance and Nabor-

[103]Alexander Hamilton, *Itinerarium,* p. 68.

[104]*Tercentenary Studies, Reformed Church in America,* p. 61.

[105]H. L. Mencken, *The American Language,* p. 427.

[106]Wm. H. Carpenter, "Dutch Contributions," *Modern Philology,* Vol. VI, No. 1, pp. 60–61. The church records at Schenectady speak of Johannes Glen, "justis van de peace." *Two Hundredth Anniversary of First-Church Schenectady,* p. 69.

hod of pochkepsen aforesaid to Bild and Maentaen a proper Mietenghous to worship . . . in the Neder Dutch Lingo . . . with the benefitt of the Mietenhous yard for a Bureall place of Christian Corps to the same belonging."[107] Obviously the person who wrote this passage was trying to write in English while thinking in Dutch. Similarly Cornelius Van Catts, of Bushwick, in his will dated 1726, left his whole estate to his wife, "But if she happen to marry," he added, "then I geff her nothing—and all will be left for the children, Cornelius Catts and David Catts, heeff and heeff."[108]

The New England communities adjacent to New York adopted many Dutch words and expressions. On Long Island or in Suffolk or Westchester it became common for the English to speak of *master* as *baas, lightning* as *blicksem, forest* as *bosch, farm* as *bouwerij, letter* as *brief, citizen* as *burger, glove* as *handschoen, church* as *kerk, channel of water* as *kil, little bed* as *krib, porch* as *portaal, ghost* as *spook, door steps* as *stoep,* and *penny* as *stuiver.*[109] In fact certain Dutch words became so embedded in English that they are in current use in the United States today. When an American boy asks for a *cruller* or a *cooky,* he does not realize that he is paying tribute to the skill of the old Dutch housewives; when the laborer speaks of his *boss,* the sports writers of *dope,* or the riverboatsman of a *scow,* they are unconsciously harking back to the early days of Father Knickerbocker.[110]

The struggle for the mastery between Dutch and English reached a climax in New York City while Dutch was still firmly entrenched in many of the smaller communities. Not only did the interruption of trade with Holland which followed the conquest bring merchants into intimate business relations with England, but in the beginning of the eighteenth century a wave of immigration added greatly to the English-speaking part of the

107Irving Elting, "Dutch Village Communities on the Hudson River," *Johns Hopkins Studies,* IV, p. 40.

108Henry R. Stiles, *History of the City of Brooklyn,* Vol. I, p. 234. The historian William Smith, writing in 1732, declared: "English is the most prevailing language among us, but not a little corrupted by the Dutch dialect" (*History of N. Y.,* p. 323).

109A. J. Weise, *History of the City of Troy,* Chap. IV.

110H. L. Mencken, *The American Language,* p. 56.

population. With English the language of commerce, of the government, of the newspapers, and with intermarriages between Dutch and English a frequent occurrence, the position of the Dutch tongue became more and more precarious.

In the Dutch families it was usually the older members who were deeply attached to their language and most concerned for its future. So early as 1726 the Consistory of the Dutch Church reproved those members who "have for some years neglected to have their children receive instruction in the Netherlandish tongue. Are not our youth, now growing up among us, living witnesses of this?"[111] Since catechising and preaching was in Dutch, this would inevitably lead to irreligion and the decay of the Reformed Church. In 1733 the Consistory appointed Gerrit Van Wagenen master of the school, "to teach the youth reading, writing and ciphering and the elements of the Dutch Reformed religion in the Dutch language." The school seemed to them vital for the "training of our youth, in order to gain them from the earliest period to the language of our Church, and to a love for the Dutch Reformed worship."[112] In 1743 they established a second Dutch school, taught by Abraham de Lanoy, for children who lived too far away to attend Mr. Van Wagenen's school. But these efforts proved unavailing. "They have had well-regulated free-schools, richly supported by the church," it was stated in 1754, "and yet in spite of their utmost efforts, parents have found it impossible to transmit it [their language] to their children. Whence it is generally feared that the very next generation will scarce furnish one person in this city, except the clergy, well acquainted with the tongue."[113]

Some of the more far-sighted members of the church began to advocate the use of English in catechising and preaching for those who desired it. Otherwise, they pointed out, the Dutch churches would be ruined. It was not to be expected that any one should long remain in a church where the services were in a tongue he did not understand. Already certain families had with-

[111] *Ecclesiastical Records, State of New York*, pp. 2340–2341.

[112] *Ibid.*, pp. 2620–2621.

[113] *Ibid.*, p. 3459. The writer was William Livingston.

drawn to give their allegiance to the Trinity Episcopal church.[114] "Most of the young people now speak principally English and go to the English church, and would even take it amiss if they were called Dutchmen and not Englishmen," wrote Peter Kalm. So early as 1748 there was talk in the Dutch church of calling a minister who could preach in English, and six years later William Livingston pointed out that the church must either use English in the services or eventually cease to exist.[115]

In May, 1762, matters reached a crisis, when Jacobus Roosevelt and Philip Livingston presented a request, signed by many of the congregation, for a minister who could preach in English. Immediately some of the older members were up in arms. Their language and their religion were indissolubly united, they said. They could not abandon the one without abandoning the other. None-the-less, the Consistory, which included such prominent names as De Peyster, Brevoort, Beekman, Roosevelt, and Van Wyck, decided in favor of the new move, and appointed a committee to seek an English-speaking minister in Holland.[116] This so infuriated the opposition that they instituted a suit against the Consistory, on the ground that the matter could be settled only by all the members of the congregation. When the suit went against them the most headstrong went over to the Episcopalian church, declaring, "If it must be English, let it be English."[117]

The Classis of Amsterdam supported the Consistory. After all, the Gospel is the important thing, they pointed out, not the particular language; certainly it is better to have preaching in English than to have the church perish because of insistence upon Dutch.[118] So they selected Reverend Archibald Laidlie, a Scotchman, the minister of the English church in Flushing, Holland. Arriving in New York in 1764, he preached his first sermon in the Nassau Street church before a large audience, including the

[114]Thos. De Witt, *Discourse Delivered in North Reformed Dutch Church,* 1856, p. 29. Rev. Gerardus Haeghoort wrote in 1731: "As to the state of my congregation, . . . many had become almost wholly English, and had thus become estranged from the Dutch Reformed Church." (*Ecclesiastical Records, State of New York,* p. 2582.)

[115]*Ibid.,* p. 3459.

[116]*Ibid.,* pp. 3841–3842.

[117]D. D. Demarest, *The Reformed Church in America,* p. 64.

[118]*Ecclesiastical Records, State of New York,* p. 3904.

Mayor and some of the Aldermen. Most of the congregation, who regarded the coming of Mr. Laidlie as the dawn of a new period of prosperity for the church, welcomed him with open arms. "Ah! Domine," they told him, "we offered up many an earnest prayer in Dutch for your coming among us, and truly the Lord has heard us in English."[119]

Mr. Laidlie was highly successful from the first. Talented, learned, affable, attentive to his pastoral duties, he became immensely popular with the English-speaking faction. So many crowded into the Nassau Street church to hear him that it became necessary to erect galleries. Even this proved inadequate, so that three years after his arrival a new and larger church was built at Fulton and William Streets.[120] In the meanwhile, Reverend Lambertus de Ronde, the Dutch minister of the Nassau Street church, alarmed at his dwindling audiences, himself began preaching in English, although haltingly and with many a Dutch word thrown in.[121] So obvious were his deficiencies, that John H. Livingston, a brilliant young theological student at the University of Utrecht, was called to assist him.[122] Domines de Ronde and Ritzema, however, continued to minister to the Dutch-speaking members of the South and Middle churches until the Revolution.

With the evacuation of New York by the British in 1783, Domine Livingston, who long remained the only minister of the Reformed church, occasionally preached to the old people in Dutch.[123] This proved so unsatisfactory to these good souls that urgent appeals were made to several Dutch ministers in other parts of New York, but all preferred to remain where they were. At last, in 1789, Reverend Gerardus Arenz Kuypers, an able scholar and preacher, came to New York, to the great joy of the dwindling Dutch contingent. Before the end of the century, however, when a mere handful were left, the Consistory requested Doctor Kuypers to begin preaching in English. Although at first he de-

[119]D. D. Demarest, *The Reformed Church in America,* p. 63.
[120]*The Collegiate Dutch Church, Centennial Anniversary,* p. 11.
[121]*Ecclesiastical Records, State of New York,* p. 4016.
[122]*Ibid.,* p. 4136.
[123]G. P. Disosway, *The Earliest Churches of New York,* p. 29.

murred strongly, the folly of speaking to empty benches became so obvious that at last he was forced to yield. His last regular sermon in Dutch, late in 1803, may be said to mark the end of the battle of languages in the metropolis of Dutch-America.[124]

Had Dutch-America been geographically as compact as German-Pennsylvania, the Dutch language would probably have survived much longer. But it stretched in a thin line up the Hudson, with tentacles thrust up the rivers of northeast New Jersey, and across the East River into Long Island. Its entire eastern flank was open to invasion from New England, while its splendid system of waterways was a standing invitation to immigrants from Europe. And the newcomers, whether from England, or Connecticut, or eastern Long Island, instead of pushing west beyond the limits of the old Dutch communities, found arable land at their very doors.

On Long Island the clash between the Dutch and the New Englanders dates from the days of Governor Willem Kieft. Kings County was long a stronghold of Dutch culture. Visitors remarked on the Dutch manners and customs of the people, on the Dutch architecture, on the use of the Dutch tongue.[125] Suffolk, on the other hand, was distinctly an outpost of New England civilization, while the common meeting-ground was Queens. "Here Yankees and Dutchmen, Presbyterians and Quakers, men of every religion and no religion, mingled together."[126] It was in the early years of the eighteenth century that an eastward movement of Dutch from Kings into Queens came into contact with the movement of New Englanders from Connecticut across the Sound and then westward.

It is rather remarkable, then, that the churches at Oyster Bay and Newtown, outposts as it were of Dutch culture, should have continued the use of Dutch until the beginning of the nineteenth century. The Baptismal Register at Oyster Bay was kept in Dutch until 1792.[127] Domine Ryneer Van Nest, who usually preached

[124] *The Collegiate Dutch Church, Centennial Anniversary,* p. 25.

[125] Nathaniel S. Prime, *History of Long Island,* p. 69.

[126] *Ibid.,* pp. 69, 70.

[127] Henry A. Stoutenburgh, *Documentary History of Dutch Congregation at Oyster Bay,* pp. 39, 92.

in Dutch, remained with the Queens collegiate churches until 1797, while English seems to have come into general use only in 1802.[128] In Kings, as was to be expected, the use of Dutch lingered even longer. Reverend Martinus Schoonmaker, who understood English imperfectly, ministered to the six collegiate churches until his death in 1824.[129] It is said that when officiating at a certain wedding, he attempted to conclude the ceremony in English with the words, "I pronounce you man and wife and one flesh," but came out with, "I pronounce you two to be one beef."[130] Benjamin F. Thompson, in his *History of Long Island,* writing in 1839, states that "Many individuals, and even families, employ the Dutch language in their ordinary intercourse with each other at this day."[131] That a large English element existed in the congregations at a fairly early date, however, is shown by their action in calling Reverend Peter Lowe in 1787, to preach in English.[132]

In the Raritan valley, the Dutch language began to give ground in the second half of the eighteenth century. At New Brunswick, Reverend Johannes Leydt preached for many years exclusively in Dutch, but before his death in 1773, began alternating with English.[133] Reverend William Jackson at times filled the pulpit after Mr. Leydt's death, apparently speaking in Dutch. One afternoon, when he was holding the congregation with an interminable sermon, a certain James Schureman gave him a hint to close. "Sit down," the minister thundered out in Dutch, "Paul preached until midnight."[134] With the pastorate of Reverend Ira Condit, which began in 1793, Dutch was abandoned in the New Brunswick church.

In some of the Raritan valley churches the transition from Dutch to English was attended by many heart burnings. The older members of the Readington church were offended when the Consistory began keeping its minutes in English, "in order that

[128]James Riker, *Annals of Newtown,* p. 242; Henry R. Stiles, *History of the City of Brooklyn,* I, p. 193; Oscar Maddans, *Collegiate Churches of Queens County,* p. 62.

[129]Bushwick, Gravesend, Brooklyn, Flatlands, Flatbush, and New Utrecht.

[130]H. R. Stiles, *History of the City of Brooklyn,* I, pp. 190, 191.

[131]*Ibid.,* p. 448.

[132]*Ibid.,* p. 189.

[133]Richard H. Steele, *Historical Discourse,* p. 70.

[134]"Zig neer, Paulus predikte tot den midder-nacht."

the succeeding generation may have them in a language which will be better known to them."[135] To appease them, it was stipulated that Reverend Peter Studdiford, who came to the church three years later, should acquaint himself with Dutch in order to preach occasionally in that tongue. Apparently he was a poor linguist, for after several lamentable efforts, he was permitted to preach exclusively in English. Thereupon some of the Dutch-speaking group got the key to the church and locked him out. But they yielded when a certain Peter Ten Brook seized an axe, saying, "If you don't open that door I will!"[136] Ninety-five years after this incident there was still one member of the congregation, Andrew Van Vliet, who could speak Dutch.

The upper Raritan valley was the meeting place of three racial groups—the Dutch, coming up the Raritan and the Millstone; Germans, who formed the southern outpost of Teutonic New Jersey; and the encircling English. Reverend Christian F. Foering, pastor of the New Millstone church at the time of the Revolution, preached successively in German, Dutch and English.[137] On the other hand, Reverend John M. Van Harlingen, who assumed the pastorate in 1787 preached only in Dutch. But the congregation was now rapidly swinging to English, which no doubt accounts for his resignation in 1795, and the appointment of Reverend James P. Cannon.

The Hackensack valley proved the last stronghold of the Dutch language. Reverend John Cornelison, who ministered to the church at Bergen from 1792 to 1828, at first preached only in Dutch, but after 1806 alternated with English.[138] Although the use of Dutch gradually diminished, so late as 1841 Reverend Thomas De Witt, of New York, delivered an address in that language at the laying of the cornerstone of the new church, to the great delight of a large portion of the audience.[139]

Farther up the valley at Hackensack and Schraalenbergh, Dutch displayed even greater virility. The inscription over the

[135]Henry P. Thompson, *History of the Reformed Church, Readington, N. J.*, p. 71.
[136]*Ibid.*, Footnote, p. 78.
[137]*Ibid.*, p. 60.
[138]Benjamin C. Taylor, *Annals of Classis of Bergen*, p. 132.
[139]*Ibid.*, p. 147.

front door of the Schraalenbergh church, built in 1801, was in Dutch.[140] "The habits, manners and customs of the people," wrote Reverend Benjamin C. Taylor in 1857, "were those of the good old Dutch, and are so, largely to this day. They continue to use quite extensively the Dutch language." In fact, so late as 1919, when Professor J. Dyneley Prince visited this region he found "Jersey" or "Bergen County Dutch" still "the vernacular of the descendants of the original Netherland settlers . . . Up to thirty years ago [1880], this was the common idiom of many rural districts in northern New Jersey, employed alike by Dutch, English, German and French settlers. It has . . . been driven from its former territory by the advent of the public schools, and now survives only in the memories of some two hundred old persons, nearly all of them over seventy years of age. The younger generation have preserved, however, the curious jerky intonation, unclear diction, and the marked singsong tone of voice."[141]

In many parts of the Hudson valley, also, Dutch resisted the encroachments of English until far into the nineteenth century. In certain isolated districts preaching continued in Dutch so late as 1835.[142] In 1788, when New York State seemed on the point of rejecting the new Constitution of the United States, the Federal Committee at Albany won over many of the older men by publishing a translation in Dutch.[143] It is related that Aaron Burr, while dining at a wayside inn at Claverack, asked his hostess for a napkin. After long consultation with her husband, the good woman decided the Colonel wanted a *kniptong,* and so brought him a pair of pincers.[144] So late as 1850 some of the children of Ulster County spoke nothing but Dutch, and when they went to the district school had to be taught English before they could start their studies.[145]

140J aaght de vreede na met allen. Den Noorden Kerke te Schraalenburgh, Gebowd in het yaar 1801. Aan alle plattse daar Ik mynes nams Gedachtenisse Stichten Sal, Sal Ik tot u Komen ende sal u Segenen. . . . .

141J. Dyneley Prince, "The Jersey Dutch Dialect," *Dialect Notes,* III, Part VI, p. 459.

142David Cole, *History of Reformed Church of Tappan,* p. 84.

143Thomas Hunt, *Historical Sketch of the Town of Clerement,* p. 22.

144F. N. Zabriskie, *History of Reformed Church of Claverack,* p. 26.

145Thomas Hunt, *Historical Sketch of the Town of Clerement,* pp. 47–48.

The case of Albany was peculiar. Originally it was wholly Dutch. But since it "is on the frontier and near the enemy, men have been sent here from other places to help in guarding it," pointed out Reverend Theodore Frelinghuysen in 1748. "Most of these are Englishmen, and do not understand the Dutch language. Since they have no preacher among them, I have undertaken by their request to preach for them in the English language."[146] By 1780 English had become so widespread that the Reformed Church called Doctor John H. Livingston as a colleague to Reverend Eilardus Westerlo to preach in that language.[147] When he declined the invitation, Doctor Westerlo began to divide his sermons between Dutch and English, and so continued until his death in 1790, when the Dutch tongue was abandoned in church services.[148] But it was by no means abandoned by the Dutch families. A distinguished citizen of Albany writes me: "When I came to this country in 1897 I met a number of old people here in Albany and in Ulster County who could still speak Dutch. The language was more or less corrupted, of course, and often ungrammatical, but the accent was correct and had a native even though dialectical flavor, quite distinct from that of the pronunciation of a foreigner."[149]

The battle of languages in the Hudson valley and northeast New Jersey shows how certain, although at times slow, is the action of the melting-pot. A racial group, if it embraces a decided majority of the people in a large enough area, may retain its identity for centuries, but eventually it is certain to be swallowed up. On the other hand, it always adds its bit to the complex amalgam of the United States. The rôle of the Dutch in the building of America was important far out of proportion to their numbers. Entrenched in what was to become, in their own language, the stoop of the United States, they were eventually overwhelmed by the multitudes who entered there. But the New Yorker of today is reminded that it was the Dutch who founded

[146]*Ecclesiastical Records, State of New York*, p. 3018.

[147]E. P. Rogers, *Historical Discourse on the Dutch Church of Albany*, p. 30.

[148]*Our Two Hundred and Fifty Years*, p. 18.

[149]Mr. A. J. F. Van Laer, Archivist, University of State of N. Y.

his city whenever he walks along the Bowery, or visits Harlem or Spuyten Duyvil, or crosses over to Gravesend or Flatbush or Flushing. The story is told of the Kentucky colonel who complained that his whiskey tasted of leather and iron, and upon draining off the barrel of Bourbon discovered a leather-headed tack. It does not take a connoisseur to detect the Dutch flavor in the complicated mixture that is New York.

Chapter IV

THE PURITAN IN NEW JERSEY

THE expansion of New England is one of the major movements of American history. Many thousands of the hardy sons and daughters of the Puritans, deserting their rather sterile hills or turning their backs upon their fishing nets or their shipbuilding tools, set out for the West to create new homes in the wilderness. Starting as a small stream which trickled over the New York border into Westchester and Dutchess, or across the Sound to Long Island, the migration gained momentum until it had spread over northern Pennsylvania, the major part of New York, southern Ohio, Indiana and Illinois, southern Michigan and Wisconsin, and created New England pockets in New Jersey, and here and there in the southern parts of the old Northwest.[1] In this way the traditions, customs, religion, institutions and arts of the Puritans were spread from the Hudson to the Mississippi.

The migration of New Englanders to New Jersey was but the continuation of the westward movement within New England itself, a movement which had begun only a few years after the founding of Massachusetts. The motives were also the same, for as it was the search for more fertile lands or better trading facilities, or a desire to escape persecution or religious error, which drove men from Massachusetts Bay through the wilderness to Rhode Island or Long Island or the Connecticut valley, so they later caused many to desert these places for the Achter Kil, the Passaic, Cape May, or the lower Delaware.

Most of the Englishmen who came to Massachusetts Bay in the great Exodus were agriculturists whose wealth consisted chiefly of flocks and herds. The ships which set sail for the New Canaan bore from ten to a hundred beasts each, and in stormy weather the prayers of the Puritan fathers must have been mingled with the lusty bleating of sheep and the lowing of cows. William

[1]Lois K. Mathews, *The Expansion of New England.*

Wood in *New England's Prospect* tells us that the 4000 inhabitants in 1634 owned 1500 cattle,[2] and in a decade this number seems to have multiplied several times over. The advance agent of each migrating group, in selecting the site for the settlement, regarded the presence of rich meadow land as the prime consideration. If one or more congregations chanced to plant themselves in too close proximity, or if the meadows proved too small, a part of the settlers moved on. When the people of Newton asked permission of the Massachusetts Court to migrate to Connecticut, they cited as their reason "their want of accommodation for their cattle, so as they were not able to maintain their ministers, nor could receive any more of their friends to help them."[3]

The peopling of Connecticut proved but a step in the quest for fertile meadows. "No sooner was Windsor strong and lusty than her men in turn planted Simsbury and Fairfield; no sooner was Wethersfield strong than her men founded Middletown, Newington, Stamford and Branford; . . . Springfield sent its own waves of migration westward to Westfield or up the valley to Hadley and Northampton and into Vermont."[4] Even before all of the best land in Connecticut and New Haven had been taken up, the settlers began to cast longing eyes upon the region west of Newark Bay.[5]

The Yankee traders who were constantly coming down through Hell Gate to New Amsterdam in their little sloops, must have looked with envious eyes upon the wide meadows and forest-covered uplands of the lower Passaic, the Elizabeth and the Raritan.[6] The Puritans of Long Island especially, who were struggling with the unfertile soil of Easthampton, Southampton and Hempstead, were prepared whenever the opportunity offered to seek their fortunes in this more favored region. "This is the handsomest and pleasantest country that man can behold," declared Secretary Van Tienhoven, of New Netherland, in 1650, "it

[2]Prince, Soc., *Publs.* I, p. 52. [3]Archer B. Hulbert, *Soil* (New Haven, 1930), p. 97.

[4]Archer B. Hulbert, *Soil* (New Haven, 1930), p. 97.

[5]At a town meeting of New Haven, Dec. 17, 1650, "The Governor said that divers felt a sense of difficulty in carrying on their family occasions in this place, that the town held more than could subsist together."—C. H. Levermore, *Republic of New Haven* (Balt., 1886), p. 96.

[6]Stephen Wickes, *History of the Oranges*, p. 31.

furnished the Indians with abundance of maize, beans, pumpkins and other fruits."[7] Daniel Denton, writing twenty years later, was no less enthusiastic. Here let one's "cattle amount to some hundreds, he need not fear their want of pasture in the summer or fodder in the winter. . . . You have grass as high as a man's knees . . . and these woods also every mile or half-mile are furnished with fresh ponds, brooks and rivers, where all sorts of cattle, during the heat of the day do quench their thirst and cool themselves."[8] With these goodly meadows almost within sight, the Long Islanders were undeterred by the fact that East Jersey was then a part of New Netherland, and that English settlers within its borders would fall under the rule of Peter Stuyvesant. Provided the Dutch gave them a clear title to the land and guaranteed religious freedom many were ready to move.[9]

But when once the tide of settlement had begun it was swelled by many devout persons fleeing religious persecution. The founders of New England, who had led their people into the American wilderness in order to establish there a religious and political system based upon the teachings of Calvin, had been unflinching in their determination that heresy should not follow them. When certain Quaker missionaries came to Massachusetts, they subjected them to pitiless repression. Mary Fisher and Ann Austin, who arrived in Boston in 1656, were merely imprisoned until they could be shipped out of the colony. But when eight others came in from London and it became apparent that New England had been picked out by the Quakers as fair territory for proselytizing, laws were passed for their suppression, with such severe punishments as whipping, boring of the tongue, banishment and execution.

The enforcement was rigid. When William Brend, after 117 blows on his bare back with a tarred rope lay dying, Reverend John Norton remarked to the pitying bystanders, "He endeavoured to beat the gospel ordinances black and blue, and it was but just

[7] *N. J. Col. Docums,* I, pp. 366–367.

[8] Edwin F. Hatfield, *History of Elizabeth* (N. J., 1868), p. 36.

[9] J. P. Wall and H. E. Pickersgill, "The Raritan Valley of New Jersey," *Americana,* XV (July, 1921), p. 215.

to beat him black and blue."[10] At Dover three Quaker women, Ann Coleman, Mary Tomkins and Alice Ambrose, were made fast to a cart's tail, stripped to the waist despite the bitter northern winter, made to trudge "half-leg-deep" through the snow, and at each of several towns whipped on their bare backs.[11] In 1659 Mary Dyer, William Robinson and Marmaduke Stevenson, who had come to Boston courting martyrdom, were sentenced to be hanged. They were conducted to the gallows and the two men executed. Mrs. Dyer, after her hands and legs had been bound, her face covered and the rope adjusted around her neck, was informed that she had been reprieved. She was taken to Rhode Island by her family, but in the following spring, having appeared once more at Boston, was executed.[12] The hanging of William Leddra, in November 1660, concluded the executions of Quakers in New England, for Charles II gave orders that the vein of innocent blood opened in his dominions should be closed.[13]

The Baptists too were subjected to severe persecution. John Clark, Obadiah Holmes and John Grandall, of Newport, upon going to Lynn to visit an aged member of their church were fined an aggregate of £60. When Holmes was receiving sentence he remarked that he blessed God that he was counted worthy to suffer for the name of Jesus, whereupon Reverend John Wilson struck him, saying, "The curse of God, or Jesus go with you."[14] For refusing to pay his fine, thirty strokes were laid upon his bare back with a three-corded whip. As he left the stake, streaming with blood, two compassionate bystanders took him by the hand, but were themselves arrested, fined, admonished and threatened with whipping.

[10]H. Norton, *New England's Ensign* (1659), p. 55.

[11]Geo. Bishop, *New England Judged by the Spirit of the Lord* (London, 1703), p. 366.

[12]Rufus M. Jones, *The Quakers in the American Colonies* (London, 1911), p. 86.

[13]*Ibid.*, p. 98. Humphrey Norton, a Quaker, was sent a prisoner from Southold, L. I., to New Haven for trial. The court fined him £20, and sentenced him to be severely whipped, branded on the hand with the letter H, and banished. (Benj. F. Thompson, *History of Long Island*, N. Y., 1843, I, p. 380.)

[14]John Clark, "Ill News from New England" (London, 1652), *Mass. Hist. Soc. Coll.* Series IV, Vol. II, p. 33.

Many Massachusetts Baptists and Quakers found refuge in Rhode Island, where the advanced views of Roger Williams protected them from persecution. But the Quakers even here found themselves in opposition to the law requiring them to bear arms and drill on training days. Some fled to Gravesend and elsewhere in the western end of Long Island, expecting there the liberal treatment usually accorded by the Dutch to all religious faiths. But they had not counted on the stubborn intolerance of Peter Stuyvesant. The governor had William Reape, a Rhode Island Quaker, arrested and imprisoned; John Tilton, of Gravesend, fined and banished for entertaining Quakers; and others treated with equal severity.[15] Robert Hodgson was arrested at Hempstead, and refusing either to pay a fine of one hundred guilders or "to work at the wheelbarrow two years with the negroes,"[16] was whipped on his bare back with a thick pitched rope until he fell to the ground where he was left until nightfall with the sun beating down on his bruised and swollen body.[17]

From the cruel intolerance of Stuyvesant and the New England clergy and magistrates, many Quakers and Baptists sought refuge in the wilds of New Jersey. In 1663 a party of twenty sailed over from Gravesend to Monmouth, and despite the protests of Dutch traders, purchased a tract of land on the Navesink and Shrewsbury Rivers.[18] The next year actual settlement began, when John Bowne, Richard Stout and others founded the villages of Middletown and Shrewsbury. Among them were many who had felt the heavy hand of the magistrates or the sting of the whip; John and Peter Tilton, Samuel Spicer, John Townsend, Obadiah and Jonathan Holmes, sons of Reverend Obadiah Holmes; Edward Wharton, who had been imprisoned and whipped in Massachusetts as a Quaker, William Reape, once deputy governor of Rhode Island; William Goulding, banished from Massachusetts because of his Baptist beliefs; William Shettock, a Quaker who had settled in Massachusetts but had been whipped and driven out;

[15]*History of Monmouth County, N. J.*, Lewis Hist. Pub. Co. (N. J. and Chicago), pp. 54–55.

[16]J. F. Jameson, *Original Narratives of Early American History*, p. 400.

[17]E. B. O'Callaghan, *History of New Netherland*, Vol. II, pp. 350–357.

[18]*History of Monmouth County*, Vol. I, p. 50.

Elakim Wardell with his wife Lydia,[19] imprisoned and whipped in New Hampshire.[20]

Middletown was the haven for the Baptists, and here the little band of exiles set up their humble church in the woods, unperturbed by the changing jurisdiction of Dutch and English or even by the influx of men of other religions or of no religion.[21] The Quakers erected their first meeting-house at Shrewsbury. When John Burnylate and George Fox visited the village in 1672 the Friends assembled from far and near, journeying through the forests or up the river by boat, to take part in the "precious meeting."[22] In subsequent years we find the Quakers establishing their meeting houses at various places along the coast, at Egg Harbor, Seaville, Cape May, and elsewhere.

Piscataway, north of the Raritan, was founded by families from New Hampshire, many of them Baptists fleeing from persecution. The Baptist church at Piscataway, established in 1680, became the "established church" of the town, its minister being paid from taxes and its affairs regulated in "town meeting."[23] Baptists also established themselves at Squam and Deal, Cape May, Waretown on Barnegat Bay, Cohansey, and elsewhere. Thus it was that religious persecution, which had been so vital a factor in the migration of thousands from Europe to America, became an important influence also in the movement of population from one colony to another.

On the other hand, whole groups came to New Jersey, not because of the severity of the New England clergy, but because of their increasing laxity. Hardly had two decades elapsed since the beginning of the Great Exodus, when to some of the leaders, men of the stamp of John Davenport, it seemed that its original purposes were failing of accomplishment, that the rule of the chosen few was tottering, that the doors of the church were opening too

[19]Wardell and his wife had appeared before the congregation at Hampton almost naked, as a "sign." Rufus M. Jones, *The Quakers in the American Colonies* (London, 1911), p. 371.

[20]*History of Monmouth County,* Vol. I, pp. 52–55.

[21]*Ibid.,* p. 322; Thos. S. Griffiths, *Hist. of Baptists in New Jersey,* pp. 15–16.

[22]*History of Monmouth County, N. J.,* Vol. I, p. 340.

[23]Ezra Hunt, *Metuchen and Her History* (N. Y., 1870), p. 6.

wide to the unregenerate, that the old Puritan code of morals was relaxing. So as the Puritans had fled from an unregenerate England to found a Zion in Massachusetts, these extremists fled from an unregenerate New England to try the experiment once more in the wilds of New Jersey.

In this new exodus the largest groups came from the so-called republic of New Haven. The founders of New Haven had been of the most extreme Puritan type. The fundamental agreement, upon which their laws were based, restricted the franchise to church members; provided for the election of twelve pious men who were to appoint magistrates, make and repeal laws and perform practically all public duties; and directed that "the word of God shall be the only rule to be attended unto in ordering the affairs of government."[24] In other words, New Haven was a Bible state, ruled by a narrow clique working in close affiliation with the clergy.

But the body of the freeholders, despite their reverence for the leaders, were not long content with this complete surrender of their rights. In 1651 a group of young men united against the magistrates, and by a series of ordinances forced through the town meeting, succeeded in shearing them of their most important powers. To the founders this seemed to doom the whole venture, and John Davenport exclaimed sorrowfully, "The cause of Christ in New Haven is miserably lost."[25]

The situation became more critical for them with the restoration of Charles II and the consequent threat of annexation to Connecticut. Davenport and his friends had regarded with sullen disapproval the liberal tendencies of their neighbors to the north, especially their acceptance of the Halfway Covenant which permitted baptism to children of pious parents who had had no definite "religious experience." So they "spurned the Christless rule of Connecticut," even though they were in sore need of support against the King's open hostility and the enmity of their neighbors. But when many of the younger men began openly to declare themselves citizens of Connecticut, when taxes could not be col-

[24]*New Haven Records,* Vol. I, pp. 11–21.
[25]Chas. H. Levermore, *Republic of New Haven,* pp. 101–107.

lected and the colony fell deeper and deeper into debt,[26] when the English conquest of New Netherland threatened the inclusion of New Haven in the provinces of the Duke of York, opposition broke down and independent New Haven came to an end.[27]

As their Zion fell in ruins about them, the uncompromising Puritan group now turned their thoughts to New Jersey. New Haven had been founded in part as a commercial enterprise, and when it was discovered that no profit was to be had from trade with the impoverished Indians along the Quinnipiac, the leaders had purchased a vast tract of land on the lower Delaware and established a post near Salem. Although sickness, together with the attacks of the Swedes and Dutch, had brought failure to this venture, New Haven had never relinquished her claims.[28] The old leaders were appealing to Colonel Nicolls for a recognition of their rights in this region when the news came of the grant of all New Jersey to Berkeley and Carteret. When this was followed by Governor Philip Carteret's promise of full civil and religious rights to all settlers, they made active preparations to turn their backs on New Haven, and with all who still adhered to the original conception of the strict Puritan commonwealth, to migrate to the shores of the Delaware.[29] Robert Treat and John Gregory, sailing down the coast, up the bay and into the river on a tour of inspection, had almost decided to lead the settlers to the vicinity of Burlington, when the governor persuaded them to take the Newark region instead.[30] After that the New Haven of John Davenport, the Puritan State ruled by the godly under Bible law, must be sought, not on the banks of the Quinnipiac, but of the Passaic. The experiment which was tried in Massachusetts Bay, and later at New Haven, was to be duplicated in the wilds of New Jersey.

This Zion, for which so many earnest men and women were willing to desert their houses and migrate into a wilderness, its founders fervently trusted was to endure to the end of time. In

[26]*Ibid.*, pp. 113, 114.
[27]Herbert L. Osgood, *American Colonies in the Seventeenth Century*, Vol. I, p. 331.
[28]C. H. Levermore, *Republic of New Haven*, pp. 90–95.
[29]*Ibid.*, p. 117.
[30]Frank J. Urquhart, *A History of the City of Newark*, Vol. I, p. 48.

fact, it collapsed in a few decades. Treat and Pierson and the rest should have realized that their ideals could not endure in a province made up of a heterogeneous population of various religious beliefs, where they were subject to laws passed by an Assembly not in complete sympathy with their views, under the administration of English governors some of them ardent Anglicans, in commercial contact with New York and touching elbows with the Dutch at Bergen. Governor Carteret, in his concessions guaranteeing full civil and religious liberty, had never intended that Newark should be an independent town, cut off from the jurisdiction of the provincial government; yet without independence the Newark envisaged by its founders could be of but short duration.

Nonetheless they went ahead with their plans hopefully and prayerfully. Guilford, Milford and New Haven provided many of the settlers, while the people of Branford migrated almost as a whole. It was appropriate, therefore, that Branford should draw up the Fundamental Agreement which became the "constitution" of the new town. First and foremost it provided "that none shall be admitted freemen or free burgesses . . . but such planters as are members of one or other of the Congregational churches, nor shall any but such be chosen to magistracy . . . nor . . . to vote in establishing laws." They then added: "We shall with care and diligence provide for the maintenance of the purity of religion professed in the Congregational churches." To these two "foundation stones," the other emigrants added another requiring all who shall "come in to us or arise amongst us . . . to subvert us from the true religion . . . quietly to depart the place."[31]

The Newark pilgrims had no such trying passage to their Promised Land as the founders of Plymouth and Boston, for the voyage from the little Connecticut towns through the Sound, past Manhattan, around Bergen Point into Newark Bay and the Passaic entailed little danger for their sloops, crowded as they no doubt were with men and women, household goods, cattle and other domestic animals. Many families made the journey in 1666 and began the work of clearing the ground, laying out the lots

[31] *Ibid.*, Vol. I, pp. 66, 67.

and erecting temporary houses, but it was only in June, 1667, with the arrival of the Branford group, that the enterprise was safely launched.

Certain historians have objected to the use of the word *theocracy* to describe the early Massachusetts, New Haven and Newark governments. Whereas in a theocracy the church rules the state, in these early Puritan commonwealths the clergy held no civil office, they point out, and were subject to laws passed by the town meeting and the provincial Assembly. In fact, the church and state were at first so closely interwoven as to be almost indistinguishable. Since none but church members could vote, the town meeting, and in New England the Assembly, were in a sense also congregations or synods. In Newark the town meeting might vote at one moment on the regulation of fences, next on repairing the church, next on providing a night watch and then on levying taxes to pay the minister's salary.[32]

The East Jersey Assembly at first was also clearly Puritanical in character, although no doubt many of the delegates were less rigid than those from Newark. At the Assembly which met at Elizabethtown in 1668, there were six representatives from the congregational towns of Newark, Elizabethtown and Woodbridge, two from the Dutch town of Bergen, and three from Middletown and Shrewsbury.[33] One of its first concerns was to draw up a stern penal code based on Leviticus.[34] Death was prescribed for murder, arson, perjury to the prejudice of life, kidnapping, witchcraft, treason, rape, and unnatural vice, and in some cases for burglary and the smiting or cursing of parents by their children.[35] For infidelity in married life the offender might be fined or whipped or banished, for lying fined or placed in the stocks, for the "beastly vice of drunkenness" fined or subjected to corporal punishment or placed in the stocks. "All prizes, stage-plays, games, marques, revels, bull-baiting, and cock fightings, which excite people to rudeness, cruelty, looseness and irreligion," were to be discouraged and punished by the courts.

[32]*Records of Town of Newark* (Newark, 1864).
[33]F. J. Urquhart, *A History of the City of Newark*, Vol. I, p. 144.
[34]This was renewed in 1675 and slightly modified in 1682.
[35]Wm. A. Whitehead, *East Jersey under the Proprietary Government*, pp. 239, 240.

Violation of the Lord's Day by domestic work, recreations and unnecessary travelling were punishable by fines, confinement in the stocks, imprisonment or whipping.[36]

The Newark Puritans from the first had great difficulty in maintaining the isolation which they considered necessary to the purity of their religion. New York was the natural market for their surplus produce, and hardly a weekday passed when one would not see their sloops tied up in the Broad Street canal while they rubbed elbows with the cosmopolitan crowd in the shops on either side. Nor could they long shut themselves off from their Dutch and Flemish neighbors of Bergen, or slam the door in the face of newcomers from Long Island or Connecticut. Their fear of contamination is revealed in a town ordinance passed in 1680 forbidding "planters" to receive or entertain any one "coming or resorting to us to settle upon the land, nor to lease any house or lot to them, nor permit them to remain in the town more than a month without especial permit."[37] Yet the same year eleven new settlers were admitted upon the payment of purchase money for land, apparently without signing the Fundamental Agreement. Strict censorship was kept over all strangers for several generations, but by 1690 it must have been obvious that the ideal of the isolated uncontaminated community had proved impracticable.

Moreover, fatal weakness appeared within. In the Puritan town, where church and state were united under one government, any serious divisions within the congregation threatened the whole system. When, then, the Presbyterian leanings of Reverend Abraham Pierson, Jr., brought him into conflict with a large part of the people, the town meeting refused to levy the usual tax for his salary and he became dependent upon voluntary contributions.

[36] *Ibid.*, pp. 240–243. These East Jersey laws are obviously based on the New Haven code, and in many cases are almost identical with it. Thus in New Jersey we find the wording: "If any man shall willfully or forcibly steal away any mankind, he shall be put to death." In New Haven the law says: "If any person steal a man, or mankind, that person shall surely be put to death, Exod. 21:16." In East Jersey the law required: "If any person be found to be a witch, either male or female, they shall be put to death"; in New Haven, "If any person be a witch, he or she shall be put to death according to Exod. 22:18; Levit. 20:27; Deut. 18:10, 11."

[37] *Records of Town of Newark*, p. 83.

Thus was opened a breach between the civil and religious functions of the government which was never fully closed. In 1700, when Reverend Jabez Wakeman was installed as the minister, the people agreed that his salary should "be raised by a rate," but though the town officers collected the money, they seem to have levied only on voluntary subscribers.

The incorporation of Newark as a township in 1713 emphasized its civil, as contrasted with its ecclesiastical character. Thereafter, separate town meetings were called for the transacting of church business, which were almost indistinguishable from ordinary church meetings. When the congregation split, one group going over to Presbyterianism and the other founding the Mountain Society, neither cared to entrust its interests to the town. In 1753 the members of the first church incorporated themselves under a royal charter and took independent control of their property interests.[38] For a few years longer the town continued its oversight of the burying ground, but after 1764 all references to the church save as an independent body disappear from the records.[39]

The really fatal blow, however, had come many years before. Colonel Josiah Ogden was a leading member of the community, a man of wealth who had represented the town in the Assembly from 1716 to 1721. Although a pillar of the church, he seems to have tempered piety with common sense. In the fall of 1733 when there had been such long-continued rains that his wheat was in danger of rotting on the ground, he did not hesitate to gather it in on a Sabbath when the sun broke through the clouds. But his neighbors, horrified at this desecration of the Lord's Day, which had it occurred a few decades earlier might have landed even the influential Ogden in the stocks, brought the matter before the congregation, and secured a verdict of public censure.[40]

The matter did not end here, however, for the colonel's friends rallied to his support, and the whole community was torn by the bitter wrangling of the pro-Ogden and the anti-Ogden faction.

[38]Walter S. Nichols, *The Old Town Church Endowment* (Newark, 1916), p. 47.

[39]*Ibid.*, p. 49; *Records of the Town of Newark.*

[40]Alexander McWhorter, *A Century Sermon* (Newark, 1808), p. 16.

The Presbytery sought to heal the breach by reversing the decision of the congregation, but it was too late. Already a sprinkling of Anglicans had appeared at Newark, establishing themselves in fine homes at Barbadoes Neck on the east bank of the Passaic, and with them Colonel Ogden united to found an Episcopal church. Jonathan Dickinson rushed in to save the day with a blast against Episcopacy, but this resulted in nothing more tangible than a wordy war of pamphlets with Reverend John Beach, of Connecticut. The new Anglican congregation found an able minister in the Reverend Edward Vaughan "missionary at Elizabethtown" and in 1743–44 had become strong enough to erect Trinity Church. This separation was "the origin of the greatest animosity and alienation between friends, townsmen, Christians, neighbors and relatives" that the town ever beheld, kindling "a flame which was not extinguished," till the conclusion of the Revolutionary War.[41]

If the Newark Zion began to crumble a few decades after its founding, other Puritan towns in New Jersey, less zealous, less homogeneous, had little chance indeed to hold out. So early as 1660 a certain John Strickland, of Huntington, Long Island, applied to Governor Stuyvesant for permission to lead a group of settlers to the western shore of Achter Kil. A conference followed which proved a failure only because they demanded, in addition to religious liberty and a large degree of local self-government, the "right to administer justice in all civil matters" without appeal to the provincial authorities.[42] The matter was still hanging fire when New Netherland surrendered to the English. This was good news indeed to those Puritan families of western Long Island, who had been anxiously waiting, many of them without homes, to move across to New Jersey to start their new town. So a group of associates, having secured Colonel Nicolls's approval, purchased a large tract from the Indians west of Staten Island for twenty fathoms of trading cloth, two coats, two guns, two kettles, ten bars of lead, twenty handfuls of powder, and four hun-

[41]Alexander McWhorter, quoted in Wm. H. Shaw, *History of Essex and Hudson Counties,* Vol. I, pp. 502, 503 (Phila., 1884).

[42]E. B. O'Callaghan, *History of New Netherland,* Vol. II, pp. 447–448.

dred fathoms of wampum,[43] and began laying out lots and erecting houses.

The men who gathered for the initial town meeting were New Englanders, of the same stern stuff as the Newark settlers. While most of them had resided for some years at Southold, Southampton or East Hampton, on the east end of Long Island, some came directly from Connecticut, and a few from Massachusetts. Many had been associated with each other in the founding of other towns, and so met again on the banks of the Achter Kil as old friends and in some cases as reunited families. Even though the desire for fertile pastures and "upland" may have been the chief motive for their migration, they were determined to establish the typical Puritan community with Town and Church indissolubly united, and, like the Newarkers, to slam the door in the face of strangers of doubtful orthodoxy.

Disillusionment came immediately, for in August, 1665, the *Philip* cast anchor off the town, bringing young Philip Carteret, with Robert Vauquellin, a French surveyor, Captain James Bollen, of New York, and eighteen servants and laborers. Carteret informed the settlers that the Duke of York had sold New Jersey to Lord John Berkeley and Sir George Carteret, who had made him governor and directed him to establish their government. The Elizabeth Associates thus found that they had prepared, not an isolated religious community, but a capital for the province. The governor was gracious and tactful at first, made no attempt to disallow the Nicolls grant and himself became an associate of the town by buying John Baily's rights, but the ideal of the isolated Puritan town with the people all of one mind and heart was lost.

A breach having been thus effected in the walls of religious conformity, other discordant elements rushed in. Reverend Seth Fletcher, the Puritan minister engaged by the town, was greatly annoyed by Quakers, "new ones coming in one after another." Since the laws of the province made it impossible to expel these intruders, Mr. Fletcher resorted to the more hazardous expedient of debate. But this too proved ineffectual, for the Quakers when-

[43]E. F. Hatfield, *History of Elizabeth,* pp. 30, 31.

ever argument went against them, "set to humming, singing, reeling their heads and bodies . . . and threatening" Mr. Fletcher that his "destruction was nigh at hand."[44] By the end of the century the Quakers had so increased in members and influence that they were able to build a meeting-house in the southern part of the village.[45]

Of more importance were the efforts of the Society for the Propagation of the Gospel in Foreign Parts to build up an Episcopal congregation. The Society fired the opening gun in 1703, when Reverend George Keith preached in Elizabeth,[46] and followed it up by sending to the province a succession of able preachers: John Brooke, Thomas Moore, Edward Vaughan, and others. The old intolerance must have been much softened by this time, for the town permitted the Anglicans to use the meeting-house temporarily, though with a proviso that none of the prayers of the Church be read.[47] In 1706 the Episcopalians laid the foundations of a church of their own, the charming old St. John's, and gradually gathered a small congregation. In 1711 Reverend Thomas Halliday reported that he had baptized seventy-two children in East Jersey, besides eleven adults, who had been so unfortunate as to be brought up "in dark Quakerism and Anabaptism." "The New England Independents," he added regretfully, "are now old and confirmed in their erroneous way," so that a small group of families from England and Scotland constituted his main reliance.[48]

With Quakers, Anabaptists and Anglicans mixed with the Congregationalists, with New England blood diluted with that of Scots, English, and an occasional Frenchman, the union between Church and Town seems to have been dissolved in Elizabeth even earlier than in Newark. The loss of the Town Book makes the point obscure, but we know that by 1694, and probably long before, the minister's salary was paid entirely by subscription. Reverend John Harriman, who was an excellent business man as well as preacher, entered every subscription and

[44] *Ibid.*, p. 207. [45] *Ibid.*, p. 288.

[46] Samuel A. Clark, *The History of St. John's Church, Elizabeth Town, New Jersey*, [Phila. and N. J., 1857], p. 15.

[47] *Ibid.*, p. 19. [48] *Ibid.*, p. 38.

every payment in his private account books, one of which was preserved by his family. Although the list of 1694, containing ninety-nine names and subscriptions totalling £83.11.0., seems to have been drawn up at the Town Meeting, Mr. Harriman had to be his own collector. It must have taken no inconsiderable part of his time to receive and capitalize on his pay, made often in meat, grain and vegetables; often in day labor on his farm, at his mill, in his garden or in repairing his house or barn; often in shoemaking, tailoring or weaving.[49] With the switch to Presbyterianism in 1717,[50] the Elizabeth church doubtless divorced itself almost completely from the Town government.

At Woodbridge not only the relationship of Church and Town, but religion as such suffered severely because of isolation and poverty. The little group of settlers, despite their earnest efforts, were long unsuccessful in securing a permanent minister, so that during the first fifteen years they enjoyed only nine months of religious services.[51] When, in 1695, a desirable minister was found in Reverend Samuel Shepard, he resigned after a brief pastorate, because his wife was so "utterly averse to settling" there.[52]

The presence of a group of Quakers hastened the breakdown of the union of Church and Town. It was in 1695 that William Webster, "pretending that it was contrary to his conscience to pay anything toward the maintenance of a minister," brought on a heated discussion. John Bishop tried to heal the breach by offering to pay Webster's tax for him, but the difference was too fundamental to be dodged. In 1700 the town meeting appointed a committee "to discourse our dissenting neighbors the Quakers, to make a final end to the difference that hath been between us and them concerning their paying to the public ministry."[53] That the ensuing agreement freed the Quakers from church dues is obvious since thereafter the minister seems to have been supported by subscription, not taxation.[54] With the coming of Anglican mis-

[49]E. F. Hatfield, *History of Elizabeth,* pp. 283–285. [50]*Ibid.,* p. 330.
[51]J. W. Dally, *Woodbridge and Vicinity,* p. 81.
[52]*Ibid.,* p. 166. [53]*Ibid.,* p. 88.
[54]In 1702 Mr. Shepard's salary was paid out of the town rates, but probably only subscribers were forced to contribute.

sionaries and the organization of an Episcopalian congregation the last hope of religious unity vanished.

In Middletown the population was too varied in its religious persuasions to permit the New England system of a united Town and Church. The musty old town book with entries dating back to 1667, although recording the votes of the town meetings on land divisions, elections of Deputies, the erection of fences, etc., is silent in the matter of meeting house or minister.[55] When the Baptists became numerous enough to organize a congregation their minister must have been supported by voluntary contributions.

In its civil capacity the East Jersey town was far more enduring. In 1700 Colonel Lewis Morris wrote: "East Jersey has in it ten towns, viz: Middletown, Freehold, Amboy, Piscataway, Woodbridge, Elizabeth Town, Newark, Agusehenouch,[56] and Bergen. . . . These towns are not like the towns in England . . . the houses built close together on a small spot of ground . . . but they include large portions of the country, of four, five, eight, ten, twelve, fifteen miles in length, and as much in breadth."[57] The town system was created by the various groups of settlers, not by the English government nor the Assembly. The New Englanders brought it with them as a matter of course, as they brought their language and their religion. It was tacitly recognized by the first Assembly in that the membership was made up of representatives of the towns, but it was only in 1693 that it took legal cognizance of it and prescribed the bounds.

One of the first steps in creating the town was the dividing of the land among the associates. The first drawing was for home lots, where the settler was to build his dwelling and cow shed, and plant his garden; the next for the meadow land or marsh where he pastured his cattle; the third for the "upland" for the planting of wheat, rye and maize. In New England the meadow was usually held in common, and its division in New Jersey indicates its wider extent there. It was a signal mark of honor

[55] *Middletown Town Book*, Vol. I, Monmouth County Hist. Assn., Freehold.

[56] Acquackanoak.

[57] S. A. Clark, *History of St. John's Church, Elizabeth Town* (1857), p. 14.

to Robert Treat that his fellow townsmen of Newark granted him a lot "next the river, adjoining to the little cove of meadow, . . . against his land near home."[58] The charter of Woodbridge directed the freeholders "equally to divide the aforesaid tract of upland and meadow amongst themselves by the first, second, and third lots or as they can otherwise agree upon."[59] In Middletown there were two divisions, the first of home lots, along a street running east and west, and the second of pasture lots in Poplar field, now known as Osborn Hill.[60]

The size of the holdings differed in various towns and according to the character of the land, but on the whole followed closely the New England precedent. In Clinton Township, Thomas Pierson, Jr., had a home lot of six acres, and thirty acres "beyond the two-mile brook;" while his next-door neighbor Samuel Lyon also had a home lot of six acres, and sixty-five acres of field and pasture land.[61] In Middletown the "out-lots" of field land varied in size from ten to thirty-two acres.[62] When Joakim Andrews of Woodbridge died in 1675, his widow Ann sold "the house, orchard, house lot, pasture for calves, and all that might be claimed by the concessions—a first lot-right—except twenty acres sold by her husband . . . and one pear-tree and some gooseberry bushes reserved for her use."[63] In Woodbridge the "home lots" varied greatly, John Pike having ten acres, John Martin eleven, Samuel Dennis twelve, Thomas Bloomfield seventeen and a half, Obadiah Ayres sixteen. The original Woodbridge associates were granted, in addition to the home lot, forty acres of meadow and two hundred and forty acres of upland.[64]

Since the town usually owned far more land than could be put under cultivation at first, the freeholders in later years often voted themselves additional lots from the commons. A committee, ap-

[58]*Records of the Town of Newark*, pp. 8, 9.

[59]*East Jersey Records, Deeds, Patents,* Liber I, Office of Secretary of State, Trenton.

[60]*Middletown Town Book*, Vol. I, Dec. 30, 1667, Monmouth County Historical Society, Freehold, N. J.

[61]Wm. H. Shaw, *History of Essex and Hudson Counties,* Vol. II, p. 690.

[62]*History of Monmouth County* (Lewis Pub. Co., N. Y. and Chicago, 1882), Vol. I, p. 323; *Middletown Town Book*, Vol. I.

[63]W. W. Clayton, *History of Union and Middlesex Counties* (Phila., 1882), p. 555.

[64]Joseph W. Dally, *Woodbridge and Vicinity,* p. 28.

pointed by the Town Meeting, was instructed to lay out the lots "as equally as maybe," but if one lot was more fertile than another "to add so much in quantity to the bad lot that may countervail the goodness of the other." When all was ready the lots were "numbered on little pieces of paper" which were placed in a bag, from which they were drawn one by one. We can imagine with what intense interest the Woodbridge freeholders stood around John Parker in 1717 as he thrust his hand in the bag and pulled out the first slip with lot No. 19 for Daniel Pierce, and how the group dispersed after the drawing to examine each his new lot, to step off the grounds, and to estimate the yield.[65]

As in New England, class distinctions in the New Jersey town were clearly marked. The man of property, or the Town magistrates, or persons of good family were singled out for honor, especially in allotting seats in that center of community life the meeting-house. In 1679, the Newark "seating committee" were instructed to place all persons "according to office, age, estate, infirmity and descent or parentage."[66] Yet, as in New England, pioneer conditions and the democracy of labor tended to break down distinctions. When it became necessary to "daub" or plaster the new meeting-house at Woodbridge, the entire male population was called upon; when the walls were to be whitewashed, it was John Pike, Clerk of the Town and a member of the Colonial Assembly, who did the work; when a new pulpit became necessary Ezekiel Bloomfield, former Assemblyman, took hammer and saw, and set it up.[67]

Like its New England prototype the New Jersey town strove to attain a large degree of economic independence and imported nothing it could make for itself. Among the early Elizabeth settlers was Roger Lambert, blacksmith; Benjamin Parkis, joiner; George Ross, carpenter; William Letts, weaver; William Looker, brewer; Benjamin Wade, clothier; John Wilson, wheelwright; William Broadwell, cordwainer; Richard Clarke, shipwright; Nathaniel Forbes, shoemaker; John Hume, mason.[68] Early Wood-

[65]*Ibid.*, p. 159. [66]*Records of the Town of Newark*, pp. 77, 78.
[67]Jos. W. Dally, *Woodbridge and Vicinity*, p. 87.
[68]Edwin F. Hatfield, *History of Elizabeth*.

bridge had five carpenters, one shoemaker, four blacksmiths, one mason, two tanners, three weavers, one millwright and one joiner.[69] So important were these workers to the town that the authorities sometimes offered them especial inducements to settle in their midst. In 1698 John Grandal moved his blacksmith shop to Woodbridge upon the invitation of the town and a gift of two acres of upland.[70]

The typical townsman produced his own grain, vegetables, fruit, milk, butter and meat; had his wheat ground at the local mill; purchased his shoes of one neighbor, his furniture of another; spun his own thread and had the best weaver make it into cloth; bought his cart from the wheelwright and his hardware from the blacksmith. We get glimpses of the economy of these early towns from an order for ammunition for Woodbridge, to be paid for "by the Constable in wheat and pork out of the Treasury,"[71] and the voting of the minister's salary in the "current pay of the country," which meant pork, peas, wheat and other provisions.

In New Jersey the freemen, even the Newark extremists, refused to surrender the control of the town to a small group of magistrates who held office for life, the "town's men" or special committees to carry on the regular functions of government being elected annually. And it was specifically ordered that their powers should not extend to the disposing of land, the admission of new inhabitants, the levying of taxes, nor the fundamental agreement.[72] In Woodbridge the first town committee was chosen in 1705, when seven men were designated to act in all matters save the disposition of land and the levying of taxes, and the presumption is that prior to that date the government was carried on exclusively by the town meeting and the town officers.[73] "Selectmen to manage the affairs of the town" were chosen in Piscataway for the first time in 1693.[74]

[69] Jos. W. Dally, *Woodbridge and Vicinity*, p. 20.

[70] *Ibid.*, p. 119. [71] *Ibid.*, p. 48.

[72] John L. Rankin, "Newark Town Government," N. J. Hist. Soc. *Proceedings*, Ser. III, Vol. X (1915).

[73] Jos. W. Dally, *Woodbridge and Vicinity*, p. 147.

[74] W. W. Clayton, *History of Union and Middlesex Counties* (Phila., 1882), p. 592.

The powers of the Town Meeting were extensive and varied. We find the freeholders assembled perhaps in the meeting-house; or, if the weather was too cold for that cheerless place, around the roaring fire in some near-by residence, appointing the "rate gatherers" for the year, or ordering the construction of "a good horse bridge," or admitting a new freeholder, or allotting land for a sheep pound, or offering rewards for the killing of wolves, or electing deputies to represent the town in the Assembly, or voting the minister his salary, or contracting for new seats in the meeting house, or regulating the erection of fences. These sturdy pioneers, in their little communities on the fringe of English civilization, little dreaming of the day when the individual was to lose his identity in the fabric of a vast, complicated and industrialized state, regulated the everyday affairs of their life in a way that would be impossible today. The New Jersey town-meeting, like its prototype of New England, was the expression of American democracy at its best.

As a social unit the New Jersey town tended to break down because of the large extent of area it embraced. In the ideal town the center of life was the village. Here the people had their homes, here was the Town Meeting house, here the blacksmith had his forge, the weaver set up his loom, the shoemaker his shop, here the militia drilled on the green, here often was the grist mill, the town landing, the school. In the morning the villager rose with the dawn, and after the reading of the Scripture, family prayers and the simple breakfast had been concluded, shouldering his hoe, or his scythe or pitch-fork, set off for his upland lots. Perhaps he found it necessary to take with him his wooden plow, drawn by slow-moving oxen, perhaps, if it were harvest time, his clumsy two-wheeled cart. When the day's work was done he trudged home to enjoy his evening meal of pork, brown bread and a mug of beer.

The agricultural village had obvious advantages. The compactness of the little community served as a safeguard against the Indians, for in case of a night alarm every man capable of bearing arms could be summoned within a few minutes. It was vital to the ideal of the Puritan Church, for the entire population, when the little bell in the cupola summoned them to worship, was within easy walking distance of the meeting-house. The minister resided in the very midst of his flock, so that it was easy for him to visit the sick, counsel the perplexed and admonish the wayward. Whereas the Virginia rector had to ride many miles on horseback through fields and forests to attend his parishioners, the early New Jersey Puritan minister need only take a short stroll to be at the home of the most distant of his congregation.

For the artisan, also, the village was of vital importance, since it enabled him to escape the itinerant stage, and to do his work in his own little shop. If the villager needed a new rim for his cart wheel, he could have it made at the smithy a few doors away; if his house needed reshingling, the carpenter was close at hand; if he had an excess of pork or beef for sale, the local cooper could make his barrels; if he wanted a new table or chair he would order one from the joiner; if his daughters had spun wool sufficient for a few yards of cloth he would take it to the weaver,[75] if he wished to purchase imported articles—a book, a watch, a few pewter platters, a pair of stockings for his wife—he stopped by at the store of the village merchant.[76]

The system began to change, however, when allotments were made in the outlying fields. It was no great matter for the yeoman to go out for work when his upland lot was adjacent to the homestead; or even when a mile or two distant, but it became burdensome in the extreme, when he attempted to put under cultivation fields in the more remote parts of the town, four, five, perhaps six or seven miles away. Even though the town took care to lay out roads to the new divisions, even though the yeoman might ride his horse or drive out in the hay cart, he could ill afford the time and energy spent in going and coming. When the Woodbridge associate received his lot at Rahway, five miles from the village, and the Newark freeholder his share of the Mountain land, they must have been perplexed as to how to make use of their new holdings.

The solution came apparently with the advent of the second

[75] *N. J. Archives,* Ser. I, Vol. XXI, pp. 724–730.

[76] See *John Brown Account Book*—Piscataway, Princeton University.

generation. When a son was married and wished to make a home for himself, the father thought of his bit of wood or field, lying idle on the outer borders of the town. In fact, it is probable that it was the need of the younger men which forced the towns to divide some of the last of the common land. The new owner, finding it impracticable to make the daily journeys from the village, decided to build a homestead on his own property. In this way began a transition of supreme importance for the future of East Jersey rural life—the transition from the agricultural village to the farm. For decades the two systems existed side by side, but as time went on the percentage of yeomen living in the villages grew less and less, the number of farms doubled many times over. The village remained, of course, but it became no longer an agricultural center but a community of traders and artisans.

The term *farm* appears in the records with increasing frequency before the end of the ninth decade of the century. So early as February, 1684, we find Jonathan Dennis of Woodbridge, conveying thirty acres to John Codington, "adjoining the grantor's *farm*."[77] Two years later, when the Town of Woodbridge was making one of its divisions of upland, the order of the survey spoke of the "farms already laid out,"[78] indicating that houses and barns had already been built upon some of the outlying lots. When the yeoman owned one or more widely separated tracts, it was customary for him to build on the largest, which he then called the home farm. Thus Joshua Clarke, of Elizabeth Town, at his death in 1714 disposed of various properties, among them the "home farm" on Thomsson's Creek.[79] In time the farmers consolidated their holdings by sales of their more distant land and the purchase of adjoining properties.

The effects of this change upon the life of the farmer were profound. It became difficult for him to attend services in the distant meeting-house, his children suffered for want of a good school, in time of illness he had to go many miles before he could find a doctor; for his shoes, cooking utensils, nails, farm

[77]*New Jersey Archives,* Series I, Vol. XXI, p. 169.
[78]Jos. W. Dally, *Woodbridge and Vicinity,* p. 108.
[79]*New Jersey Archives,* Ser. I, Vol. XXIII, p. 95.

implements, salt, he had to make the trip to the village, he and his family were cut off from the intimate social contact so interesting in the old type of town. In time there developed in various localities local centers or hamlets, with the church, mill, school and perhaps a shop or two. In 1701 Rahway began to emerge as a civic center, when the Woodbridge town meeting granted the people there the privilege of building a pound, and set aside a small lot for a school building.[80] When the "westfields" of Elizabeth Town were first laid out and farmhouses built, it is stated that many of the settlers often trudged seven or eight miles through the woods to be in their regular seats in the meeting-house on Sunday. But this was strenuous indeed in the winter months, and for aged and feeble it was impossible, so about 1727, the people divorced themselves from the mother congregation by constructing a rude meeting-house of their own.[81] In this way began the village of Westfield. In a similar way village centers grew up at New Providence, Springfield, Connecticut Farms and elsewhere.[82]

The New England town system in New Jersey has undergone many changes, made necessary by the growth of population, the creation of State and national governments and the development of industry. The townships, as the towns are now called, persist throughout the State, side by side with the municipalities and counties. In many cases, however, the township has been absorbed entirely or in part by the creation of cities. New Brunswick had been a town but six years, from 1724 to 1730, when it became a municpality. Newark clung to its original form of government until it was made a city in 1836.[83] Elizabeth was incorporated in 1740 as a "free borough and town," but the change was in name more than in fact, the Town Meeting continuing as before to levy the taxes, control town lands, and appoint the Town Committee until 1855 when the place became a city.[84]

[80]Jos. W. Dally, *Woodbridge and Vicinity,* pp. 144, 180.
[81]W. W. Clayton, *History of Union and Middlesex,* p. 336.
[82]Union County Hist. Soc., *Proceedings,* Vol. II, p. 148.
[83]Austin Scott, "Early Cities of New Jersey," N. J. Hist. Soc., *Proceedings,* 2d Ser., Vol. IX (1887), p. 165.
[84]W. Woodford Clayton, *History of Union and Middlesex Counties* (1882), p. 184.

The expansion of New England to East Jersey did not stop with the founding of towns on the Passaic, Achter Kil, the Raritan, and Shrewsbury River. From these early centers settlers went out to the north and west until Puritan New Jersey embraced all southern and central Essex, three-fourths of Morris, almost all of Union, and all northern Middlesex. The spear-head of New England expansion penetrated some thirty-five miles through northern New Jersey toward the west, but there it came to a stop, the eventual outlet from Connecticut and Massachusetts being through southern New York, and the Mohawk and Genesee valleys to the Great Lakes.

The failure to break through to the Delaware with a chain of settlements is explained in large part by the geography of northern New Jersey. The New Englanders, although they made settlements at the mouths of the two chief rivers of the region, the Passaic and the Raritan, were largely elbowed out of the upper reaches of both by the Dutch and Flemings. They had to advance, therefore, not up fertile river valleys, with the means of transportation at hand, but across high hills running northeast and southwest. This so slowed up their progress that before they could cross the Musconetcong mountains, they were met by other groups from the Delaware Valley. It is true that many New Englanders established themselves in Bucks County, Pennsylvania, but they too found themselves hemmed in by successive waves of German migration.

Even within the confines of Puritan New Jersey the population was not exclusively New England. Among the first settlers at New Providence were some from England, a few from Wales, a few from Scotland, and some from Ireland.[85] The stern repression of the Covenanters in Scotland at the time of the second Stuart despotism, drove a number of deeply religious men to Plainfield, Westfield, Scotch Plains, and elsewhere in East Jersey.[86] The presence among the early settlers of Robert Vauquellin, Peter Noe,[87] Rene Peeat, Peter de la Noy, Peter de Signey, and others bearing French names, indicates the presence of a sprin-

[85] W. W. Clayton, *History of Union and Middlesex*, p. 345.

[86] N. J. Hist. Soc., *Proceedings*, 2d Ser., Vol. V, p. 66.

[87] Neau.

kling of Huguenots. At Elizabeth Town seven of the eighty freeholders listed in 1673 were Dutch.[88] Yet New England blood, culture, institutions, religion were indelibly impressed on the region. "Tho' some of these settlements were made, with some intermixtures, above a hundred and twenty years ago," wrote John Rutherfurd in 1786, "they still retain the manners, language and worship of their predecessors."[89]

The New England spirit was maintained in part by continued migrations from Massachusetts, Connecticut and Long Island. The search for fertile land was even more intense in the eighteenth century than it had been in the seventeenth, and when new areas were opened in Morris County, the stream of settlers from New England set in afresh. "Up to the period of the Revolution the population was of New England origin," says Joseph F. Tuttle, the Morris County historian, "coming from Newark, Long Island, or directly from the New England States."[90] How large was the proportion of Yankee immigrants is shown by the list of jurors drawn in Morris County in 1742 in one of the suits in the celebrated Elizabeth Town Bill of Chancery case. Caleb and Zachariah Fairchild were "of Connecticut colony"; Abraham and Benjamin Hathway were of "the Massachusetts colony"; David Trowbridge was listed as from New England; Samuel Swesey was from the east end of Long Island; Joseph and Benjamin Coe were of Jamaica, Long Island; Peter Beach and Benjamin Winchell were born in Connecticut but raised in Morris County; Job Allen and Joseph Hayward were born in New England and came as children to New Jersey; John Ball, Caleb Ball and Nathaniel Dalglish were from Newark; Nathaniel Drake was born in Piscataqua and raised in Morris; Jonathan Osborn was born in Essex; John Lindsley, Jr., had lived "long since in Newark," Robert Goble and Thomas Guerin came from South Carolina; Robert Young was a native of Ireland; Jacob Ford and Joseph Kitchel had been reared in Morris and were of New England ancestry.[91]

[88] E. F. Hatfield, *History of Elizabeth*, p. 159.

[89] N. J. Hist. Soc., *Proceedings*, 2d Ser., Vol. I, p. 88.

[90] Joseph F. Tuttle, "Washington in Morris County," in *Centennial Collections of Morris County*, p. 93.

[91] New York Historical Soc. Manuscript—Elizabeth Town Bill and Chancery Case.

Of the New England and Long Island immigrants to Morris County in the colonial period we find that the Cobbs, Paddlefords, Miricks, Leonards and Deans came from Taunton, Mass.; the Farrands from Connecticut by way of Newark; the Richards, Allens, Hubbles, Stiles, and Canfields directly from Connecticut; the Osborns came from Connecticut to Easthampton, thence to Elizabeth Town, thence to Morris; the Greens came from Malden, Mass.; the Howells from Southampton, Long Island; the Davenports from Kingston; and one branch each of the Motts and Budds from Westchester County, N. Y.[92] These facts seem to warrant the statement in a report from the government of New Jersey to the Board of Trade in 1721 that "the inhabitants daily increase in great numbers from New England."[93]

The New England influence was constantly renewed also through the stream of Calvinist ministers who answered the call of New Jersey towns. For eighty years after the founding of Elizabeth and Newark, the Puritan congregations of East Jersey could look only to the graduates of Harvard and Yale for their spiritual leaders. Woodbridge was but following the usual custom when, in 1693, it voted to send Ephraim Andrews to New England as a messenger for the town to search for a minister, providing him "with money sufficient for his journey and a horse to ride on."[94] It was Theophilus Pierson, "sent to New England to endeavor to procure a minister," who brought Reverend Nathaniel Bowers to Newark.[95]

Among the New England preachers who responded to the East Jersey call were Reverend Samuel Shepard, at Woodbridge; John Prudden, and Jabez Wakeman, both Harvard graduates and Joseph Webb, of the Yale class of 1715, at Newark; Jonathan Dickinson, James Peck, Seth Fletcher and Elihu Spencer at Elizabeth Town; Nathaniel Hubbell of Yale, 1723, and Jacob Green,[96] Harvard, 1744, at Whippany, the first permanent settlement in

[92]For these facts, I am indebted to that indefatigable student of Morris County history, Philip H. Waddell Smith.

[93]*N. J. Archives,* Series I, Vol. V, p. 22.

[94]Jos. W. Dally, *Woodbridge and Vicinity,* p. 86.

[95]Jonathan F. Stearns, *Historical Discourses,* p. 116. New England "had been from the beginning the great clerical hive."

[96]Green was chairman of the committee which framed the constitution of the state in 1776.

Morris County. These men became the spiritual, moral and educational leaders in their communities, and their influence in strengthening the original New England tradition can hardly be exaggerated. It was only with the founding of Princeton in 1746 that the New England regions of New Jersey began to break away from the intellectual and religious dominance of the parent section. Even then the close "intercourse of minds" continued, and it is significant that the early Princeton presidents Jonathan Dickinson, Aaron Burr and Jonathan Edwards were all New Englanders.

On the other hand, there seems to have been comparatively little contact with the "mother colonies" through the medium of trade. With Acter Kil, New York Bay, East River and Long Island Sound providing a short inland waterway from Perth Amboy to the Connecticut ports, with the East Jersey farms and woods supplying wheat, flour, and timber in considerable quantities, one would expect to find the Yankee merchantmen constant visitors in Newark Bay and Raritan Bay. There is some evidence that in the seventeenth century they did participate in the carrying trade between East Jersey and the West Indies, but they were soon elbowed out of it. The proximity of New York, with its splendid facilities for commerce, tended from the first to draw into the North and East rivers the lion's share of the surplus products of the region. So early as 1708 Lord Cornbury stated that East Jersey had no trade save with the "neighboring province of New York." The New Jersey legislature sought to build Perth Amboy into a great port, so as to break the hold of New York, but without success. The farmer of Woodbridge or Newark found it advantageous to load his flour, or bread, or beef, or staves on a little shallop, sail the ten or fifteen miles to New York, and there dispose of them to one or other of the great exporters. With his vessel unloaded, and his pockets jingling, he could step into a near-by store to purchase whatever was needed for his farm—nails, hinges, hoes, a flail, a chair, perhaps a pot or two and a few pewter spoons. With good luck he could be back at home with the setting of the sun. In 1741 Governor Lewis Morris wrote: "The province of New Jersey sends but few vessels abroad, what they raise is chiefly sent, from the Eastern division to New York, from the Western to Philadelphia, from which places they are for the most part supplied with what European commodities they want."[97] The trade from Perth Amboy to New England gradually declined until at the end of the colonial period not one vessel in five years cleared for Boston, New Haven or New London. About ten times a year a small Rhode Island vessel would put in with rum, sugar, molasses and manufactured goods and take off hogshead hoops and staves, but the amounts were insignificant.[98]

Thus was East Jersey almost completely isolated commercially from Connecticut, Long Island and Massachusetts. The intercourse between Virginia and England through the tobacco trade, had no counterpart in the relations of East Jersey with the parent colony. The appearance of a Rhode Island sloop at Perth Amboy every month or so could have but little influence in strengthening the cultural domination of New England in the province. Even though the masters and sailors may have come ashore to mingle with the people, bringing the latest gossip of Newport, their contacts must have been limited to the mercantile group of this one village. Commercially Newark, Elizabeth, Woodbridge and even Perth Amboy were as completely cut off from their "mother colonies" as though they had been located in the wilds of Ohio, rather than upon navigable waters within a day's sail.

The transit of New England culture to East Jersey was affected, then, by various factors, some tending to strengthen, some to weaken the influence of the mother provinces. The settling of large areas with New England stock, and the contact with Connecticut, Massachusetts and Long Island through continued migrations, especially of influential clergymen, tended to make Essex, Union and Morris counties replicas of the original Puritan colonies. On the other hand, the renewed struggle with the wilderness; immigrations of Scotch, English and Scotch-Irish; the contact with the Dutch on the Passaic and the Raritan; the

[97] *Letters of Governor Lewis Morris*, p. 135.

[98] *Custom House Series*, 16, Vol. 8, Library of Congress Photostats; *N. J. Archives*, Ser. X, p. 443.

presence of Quakers and Baptists, and the lack of extensive commercial intercourse with New England, all made for the development of a distinct East Jersey culture. Visitors to Newark or Elizabeth in the middle of the eighteenth century, while recognizing at once the kinship of these places with New England, testify to the differences which had developed—in town government, in religion, in blood, in architecture, in customs.

To understand the region between the Passaic and the Raritan one must realize that it was settled in large part by groups of habitual pioneers. Some of them had migrated from England to Massachusetts, whence after a few years they had moved to Connecticut or New Haven; while those colonies were still struggling with the wilderness they had migrated to Long Island, and from there in time they had come to East Jersey. Some of the original Elizabeth Town settlers remembered England but dimly, some had been born after their parents had left the Old World; few indeed knew Massachusetts save as a raw pioneer region with its government, its architecture, even its religion in the period of formation; they could not establish New Haven culture in their new homes for they had deserted that colony, many of them, before its culture had taken form; those who came from the eastern end of Long Island left when the infant towns of that region were struggling with the surrounding Indians and forests.

In nothing is this more clearly shown than in the architecture of East Jersey. One may wander through the region from Chester township in Morris County to Newark Bay and from Bloomfield to the Raritan, and he will find few, if any, examples of seventeenth-century New England houses. He will look in vain for the pronounced overhang and dewdrop of Massachusetts, or the shallow overhang and the lean-to of Connecticut. It is true that time, the torch of the British invaders, and the advance of modern industry have left little of the earliest East Jersey architecture, but enough has come down in pictorial form and in the descriptions of contemporaneous writers to reveal its chief characteristics. There are still many homes standing which bear unmistakably the imprint of New England influence, but they are the product of eighteenth-century migrations, rather than of the continuance of the New England tradition brought by the first settlers.

The early architecture of Essex and Union counties was essentially pioneer architecture showing New England, Long Island and Flemish influences. The very first structures were, of course, mere temporary shacks or "wigwams" as the colonists called them. "I put up a wigwam in twenty-four hours," wrote Thomas Gordon in 1685, "which served us till we put up a better house."[99] He then gives a brief description of the "better house," which seems to have been typical of the region in its early days. It is "twenty-four foot long and fifteen foot wide, containing a hall and kitchen both in one, and a chamber and a study, which we put up pretty well with pallisadoes on the sides and shingles on the roof."[100] What Gordon meant by "pallisadoes" is explained in a letter from Governor Lowrie. "The walls are of cloven timber," he says, "about eight or ten inches broad, like planks set one end to the ground, and the other nailed to the raising."[101] Another writer says that "most of the country houses are built of wood, only trees split and set up on end on the ground."[102] Although apparently none of these pallisaded houses have survived, a painting of the Camp homestead, Newark, shows that the barn was of this type of construction.[103] There is no reason to believe that any of the seventeenth-century houses of this region were made of logs, notched at the ends and laid horizontally. Dankers and Sluyter, who visited the colony in 1679 and 1680, give a full description of the Swedish log houses on the lower Delaware, but mention no similar construction in East Jersey.[104]

When the colonists became more firmly established, when the woods were cleared, meadows fenced, and meeting houses erected, the pallisaded house gave way to the frame house, covered with clap-boards or shingles. If we may rely on Dankers and Sluyter who spent a most uncomfortable night in one of these frame

[99]Geo. Scot, *The Model of the Government of the Province of East New Jersey* (Edinburgh, 1685), reprinted in Whitehead's *East Jersey under the Proprietary Governments* (1846), p. 254. [100]*Ibid.*, p. 420. [101]*Ibid.* [102]*Ibid.*, p. 424.

[103]Wm. P. Tuttle, *Bottle Hill and Madison*, p. 99.

[104]Jaspar Dankers and Peter Sluyter, *Journal*, etc. (Brooklyn, 1867), p. 175.

cottages, they must have been crude indeed. "Most of the English, and many others, have their houses made of nothing but clapboards, as they call them, in this manner: they first make a wooden frame, the same as they do in Westphalia, and at Altona, but not so strong; they then split the boards of clapwood, so that they are like cooper's pipe staves, except they are not bent. These are made very thin, with a large knife, so that the thickest end is about a little finger thick, and the other is made sharp like the edge of a knife. They are about five or six feet long, and are nailed on the outside of the frame, with the ends lapped over each other. They are not usually laid so close together as to prevent you from sticking a finger between them, in consequence either of their not being well jointed, or the boards being crooked. When it is cold and windy the best people plaster them with clay."[105]

It was the general custom to build of wood, for around every settler was a wealth of oak, cedar, and chestnut. Usually the heavier timbers were hewn out with the axe, perhaps from heart oak, for even where saw-mills were within reach, the blades of that day could not be trusted to cut the heavier beams.[106] Although the people of East Jersey, like those of New England, seem to have built no half-timber houses, the early frames were doubtless often identical with the English half-timber frames. A drawing of the Tennent parsonage, made when the building was in a state of great disrepair, with many of the beams exposed, reveals a framework of heavy hewn uprights and girts with lighter studs and diagonal props. Shorn of its coating of shingles and filled in with wattle, daubed with a mixture of clay, straw and lime, it would have fitted quite naturally into the landscape of Essex or Cambridgeshire.[107] But the New Jersey settlers found clapboard shingles to be the cheapest and most convenient cover-

[105] *Ibid.*, p. 173.

[106] "I have sent you a piece of timber, scored and forehewed, unfit to join to any piece of handsome work," wrote Leon Gardiner to Robert Chapman in 1660, "but seeing I have done the hardest work, you must get somebody to chip it and to smooth it, lest its splinters should prick some men's hands." Benj. F. Thompson, *Hist. of Long Island* (N. Y., 1843), Vol. II, p. 306.

[107] Frank R. Symmes, *History of the Old Tennent Church* [Cranbury, N. J., 1904], p. 147; Basil Oliver, *The Cottages of England* (N. Y., 1929), p. 31.

ing for their outer walls. Peter Kalm says the houses at Woodbridge "had a covering of shingles on the outside . . . round at one end, and all of a length in each row."[108] Occasionally the well-to-do built of stone, for there were quarries of excellent brown sandstone in Belleville, Newark, the Oranges and elsewhere, and the Flemish settlers on the Passaic and Hackensack had already set the example. The severe winters and hot summers in time forced those who could afford it to insulate their outer walls by filling in the framework with brick or clay before adding the final coat of shingles. Washington's Headquarters at Rocky Hill and other houses still standing were so treated. The famous old Meeker house, at Newark, had eighteen-inch walls of brick laid on stone foundations and covered over with boards to which shingles were attached[109] (Plate 10). The roofs were usually covered with wooden shingles, but here too an occasional settler imitated his Dutch neighbor by substituting pantiles,[110] or perhaps went back to English precedent by using thatch.[111]

The crudeness of the seventeenth-century houses was the inevitable consequence of pioneer life. The New Jersey farmer or artisan could not, like his descendants of today, contract with a builder for his house, with the certainty of moving in within a few months. In many cases he was his own contractor, bargaining for bricks or shingles or nails wherever he could find them, paying the carpenter or mason by the day or week, often doing the major part of the construction himself. We gain a vivid idea of these difficulties from the story of the erection of the Quaker meeting house at Woodbridge. The first impetus came in 1706 when William Sutton donated a year-old steer to the project, but actual construction got under way only three years later when a carpenter agreed to make the "outside" for £37.

Since the congregation had to supply the materials, William Robinson was "appointed to draw the meeting-house timber to the place," and Nathaniel FitzRandolph to get "shingling nails" and "clap-board nails." To Robinson fell the further task of

[108]Peter Kalm, *Travels into North America* (2d Edit., London, 1772), Vol. I, p. 181.
[109]See photograph in possession of N. J. Hist. Soc., Newark.
[110]Wm. A. Whitehead, *Model of the Government of East New Jersey*, p. 424.
[111]*Our Home* (Mag.), Vol. I, p. 289.

getting boards for the floor, and of speaking to the "brick maker for bricks for the chimney." He reported that the brick-maker "as soon as he has done burning a kiln at Elizabeth Town will burn some here," so two of the brothers were appointed to "get wood for the kiln" and "to agree with John Pike for his oyster shells" for lime for the mortar. In February, 1711, the meeting ordered to be paid, "one week's diet to the bricklayers, and 4^s, 3^d to John Pike for shells, and 5^s due to Moses Rolph for two days' work of his negro tending the mason, and 9^d for watching the kiln, and 13^d for a bottle of rum and 2^s for his horse and boy to draw water for the bricklayer." In May, 1712, oyster shells were ordered for lime "to plaster the meeting house," and in February, 1713, five years after construction had begun, the structure was so far advanced that the congregation could occupy it.[112]

In view of the difficulties in building it was to be expected that the homes of the people of East Jersey, even those of the well-to-do, should be in the main small, unpretentious buildings devoid of ornament or embellishment. For this there was precedent enough in both New Haven and Long Island. Although many of the well-to-do had erected there rather pretentious two-story houses, after the manner of the famous Henry Whitfield house, Guilford, the Baldwin house, Branford,[113] and the Payne house, Easthampton,[114] the humbler citizen had contented himself with a little cottage. The typical small house was one story high with loft, the roof often devoid of dormers, the sides covered with weather-boarding or shingles, the chimney centrally placed, the roof lines rather low, the front door flanked on either side by two windows. One finds surviving examples at Groton Center, Essex, and elsewhere in Connecticut and at Orient, Laurel, and East Marion, Long Island.[115]

The main feature of these cottages is the great central chimney, with its lone stack and its numerous fireplaces, around which are grouped all the rooms. Upon stepping through the front door

[112] J. W. Dally, *Woodbridge and Vicinity*, pp. 66–69.

[113] Norman M. Isham, *Early Connecticut Houses* (Providence, 1900), pp. 112, 125; *The White Pine Series*, Vol. V., Nos. 1, 2.

[114] *The White Pine Series*, Vol. V, No. 2.

[115] *The White Pine Series*, Vol. VI, Nos. 1, 6.

one finds himself in a tiny entry, with steep ladder-like stairs facing him, and with doors to right and left leading to two front chambers. In the rear is the living-room, flanked on either side by small bed-rooms, while above is the loft.

The East Jersey cottage, although retaining some of the features of the small New England house, shows a strong Flemish influence. The typical house was perhaps forty-five feet by eighteen, one story high with loft, with few or no dormers, the windows set with tiny panes, the chimneys usually, though not always, at either end and invariably placed in, not on the outside of the wall, the roof often sloping down behind to cover a narrow annex on the rear. Among the most interesting of the old homes in the Newark region was the Meeker house, in Potpie Lane, near Dividen Hill (Plate 10). This long, low structure is said to have been built prior to 1677 or even to date back to the first years of the Newark settlement. Stripped of the shingles which covered the brick walls, its similarity to the Abraham Hasbrouck house, New Paltz, would have been striking. In its original form it was probably typical of the early houses of East Jersey.[116] Reverend Joseph W. Dally, writing in 1873, describes one of the oldest houses then standing in Woodbridge, which must have resembled the Meeker house closely. "It is a one-story building and shingled on the outside, where from old age the shingles have not rotted from the nails and fallen off. The door is double after the ancient style, the upper part swinging open while the lower remains shut. There are two rooms below . . . and an attic above reached by a flight of stairs. The ceiling is low, and the heavy timbers overhead make it seem still more so."

The Camp home, which stood on the corner of Broad Street and Clinton Avenue, Newark, although in some respects quite different (Plate 11), also shows an interesting blending of the Cape Cod cottage and the Bergen County Flemish farmhouse. The broad, low-lying roof, originally no doubt without dormers, the central door flanked by two windows on each side, and the two-room depth suggest New England; while the end chimneys, the use of stone, the door stoop with its side benches are unmistakably

[116]See photograph in possession of New Jersey Hist. Soc.

Flemish.[117] The Flemish influence was strongest in northern Essex and Morris and on the north bank of the Raritan, where New Englanders and Flemings lived side by side, had close business relations and even intermarried. Here one still has difficulty in classifying this house as definitely New England in origin and that house Flemish, the chief, if not only, clue being the propensity of the Connecticut settlers to sheath all or a part of the stone walls with weather-boarding.

In contrast to the New England arrangement of rooms around a central chimney, the East Jersey houses were usually but one room deep, having a living-room on one side of a narrow entrance hall, and a bedroom on the other. Additions were made not in the form of an L, as in New England, but in true Flemish style, to the right or left of the main building, sometimes as extensions of the original lines, sometimes as small wings, sometimes as larger and more pretentious structures.

Some of the later settlements, made in part by fresh migrations from Connecticut, furnish the purest examples of New England architecture. Of these the most interesting is the Wick house, at Morristown, recently restored by the National Park Service (Plate 12). The broad sweep of the roof, the absence of dormers, the central chimney, the arrangement of rooms, the ladder-like stairs, the shingled front walls all betray its origin. Yet even in this cottage, which would feel quite at home amid the sand hills of Barnstable or Harwich, the interior carpenter's work, as evidenced by the arrangement and notching of the beams, is Dutch in character.

In Elizabeth Town, Woodbridge and Middletown, the influence of Long Island and Staten Island architecture is obvious. The parsonage of St. John's church, Elizabeth Town, a long, low structure, with end chimneys and water-shed dormers, must have been very similar to the Nicholas Brittin house, New Dorp. In Marlprit Hall, at Middletown, built in 1684, the rear lean-to suggests the influence of Easthampton, the flaring front eaves must have been a conscious imitation of the Dutch houses of New Utrecht or Jamaica.

[117]Wm. P. Tuttle, *Bottle Hill and Madison*, p. 99.

PLATE 10. MEEKER HOUSE, NEWARK

PLATE 11. CAMP HOUSE, NEWARK

PLATE 12. WICK HOUSE, MORRISTOWN

PLATE 13. *Top Left:* Washington's headquarters, Morristown. *Top Right:* Springfield Church. *Lower Left:* New England type house near North Plainfield. *Lower Right:* Cannon Ball Inn, Springfield

The New England "salt-box" house, two stories high in front and one story behind, with the front slope of the roof comparatively short, and the back slope falling in a broad windowless expanse for twenty-five or even thirty-five feet, was rare in East Jersey. Although the Moulthrop house, New Haven, built prior to 1700, the Starr house and the Philo Bishop house, Guilford, both built in 1665; and the Baldwin house, Branford, built probably about 1645, were undoubtedly known to some of the emigrants to East Jersey,[118] they found them too pretentious for their pioneer towns, or perhaps thought them unsuited to the New Jersey climate. Yet they did erect a "salt-box" here and there, as the old parsonage at Bottle Hill, shown in a sketch in Tuttle's manuscript history[119] and other examples testify.[120]

In the first half of the eighteenth century, when New England had developed a fairly uniform type of farmhouse, moulded along Georgian lines, the fresh waves of migration brought it but slightly altered to New Jersey. Whereas one has difficulty in finding a close analogy between the early East Jersey and early Connecticut houses, we recognize at a glance the Yankee origin of pre-Revolutionary houses of Morristown or Union or Plainfield. In each case we have the two-story frame house, the roof shingled, the walls usually weather-boarded but sometimes shingled, the central door flanked on each side by two evenly spaced windows.

Typical of the New England Georgian is the Cannon Ball Inn, at Springfield (Plate 13). As though the builder were reluctant to give up early East Jersey traditions, the front of this old house is shingled; yet above, in strange contrast, the elaborate cornice proclaims the influence of the new style. If we ignore the front porch, which is undoubtedly a late addition, the house would fit perfectly into one of the charming elm-lined streets of any old Connecticut village. Clearly New England and Georgian in origin, also, are the original wing of the Washington Head-

[118] John Mead Howells, *Lost Examples of Colonial Architecture* (N. Y., 1931), plate 183; *The White Pine Series,* Vol. V, pp. 4, 5, 9.

[119] Reproduced in W. P. Tuttle's *Bottle Hill and Madison,* p. 57.

[120] An excellent example of a "salt-box" is shown in John Whitehead's *The Passaic Valley,* p. 242.

quarters at Morristown (Plate 13); the Clinton Headquarters, Freehold; the Wallace house, Somerville, and many others.

In New England the advent of the Georgian gradually brought about a change in the interior arrangement, the central hallway running through the house, with rooms on either side, necessitating the substitution for the one central chimney of end chimneys or chimneys between front and rear rooms.[121] In East Jersey, where the central chimney from the first was rare, the transition to the new arrangement was easy.

As though to show that they were not entirely dependent upon other colonies for their architectural ideas, the New Jersey builders developed an interesting feature of their own,[122] by leaving the lower portion of their chimneys bare while covering the upper portion as far as the roof with the regular shingling or weather-boarding of the gable end (Plate 13). Thus one gains the impression of an oblong square of stone or brick in an expanse of wooden wall. The reason for this treatment is not apparent, unless to economize in shingles or weather-boarding, or to lessen the danger of fire. It cuts across various architectural strata, in both northern and southern New Jersey, in such widely distant places as Morristown, Princeton, Greenwich, Plainfield, Raritan.

Ecclesiastical architecture in the parts of East Jersey settled by New Englanders, adhered more closely to the Connecticut and Massachusetts models than domestic architecture. Perhaps the Puritans, although willing to accept new ideas from their neighbors in the construction of their homes, would permit no liberties with the established ideal of a house of worship. Since the New England meeting-houses were severely plain, in keeping with the spirit of Calvinism, they found little difficulty in imitating them, as soon as the first pioneer hardships had been conquered.

We have a fair idea of what the first meeting-house at Newark was like, since the town records have come down to us. It was a very crude structure, in keeping with the little frontier village,

[121]Note the Sheldon Woodbridge house, Hartford, and the Webb house, Wethersfield. (Isham and Brown, *Early Connecticut Houses,* pp. 76–86.)

[122]This feature is not unknown in New England, but it became so universal in New Jersey as to become a distinguishing characteristic of the architecture of that colony.

"twenty-six feet wide and with a lean-to to it, and thirty-six feet long, and thirteen feet between joists," the roof rising, not on all four sides as was so common in New England, but on two sides to a ridge.[123] The flooring was "of good chestnut or oak, of two inches and a half plank" laid down on "seven good sleepers," the walls "lathed and filled up with thin stone and mortar below the girts," the roof shingled, and the interior in 1704, fitted with a gallery.[124]

The second building, erected probably in 1715 or 1716, seems to have been a typical New England square meeting house, after the style of the "Old Ship," at Hingham, and the "Old Tunnel," at Lynn. Constructed of stone, forty-four feet square, with the roof receding on four sides to a platform on which rested the cupola or belfry, Reverend Joseph Webb, Reverend Aaron Burr and its other New England preachers must have felt perfectly at home in it.[125] The interior arrangement also was according to tradition, for the pulpit, which was placed against the west wall opposite the door, was flanked by two square pews, one for the minister's family and the other for the leading family of the congregation, while the rest of the house was seated with long benches. The bell rope descended from the cupola to the middle of the central aisle. It is said "pride and prejudice" were not unknown even in this old sanctuary, for the ladies of the "leading family" were wont to "pass up the aisle with rustling silks and tossings of head, to take the undisputed place of preferment."[126] Doctor Mac Whorter tells us that "it was an exceedingly great exertion for the people to build" this meeting house, which was "the most elegant edifice for public worship at that time in the colony."[127] When Whitefield came to Newark for his second visit, the church could not hold the crowd, so that a window back of the pulpit was

[123] *Records of the Town of Newark* (Newark, 1864), p. 12.

[124] *Ibid.*

[125] The Map of the Town of New-Ark, published in 1806, shown in W. H. Shaw's *History of Essex and Hudson,* Vol. I, p. 448, shows the second meeting house. Since there is an obvious attempt to depict the chief buildings as they were, we may assume that the map gives us a crude but fairly accurate idea of what the building was like.

[126] Jonathan Stearns, *Historical Discourses* (Newark, 1853), p. 247 note.

[127] Alexander MacWhorter, *A Century Sermon* (Newark, 1807), p. 14.

taken out through which he preached to the people assembled in the burying ground.[128]

Very little is known about the early colonial meeting houses of Elizabeth Town. The first crude wooden structure built no doubt soon after the founding of the town, gave place to a larger building in 1724. The latter was originally fifty-eight feet by forty-two with "the audience room" twenty-four feet in height.[129] In 1766 an addition of sixteen feet made the length seventy-four feet. It has been described as a small, frame, shingle-covered building, with a steeple which carried the town clock. We may surmise, then, that it did not follow the early square type, but more nearly resembled the Long Lane Meeting House, Boston, or the old Cambridge Meeting House. It went up in flames on the night of January 25, 1780, when a party of British and Tories, who had crossed over on the ice from Staten Island, applied the torch to it.[130]

In the eighteenth century, New England church architecture fell in part under the influence of Sir Christopher Wren. The Gothic was still anathema to the Congregationalists and Presbyterians, since they associated it with Catholicism, but the new school of English architecture offered them an escape from the homely simplicity of early Puritan meeting houses. They might add a steeple and spire, perhaps even a Georgian cornice or a pedimented door and a rounded window, without doing too much violence to the spirit of Cotton and Bradford, and though they were still suspicious of ornateness, their churches now began to take on a gracefulness and charm hitherto lacking. Old North and Old South, in Boston, seem to have led the way, providing admirable examples for the New England builders to follow.

Whether the New Jersey congregations consciously imitated the eighteenth-century New England church or whether they drew their inspiration directly from English architects or English books of designs is a matter of conjecture. But the typical East Jersey Presbyterian church of the later colonial period bears a

[128] *Ibid.*

[129] Everard Kempshall, *Caldwell and the Revolution* (Eliz., 1880), p. 9.

[130] Nicholas Murray, *Notes on Elizabeth Town*, p. 105.

striking resemblance to those of Massachusetts and Connecticut. In fact, a comparison of the Newark, Elizabeth and Morristown churches, all built soon after the Revolution, with Old North and Old South, leads one to suspect that the former were consciously patterned after the latter.

Reverend Alexander MacWhorter described the Newark church of 1791 as "one hundred feet in length, including the steeple, which projects eight feet. The steeple two hundred and four feet high, two tiers of windows, five in a tier on each side, an elegant large Venetian window in the rear behind the pulpit, and the whole finished in the inside in the most handsome manner in the Doric order."[131] The building, which is now dwarfed by the skyscrapers of Broad Street, is admirable in its proportions and details. Save for the fact that it is built of brown stone set off with quoins, and that the Palladian window smacks more of Philadelphia than of Connecticut or Massachusetts, it would seem to be clearly of New England origin. The square tower, which is partly sunk in the front gable end, is entered through an arched doorway, above which is an arched window under a pediment which unites with a cornice across the gable end. Still higher is a round window, above which is the clock, and over it the square section gives way to two wooden octagonal sections, surmounted by a slender spire. The tower is flanked by two oval windows in the gable end, while originally urns graced the four corners of the roof.[132] The Morristown church, built in 1791, the charming Elizabeth church, and the Bloomfield church, all follow essentially the same design.[133]

In the simpler New Jersey churches the builders, instead of rearing a tower from the ground projecting from or partly sunk in the front end of the church, often superimposed it on the front end of the roof straddling the ridge. Although this deprived the building of the grace that is so noticeable with the Newark

[131] J. F. Stearns, *Historical Discourses* (Newark, 1853), p. 249.

[132] J. Urquhart, *A History of the City of Newark*, Vol. I, p. 398; *Historic Newark* (Newark, 1916), p. 11; J. F. Stearns, *Historical Discourses*, pp. 248, 249.

[133] It is noteworthy that old St. Paul's, New York City, is similar in design to these New Jersey churches. It is distinguished from them, however, by its greater ornateness—the beautiful Wren tower, the roof, balustrade, etc.

and Elizabeth churches, it preserved much of the simple charm of the earlier meeting houses. The Presbyterian church at Springfield (Plate 13), with its tiers of windows each fitted with thirty little panes, its three simple front doors, its shingled sides, its cornice which is extended across the front wall, the gable end pierced by one large arched window surmounted by one rounded window and flanked by two oval windows, the octagonal cupola on a square base, perched on the ridge like a sentry box, is one of the most charming church buildings in the state.[134]

The settlement of parts of East Jersey by New Englanders is of especial interest in colonial history as it marked the first important movement of population from one section to another. It was antedated by the migrations from Massachusetts to Rhode Island and Connecticut and from New Haven to Long Island, but this was rather the filling out of New England than the transplanting of New England culture in a new section. Despite clearly marked differences the people of Connecticut, Rhode Island and eastern Long Island were no less New Englanders than the people of Massachusetts, but the descendants of the Puritan founders of Newark or Elizabeth or Morristown, while clearly showing their New England origin, and clinging to many Puritan traditions, by the advent of the Revolution had become a part of the civilization of the Middle Colonies.

Thus early was it demonstrated that the transit of civilization from one section of the country to another was subject to the same laws as the transit from Europe to America. There was the same determined effort to maintain the old culture amid new surroundings; the same moulding influence of climate, soil, isolation, geographic configuration; the same reshaping of culture by contact with the original source of migration; the same yielding to the power of the melting-pot. When the Revolution brought into close contact men from widely separated colonies, in Congress or around the camp fire, the East Jerseyman, while less distinctive perhaps than the Charlestonian, the Virginia planter, or the Boston merchant was nonetheless an East Jerseyman.

[134]The effect of the cupola is decidedly pleasing and does not mar the lines of the building, as does the cupola of the church at Aquia, Va.

The Puritan, when he moved into the New Jersey forests, vowed to maintain there the religious and political tenets which he considered essential to his salvation; he set up as a matter of course the New England town system with its distinctive method of land distribution, its community life, its town meeting; he expected to continue in his new home his vocation in the old, whether farming, shipbuilding, fishing, trading, shoemaking, carpentry, tanning. But he found himself in the grip of forces he could not resist, the forces of new environment. He must encounter the hardships of the frontier; he found a different and more fertile soil; his meadows were larger and easier to purchase; for his houses and churches different building materials were at hand; he discovered that there were no rich fishing banks near by; his commercial ambitions were stifled by the competition of New York and New England; he had to rub elbows with Dutch, Scotch, Germans, Scotch-Irish; he learned toleration by contact not only with Dutch Reformed, Quakers, and Lutherans, but with Baptists, Mennonites, and Roman Catholics. So in time the church began to separate from the town, Congregationalism gave way to Presbyterianism and the agricultural village to the farm, Anglican church buildings appeared in the old Puritan centers, houses here and there showed Dutch influence, the stern Puritan code of laws was less rigorously enforced. In short the transit from New England to the near-by province of East Jersey produced a distinct culture, shaped in part by the New England inheritance, in part by local conditions on the banks of the Passaic or the Raritan, and in part by the melting-pot.

Chapter V

WHEN CALVINIST MEETS CALVINIST

WHEN the disciples of Calvin went out from Geneva to carry his message to the nations of western Europe, they were in complete accord as to matters of doctrine. They had in their hands the *Institutes of the Christian Religion,* they had had every point explained by the great teacher himself. Wherever they went, to Holland, to France, to Scotland, to the wilderness of America, they held fast to these tenets as the only sure guide to salvation.

In regard to church polity there was more uncertainty. True they had before them the example of the Genevan system, in which the right of discipline was vested in preachers and elders and every member of the State was also under the jurisdiction of the Church. But Calvin had won the almost undivided support of the people of Geneva, and so had a free hand to put into effect his ideas of the Christian republic. But his followers found the situation far different in other countries, where the government was in hostile hands. In France, in England, in Scotland they had to contest the ground with Roman Catholics or with high-church Anglicans. Upon their success in combating these influences depended their church organization.

In Scotland the reformed Church had its origin, not in separate congregations, but in the Confession of Faith adopted by Parliament in 1560. With Calvinism, as interpreted by John Knox in the *First Book of Discipline,* thus legally established, the organization of the Scottish Kirk followed immediately. In December, 1560, a group of ministers and laymen formed themselves into a General Assembly, and assumed complete control over all church affairs. The hierarchy was struck down, at least nominally, and bishops, abbots and priests were placed upon a parity. A mere vestige of the old order survived in the institution of Superintendents, or itinerant bishops with very limited powers, whose function it was to enforce discipline, induct ministers and appoint lay readers.

With the arrival from Geneva of that arch enemy of prelacy, Andrew Melville, the revolution in the Church was completed by the abolition of the office of Superintendent and the introduction of the Presbyterian system. It was in 1577 that the *Second Book of Discipline* was adopted, under which the congregations were organized into Presbyteries, and the Presbyteries into Synods, all under the supreme authority of the General Assembly. Should the civil authorities prove lax at any time in suppressing heresy, schism or immorality, it was the right and the duty of the General Assembly to act alone.

Thus from its inception authority in the Scottish Church was highly centralized. The Synods, the Presbyteries, even the congregations in a sense were the creations of the General Assembly, and so forever after must submit to its rulings. In fact, there was little desire for localism, for every good Scottish Calvinist realized the urgent need for the strength which comes with union. To him Presbyterianism meant protection for the middle and lower classes against the oppressions of the aristocracy and the Crown. When John Melville stood forth as the champion of the Church, he became also the champion of the rights of the people. When he plucked James VI by the sleeve, calling him "God's silly vassal," it was the people who applauded. When, in his sermon before the General Assembly of 1582 he thundered against "the bloody knife of absolute authority, whereby men intended to pull the crown off Christ's head, and wring the sceptre out of his hand," that body drew up a protest to the Throne and appointed him to deliver it. So the intense loyalty of the average Scotchman to his own form of Church polity had its roots not only in the Genevan system, but also in the important rôle of Presbyterianism in establishing Calvinism and in defending both religious and civil rights. Wherever the Scotch went, to Ulster, to Pennsylvania, to the Shenandoah valley, they clung to their Synods and Presbyteries as though they were indispensable in keeping ajar the gates of heaven.

In England events followed a very different course. When

Henry VIII broke with the Roman Catholic Church, Parliament merely transferred the jurisdiction of the Pope to the King. In matters of doctrine and Church organization, however, Henry was entirely out of sympathy with the Protestant reformers, secured an act directed against them, and actually sent several to the stake. It was only under Edward VI that the new doctrines were introduced into the Anglican Church with the First Book of Prayer. After the interlude of Mary's reign, a final settlement was reached under Elizabeth in 1563, fixing the Anglican creed in the famous Thirty Nine Articles. The episcopal organization and the ritual were largely retained from the Roman Catholic Church, while the creed itself was far closer to Lutheranism than to Calvinism.

This was entirely unsatisfactory to the many English followers of the Genevan school, who demanded the "completion" of the Reformation by the sweeping away of the hierarchy and the acceptance of a creed based on Calvin's teachings. When James I came down from Scotland to take the Crown of England, many hoped that he would introduce some form of Presbyterianism, and Andrew Melville, at the Hampton Court conference, urged the calling of a General Assembly. But the Scottish system was just what James did not want. "If you aim at a Scottish Presbytery," he told the Puritan representatives, "it agreeth as well with monarchy as God with the devil." "If this be all that they have to say," he added, "I shall make them conform themselves, or I will harry them out of the land, or else do worse." With the remark, "It is my aphorism, no bishop, no King," James began the close alliance of the Crown with episcopacy which was to mark the seventeenth century.

So the Puritan preachers left the conference with the sad realization that for the time being, at least, there was no hope of reshaping the Anglican church to make it conform to their views. Could they bring a majority of the English people to their way of thinking, they might eventually secure the co-operation of the House of Commons, and through it force the King to yield. But this at best would entail a long and bitter struggle, which in the end might be unsuccessful. Yet they hesitated to withdraw from the organization, give up their parishes and their incomes, and place themselves definitely in the position of dissenters. This would have been like deserting the ship merely because they distrusted the pilot, and before he had run it on the rocks. Moreover, had they attempted a separate Church organization, akin to Presbyterianism, it would have brought on immediate repression and perhaps violent persecution.

Out of this predicament grew Brownism, or Separatism. Robert Browne, an earnest Calvinist, contending that the Church of England was inwardly corrupt and outwardly under subjection to an unscriptural hierarchy, declared it the duty of true Christians to strive for its reformation. Failing that, they should separate from it to form independent congregations. Such persons, he said, could rightly constitute a church by covenant with God, and by placing all authority in Him, as manifested through the votes of the individual members of the congregation. In other words, Browne, seeing no hope either that the Calvinists might control the Anglican Church or establish an organization of their own, turned to extreme localism and extreme democracy in matters of church government. Under the Brownist system there was close fellowship between the congregations, since all were united under the kingship of Christ, but none was to exercise authority over the other.[1]

Although persecution prevented the full development of Brownism in England, it was reported in 1640 that about eighty "conventicles" of humble people were meeting in or near London. The chief importance of the movement lies in the influence which it exerted on Congregationalism, in Holland among the exiled English groups, in England itself, and especially in New England through the original church at Plymouth. But Brownism bore within itself the seeds of disintegration, since it was purely negative, the mere assertion of the right to assemble and to worship. It offered the English Calvinists nothing with which to combat prelacy—no scheme of union, no form of organization within the separate congregations.

[1]Henry M. Dexter, *The Congregationalism of the Last Three Hundred Years* (N. Y., 1880), pp. 101–109.

Recognizing this weakness and distrusting democracy, Henry Barrowe, John Greenwood, and other leaders advised the creation of officers within each congregation who were to be invested with large, if not supreme, control. So, retaining Browne's idea of the separate church, they turned to Presbyterianism for this group of rulers—pastors, teachers, elders,—who were to see that "God's ordinances be truly taught and practiced," and "that the people obey willinglie and readily."

In 1596 the London Congregationalists united with the exiles in Holland to issue a *True Confession,* giving the main points of their church polity. A church was described as a congregation made up of those who convenant together to be in communion. Such a church should appoint suitable persons for pastor and elders, "to governe, oversee, visite, watch, &c.," and in case of need excommunicate. And "though congregations bee thus distinct and severall bodyes, every one as a compact Citie in it self, yet are they all to walke by one and the same rule, & by all meanes convenient to have counsell and help one of another in all needfull affayres of the Church."[2]

The *True Confession* then gives the Congregationalist theory of what is the proper relation between Church and State. Ignoring the fact that they themselves would be the first victims of religious persecution, its authors declared it the duty of civil magistrates to expurgate heresy. They ought to "suppress and root out by their authoritie all false ministries, voluntarie Relligions, and counterfeit worship of God, . . . establish & mayntein by their lawes every part of God's word, . . . and enforce al their subjects, whether ecclesiasticall or civile, to do their duties to God and men." In other words, they demanded that the government should establish the Church in accordance with their views, support and aid it in every possible way, and suppress all others.[3]

Thus it was to the government that the Congregationalists looked for real organization and strength, rather than to a compact and powerful church organization as in Scotland, and so long as the government remained hostile their ideal was impossible. They must either continue in the Anglican organization,

[2] *Ibid.,* pp. 281–282.

[3] *Ibid.,* p. 282.

submitting to the dictates of the archbishops, or withdraw into isolated congregations having no official bond of union one with the other. It was this situation which convinced many of the most farsighted Calvinists that should their effort to bring the King and Parliament to their support definitely fail, their only recourse was to migrate to some other part of the world and there establish both Congregationalism in its purest form, and a government in full sympathy with it.

This explains the insistence of the leaders of the exodus to New England upon securing a charter guaranteeing not only the right to worship as they chose, but to control the civil government. It explains also the buying up of the shares of the Massachusetts Bay Company by the emigrants themselves and its transference to the colony. Without this assurance that the civil magistrates would enforce whatever the Church advocated, there would have been little point in leaving home. "We came hither because we would have our posterity settled under the pure and full dispensations of the gospel," John Cotton declared, "defended by rulers that should be of ourselves."[4] The ministers were to point the way to heaven; it was to be the duty of the civil authorities to close the door to hell.

When the Puritans arrived in New England they had the choice of any form of Church polity. They might have set up Scottish Presbyterianism, with power concentrated in an ecclesiastical General Assembly. But they preferred to continue their own Congregationalism, which circumstances in England had forced on them, adding the necessary strength through the Church's influence over the civil authorities and the power of the civil authorities to interfere in religious matters. None should vote nor hold office save those admitted to the Lord's Table in some recognized congregation, and no new congregations were to be established without the consent of the other churches. The government, resting on this base, was to maintain "the purity and unity of religion, . . . by the advice and with the consent of the churches, and to suppress the contrary."[5]

[4]Cotton Mather, *Magnalia,* Vol. I, p. 219.

[5]Massachusetts Historical Society *Collections,* Vol. V, 1798, p. 173; *The Laws of Mass.,* John Cotton, 1641.

In 1648 a Synod comprised of elders and messengers from fifty New England churches met in Harvard College to consider matters of church government.[6] After rejecting Presbyterianism, they emphasized the importance of the rôle of the civil authorities in church affairs. It was their duty to restrain and punish heresy and open contempt of the word preached. "If any church, one or more, shall grow schismatical, rending itself from the communion of other churches, or shall walk incorrigibly and obstinately in any corrupt way of their own, contrary to the rule of the Word, in such case the magistrate is to put forth his coercive power."[7] How ready the magistrates were to live up to the letter of this injunction is shown in innumerable cases—in the banishment of John and Samuel Browne, Roger Williams, and Anne Hutchinson, the persecution of the Quaker missionaries.

Under this shelter the individual congregations enjoyed a large degree of independence. True, from time to time Synods were called, but their authority was limited chiefly to giving advice. The first Synod, which met in 1637 to consider the case of Anne Hutchinson and her followers, merely *testified* to their errors and left the rest to the civil authorities. And though the Synod of 1648 drew up the Cambridge Platform, or System of Discipline, as it was called, this merely reaffirmed the state of affairs as it then existed. The New England church polity is thus described by John Cotton: "Though we doe not subject our selves to the government of the Elders of the other churches, we acknowledge and reverence such churches in the Lord, . . . and are willing to make use of their Brotherly counsell and help. . . . Nor is Independency a fit name of the way of our churches . . . in that it confineth us within our selves . . . whereas indeed we doe professe dependence upon Magistrates."[8]

At the same time the New Englanders refused to adopt the Brownist system of democratic rule within the separate congregations. The church, after its first organizing, selected a pastor,

[6]J. W. Platner, "The Congregationalists," *The Religious History of New England* (Cambridge, 1917), p. 18.

[7]Charles Hodge, *The Constitutional History of the Presbyterian Church,* Vol. I, p. 37 (Phila., 1839).

[8]John Cotton, *The Way of the Congregational Churches,* p. 10 (London, 1648).

a teacher, and two or more ruling Elders. These officers constituted the Presbytery of Elders who were the ruling body of the congregation. To the church members was reserved the "privilege of submission to all God's Ordinances." It was thus quietly assumed that Christ would reveal His will to the Elders, but not to the church-members. If any member did not submit he was called "factious" or "obstinate" and after admonition his vote was nullified. The Presbytery of Elders had power to call the church together, to prepare matters for its hearing, to administer ordination, to censure, to examine applicants for membership and enforce discipline.[9]

In time the congregations tended to become more democratic, the body of Elders losing much of their influence or in some cases ceasing to exist.[10] From the first these free-born Englishmen must have surrendered their rights to this little oligarchical group only with keen disrelish. As representative government in civil affairs gained ground in the colony, the people demanded and obtained more democracy in congregational control. In 1717, when John Wise, of Ipswich, published his *Vindication of the Government of New England Churches,* he calmly assumed "that the People, or Fraternity, under the Gospel, are the first Subject of Power," and declared "that a Democracy in Church or State, is a very honorable and regular Government."[11] This was a long cry from John Cotton's statement: "Democracy I do not conceive that God did ever ordain as a fit government for either church or commonwealth."[12]

The close cooperation between Church and State in Massachusetts made it unnecessary to build up a Presbyterian system in which the individual congregations must submit to the authority of Synods or Assemblies. The sentiment in favor of the Congregational way was from the outset overwhelming, and had not the Puritans in England, at the Westminster Confession, accepted

[9]H. M. Dexter, *The Congregationalism of the Last Three Hundred Years,* p. 424; "These Presbyters may preach, pray, administer the sacraments, order speech and silence of the people, put questions to vote, pronounce sentence of censure, receive penitents, and bless the people." *Ibid.,* 427. [10]C. A. Briggs, *American Presbyterianism,* pp. 95–96.

[11]H. M. Dexter, *The Congregationalism of the Last Three Hundred Years,* p. 498.

[12]Thomas Hutchinson, *The History of the Colony of Massachusetts Bay,* Vol. I, p. 437 (Boston, 1764–1828).

Presbyterianism as the price of Scottish aid against the King, there probably would have been no efforts in New England to discard it for a closer Church government. As it was, the Newbury congregation, by threatening to appeal to Parliament, forced the calling of an Assembly at Cambridge to consider the Church constitution.[13] But this body expressly repudiated Presbyterianism, and in the Cambridge Platform, reaffirmed the autonomy of the individual church. There is no visible universal Church, they declared, but the group of congregations have a collective life because of their fellowship under God.[14] After this blow Presbyterianism did not dare raise its head in Massachusetts for half a century.

With the gradual weakening of the old spirit, following the loss of the colonial charter, the influx of newcomers, the growth of rationalism and commercialism, some of the ministers once more urged the advisability of a closer Church organization. In 1705 a group of Boston ministers adopted certain proposals which they publicly recommended to the consideration of the New England churches. But their plan, which envisaged local Associations of ministers and a Standing Council clothed with final authority over the congregations smacked too much of Presbyterianism. That the plan should even be suggested testifies to the fear of the ministers that the civil government would fall more and more into the hands of "godless" men, thus depriving the Church of the prop which was the backbone of Congregationalism. Although the Proposals had the support of the powerful Mather family, they were received coldly in Massachusetts, and finally fell before the attacks of John Wise in his *The Churches Quarrel Espoused,* in which he declared that they were "enough to strangle a freeborn Englishman."[15] The colony definitely and finally rejected Presbyterianism.[16]

[13]"The principal occasion was because some of the elders went about to set up some things according to the presbytery, as of Newbury." H. M. Dexter, *The Congregationalism of the Last Three Hundred Years,* p. 432; William Hill, *A History of . . . American Presbyterianism* (Washington, 1839), p. 51.

[14]John W. Platner, "The Congregationalists," *The Religious History of New England* (Cambridge, 1917), pp. 18–19.

[15]H. M. Dexter, *Congregationalism of the Last Three Hundred Years,* p. 497.

[16]John W. Platner, "The Congregationalists," *The Religious Hist. of New England* (Cambridge, 1917), p. 36.

In Connecticut events took a somewhat different course. This colony was dual in character, since it embraced the comparatively liberal group of the Hartford region, and the rigid churchmen of New Haven. From the date of its foundation by Thomas Hooker, Connecticut had granted the franchise to a comparatively wide group, embracing some who were not admitted to full communion in the churches. When New Haven was annexed the people tried in vain to escape this provision. The government agreed that none should vote save men of religious carriage certified by the deacons of their church and two of the selectmen of their town, but that was all.[17] As a result, in time the government, although still made up of men sympathetic with the Church, was less willing to enforce its every wish, was less fitted to serve as a civil frame-work for the ecclesiastical structure.

Perhaps this explains why it was that the Presbyterianizing efforts of the day met with a warmer reception in Connecticut than in Massachusetts. It was in 1708 that the General Court called a Synod of twelve clergymen and four laymen to meet at Saybrook. This group drew up the Saybrook Platform, suggesting that churches "which are neighboring to each other" form Consociations having large powers over the congregations, that the ministers unite in local Associations for consultation, licensing and ordination, and that the Association elect delegates to a General Association of the whole colony.[18] The acceptance of this "constitution" made the Connecticut Church in theory rather Presbyterian than Congregational, but in practice there was no vital change. True, the Consociations became influential bodies, but their chief function was for "mutual affording to each other of assistance," and not the disciplining of the congregations.[19] That Connecticut Presbyterianism was a very different thing from Scottish Presbyterianism became apparent when the two came into collision in the middle colonies.

With the settlement of parts of Long Island, Westchester, and

[17] Isabel M. Calder, *The New Haven Colony*, p. 239.

[18] *Records of the Presbyterian Church* (Phila., 1904), p. 8; H. M. Dexter, *Congregationalism of the Last Three Hundred Years*, pp. 488–490.

[19] *Records of the Presbyterian Church, Part Four*, p. 8; Wm. J. Cumming, *The Presbyterian Church . . . of Westchester* (Hartford, 1889), pp. 12–15.

the region between the Passaic and the Raritan by New Englanders, American Congregationalism experienced a very trying test. Could it maintain itself, with all its decentralizing features, in provinces where the government was either indifferent to its welfare or actually hostile? The little churches of Kings could not expect Peter Stuyvesant to enforce all their Sabbath laws, or expel heretics or to sanction the limiting of the franchise to communicants, in imitation of the General Court of Massachusetts. As for the English conquest, it merely aggravated the situation. Despite the violent protests of the settlers, eastern and central Long Island was wrested from Connecticut and handed over to the Duke of York, while a long series of governors exerted their influence to undermine the Calvinistic congregations and to encourage the Anglican Church.

Under such conditions Congregationalism was hopelessly handicapped. Should a minister lead his flock into "error" and remain "obstinate," there was no way whatsoever to bring him or them to reason. If the people of a town refused to pay taxes for the minister's support, he would probably have to fall back on voluntary contributions. When Lord Cornbury seized the church building at Jamaica and turned it over to the Anglicans, the congregation regained possession only after litigation lasting many years.[20] In other words, these transplanted New England congregations began to realize that one of the most vital elements of their Church polity was lacking, without which there would be no real strength nor coherence.[21]

The situation was the more serious in that frontier conditions made unity of the greatest importance. Isolated in the wilderness, many of them, struggling to conquer the forests and to build homes, cut off from close contact with each other and with the New England churches, often unable to secure ministers or to erect suitable church buildings, combating the proselyting efforts of other sects, they must have been keenly conscious of the weakness of their position. Obviously a stronger form of church

[20]The "Concessions and Agreement" of Berkeley and Carteret, of 1664, provided "that no Person—shall be molested—or called in question for any Difference in Opinion or Practice in matter of Religious Concernment."

[21]Wm. Hill, *A History of . . . American Presbyterianism* (Wash., 1839), pp.116–117.

organization, something akin to Presbyterianism was absolutely necessary. When the Presbytery of Philadelphia was organized, the New Jersey congregations recognized in it the needed unifying force, and one after the other gave it their allegiance.

It is significant that the first steps for organization came not from the Congregational churches of New York and New Jersey, but from the still more isolated groups of Pennsylvania, Delaware and Maryland, under the leadership of a Scotch-Irish missionary, Francis Makemie.[22] Makemie drew around him John Hampton and George McNish, just sent over as missionaries by a group of London ministers, and four Calvinist ministers already at work in the region, Jedediah Andrews, John Wilson, Nathaniel Taylor, and Samuel Davis, to form the Presbytery of Philadelphia. This little body, meeting for the first time in the spring of 1706, marks the birth of the Presbyterian Church in America.[23] A storm of controversy has long raged as to whether it was a real Presbytery in the Scotch sense, or merely a body for consultation more like a New England synod. It is probable that the members themselves had no definite thoughts on the subject.[24] Their object was to "consult the proper measures for advancing and propagating Christianity" and to create a rallying-point for Presbyterianism in the Middle Colonies, and they could afford to leave matters of Church polity to the future.[25]

The New Jersey congregations and some of the Long Island churches were not long in seeking admission to the presbytery —Freehold, Cohansie,[26] Woodbridge, Elizabeth, Newark, Newtown, Southampton. There were serious misgivings on the part of many who had been reared in the New England way, but these were borne down by the obvious need for cooperation. Makemie went to great pains to disarm suspicion. "We would not have anything should be advanced that may be justly disgustful to

[22]Francis Makemie was born at Ramelton, Ireland, and studied at the University of Glasgow. Coming to America in 1683, he had a varied experience as an itinerant preacher in Maryland, Virginia, and Barbadoes. His *A Plain & Friendly Perswasive to the Inhabitants of Virginia and Maryland for Promoting Towns,* in order to foster religion, published in London in 1705, appears in the *Virginia Magazine of History and Biography,* Vol. IV, pp. 264–265.

[23]As an organized body.

[24]Chas. A. Briggs, *American Presbyterianism* (N. Y., 1885), p. 143.

[25]*Journal of Presbyterian Historical Society,* Vol. IX, p. 396.

[26]Or Fairfield.

any pious soul, but on the contrary, so it is our universal desire to walk in the nearest union and fellowship with the churches in those parts where you inhabit," he wrote the Connecticut ministers, "not knowing any difference in opinion so weighty as to inhibit such a proposal."[27]

In Newark the change to Presbyterianism was attended by long and bitter disputes which eventually split the church. Abraham Pierson, the first minister, seems to have been at one with his flock in his attachment to the New England way, but his son, Abraham Pierson, Jr., who took over his work in 1678, was more inclined to the Presbyterian Church organization. In this he was encouraged by a few Scotch immigrants, who had fled from the persecutions of Charles II, and whose piety and religious zeal had gained them admission to the privileges of the town.[28] But the time was not ripe for the change, and in 1692 the opposition to Mr. Pierson's views became so strong that he was obliged to resign.

In his place the church chose Reverend John Pruden, a Connecticut Congregationalist, who had preached at Jamaica, and was known to many of the Newark families. Nonetheless, the dissensions continued and in 1699 had become so bitter that Mr. Pruden thought it wise to resign.[29] His successor, Reverend Jabez Wakeman, seems for the moment to have stilled the strife by his brilliant sermons, but unfortunately he died in 1704, when but twenty-six years old.[30] Reverend Nathaniel Bowers also was able to prevent an open breach, but the storm broke in 1716 with the election of Reverend Jedediah Buckingham. A great change had taken place since the days of the younger Pierson, and a majority of the congregation had become convinced of the desirability of some kind of Presbyterian organization. Only the farmers, many of whom lived in the western part of the town known as the mountain, remained true to the original principles. When Mr. Buckingham was forced to resign because of his strong Congregationalist leanings, this group withdrew from the church and

[27] C. A. Briggs, *American Presbyterianism* (N. Y., 1885), pp. 159–160.

[28] Jonathan F. Stearns, *The First Presbyterian Church in Newark* (Newark, 1853), p. 86n.

[29] David L. Pierson, *Narratives of Newark*, p. 154.

[30] *Ibid.*, p. 155.

organized the Mountain Society. The remainder of the congregation called Reverend Joseph Webb, who had been ordained by the Presbytery of Philadelphia,[31] and openly acknowledged themselves a Presbyterian church. The Mountain Society continued as a Congregationalist church for about thirty years, when it too succumbed to the trend of the day, called a Presbyterian minister[32] and joined the Presbytery of New York.[33]

In joining the Presbytery of Philadelphia, the Congregational churches of New York and New Jersey were very far from accepting Scottish Presbyterianism. All they desired was a degree of union for mutual protection, and they had no intention of surrendering their independence to any superior body—Presbytery, Synod, or Assembly. They no doubt thought of the Presbytery of Philadelphia as akin to the Consociations of Connecticut, with their limited power over the congregations, rather than a Scotch or a Scotch-Irish Presbytery. In short, they expected to remain essentially what they had always been—New England Congregationalists.

In the early days of the Philadelphia Presbytery, when it represented but a few scattered churches struggling against adverse conditions, this position seems to have gone unchallenged. If the Scotch and Scotch-Irish ministers objected, at heart wishing for a more powerful and active Church organization, they realized that the time for decisive action had not come. But matters gradually changed as Scotch-Irish in increasing numbers began to arrive in the colonies. These sturdy settlers, driven out of Ulster by economic and religious persecution, were coming in large numbers in 1718, and by 1730 there were probably 12,000 in Pennsylvania alone.[34] Presbyterians of the strict Scottish type, the newcomers, both ministers and laity, were dissatisfied with the looseness of the existing Church organization.[35] The original Presbytery had now grown into the Synod of Philadelphia, but there was no written constitution, no established creed, no prescribed form of

[31]Jonathan Stearns, *The First Presbyterian Church in Newark*, p. 123.
[32]Rev. Caleb Smith.
[33]Stephen Wickes, *History of the Oranges*, pp. 118–120.
[34]Jas. T. Adams, *Provincial Society* (N. Y., 1927), pp. 186, 187.
[35]William Hill, *A History of . . . American Presbyterianism* (Wash., 1839), p. 110.

discipline, so that each congregation was practically free to regulate its own affairs.[36]

In 1721, Reverend George Gillespie, of White Clay, a native Scotchman, proposed that any member of the Synod might introduce legislation, which, if passed, should be binding on the Presbyterians and congregations. The adoption of this measure so startled Jonathan Dickinson and others of Congregational tendencies, that they entered a protest.[37] Later the dissenting group presented four articles, which may be regarded as the conditions under which the New England group were willing to accept Presbyterian discipline. They acknowledged the authority of Synods and Presbyteries, and accepted Church discipline and the right to appeal from lower to "higher judicatories." But they reserved the right to disregard the "acts" of Synods and Presbyteries, if they conscientiously dissented, and insisted that the churches might resist discipline if they "think they have a right to do so." With what sour countenances the Scotch group approved and recorded these articles may well be imagined, but they were in no position as yet to force the New Englanders to submit or withdraw.[38]

They returned to the charge with renewed vigor in 1727, however, when Reverend John Thomson, of New Castle Presbytery, proposed to the Synod that it adopt publicly the Westminster Confession of Faith, requiring every candidate for the ministry and every minister "coming among us" to subscribe to it. The New England ministers were able to stave off this measure for two years, but in 1729 it came before the Synod with the proposal that all ministers who refused to sign it should be expelled. It was in vain that Jonathan Dickinson expostulated: "The churches of New England have all continued from their first foundation nonsubscribers, and yet retain their first faith and love. . . . Tho subscription may shut the door of the church communion against many serious and excellent servants of Christ . . . yet its never

[36]Wm. H. Brown, "Early New Jersey Congregationalism," *Congregational Quarterly* Vol. XIX, No. 4, p. 539.

[37]Jonathan Stearns, *The First Presbyterian Church of Newark*, p. 131.

[38]*Ibid.*, p. 133; Chas. A. Briggs, *American Presbyterianism*, pp. 202–216

like to detect hypocrites, nor keep concealed hereticks out of the Church."[39]

It was probably Dickinson who so worded the act adopting the subscription resolutions that he and other ministers who were not in sympathy with strict Scotch Presbyterianism could agree to it. The Adopting Act required all candidates for the ministry to declare themselves in agreement with the Confession, but only in "essential and necessary articles."[40] This gave the American group a loophole, so that they could join with the Scotch and Scotch-Irish to make the vote unanimous.[41] Once more the Synod had found a formula to which both Scottish and New England Presbyterians could subscribe, once more the day of division had been postponed.

But the Scotch-Irish were now pouring through the port of Philadelphia, adding strength every year to the Scotch faction in the Synod. It was inevitable that ere long they would overwhelm the New Englanders, forcing them either to conform to their views of Church government or to withdraw. The old breach was forced upon the attention of the Synod by the trial for heresy of Reverend Samuel Hemphill, who had declared his assent to the Westminster Confession, but later proved to be an Arminian, drifting toward Deism. The Scotch-Irish placed the blame squarely on the loopholes left by Dickinson and the other New Englanders in the Adopting Act, and demanded their elimination. Therefore, in 1736, the Synod passed a supplementary act, declaring that they "have adopted & still do adhere to the Westminster Confession . . . without the least variation or alteration." Despite this defeat, the liberal subscriptionists, most of whom were absent when the resolution was passed, did not withdraw, determined to make no resistance until forced to do so by some act of coercion against one or more of their ministers or congregations.[42]

The final breach was hastened by the wave of religious emo-

[39] *Ibid.*, p. 213. [40] *Ibid.*, pp. 216–221. [41] *Ibid.*

[42] *Ibid.*, pp. 230–238. Voting for the act were fourteen Scotch-Irish, two Scotchmen, one Welshman and three New Englanders. Pumroy, Dickinson, Pierson, Webb, Pemberton, Hubbel, Horton, Wales, Morgan, Chalker, and Nutinan, all from New England, were absent. *Ibid.*, 237n.

tionalism which swept over the colonies known as the Great Awakening. Originating in the Pietism of the European Continent, the demand for a vital and practical religion spread to almost every part of the British Empire. In England its chief exponents were Wesley and Whitefield, two emotional evangelists who awakened the people to the hollowness of mere ritual and form in religion. Although Pietism reached the shores of America even in the seventeenth century through the preaching of the Dutch missionary William Bertholf and later through the activities of Domine Theodorus J. Frelinghuysen, its chief impetus came by way of England and New England in the fourth decade of the eighteenth century. Whitefield himself came to America, touring through the colonies and preaching to enormous throngs of excited listeners.

Among the Presbyterians, as among the Dutch Reformed and the New England Congregationalists, there were many clergymen who resented the Great Awakening and resisted it with bitter determination. They were not ready to admit that God reveals himself directly to the individual without regard to the Church organization, that they themselves were more interested in dead orthodoxy and abstract theology than in evangelical faith, and that religious emotionalism was more to be desired than formalism. Others, however, embraced the new movement with enthusiasm, New Englanders and Scotch-Irish alike. In the Middle Colonies not only Dickinson, Aaron Burr, and other former Congregationalists aligned themselves with Frelinghuysen and Whitefield, but also the famous Scotch-Irish Tennent family and their fellow-countrymen John Cross, George Gillespie, and Alexander Craighead.[43]

Thus the old conflict within the Presbyterian church between the centralizing tendencies of the Scotch-Irish, and the Congregational traditions of the New Englanders was complicated by the clash of the evangelical New Lights with the formalist Old Lights. The situation was the more critical in that it involved also the old question of yielding to or resisting the forces of Americanization in the Church. The Tennent group contended

[43]Jonathan Stearns, *The First Presbyterian Church of Newark*, p. 167.

that pious young men who desired to enter the ministry should be encouraged to do so, even though they should find it impractical to go to New England or to Europe for a theological education. The people who were daily pushing out to the frontiers were demanding the Gospel and cared little whether or not the missionaries who came to them were thoroughly tutored in theoretical orthodoxy. But when William Tennent's Log College, at Neshaminy, Pennsylvania, began to turn out evangelical ministers, the Old Lights in the Synod passed a resolution designed to exclude them.[44] The New Lights retorted by holding revival meetings in neighboring pastorates in which they inveighed pointedly against the dangers of empty formalism and "an unconverted ministry." In the Synod they sought to protect themselves by appealing to the Adopting Act, and so went over definitely to the decentralizing position of their New England allies.

The contest thus took on a triple aspect. On the one hand a demand for the traditional Congregational localism in Church government, for a new birth of piety and evangelism, and for a response to the demands for more ministers and missionaries; on the other the Scotch system of Church centralization, a dependence upon formalism and orthodoxy, and resistance to the forces of Americanization. The crisis came in the 1741 meeting of the Synod, when the Old Lights, taking advantage of the absence of many of the New Jersey members, expelled eleven of the opposing group, including the entire Presbytery of New Brunswick.[45] At subsequent meetings, in 1742 and 1743, members from the Presbytery of New York made earnest efforts for compromise, but in vain. The Old Lights refused to restore the ejected ministers. Thereupon, Jonathan Dickinson, Aaron Burr, Ebenezer Pemberton and John Pierson, New Englanders all of them, declaring that they could not see their "way clear to sit" in the Synod when others were unjustly excluded, quietly withdrew. In

[44]Chas. A. Briggs, *American Presbyterianism*, p. 243.

[45]Chas. A. Briggs, *American Presbyterianism*, p. 267. The expelled members were: William Tennent, Jr., and Richard Treat, of the Presbytery of Philadelphia; Alexander Craighead and David Alexander of the Presbytery of Donegal; William Tennent, Sr., Gilbert Tennent and Eleazar Wales, of the Presbytery of New Brunswick; Charles Tennent, Samuel Blair, George Gillespie, and Alexander Hutchinson, of the Presbytery of New Castle.

1745 this group united with certain of the ejected members and other New Lights at a meeting in Elizabeth to organize the Synod of New York, with three Presbyteries and twenty-two ministers.[46] The Synod of Philadelphia promised to "maintain charitable and Christian affections toward them," but the bitterness attending the separation was too deep-seated to be cloaked by empty words.

Perhaps few of the angry ministers, as they turned homeward by boat or horseback from the fatal Synod of 1741, reflected upon the strange course of events leading up to the breach in their Church—the organization of a national Kirk in Scotland, the migration of colonists from Scotland to Ireland and thence to America; the struggle of the Calvinists in England for the control of the Anglican Church, their failure and consequent organization of Congregationalism, the exodus to New England, the migrations thence to New York and New Jersey, the meeting of Scotch Presbyterianism and English Congregationalism in the Synod of Philadelphia. No doubt these good men would have been more conciliatory had they realized that their own views and the views of their opponents were but the result of fate, a fate which gave to the Scottish Calvinists a strongly centralized form of Church government and denied it to the Calvinists of England.

The division of the Church by no means followed geographical lines. The Synod of New York was especially strong in the New England districts of New York and New Jersey, but it extended its influence also into Pennsylvania and far into the Scotch-Irish regions of the South.[47] If a struggling little congregation in the Shenandoah or in western Maryland appealed to the Synod of Philadelphia for a minister, they could expect only disappointment, since the number of available college trained men was very limited. If the appeal went to the newer body,

[46]The Presbytery of New York was formed in 1738 by uniting the Presbyteries of Long Island and East Jersey. It embraced the churches of Elizabeth, Woodbridge, Wallkill (N. Y.), Westfield, Hanover, New York, Newark, Bethlehem (N. Y.), Connecticut Farms, Setauket (L. I.), Newtown (L. I.), Mattituck (L. I.), Southampton, Jamaica, and Goshen (N. Y.). S. D. Alexander, *The Presbytery of New York* (N. Y., 1887), pp. 3–8.

[47]Zebulon Crocker, *The Catastrophe of the Presbyterian Church* (New Haven, 1838), p. 51.

it was seldom in vain, and in good time some zealous, godly young pastor would come out to them. There were loud reproaches from the Old Lights of "taking men from the last and the loom" and putting them into the ministry, but this mattered little to most of the congregations so long as their lives were holy and their preaching inspiring.[48]

But the New Lights were not blind to the advantages of an educated ministry, and sought to erect a seminary of learning to take the place of the Log College. Accordingly in 1746 the College of New Jersey, the present Princeton University, was put into operation with Jonathan Dickinson as its first president. In a short while it had become a powerful influence for good in the Church, and its graduates were filling pulpits from the Hudson to the James and the Roanoke.

This progressive spirit, this ready response to the needs of the Church in America, made the Synod of New York a really vital, growing body. Comprising only twenty ministers at its formation in 1742, in seventeen years it had increased to seventy-two, many of them graduates of Princeton and Yale. The Synod of Philadelphia, however, with no adequate provision for training a native ministry, reacting into barren ecclesiasticism, in opposition to the active forces of the age, found it difficult to secure recruits. They had lost ten members by death by 1759, and had added only fourteen, none of whom was a graduate of an American college.[49]

Throughout the period of separation, the New York Synod continued to make overtures for a reconciliation. At first the personal irritation of the Old Side, especially against the Tennent group, prevented the acceptance of these overtures, but at last, in 1758, a plan of union was drawn up and put into operation the following year. Many of the moving spirits in the schism were now dead, animosities had softened, the evils of separation had taught forbearance. Despite their weakness the Philadelphia Synod carried some of their chief points in the plan of reunion—the final jurisdiction of the Synod and the Presbyteries, the in-

48Jacob Green, *A View of a Christian Church* (Chatham, 1781), p. 47.

49Chas. A. Briggs, *American Presbyterianism* (N. Y., 1885), pp. 314–316.

sistence upon subscription, the prohibition of intrusion into the congregations of other ministers. On the other hand, the New Lights inserted a provision that candidates for the ministry should be examined upon their "experimental acquaintance with religion," as well as upon learning and orthodoxy.[50] The reunited group took the name of Synod of New York and Philadelphia.

Despite this outward reconciliation, there remained many serious misgivings on the part of both groups. Some of the New Jersey and New York ministers, mindful of their Congregational traditions, chafed at the restrictions put upon them by the Synod, and this finally led to a minor secession and the formation of an independent Presbytery. It was in 1779 that four ministers, Jacob Green, Joseph Grover, Amzi Lewis and Ebenezer Bradford, withdrew from the Synod. They objected to that body's assuming legislative power, ordering instead of desiring contributions, enjoining ministers not to use notes in preaching, and forcing subscription "without any liberty for explanation"; in short for governing after the manner of the "General Assembly of the Church of Scotland."[51] In 1780 the seceders formed what later took the name of Presbytery of Morris County. Striking a sympathetic chord with persons of strong Congregationalist leanings, the new body grew rapidly, especially in Dutchess and Westchester Counties.[52] It was eventually swallowed in the Plan of Union of 1801. The movement, short-lived though it was, is significant of the uneasiness with which English Calvinists dwelt under the same roof with Scotch Calvinists.

Nonetheless, it is probable that the reconciliation of 1759 might have been permanent, had not the conditions which created the rupture of 1741 repeated themselves. It was in the last decade of the eighteenth century that thousands of New Englanders, discouraged by the barrenness of their farms or thrown out of work by the interruptions in trade, gathered their meager belong-

[50]Robert E. Thompson, *American Church History. The Presbyterian Churches* (N. J., 1907), pp. 43–44.

[51]Jacob Green, *A View of a Christian Church* (Chatham, 1781), pp. 49–51; Chas. A. Briggs, *American Presbyterianism* [N. Y., 1885], pp. 362, 363.

[52]Ezra H. Gillett, *History of the Presbyterian Church in the U. S.* (Phila., 1864), Vol. I, pp. 213, 214.

ings and moved out into the fertile valleys of western New York. Here they came into contact with other settlers from the Hudson and lower Mohawk, and later with a stream of settlers from Pennsylvania, New Jersey and Maryland, coming up the Susquehanna. In 1800 the region west of Oneida and Oswego had 60,000 inhabitants, in 1810 the number was 200,000, and ten years later it had swelled to half a million.[53]

Like other pioneers, these people often found it expedient to ignore denominational differences in order to unite in building churches and securing ministers. And like their fellow New Englanders in East Jersey, the Congregationalists recognized the need of a degree of Presbyterian organization. Thus many Presbyterians joined what were essentially Congregational churches, while these in turn organized Presbyteries and accepted the Presbyterian name. The process of amalgamation was hastened by the Plan of Union of 1801, which was ratified by both the General Assembly of the Presbyterian Church and by the General Association of Connecticut. It prescribed regulations for the amalgamated churches of the new settlements, and made it possible for them to join the organized Presbyterian Church.[54] As a result there were created the Synod of Geneva in 1812, the Synod of Genesee in 1821, the Synod of the Western Reserve in 1825, and the Synod of Utica in 1829.[55] Despite this Presbyterian organization, however, the people of the region were Congregational in tradition and continued fundamentally Congregational in church polity.[56]

Although there were some mutterings of discontent, the Plan of Unity seems to have been satisfactory until, in the fourth decade of the century, large groups of Scotch-Irish, moving up the Susquehanna, settled in western New York. When they found the Presbyterian churches there in reality Congregational, they were prompt in entering complaints with the General Assembly. Nor were they long in finding ardent backers among the Old Lights

[53]Alex. C. Flick, *History of the State of N. Y.*, Vol. V, pp. 165, 166.

[54]Isaac V. Brown, *Old School Vindicated*, pp. 32, 33.

[55]*Ibid.*, pp. 51–55.

[56]Isaac V. Brown is obviously wrong in classifying more than half the churches as Presbyterian. Had this been the case there would have been no point in ejecting the four synods from the Church in 1837, in which he himself took so prominent a part.

of the Middle States and South. The Plan of Union "was originally intended not as the medium through which Congregationalism would be perpetuated in the Presbyterian Church," they stated somewhat naïvely, "but to give opportunity for the Congregationalists (if after learning the character of our system, they approved of it) to become Presbyterians."[57] But the Old School now, when they found the Church chained to a lion rather than a lamb, demanded the rescinding of the Plan of Union and the ejection of the northwestern synods from the Church. "No reasonable man . . . could expect that two religious bodies, under a fictitious, not a real union, each retaining its own peculiar and irreconcilable features, should continue long to act harmoniously together. . . . By this apparently conciliatory device . . . the Presbyterian Church threw down their wall of defense, they opened their bosom to the ingress of strangers."[58]

The battle began in earnest in the meeting of the General Assembly in 1834, with the presentation of the so-called *Western Memorial,* complaining of Congregational practices under the Plan of Union of 1801—the loose interpretation of ecclesiastical formulas, the ordaining of men by one Presbytery for work in some other, the ordaining of Congregationalists as Presbyterian ministers. The memorialists inveighed especially against the American Home Missionary Society, because of Congregational influences working within it, and demanded that missionaries be commissioned only by the General Assembly. When the New School majority in the Assembly refused to listen to these complaints, the Old School group embodied them in a paper entitled *Act and Testimony* which was published in the *Presbyterian.* Immediately the Church, from one end of the country to the other, was rent by angry contentions, the Old School party hailing the articles as "an imperishable bill of Presbyterian wrongs and rights," their opponents "pouring forth denunciations like repeated peals of thunder . . . in their assemblies, tribunals and journals."[59]

[57]Isaac V. Brown, *The Old School Vindicated,* p. 49. Statement of Rev. James Wood.
[58]*Ibid.,* p. 35.
[59]*Ibid.,* pp. 99–144; Robert E. Thompson, *A History of the Presbyterian Churches in the U. S.* (N. Y., 1895), p. 111.

In the end the victory rested with the Old School. Gathering their full strength, especially from Pennsylvania and the South, where the Scotch-Irish were numerous, they secured a substantial majority in the General Assembly of 1837. Meeting first in caucus in the Philadelphia Sixth Presbyterian church, they drew up a program of action which they agreed to force on the Assembly, to expunge Congregationalism from the Church. "Our present evils have not originated within," they declared, "but have been brought from without, and are, in a great degree, the consequences of an unnatural intermixture of two systems of ecclesiastical action, which are in many respects entirely opposite. . . . Two important families in the great Christian community . . . have been brought beneath the same roof. . . . Contact has not produced real union. . . . On the contrary, original differences of opinion and prejudices in relation to the principles of government . . . have for a number of years been widening." Declaring that they could not remain in a union which menaced their existence as a Church, they urged the abrogation of the Plan of Union of 1801, the taking over of missionary work by the General Assembly, and the dissolving of "non-Presbyterian" churches, Presbyteries and Synods. This program they carried through the General Assembly almost unchanged in the face of the bitterest opposition, and ended by severing all connection with the Synods of Utica, Geneva, Genesee and the Western Reserve.

The New School party was not yet defeated, however, and at the General Assembly of 1838 made a bold attempt to take over the Church organization. The delegates of the ejected Presbyteries pushed into the meeting, filling the floor and overflowing into the gallery, "making motions, stamping feet, uttering conflicting and unearthly sounds, from all sexes, ages, positions and directions, overwhelming all business, impressing the . . . Assembly with astonishment and dismay."[60] When the moderator refused to recognize them, the delegates, with other New School men, proceeded to organize the Assembly to their own liking and then adjourned to the First Church. The matter was taken to the civil

[60]This description from the hostile pen of Isaac V. Brown is no doubt somewhat colored. See I. V. Brown, *Old School Vindicated*, p. 260.

courts, where it was eventually decided in favor of the Old School party, who thus retained possession of the Church Organization. When the separation was complete it was found that about five-ninths of the churches, located chiefly in the Scotch-Irish regions, still adhered to the Old School, while the groups with New England antecedents joined hands with the New School Assembly.[61]

This bitter clash between Scottish Presbyterianism and Congregational principles, occurring thus in the fourth decade of the nineteenth century, is a striking illustration of the persistence of Old World traditions. Had there been any perceptible difference in matters of faith or of worship, the inability of the two groups to work in harmony would have been quite understandable. But the chief, if not the only real, divergence was in the matter of Church polity, of the power of the General Assembly, of the Synods and Presbyteries, of the organization of individual congregations. But the Scotch-Irish, reared in the Scottish tradition where all power in the Church came from above, could never reconcile themselves to the localism of the Congregational system, which seemed to them spineless and inviting chaos in doctrine as well as government. On the other hand, the New Englanders became restive in an organization where obedience to the Church as a whole was sternly exacted of individuals, congregations, Presbyteries and Synods.

It seems strange that there should have been so much trouble in reconciling the two systems when both found themselves in new surroundings so different from those in which they were nurtured. The men who faced each other angrily in the Pittsburgh Assembly, men still living amid frontier conditions, some of them, should have stopped to consider that the need was for a system suited to America, rather than for Scotland or for England in the sixteenth and seventeenth centuries. But since they were descendants of Scotchmen or of English Puritans, with all the stubborn strength of Scotchmen and English Puritans, they regarded compromise as a fatal weakness, as the opening wedge for ruin. When, at last, common misfortune, after the secession

[61]Robert E. Thompson, *A History of the Presbyterian Churches in the U. S.*, pp. 120, 121.

of the Southern Presbyterians, had produced a reconciliation and reunion of the Old School and the New School groups in the North, many sincere men still opposed it with bitter determination. Doctor Charles Hodge, "rode nine miles to meet the Presbytery in Cranberry, on October 5, 1869, with the *anthrax malitiosissimus* on the back of his neck, for the purpose of casting his final vote against" reunion.[62] And though the sturdy doctor and others like him were voted down, though reunion became a fact, though the process of Americanization has gone on, though time has softened the intensity of beliefs and traditions, one has no difficulty even today in distinguishing within the Church, on the one hand ideas which hark back to John Knox and Andrew Melville and, on the other, those which found their roots in Robert Browne, Henry Barrowe, John Robinson, and John Cotton.

[62]*Ibid.*, p. 180.

Chapter VI

PENN'S HOLY EXPERIMENT

IN PLANNING his colony on the bank of the Delaware William Penn was actuated by a desire not only to establish a refuge for his oppressed fellow Quakers, but to make a hitherto untried experiment in government. Believing that great harm had resulted from the tendency of governments to make expediency rather than right their guiding star, he based the political structure of his colony on truth, justice and righteousness. There must be no compromise with wrong. If war is wrong, then there must be no war whatever the cost; if intolerance is unjust, there must be religious freedom even though it should ultimately overthrow the Quaker principles themselves.

Penn and his followers reserved to themselves, however, the all-important privilege of deciding what was right and what was wrong, and so founded the government of Pennsylvania on Quaker principles. Fortunately these principles were in the main enlightened and liberal, although some were perhaps impractical, and some actually reactionary. When once the government had been established and the Quaker code enacted into law, it remained to be seen whether the experiment would be successful. Penn himself had his moments of doubt. If another government committed a wrong against his province, could it reply always with right; if it became the object of aggression, could it defend itself only with protestations of friendship; could it answer injustice with justice?

The Quakers lay down as a main fundamental in religion that God gives every man a "light within," or "manifestation" to inform him of his duty and to enable him to do it. By this "they understand something that is divine, and though in man, yet not of man but of God; and that it came from him, and leads to him all those that will be led by it."[1] Since God speaks directly to the

[1] William Penn, *Primitive Christianity Revived* (Phila., 1783), pp. 7, 8.

individual, and not indirectly through the Church, salvation may be attained without the intervention of an ordained priesthood. Baptism, the Lord's Supper and other sacraments, and all forms and ceremonies are unnecessary.[2]

From these views the advocacy of religious freedom followed as a matter of course. Penn promised that no person in his colony who believed in God should be molested for his "persuasion or practice,"[3] not only because of his own sufferings for conscience sake, but because the Quakers could not consistently establish a State Church. The Puritans in migrating to Massachusetts Bay had as one of their main purposes the setting up of a Church which could be defended from heresy by the stern hand of the law. Persecution was the logical consequence of their belief that salvation was possible only through this Church and the observance of its ordinances. The Quakers, on the contrary, averring that religion was a matter between the individual and his Maker, could not interfere with this holy relationship by prescribing for it rules and regulations. So Pennsylvania was thrown open to Christians of all denominations, and Anglicans, Presbyterians, Lutherans, Mennonites, Moravians, Reformed rushed in.

But though the Quakers made no effort to enforce their own tenets by law, they had emphatic views as to morality, and enacted them into laws backed by severe penalties. The theatre was prohibited. "How many plays did Jesus Christ and his apostles recreate themselves at? What poems, romances, comedies and the like did the apostles and saints make or use to pass away their time withal?" wrote the youthful William Penn from his cell in the Tower.[4] "Plays, parks, balls, treats, romances, musics, love-sonnets, and the like, will be a very invalid plea. . . at the revelation of the righteous judgment of God." The Quakers objected to plays, not only as tending to immorality, but because of the simulating of passions, joys and grief by the actors. Christianity requires simplicity and truth, they said, and it is contrary to its spirit to create imaginary scenes and episodes.[5]

[2]William Penn, *A Key, etc.* (Phila., 1849), pp. 24–26.
[3]*Great Law of Pennsylvania,* Chapter XXXV.
[4]William Penn, "No Cross, No Crown," *Friends Library,* Vol. I, p. 266.
[5]Thos. Clarkson, *A Portraiture of Quakerism* (N. Y., 1806), p. 90.

Gambling in any form was severely condemned, the Great Law of Pennsylvania prescribing a fine or imprisonment for "playing cards, dice, lotteries, or such like enticing, vain and evil sports and games." The practice of duelling the Quakers made punishable with hard labor in the house of correction. Profanity was considered so serious an offense that those guilty of it were often given an opportunity to cleanse their vocabulary in prison on a diet of bread and water.[6] Drunkenness was punishable with fine or imprisonment.

But the Quakers were even more concerned with preventing legislation inconsistent with their principles than with these positive prohibitions. There must be no law requiring the taking of oaths, no prohibition of wearing hats in court or in the presence of the governor, no infringement of religious liberty, and above all no policy of belligerency towards the Indians or foreign powers and no participation in war. We "believe that war ought to cease," said William Penn. Jesus taught his disciples to forgive and to love their enemies, not to war against them and kill them, therefore Christians should substitute love and persuasion for weapons and war. Since the very worst of men will not hurt those who really love them, peace must in the end have the victory.[7]

As for the wearing of hats, the taking of oaths, and the use of "thee" and "thou," matters which today may seem inconsequential, in the religious philosophy of Fox and Penn they were fundamental. "We dare not swear because God forbids it," said Penn.[8] "It is needless as well as evil. . . . The true Christian's yea being yea, the end of an oath is answered." To the Quaker the removing of one's hat in court or at church or in the presence of officials was not only degrading, but an encouragement to vanity. So they resolutely kept their hats on their heads, even in the presence of the King and Queen. When Admiral Penn tried to secure a promise from his son that he would uncover his head at least before King Charles, the Duke of York and himself, the youthful William refused to lay even this one "grain of incense"

[6] *Great Law of Penna.*, Chapters. III and IV.
[7] William Penn, *Primitive Christianity Revived*, p. 63.
[8] *Ibid.*, p. 62.

on the "altar of human arrogance."[9] But the price paid was heavy. The Quakers were derided and abused; their hats were knocked from their heads, their shops were boycotted.[10]

The refusal to address individuals with the plural "you" as a token of respect was based on the same objection to "vanity, pride and ostentation." It had long been the general custom in England to address a person of rank or wealth in the plural, and as Fox says, "it was a sore cut to proud flesh and those who sought self-honor" when the Quakers came out with the "thou" reserved for humbler persons. "Why, you ill-bred clown do you 'thou' me? . . . I'll 'thou' thy teeth down thy throat," was the frequent angry reply. For their persistence in this seemingly trivial matter the Quakers were abused, beaten, imprisoned and stigmatized as ill-mannered and irreverent.[11]

So the Pennsylvania Quakers had no desire to have the government of the province fall into the hands of other denominations. Were the Anglicans to gain control they might, with the aid of the British government, attempt to rescind or at least to weaken the guarantees of religious freedom. Should a coalition of Anglicans, Lutherans, Presbyterians and Reformed fill the Assembly, many of the precepts dear to the hearts of the Quakers would be endangered, the province might be forced into war and Quakers punished for refusing to bear arms. In other words the Friends dared not weaken their grip on the government lest they suffer in their own refuge the same persecutions and abuses as in Europe, lest they find themselves balked in carrying out their basic principles and policies.

For the safety of many of their customs and beliefs which involved them in no serious conflict with law or with the interests or principles of others, the Friends had no apprehension from the government. Their neighbors might smile or even openly deride their prejudice against music, ornamental furniture, novels, dancing, elaborate dress, holy days, titles; their taciturnity; their quiet, sedate manner; their discarding of the "pagan" names of

[9]Albert C. Applegarth, "Quakers in Penna.," *Johns Hopkins Univ. Studies,* Tenth Series, Vols. VIII-IX, pp. 7, 8.

[10]Thos. Clarkson, *A Portraiture of Quakerism,* Vol. I, p. 324.

[11]*Ibid.,* pp. 275–278; A. C. Applegarth, "Quakers in Penna.," pp. 9, 10.

the months and the days of the week, but these things were unlikely to call forth hostile legislation. Their continuance depended upon something even more fundamental than the control of the government, they depended upon the supremacy in the colony of the Quaker spirit. If the policy of religious freedom together with the open door to immigrants made the overthrow of this supremacy inevitable even in Philadelphia itself, the Friends could do little more than foster and protect their ideals within their own Society. Yet the struggle for Quaker control, both legislative and moral, continued throughout the colonial period.

In the eyes of Fox and Penn dancing was a sin of grievous consequences. They agreed with Saint Augustine that the steps of the dancer were just so many "leaps to hell," that the good man who enters a ballroom "cometh forth a corrupt and wicked man."[12] The young Friend who so forgot himself as to attend a dance was certain to receive a visit from a committee of overseers, and if he persisted, to be "disowned" or expelled from the Society.

Music was viewed with suspicion. Fox warned the pious against its insidious, sensuous, frivolous influence, while Penn thought it almost as sinful as dancing itself. To bewitch the heart with temporal delight by playing upon instruments and singing, was to forget God. Moreover, to sacrifice the time necessary to acquire efficiency in either vocal or instrumental music was inconsistent with the Quaker pattern of life, in which each moment must be devoted to some useful task or to good thoughts. It was right that the individual "saint" should sing the praises of God, but not a "mixed multitude" in which there might be some unregenerate.[13]

Plainness in dress was at first not considered essential by the Friends, for some contended that it was "no vanity to use what the country naturally produced." Some of the early Quaker men wore wigs, while the women sometimes arrayed themselves in white satin petticoats embroidered with flowers, pearl satin gowns and peach-colored cloaks.[14] Nonetheless, vanity of this kind was

[12]William Penn, "No Cross, No Crown," p. 306.

[13]A. C. Applegarth, "Quakers in Penna.," pp. 12, 13; Thos. Clarkson, *A Portraiture of Quakerism*, pp. 59, 82.

[14]A. C. Applegarth, "Quakers in Penna.," pp. 26, 27.

bitterly condemned by Penn. "How many pieces of riband and what feathers, lacebands and the like did Adam and Eve wear in paradise, or out of it?" he asked. "What rich embroideries, silks, points, etc., had Abel, Enoch, Noah, and good old Abraham? Did Eve, Sarah, Suzannah, Elizabeth and the Virgin Mary use to curl, powder, patch, paint, wear false locks of strange colors, rich points, trimmings, laced gowns, embroidered petticoats?"[15]

Unable to resist this reasoning, the Quaker gentlemen discarded their handsome attire for broad-brimmed hats, coats with straight collars, drab stockings and shoes fastened with leather straps,[16] while the women contented themselves with caps or hoods, plain gowns of a drab, gray or buff color, and green aprons.[17] In time the man who appeared at meeting with silver buckles, metal buttons or ruffled collar, or the woman who wore satin or lace at once became objects of suspicion. "O that our young women would cease from all unseemly and immodest appearance in their apparel," said the Philadelphia Meeting, "certainly both males and females who take such undue liberties flee from the cross of Christ."[18]

The good Friend was supposed to avoid excess in food and drink as in other things, and George Fox warned all "God's freemen and women" to beware of "feastings and revellings, banquetings and wakes."[19] The Quaker's home should be plain and unostentatious, devoid of costly silver and gold utensils and of richly carved furniture. In his conversation he must be reserved, even taciturn, free of all idle gossip or vain boastings; in his bearing quiet, sedate and dignified. The good people of Burlington were deeply concerned when some of the young men came to meeting "galloping and riding after an airy flurting manner" inconsistent with the "moderation and gravity" becoming the Friends.[20]

With tenets and principles so different from those of other sects the Friends were determined to retain their ascendancy both

[15] William Penn, "No Cross, No Crown," p. 266.
[16] John F. Watson, *Annals of Philadelphia* (Phila., 1856), Vol. I, p. 510.
[17] Thos. Clarkson, *A Portraiture of Quakerism*, Vol. I, pp. 244–248.
[18] *Christian Advices*, by the Yearly Meeting of Friends (Phila., 1808), p. 79.
[19] *The Friends' Library*, "Institution of Discipline," Vol. I, p. 135.
[20] "Friends in Burlington," *Penna. Magazine*, Vol. VII, p. 354.

political and moral. After all the colony had been founded by a Quaker, in part as a refuge for members of the Society, in part as a proving ground for Quaker concepts. Penn had wished to demonstrate to the world that it was practical to live under a government based on religious freedom, democratic principles, good will and conciliation in foreign relations; to establish a social life dominated by piety, simplicity, sincerity, moderation and strict adherence to moral law. It was not only entirely right and just, but absolutely necessary, so his followers reasoned, for the control of the colony to remain in their own hands.

The first serious threat to the Holy Experiment came not from the non-Quaker elements, however, but from within the body of the Society itself. The man who challenged the leadership of Fox and Penn, denied some of their fundamental tenets and drew off hundreds in Pennsylvania and New Jersey was George Keith. Born in Scotland, graduated from Aberdeen University, a man of deep learning, Keith deserted the Presbyterian Church for the Society of Friends as a young man of twenty-five or twenty-six. Coming to America in 1684, he attracted wide attention by a series of able discourses and sermons and gradually drew around him a group of devoted followers. Had he not strayed from the accepted doctrines and practices of the Friends, he would no doubt rank second only to Penn in the history of the Society in America. But his restless mind, his love of controversy and his unrestrained temper got him into trouble. Charging the visiting Quaker ministers with placing all their emphasis upon the "inner light" to the neglect of the historic Christ and the Scriptures, he gave way to bitter and intemperate language. There were "more damnable heresies and doctrines of devils among the Quakers than among any profession of Protestants," he said.[21]

Had Pennsylvania been a Puritan colony the remedy would have been simple; for the Church would have tried Keith, and left it to the civil authorities to drive him into banishment. But this would have been inconsistent with Quaker ideals. Knowing this, Keith dared them to do their worst, declaring that "his back had

[21]R. M. Jones, *The Quakers in the Amer. Cols.*, p. 448; Albert C. Myers, *Narratives of Early Penna.*, pp. 335, 336.

long itched to be whipped." Some of the Quaker magistrates took him at his word so far as to arrest and convict him on a charge of disturbing the peace, but they soon saw their mistake and refused to enforce the penalty.

There was no reason why the Society as a religious body should not take action against him, however, so the Yearly Meeting, after condemning "that spirit of reviling, railing, lying, slandering and falsely accusing which hath risen . . . in George Keith and his adherents," disowned them as Friends. Although Keith was now the leader of a new sect and set up Meetings in Philadelphia, Burlington and Bucks County, he still had hopes of winning the seal of orthodoxy from the parent Society in England. But the English Yearly Meeting condemned him as a deserter from the "holy fellowship," and soon after he made another major shift by joining the Anglican Church. Upon receipt of this news some of his bewildered followers in America returned to the Quaker fold, some became Baptists, many united with the Episcopalians.[22]

The Keith schism seems to have awakened the Friends to the necessity of solidarity. Should they split up permanently into two or more factions, if Meetings should be divided and old friends turned into enemies, the Holy Experiment would be doomed. They must stand shoulder to shoulder to combat any encroachments of the British government, the Anglican Church or the Presbyterian Church; they must bring the threat of expulsion against Friends who showed an inclination to laxness, and social ostracism against non-Quakers whose conduct they considered scandalous or a reproach to the colony.

The so-called *Discipline* of the Friends grew out of the letters of George Fox and the official epistles of the London Yearly Meeting giving advice on matters of doctrine, morals and organization. There were admonitions as to dress, language, the treatment of the poor, bearing arms, salutations, amusements, etc. To the American Friends they had a sanctity second only to the Bible, so that in time they were codified into the *Discipline* which

[22] R. M. Jones, *The Quakers in the Amer. Cols.*, pp. 437–458; A. C. Thomas, *Hist. of the Soc. of Friends in Amer.*, The Amer. Church Series, Vol. XII, pp. 232–234; John Gouch, *Hist. of People Called Quakers*, Vol. III, Chapters 6, 7, 8.

became obligatory upon all the Meetings.[23] It was the duty of the overseers to inquire into cases of "drinking to excess, swearing, cursing, lying," of "superfluity of apparel and furniture," of "calling the days and months contrary to Scripture," of "smoking tobacco in streets, roads and public-houses," of "tale-bearing," of "keeping vain and loose company," of not using "the plain Scripture language of *thee* and *thou*," and other infringements of the *Discipline*. Offending members were admonished and, in cases of obstinacy, expelled by the Monthly Meeting.

The Quaker youth who cast an eye upon a maid of another sect was inviting trouble, for mixed marriages were forbidden. "Let our dear youth avoid the too frequent and familiar converse with those from whom may arise a danger of entanglement, by their alluring passions and drawing the affections after them," said a book of *Advices,* for "marriage implies union as well in spiritual as temporal concerns."[24] No doubt the pleadings of parents or the warnings of the overseers broke up many a budding love affair, but if the erring Quaker youth or maid persisted, expulsion from the Society was the penalty.[25] This exclusiveness tended ultimately to stagnation and isolation, but for the moment it seemed to bring compactness and unity and so to enhance the influence of the Society.

Strength came also from the fact that the Quaker organization was benevolent as well as religious. Penn's admonition to the Monthly Meetings "to supply the wants of the poor," and to care for "widows and orphans and such as are helpless,"[26] was so well heeded that need among the Friends was practically eliminated. George Keith says in his *Journal* that great sums were collected, not only for the Quaker poor, but as a means of winning converts from the indigent of other sects.

Money was contributed with a liberal hand to pay the expenses of travelling ministers, many of them pious and learned men from England, who exercised a powerful influence in solidifying the Society and inspiring the members. Since the Friends would have no "paid priests," as they called the ministers of other de-

[23]R. M. Jones, *The Quakers in the American Cols.*, p. 438.
[24]*Christian Advices* (Phila., 1808), pp. 45–47.
[25]William Penn, *Primitive Christianity Revived,* p. 64. [26]*Ibid.*, p. 65.

nominations, these visitors, who were always listened to with reverent attention, played a vital rôle in interpreting and defending Quaker tenets, answering criticisms and linking Meeting with Meeting, and province with province.[27]

The Meetings kept a strict eye upon the reading of the members, not only discouraging "the reading of plays, romances, novels and other pernicious books," but importing from England the works of eminent Quaker writers. Penn's *No Cross, No Crown,* Fox's *Journal,* Robert Barclay's *Apology* and similar writings served to fortify the faith of the Quakers themselves and to make new converts. If an Episcopalian or a Presbyterian had Quaker friends or relatives, he was apt to be plied with the *Apology,* which one critic termed the "glory and Alcoran" of the Friends.[28]

Thus were the ranks of the Quakers solidified into a well-disciplined phalanx. The strength imparted to some denominations by the hierarchy, or by a close alliance of Church and State, the Friends attained by other means, by a compact organization which extended its control over the thoughts, the lives, the education of the members. And in the hearts of all was constantly the thought that upon them depended the success of the Holy Experiment, the experiment which eventually was to transform the world.

No doubt many of the more thoughtful Quakers realized that not all the solidarity of their Society, not all their pride of accomplishment, not even their simple faith were enough to overcome the difficulties which lay ahead. With the control of a great and growing province entrusted to their hands, could the Quaker magistrates retain the old humility; with wealth increasing rapidly could the Quaker merchant refrain from luxury and ostentation; with broad frontiers open to the attacks of French and Indians and a broad river leading into the heart of the colony inviting hostile fleets, could the Assembly hold to its resolution not to arm the people?

Penn's colony had been in existence but a few decades when its rich soil and splendid facilities for trade began to expose the Society to the dangers of rapidly increasing wealth. Penn himself

[27] R. M. Jones, *The Quakers in the Amer. Cols.,* pp. 540–543. [28] *Ibid.,* pp. 544, 545.

could only guess at the potentialities of the vast domain to which his charter entitled him. And even though only the eastern fringe of the colony was settled in his day, he lived to see it surpass some of the older colonies in population and wealth. In the four years from 1681 to 1685 the population grew from 2000 to 7200; by 1700 it had doubled again; by 1740 it was exceeded only by that of Virginia, Massachusetts and Maryland.[29]

The settlers spread out over the agricultural lands of Chester, Bucks and Philadelphia Counties along the west bank of the Delaware River and up the Schuylkill and Brandywine, and in the "lower counties" comprising the present State of Delaware. With incredible swiftness trees were felled, crops laid out, houses, barns and fences built, and the wilderness converted into thriving farms. The soil was found to be excellent, not only for Indian corn but for wheat and other English grain, and for various kinds of fruits and vegetables. The reports of the settlers were enthusiastic. "Our lands have been grateful to us and have begun to reward our labors with abounding crops of corn," wrote one; "If God continues his blessing to us this province will be certainly the granery of the world," said another; it would gladden Penn's heart to see how the country was "becoming a fruitful field and a pleasant garden," said a third.

One writer became so enthusiastic that he expressed himself in verse:

> The fields, most beautiful, yield such crops of wheat,
> And other things most excellent to eat,
> As barley, rye, and other sorts of grain;
> In peace we plow, we sow, and reap again,
> Good Indian corn, which is a larger breed,
> It doth our cattle, swine and horses feed,
> Buck-wheat and oats, beside, good store of reed,
> A plentiful land, O plentiful indeed
> For plants, and roots, and herbs, wee'l let them be,
> To name the fruit that grows upon each tree:
> The fruit trees do flourish, and are green,
> Where apples, peaches, quinces, plums are seen."[30]

[29]S. G. Fisher, *Penna. Colony and Commonwealth,* p. 135.
[30]A. C. Myers, *Narratives of Early Penna.,* p. 301.

This rich land poured its bounty into Philadelphia. In late summer and early fall the river and bay were dotted with picturesque sails as the little wherries plied back and forth with their cargoes of farm products or European manufactured goods. Even the New Jersey trade, despite all efforts to develop Burlington into a great port, was in large part diverted to Philadelphia. The riverfront must have presented a busy scene indeed: here a 200-ton ship from London tied up at the Chestnut Street wharf while busy sailors unload boxes of cloth, hardware, and farm implements; here a brig just coming in from the West Indies with sugar, molasses and wine; here a swarm of wherries waiting to dispose of their barrels of wheat, flour or pork; there a Philadelphia-owned ship taking on staves, bread and beef for Jamaica or Barbados. In October, 1753, there were no less than 117 seagoing vessels in the harbor at one time. The vessels of overseas and inland commerce almost touched noses, for while the prows of brigs and ships came up within a few feet of the storehouses of Samuel Carpenter or William Fishbourn, Conestoga wagons in long lines were discharging the products of the German farms at the door.

By far the most important export was flour, but Indian corn, bread, staves, and iron were also shipped out in considerable quantities. "They send great quantities of corn (wheat) to Portugal and Spain, frequently selling their ships as well as cargo, and the produce of both is sent thence to England where it is laid out in goods and sent home to Pennsylvania," it was stated in 1731. "They trade to our provinces of New England, Virginia, Maryland, Carolina, and to all the islands of the West Indies (excepting the Spanish ones) as also to the Canaries, Madeira and the Azores Isles; likewise to Newfoundland for fish which they carry to Spain, Portugal and the Mediterranean. . . . Lastly, the Pennsylvanians build about 2000 tons of shipping a year for sale, over and above what they employ in their own trade, which may be about 6000 tons more."[31] One has only to select at random an issue of *The Gazette* to realize the extent of Philadelphia's trade. The number of March 16, 1758, shows incoming vessels

[31]*The Importance of the British Plantations in America.*

from Barbados, Antigua, Jamaica, Liverpool, North Carolina, South Carolina, London, Boston, New York and Saint Christopher.[32]

The quiet, simple Quakers, most of them from the humbler walks of life, suddenly found wealth dumped in their laps. The former Somerset yeoman now became a landed proprietor; the London clerk became a great merchant with a large storehouse on Front Street and perhaps a brig or two engaged in the West India trade. Men who had lived in frame cabins and had been content with pewter utensils and the plainest furniture now erected "stately piles of brick" and surrounded themselves with costly silver and Chippendale chairs and highboys.

The insidious effects of wealth in undermining the old Quaker spirit, if not Quaker principles, is interestingly described by John Smith, of Marlborough, writing in 1760. The Friends were originally "a plain lowly-minded people," he said, whose meetings were marked by "much tenderness and contrition." By 1720, however, "the Society increasing in wealth and in some degree conforming to the fashions of the world, true humility was less apparent, and their meetings in general were not so lively and edifying." In twenty more years "many of them were grown very rich, and many made a specious appearance in the world," so that "marks of outward wealth and greatness appeared in some in our meetings of ministers and elders." In fact "there had been a continual increase of such ways of life" until "weakness" and "barrenness overspread the Society."[33]

The Friends seem to have been fully aware of the danger, and tried to meet it by stiffening their warnings against pride and ostentation. "Our forefathers were drawn out of the vain fashions and customs of the world," they said. "If our youth and others should make light of that plainness of speech, apparel and furniture . . . they will find that so far as they embrace such vanities they weaken themselves in the practice of religious duties."[34] Yet many a good Quaker, despite an almost ostentatiously plain exterior, lived in a style which to visitors seemed luxurious. "This

[32] *Penna. Gazette*, Princeton University Library.
[33] R. M. Jones, *The Quakers in the Amer. Cols.*, p. 525.
[34] *Christian Advices*, pp. 75, 76.

plain Friend and his plain though pretty wife, with her Thees and Thous had provided us the most costly entertainment," a guest of Miers Fisher tells us, "ducks, hams, chickens, beef, pig, tarts, creams, custards, jellies, fools, trifles, floating islands, beer, porter, punch, wine, and a long etc." We know that many Quakers entered fully into the gayety and enjoyment of life in Philadelphia. "Hiltzheimer's horse-racing, fox-hunting, punch-drinking and city-governing friends were three fourths of them Quakers; all of them were substantial citizens."[35] So early as 1724 Christopher Sauer noted the change. "According to appearances plainness is vanishing pretty much," he said. "The dear old folks, most of whom are dead by this time, may have spoken to their children a good deal about plainness. It is still noticeable in the clothes except that the material is very costly, or is even velvet."[36]

In the quarter of a century from 1750 to 1775, Philadelphia assumed an air of elegance which excited the admiration of visitors from other colonies and even from Europe and was the despair of old-line Quakers. Stately buildings arose in the public square, handsome homes of brick set off by marble appeared on the residential streets, and charming country seats in the suburbs. The traveller Burnaby as he approached the city found the whole country "covered with villas, gardens and luxuriant orchards."[37] Music and dancing were indulged in without qualms, while the city became famous for the sumptuousness of its dinners. Chastellux, who spent some time in Philadelphia during the Revolution, describes one of the assemblies or subscription balls. "At Philadelphia, as at London, Bath Spa, etc. there are places appropriated for the young people to dance in," or to "play at different games of cards. . . . A master of ceremonies presides at these methodical amusements." He presents to each dancer a billet which "decides the male or female partner for the whole evening. . . . These dances, like the toasts we drink at table, have some relation to politics: one is called the success of the campaign, another the defeat of Burgoyne."[38]

[35]S. G. Fisher, *Penna. Colony and Commonwealth,* p. 280.
[36]*Penna. Magazine,* Vol. XLV, pp. 252, 253.
[37]R. R. Wilson, *Burnaby's Travels through North America* (N. Y., 1904), p. 88.
[38]Marquis de Chastellux, *Travels in North America* (N. Y., 1827), p. 147.

"I have seen balls on the President's birthday where the splendor of the rooms and the variety and richness of the dresses do not suffer in comparsion with Europe," said the Duke de la Rochefoucault-Liancourt. Sturdy John Adams, while gaining confirmation from his visits to Philadelphia of his belief in the superiority of everything New England, was impressed by the elegance of the life around him. "Philadelphia, with all its trade and wealth and regularity, is not Boston," he jotted down in his *Diary*. "The morals of our people are much better; their manners are more polite and agreeable; they are purer English; our language is better, our taste is better, our persons are handsomer; our spirit is greater, our laws are wiser, our religion is superior, our education is better."[39] But when he dined at Cliveden he noted with admiration the "grand entry and stair-case," the "elegant and most magnificent chambers," and the rich furniture. Nor did his Puritan tastes keep him from enjoying the "flummery, jellies, sweetmeats of twenty sorts, trifles, whipped sillabubs, floating islands, fools, etc., and then a dessert of fruits, raisins, almonds, pears, peaches," with "wines most excellent and admirable."[40]

The Quaker who remained faithful to the precepts of Fox and Penn must have been shocked indeed when he met on the streets the Philadelphia fop described in an article in 1772. The "hair is loaded with powder and pomatum . . . the rest of it chiefly consists of French silk, gold lace, fringe, silk stockings, a hat and feather and sometimes a cockade, and then it is quite irresistible. White hands, a diamond ring, a snuff-box, a scented handkerchief, and a cane. Its employment is to present that snuff-box, to wield that cane, to show its white teeth in a perpetual grin, to say soft things in every sense of the word to ladies, to follow them everywhere like their shadow, and to fetch and carry like a spaniel."[41]

But for one fop of this kind the opulence of Philadelphia created scores of cultured, able men, whose beautiful houses and gardens, extensive libraries and interest in art, literature and

[39]*Works of John Adams,* C. F. Adams ed., Vol. II, p. 395. [40]*Ibid.,* p. 381.
[41]Scharf and Wescott, *Hist. of Phila.,* Vol. II, p. 889.

science excited the admiration of visitors. Typical of the wealthy gentlemen was James Logan, scholar, philosopher, man of affairs, Secretary of the province, Chief Justice, President of the Council. At Stenton, his country estate, he gathered a fine library, wrote books, studied botany and corresponded with learned men in Europe.[42] Isaac Norris, the Speaker of the Assembly, had at his home, Fairhill, a very extensive library, which he housed in an especial building in the garden. As Mrs. Deborah Logan tells us, it "was a most delightful retreat for contemplative study, the windows curtained with ivy, the sound of bees" coming in from the outside. Here he spent every moment which could be spared from public business.

The line drawn by the Quakers between practices to be forbidden by law and those to be opposed only by moral pressure was drawn arbitrarily. A theatrical play was a matter for the police; dancing and fencing only for admonition or reproach. When Thomas Kinnett advertised in 1746 that he was prepared "to teach the noble art of defense with small swords, and also dancing," the Friends were horrified. Yet they contented themselves with expressing their surprise at "his audacity and brazen impudence in giving these detestable vices those high encomiums." Despite all their efforts both seem to have gained in popularity. In January 1758 George Abington, "late from London," gave notice of his intention to open a dancing school,[43] while a few months later John Egerton, "master of arms" started "a school for the practice of the small sword" at Thomas Riche's store, on Water Street.[44] When Ludewig Kuhn opened a music school at the "sign of the Golden Rose," Third and Arch Streets, to teach the German flute and guitar,[45] he too was probably regarded by the Quakers as an evil influence.

Against the theatre the Quakers waged unrelenting war. It was enacted as a part of the Great Law of the colony in 1682 that "whoever shall introduce into this province or frequent such rude and riotous sports and practices as prizes, stage-plays, masques," shall suffer "imprisonment at hard labor" or "forfeit twenty shil-

[42]S. G. Fisher, *Penna. Colony and Commonwealth,* p. 132.
[43]*Penna. Gazette,* Jan. 12, 1758.
[44]*Ibid.,* Sept. 7, 1758.
[45]*Ibid.,* June 25, 1772.

lings." Although this law was vetoed by William and Mary it was re-enacted in 1696. In the end, however, after repeated efforts by Penn and the Assembly to ban the theatre, the British government made it clear that they would not tolerate this restriction upon "healthy and innocent diversions."[46] Nonetheless, within the bounds of the borough of Philadelphia plays were prohibited by the Quaker magistrates. When, in 1749, it was reported to the Common Council "that certain persons had lately taken upon them to act plays," the shocked city fathers "unanimously requested the magistrates to take the most effectual measures for the suppressing of this disorder."[47]

When, some years later, it was proposed to erect a permanent theatre, a site was selected on South Street just outside the city limits in order to escape the clutches of the Philadelphia authorities. Aroused by this bold move, various denominations, Presbyterians, Lutherans and Baptists as well as Quakers, protested vigorously. And although the theatre was built and plays presented, the good Quaker, whenever business took him in its vicinity, gazed upon it with sorrow and repulsion, as upon a jail or a brothel. A correspondent pointed out in *The Gazette* that Tertullian, St. Cyprian, St. Cyril and other fathers of the Christian Church had considered theatrical performances "corrupting to morals and an impediment to salvation."[48] "Philadelphus" ran a long series of letters in *The Chronicle* denouncing the drama for its "blasphemous speeches, wanton amours, profane jests and impure passions."[49] David Douglas, one of the actors, wrote *The Gazette,* protesting against the "torrent of incomprehensible abuse which has been of late so plentifully bestowed upon the theatre," and putting up a vigorous defense.[50]

There were many in Philadelphia to take his side and all the frowns of the pious, all the efforts for restrictive legislation could not keep the growing number of pleasure-loving people from attending the theatre. Hamlet, the Merchant of Venice, the Con-

[46]William S. Dye, "Penna. versus the Theatre," *Penna. Mag.,* Vol. 55, p. 350.

[47]Scharf and Wescott, *History of Phila.,* Vol. II, p. 865.

[48]*Penna. Gazette,* Feb. 5, 1767.

[49]Geo. C. Seilhamer, *Hist. of the Amer. Theatre,* Vol. I, p. 174.

[50]*Penna. Gazette,* March 5, 1767.

stant Couple, King Lear, the School for Lovers, the Lying Valet, She Stoops to Conquer, the Taming of the Shrew and many others appeared in rapid succession.[51] During the Revolution Congress passed an act to prohibit the "exhibition of shews, plays," etc., which was seconded by a Pennsylvania State law forbidding the erection of theatres or the production of "any tragedy, comedy or tragi-comedy, farce, interlude or other play."[52] Although the old stumbling block of the royal veto was now a thing of the past, the coming of peace brought a renewal of the conflict. The law was repeatedly evaded by the production of plays disguised as lectures, concerts or moral readings.[53] During the sessions of the Constitutional Convention Washington attended at least three musical comedies or farces.[54]

In 1788 the Quakers returned to the attack, pointing out to President Franklin that the government was "insulted by the open contravention of the law in the exhibition of stage plays, under whatever evasive name disguised."[55] Shortly after, when Hallam advertised a "lecture on Richard Plantagenet," the authorities seem to have moved against him, for the play was withdrawn. This brought on another wordy battle in the gazettes. The champions of the theatre protested against interference with the "right of every freeman to dispose of his time and money according to his own taste and disposition." Plays "are innocent, entertaining and instructive; those who think otherwise are at liberty to stay at home."

The answer of the anti-theatre party to this blast was a petition against repeal signed by no less than 4000 persons. Although many of these were said to be "school boys, bound servants, negroes, etc.," the Legislature was deeply impressed until a counter-petition with about 6000 names was presented. Convinced that numbers were on the side of the theatre, they passed an act in March, 1789, legalizing plays, and the century-old struggle was over.[56] A practice which William Penn had denounced as wicked

[51]*Penna. Gazette,* see advertisements.
[52]*Statutes at Large of Penna.,* 1682–1801, Vol. XII, pp. 313–322.
[53]Arthur Hornblow, *A Hist. of the Theatre in Amer.,* Vol. I, p. 174.
[54]*Penna. Magazine,* Vol. 55, p. 363.
[55]*Penna. Archives,* Vol. XI, p. 342. [56]*Ibid.,* p. 368.

and immoral, from this date was not only permitted by law, but sanctioned by a majority of the population in the city where he had hoped that Quaker principles would be upheld for all time as an example to a sinful world.

Thus not only did the growth of "worldliness" defile the Quaker city and corrupt many of the Quakers themselves, but it placed the Society of Friends in a defensive position which restricted its influence and curtailed its growth. It forced upon them the adoption and strict observance of rules of conduct which tended to mere formalism. It caused them to draw a sharp line between their own members and the unregenerate of the world, to insist more firmly upon Quaker dress, language, customs, to repudiate those who married outside the fold. The Pilgrim fathers left Holland for America in part to avoid contamination from the religious beliefs of the surrounding population; the Friends now found themselves in the midst of worldly influences in the community which they themselves had founded.

The adoption of this defensive policy against worldly contamination caused the Society to sacrifice aggressiveness and growth for purity. With the political control of Pennsylvania largely in their hands, with a wealthy membership and overflowing treasury, the Society might have opened a missionary campaign especially on the frontiers which would have expanded their influence indefinitely. But efforts of this kind came almost to a complete stop; the energies of the Society were spent in warning and encouraging the members to be faithful; the ministers from England confined their visits chiefly to the old congregations.[57]

Their growth was retarded also by their educational policies. The New England Puritans, the Anglicans of Virginia, the Presbyterians, the Dutch Reformed all recognized the need of institutions of higher learning where young men could be educated for the ministry or for other forms of leadership. But the Friends, who had no established ministry, placed the emphasis upon secondary rather than higher education. As for their visiting ministers, it was a widely accepted view that their spiritual insight

[57]A. C. and R. H. Thomas, *Hist. of Soc. of Friends in Amer.*, The Amer. Church Series, Vol. XII, p. 239.

and power would be diminished rather than heightened by scholarship. It was more than two centuries after the founding of Harvard and a century and a half after the founding of William and Mary, that the first Quaker college in America opened its doors.[58]

George Fox seems to have understood the value of higher learning and urged the founding of institutions for the teaching of "everything civil and useful in creation." But he failed to press the point, his followers were convinced that colleges were unnecessary and so the Quaker youths found themselves cut off from cultural opportunities. In time the Society had good reason to regret this narrow policy, for it weakened their leadership and placed them at a disadvantage with other groups.

On the other hand, the Friends always placed great emphasis upon secondary education. One of the first laws of the province required parents to provide instruction for their children in reading and writing "so that they may be able to read the Scriptures," and at the age of twelve to begin their preparation for "some useful trade or skill."[59] Hardly had the first foundations been laid in Philadelphia when Governor and Council erected a large schoolhouse and employed Enoch Flower as teacher, allowing him "for boarding a scholar, that is to say, dyet, washing, lodging and schooling, ten pounds for one whole year."[60] Such immediate success attended the venture that three years later children were enrolled, not only from several neighboring provinces, but from far-off Barbados.[61]

Before the end of the century there were several schools in Philadelphia,[62] but it was the famous William Penn Charter school which the Quakers controlled and to which they sent their children. It was run at the "costs and charges of the people of God called Quakers, but was open to all, the rich at reasonable rates and the poor . . . for nothing."[63] The firebrand George Keith, who was made master, found his duties uncongenial and after the first year resigned. Thomas Makin, who succeeded him,

[58]Isaac Sharpless, *A Quaker Experiment in Govt.*, p. 36.
[59]Isaac Sharpless, *A Quaker Experiment in Govt.*, p. 37.
[60]*Colonial Records*, Vol. I, p. 91.
[61]*Penna. Magazine*, Vol. 49, p. 121.
[62]*Narratives of Early Penna.*, p. 331.
[63]*Colonial Records*, Vol. I, p. 532.

described as "a good Latinist," continued for many years to wield the ferrule, his career ending suddenly in 1733 when he fell from a wharf while stooping to get a bucket of water and was drowned.[64] Other Meetings followed the example of Philadelphia, so that it became a rarity to find an illiterate Quaker, even in the more thinly settled districts.

On the other hand, with the passing of the first generation, there were few really well-educated men among the Friends. The sons of the settlers, having no local college to serve them, engrossed with developing their farms or expanding their business, cut off in part from England, had few cultural interests. With the exception of the visiting ministers, James Logan and Henry Brooke long stood almost alone among the Quakers as men of learning. This was especially damaging to the Society since Penn's insistence upon freedom of religion and thought brought to Philadelphia a group of men of great intellectual activity. One looks in vain for a spiritual leader among the Quakers comparable to Cotton Mather or Jonathan Edwards among the Congregationalists, Theodorus J. Frelinghuysen among the Dutch Reformed, Gilbert Tennent among the Presbyterians, or James Blair among the Anglicans.

At last, during the Revolution, when there was an awakening to the situation, the opportunity for the Society to win its rightful place in the civilization of America had passed. And even at that late date conservatism was not lightly to be overcome. No one seemed capable of breaking away from the ideal of a "guarded education," with its plan for handing on "safe ideas" at the expense of constructive thought and intellectual curiosity. It was the kind of conservatism which Rufus M. Jones illustrates by an incident in a Philadelphia Quaker meeting. A liberal spirit tried to introduce a slight innovation. As he pleaded with eloquence and with vivid illustrations not a face changed; all was peace, patience and resignation. And when he had concluded the clerk arose and said: "The interruption having ceased, we will now proceed with the business."[65] For a group such as this the

[64]F. Watson, *Annals of Phila. and Penna.*, Vol. I, p. 287.
[65]R. M. Jones, *The Trail of Life in College*, p. 117.

founding of a liberal college was a radical step indeed, so radical that a full half-century more was to elapse before the first real steps were taken.

Even then it required a blow which shook the Society to its foundations. One of the most eloquent and forceful Quaker preachers of the early national period was the Long Island carpenter, Elias Hicks. Addressing immense audiences in various parts of the country, he placed such emphasis upon the inner light as to minimize the importance of the historic Christ or even to question his divinity.[66] When these doctrines were condemned by the more conservative group, the Society, in 1827 and the years immediately following, was split into two separate bodies, the so-called Hicksites and Orthodox. The latter group, convinced that the neglect of higher education was in part responsible for this breach, founded the Friends' Central school, where Quaker youths were to receive "an education equal in all respects to that which can be obtained at college."[67] It was only in 1856, however, a century and three-quarters after the founding of Philadelphia, that the school expanded into Haverford College, and the traditional educational policy of the Quakers was reversed.

In the meanwhile Philadelphia had become one of the chief cultural centers of the colonies, largely through the efforts of the non-Quaker groups—the Anglicans, Presbyterians, Lutherans. Here was established the American Philosophical Society, here the University of Pennsylvania, here the famous Carpenters Company, here lived Benjamin Franklin, David Rittenhouse, Benjamin Rush, Thomas Godfrey, John Dickinson, Andrew Hamilton, Charles Wilson Peale, Gilbert Stuart, William Smith, Trench Cox and many others distinguished in science, art and letters. While within the meeting house an atmosphere of conservatism prevailed, without was stirring the spirit of inquiry, of artistic appreciation, of intellectual curiosity.

The city had not completed its first half century when Franklin organized a group of friends into the Junto,[68] or club for "mutual improvement." Their meetings on Friday evenings, perhaps at a

[66] *Dictionary of American Biography,* Vol. IX, p. 6.

[67] P. C. Garrett (ed.), *Hist. of Haverford College,* p. 56.

[68] 1727.

tavern, perhaps at the home of one of the members, must have presented a picturesque and lively scene. We may imagine them seated around a table, with their mugs of beer and their pipes, arguing over the nature of "vapors," or the dangers of fiat money, or whether sound is "an entity or a body." Here is the youthful Franklin, here the surveyor Nicholas Scull, here the joiner William Maugridge, here William Parsons, the shoemaker who took up mathematics as an approach to astrology, here Thomas Godfrey the inventor of the quadrant. At times arguments must have become heated, for a rule was made banning "expressions of positiveness" or contradictions, and when Godfrey "expected universal precision in everything" or kept "distinguishing upon trifles," the club quietly let him withdraw.[69]

Out of the Junto grew the American Philosophical Society, the oldest scientific body on the Western Hemisphere and patterned after the Royal Society of London, whose example they considered it an "honor to follow." But though humbly content to emulate the scientist of the mother country, the founders struck a distinctly American note when they declared it their intention to inquire into the resources of the country in order to promote production. At the same time, they gave their attention to "other useful subjects, either in physics, mechanics, astronomy, mathematics, etc.," in order to encourage inquiries and experiments and to honor those who made them.[70]

The founding of the Society created great interest, not only in Philadelphia but throughout the colonies and in England itself. The list of names included so many prominent Philadelphians that it "read like a social register" of the city, while distinguished men from Nova Scotia to Antigua were proud to join as nonresident members. Among the officers in 1770 and 1771 were Benjamin Franklin, Doctor Thomas Bond, Philip Syng, Provost William Smith, Doctor Benjamin Rush, Owen Biddle, and David Rittenhouse. The day had passed when leading colonists were occupied only with pushing out the borders of civilization into the wilderness; they were now seeking to contribute their

[69]John Bigelow, *Works of Benj. Franklin* (N. Y., 1888), Vol. I, pp. 142, 143, 152.
[70]Amer. Philosophical Soc., *Transactions,* Vol. I, pp. xv–xix.

share to the development of civilization itself. Philadelphia had become a center of scientific interest and experimentation, a minor center it is true, but nonetheless one of which young America had reason to be proud.[71]

Here Franklin made his famous experiments with the Leyden jar which covered all the "essential phenomena of the condenser," here he demonstrated that lightning is electrical, here David Rittenhouse observed the transit of Venus with instruments some of which were of his own construction, here he made the famous orrery for Princeton College. In the *Transactions* of the Philosophical Society appeared articles on vine culture and wine-making in America; on the "fly-weevil that destroys the wheat," by Colonel Landon Carter, of Virginia; on the native silk-worm, by Moses Bartram; on the climatic changes of the Middle Colonies; on a "Machine for Pumping Vessels at Sea;" on canals in Pennsylvania and Maryland.[72] When the news of Franklin's brilliant discoveries crossed the Atlantic Europe awoke to the fact that the colonies had produced a scientist of the first caliber.[73]

As Franklin was the real founder of the American Philosophical Society, so was he the father of the University of Pennsylvania. In 1749 he published in his *Pennsylvania Gazette* the prospectus of his plan for the higher education of youth. "In the settling of new countries, the first care . . . must be to . . . secure the necessaries of life," he wrote, "this engrosses their attention and affords them little time to think of anything further. . . . Agriculture and mechanic arts were of the most immediate importance; the culture of minds by the finer arts and sciences was necessarily postponed to times of more wealth and leisure. Since these times are come . . . it is thought a proposal for establishing an Academy in this province will not now be deemed unseasonable." This appeal met with a hearty response and the work was taken in hand by twenty-four trustees, men of influence and distinction, most of them members of the Episcopal Church.

Taking over the charter and building of a Charity School

[71] *Ibid.*, pp. xiii, xxii. [72] Amer. Philosophical Soc., *Transactions*, Vol. I.
[73] Fred. E. Brasch, in *The Scientific Monthly*, Vol. XXXIII, pp. 336–355, 448–469.

which had been authorized in 1740 but never put into operation, they opened school in 1751. Four years later, with Doctor William Smith as Provost, regular college courses were inaugurated.[74] The institution from the first exercised a profound influence upon the life and thought of Philadelphia and the Middle Colonies, its graduates taking a leading part in many fields of activity. It had the honor of establishing the first American chair of botany and natural history, of initiating the first systematic instruction in medicine, and the first law school.[75]

It must not be assumed that the Quakers as individuals had no share in the intellectual movement which brought such distinction to Philadelphia. John Bartram, the botanist, Thomas Godfrey, the inventor of the quadrant, John Dickinson, famous for his *Farmer's Letters,* Benjamin West, the painter, were Quakers.[76] But the inspiration came from other groups.[77] Long before the Quakers had relinquished their political control in Pennsylvania, the intellectual leadership in the city of Penn itself had fallen into the hands of rival sects, especially of the Episcopalians. While Franklin and his circle were attracting wide attention by their achievements in science, art, education, architecture and the artistic crafts, the Quakers as a body retired more and more within themselves as a "peculiar people," whose purpose it was to avoid contamination and to preserve the truth in the midst of a wicked and perverse world.

But they retained a firm control in political matters throughout the colonial period, despite the vigorous attempts of other groups to loosen it. The Friends always remembered that Pennsylvania had been founded by their great leader as a Quaker Utopia, where their ideals in both religion and government were to be maintained forever. But they had to battle unceasingly against the attacks of other groups, for some of their beliefs made them especially vulnerable. Was it right that a sect which refused to protect the province from foreign enemies should dominate the government, their opponents asked? Should they be entrusted to ad-

[74]C. W. Dulles, in Univ. of Penna. *Medical Bulletin,* Dec., 1904, pp. 14, 15.

[75]H. M. Lippincott, *The Univ. of Penna.* (Phila., 1919), pp. 31, 45.

[76]S. G. Fisher, *The Quaker Colonies* (New Haven, 1919), pp. 58, 59, 60.

[77]R. M. Jones, *The Quakers in the Amer. Cols.,* p. 494.

minister important offices or act as judges, when they refused to take oaths?

The colony was still in the pioneer stage when Penn's charter was threatened by the intrigues and complaints of a faction headed by that habitual trouble-maker Colonel Robert Quarry, judge of the Admiralty court, and John Moore, the Admiralty advocate. Acting as the mouthpiece of the Anglicans and other non-Quaker groups, Quarry poured complaints into the ears of the Board of Trade. The Quakers had harbored pirates, he said, had winked at open violation of the Navigation Acts, had provided no military defense even in times of war, were administering justice through officials who had not been sworn. Prudence and sound policy alike dictated that the government should be taken out of the hands of such men and placed directly under the Crown.

But Quarry did not reckon on the astuteness and the ability to strike swift and telling blows hidden beneath Penn's placid exterior. The Proprietor, when he returned to Pennsylvania in 1699, found Quarry in the midst of a violent altercation with some of the local justices concerning the jurisdiction of the Admiralty court. Penn pretended to side with the Judge, suspended the chief offenders and promised to do all in his power to uphold the Court in suppressing illegal trade and piracy. In fact, he showed such seeming eagerness not only to cooperate with Quarry but to be guided by him, that the Judge was lulled into a false sense of security.[78]

While in this state of mind he made a blunder which delivered him into Penn's hands. Quarry and his officers seized a ship, the *Providence,* upon some slight irregularity in the registry, expecting that Penn would take his third of the prize-money which the law allowed him. But the Proprietor at once returned the money to the owners, telling them that he would not take advantage of a mere oversight, and advising them to buy off Quarry for £200. Having taken care to place the evidence of this affair in the hands of the Board of Trade, he proceeded to open every gun

[78]Scharf and Wescott, *History of Phila.,* Vol. I, pp. 168, 169; *Penna. Archives,* Vol. I, pp. 131, et sec.

in his battery upon the unsuspecting Judge. In personal letters to Chief Justice Holt, Lord Somers, Lord Romney and the Lords of the Admiralty, he poured out his complaints and accusations. "If it were worth while at first to erect a Court of Admiralty in America," he said, "it would be for the King's service to have experienced officers in it," but those now in Pennsylvania greatly discourage trade, "four ships having gone to other ports that were bound hither, by which I lost £50 and the country £100 by each." Quarry often condemned vessels unjustly merely to get his fee, trying to silence him with his "third." "I am too far off to make trips to Whitehall, otherwise Westminster, the Parliament, etc., should have rung of it as well as the Exchange." These bitter attacks proved successful, Quarry was removed and his place filled by Roger Mompesson, Penn's own selection.[79]

Although Penn triumphed in this matter, his accumulating troubles, mounting debts, imprisonment, the intrigues of his enemies, the apparent ingratitude of the colonists, in the end wore down his resolution. He himself proposed to escape from the whole perplexing question by giving up his charter and selling his rights to the Crown. Fortunately for the Quakers and for Pennsylvania illness prevented, and after his death, when his estates and franchises became very valuable, his family clung to them tenaciously. But later, when the Penns deserted the Society of Friends to join the Church of England, party alignments in Pennsylvania shifted to keep step. Although the Quakers continued to control the Assembly, most of the administrative offices were turned over to the Anglicans. This accentuated the differences between the people and the proprietors, evident even in William Penn's day, and lent bitterness to the incessant quarrels over taxing the proprietors' estates, the oath for judges and officers, the colonial militia, war subsidies and the control of the purse. So far had the Quakers become estranged from the Penns before the end of the colonial period that the Assembly itself started a movement to change Pennsylvania into a royal province, and, in 1764, sent Franklin to England to push the matter with the government.

[79] Scharf and Wescott, *Hist. of Phila.*, Vol. I, pp. 168, 181.

Yet with the increasing ascendency of the Assembly in the colonial government the importance of the defection of the Penn family gradually diminished. The Quakers proved not one whit behind the Virginians or the New Englanders in the art of cajoling, threatening, starving their governors. By withholding appropriations for military purposes or even for the governor's salary, they whittled down the executive power and converted Pennsylvania into a little republic, in local affairs largely independent of England and the proprietors alike. And in this republic the Quakers continued to rule, despite many attacks on their power, until the collapse of the old order in the maelstrom of the American Revolution.

The chief source of concern to the Friends was the rapid increase of the non-Quaker population. If the time should come when they were outvoted in the Assembly the Holy Experiment would be at an end. Penn himself so early as 1700 expressed concern because the "church party" had "three of the five counties," the Territories as Delaware was then called being largely non-Quaker. With the separation of Delaware in 1702, the predominance of the Friends in Pennsylvania was restored. But their own liberal policy, both in the matter of religion and civil liberty, together with the growing prosperity of the province brought the problem back in a more perplexing form than ever. Immigrants began to pour in—persecuted Mennonites from Switzerland and the Palatinate, German Lutherans, Reformed and Dunkers; Scotch-Irish Presbyterians fleeing the oppressions of the English government in Ulster; sailors, day laborers, artisans flocking to Philadelphia in search of work. In 1702 James Logan estimated that only one-third of the population of the city was Quaker, although in Philadelphia County the Friends had a large majority. As the immigrants continued to pour in, passing on to the frontier counties, the proportion of non-Quakers in the province as a whole grew larger and larger until at the conclusion of the French and Indian War it was estimated at eight to one.[80]

In the face of this discrepancy the Friends kept their grip upon

[80] R. M. Jones, *The Quakers in the Amer. Cols.*, p. 524. Franklin estimated the non-Quakers as three to one.

the Assembly by the compactness and efficiency of their organization, by the support of a large part of the Germans, by restricting the franchise and by limiting the number of representatives from the newly settled districts. From the first the Quakers showed an aptitude for politics. During the first thirty years, when their hold on the Assembly was almost undisputed, they often divided into factions, and made such an ado over unessential points that Penn advised them not to be so "governmentish." As their majority in the province dwindled they laid aside their factional differences and organized themselves into a smoothly running political machine.[81] It was said by opposing groups that every Quaker meeting was turned into a political caucus, where candidates were nominated and policies decided upon, but this the Friends emphatically denied. "We have as a religious society ever carefully avoided admitting matters immediately relating to civil government into our deliberations," they said. But whether their political planning was done in the meeting or out, it was so effective their enemies declared that "they have got the political reins into their hands and tamely tyrannize over the good people of this province."[82]

The Quaker leaders early saw the necessity of taking some measures to hold their ascendency in Philadelphia. The growing city was an attractive place for seamen, servants, small shop-keepers, carpenters, bricklayers, tailors, cabinet-makers and other craftsmen. As "the trade of the city much increased there was full employment for laboring people and others in low circumstances, of whom a great number, both from Europe and most parts of America flocked to the city and suburbs."[83] Some were drawn into the Quaker fold, especially through the various Quaker charities, but most of them remained a hostile and at times bitterly dissatisfied element.

To withhold from this group all participation in the government it was only necessary to place a high property qualification on the franchise. So a clause was inserted in the Frame of Gov-

[81] Isaac Sharpless, *Quakerism and Politics,* p. 85.
[82] *Penna. Archives,* Eighth Series, Vol. VII, pp. 5758, 5760.
[83] *Ibid.,* p. 5830.

ernment making the right to vote contingent on the ownership of £50 "lawful money" or fifty acres of land.[84] This was comparatively low for the country districts where the Friends were strong in numbers, but so high for the city that none but the well-to-do could meet it. It has been estimated that in the farming districts one person in ten had the right to vote and in Philadelphia only one in fifty.[85] No doubt many Quakers in the city were disfranchised along with the mass of people of other faiths, but so many others had acquired property that the law operated to their advantage.

Had the Friends used their power in the city merely to uphold the principles upon which the colony was founded, there would have been some justification for this undemocratic system. But there were at times loud complaints that they controlled legislation and trade with an eye to their own economic interests, and the hatred against them flared up in election riots when the lower and middle classes backed up their wishes with sticks and stones rather than with the forbidden ballot. It was well enough for the ruling class to denounce them as an "outrageous multitude," who by "rude and disorderly behavior" disturbed the elections; we see them today as sturdy Englishmen taking the most ready method to demand their rights.[86] Their day was to come with the Revolution, when by uniting their cause with the cause of independence, they secured a more democratic régime in Pennsylvania.

The Quakers met the menace of the newcomers who were filling up the "west" by the simple expedient of withholding from them their proportionate share of representation in the Assembly. There was an obvious reluctance to admit new counties even in the German districts, and the number of representatives from each was narrowly limited. By 1752 Lancaster, York, Cumberland, Berks and Northampton had been admitted with a total of ten seats as compared with twenty-four for Chester, Bucks and Philadelphia, the Quaker counties, and two for Philadelphia city.[87] We need no further explanation of the fact that in 1755

[84] F. N. Thorpe, *Federal and State Constitutions*, Vol. V, p. 3071.
[85] J. Paul Selsam, *The Penna. Constitution of 1776*, p. 33.
[86] A. E. McKinley, *The Suffrage Franchise in the Thirteen Eng. Cols.*, p. 284.
[87] J. P. Selsam, *The Penna. Const. of 1776*, pp. 34, 35.

twenty-eight of the thirty-six members were Quakers.[88] The injustice of this "rotten borough" system is revealed by the fact that in 1760 the five new counties, with more than half the taxables in the colony, had less than a third of the representatives.[89]

The situation was made the more acute by religious, racial and economic differences. Much of the new region was inhabited by Scotch-Irish Presbyterians who regarded the Quakers as dangerous fanatics, and were in turn heartily disliked as Calvinists who were of the same stamp as the New England Puritans who had whipped and hanged Quakers in the seventeenth century. Moreover, the trade connections of the Susquehanna valley with Maryland tended to weaken the economic tie with eastern Pennsylvania and so to render political bondage all the more galling.[90] The troubles of the French and Indian War, when the frontier counties complained bitterly of Quaker pacifism and unfitness to govern, was but one phase of a political struggle which lasted half a century. "Why should we be taxed for many thousands of pounds by the Assembly," the westerners complained, "to be spent at the dictation of a Quaker minority maintained in power through unjust means?" "What lies at the bottom of all their grievances, and must be complained of as the source of all their suffering, is their not being fairly represented in the Assembly," stated a petition in 1764 from "upwards of twelve hundred inhabitants" of Cumberland County. But their pleadings were in vain. It is true the Assembly admitted three more counties in 1771, 1772 and 1773, but with a total of only five representatives, so that when the old charter government fell, the members from the Quaker districts outnumbered those from the non-Quaker counties by twenty-six to fifteen.

With the Germans and Swiss the Quakers had very little trouble. The industrious peasants and craftsmen from the Palatinate, Alsace or Baden had never participated in governmental affairs at home, and had little inclination to do so in Pennsylvania. Accustomed to persecution and oppression, they considered them-

[88] *Penna. Magazine,* Vol. X, p. 291.
[89] J. P. Selsam, *The Penna. Const. of 1776,* p. 36.
[90] C. H. Lincoln, *The Revolutionary Movement in Penna.* (Phila., 1901), p. 40.

selves fortunate indeed to have found a land where their earnings were not confiscated and their worship was undisturbed. For the Quakers, who had invited them to share the country, they had a lively sense of gratitude which they habitually expressed at the polls. There would seem to be little reason to accept the accusation of Governor George Thomas that the Quakers held the German vote by their opposition to a militia law which would drag them from their farms for drilling and work on fortifications.[91]

The most vulnerable point in the Quaker armor was their opposition to war. It was one thing for a religious society to forbid its members to bear arms, it was a far more serious matter when that society was the ruling power in a great province and tried to shape its policies in conformity with their views. How could they keep Pennsylvania in peace when the British government declared war? How could they refuse to take measures of defense with French and Spanish privateers making captures in the Delaware Bay? How could they withhold appropriations for troops, arms, ammunition and forts, with the Indian warwhoop resounding along the frontiers? The Friends in the Assembly found these questions hard to answer, so hard that it led them into evasions or to compromising with their convictions. On one occasion they caused a number to withdraw from public life.

The great bugbear of requests from the Crown for subsidies for war purposes recurred as often as England became embroiled with other nations. So early as 1693 Governor Fletcher suggested the way out. "If there be any amongst you that scruple the giving of money to support war," he told the Assembly, "there are a great many other charges in that government . . . your money shall be converted to these uses and shall not be dipped in blood."[92] It was not long after this that the Assembly solemnly voted £300 "for the relief of the distressed Indians" of the Six Nations, although they were fully aware that "relief" was to take the form of bullets and other war supplies.[93]

Franklin was a frequent witness of the embarrassment of the

[91]S. G. Fisher, *Penna. Colony and Commonwealth,* pp. 91, 92.
[92]*Colonial Records of Penna.,* Vol. I, p. 361.
[93]A. C. Applegarth, *Quakers in Penna.,* p. 42.

Quaker majority on these occasions. "They were unwilling to offend the government on the one hand, by a direct refusal, and their friends, the body of the Quakers, on the other, by a compliance contrary to their principles; using a variety of evasions to avoid complying, and modes of disguising the compliance, when it became unavoidable. The common mode at last was to grant money under the phrase of its being for the King's use and never to inquire how it was applied."[94] In 1745, when the Assembly was asked to aid the expedition against Louisburg, they voted £4000 "to be expended in the purchase of bread, beef, pork, flour, wheat or other grain."[95] When Governor Thomas was told of this he remarked: "I understand very well their meaning; other grain is gunpowder."[96]

On the other hand, the Friends sometimes remained adamant even in the face of threats and dangers. In 1706, Governor John Evans, who wished to secure authorization to organize a body of militia, attempted to bring them over to this measure by a rather stupid hoax. Believing that the Quakers would yield could it be demonstrated that they would rush to arms like other people when their lives and property were endangered, he instructed a messenger to rush into the crowd assembled for the annual fair with the news that French warships were moving upon the city. A panic ensued. Valuables were thrown into wells, small river boats rushed to cover up the creeks, large vessels took refuge at Burlington. But the Quakers as a whole were calm, many of them attending their religious meeting, only four with arms, and the result of the farce was to strengthen them in their opposition, and to bring discredit on the governor.[97]

With the advent of the war with Spain in 1739 the old question of aid once more came up. The Quakers made their position clear. We "do not (as the world is now circumstanced) condemn the use of arms in others, yet are principled against it" ourselves. Those who wish to fight have "an equal right to liberty of conscience with others." Therefore they would not consent to a com-

[94] John Bigelow, *Works of Benj. Franklin,* Vol. I, p. 220.
[95] S. G. Fisher, *Penna. Colony and Commonwealth,* p. 95.
[96] John Bigelow, *Works of Benj. Franklin,* Vol. I, p. 221.
[97] S. G. Fisher, *Penna. Colony and Commonwealth,* pp. 43–45.

pulsory militia law, but did not oppose those who wished to organize voluntary companies.[98] Five years later, when France had joined Spain against England, Franklin actually recruited 1200 men with the tacit approval of the Assembly. "These all furnished themselves as soon as they could with arms, formed themselves into companies and regiments, chose their own officers and met every week to be instructed in the manual exercise."[99] In this matter the Assembly was much in the position of the Quaker boat captain who, when he was being crowded out from a place at the wharf, called to his mate in despair, "Thee will have to come here and use some of thy language."

But the crucial test came with the French and Indian War. The Quakers prided themselves upon their Indian policy. While other colonies had cheated the Indians, robbed them of their lands, debauched them with rum, made treaties only to break them, waged wars of extermination, the Friends had shown fairness and kindness. Penn's famous treaty, supposed to have been signed under the great elm at Philadelphia, was adhered to faithfully both in letter and in spirit. "This was the only treaty between these people and the Christians that was not ratified by an oath and that was never broken," wrote Voltaire. On their part the Indians loved and revered Penn, carried out their obligations, and looked upon the Quakers as their allies and protectors. It seemed a conclusive answer to those who said that the Quaker policy of amity and peace was impractical.

But matters assumed a different aspect when some of the immigrants, tempted by the fertility of the soil, began clearing land and erecting their cabins on tracts belonging to the Indians. The proprietors tried to buy the land as fast as it was settled, but the complaints of the Indians grew louder and louder. The situation was aggravated when, in 1737, by the fraudulent Walking Purchase the proprietors got title to a vast tract in the Minisink region north of the Lehigh River. When the Delawares who lived there refused to leave, the Six Nations were bribed with a present of £300 to drive them off. This they did with threats and insults which sank deep into the hearts of the Delawares, and brought

[98]*Ibid.*, p. 88. [99]John Bigelow, *Works of Benj. Franklin*, Vol. I, p. 214.

them back later, tomahawk in hand, to seek revenge upon both the Six Nations and the whites. When this was followed by a purchase at the Albany Conference of 1754 of vast areas west of the Susquehanna, in which the tribes concerned were not even consulted, the situation reached the breaking point.

This favorable moment was selected by the French to occupy the Ohio valley and to incite the Indians against the English. George Crogham, the Indian trader, urged the Assembly to build a fort at the forks of the Ohio, but the Quakers not only refused, but would do nothing to aid Washington when Virginia undertook the work. Aroused at last to the gravity of the situation, they would have voted funds to aid Braddock's expedition, had not an inopportune controversy with Governor Morris over constitutional rights interfered. Franklin was sent out to procure wagons and pack-horses which proved invaluable, but in the battle which opened the Pennsylvania frontier to the Indian terror there were no Pennsylvania troops to fight beside the British and the Virginians. It is true that had Colonel Dunbar, who succeeded Braddock, not fallen back to Philadelphia leaving the frontiers exposed, disaster might still have been averted. But the Scotch-Irish frontiersmen, who were exposed to the fury of the Indian raids, laid the blame upon the Quaker Assembly.

The outlying farms were widely scattered and quite unprotected—a rude log cabin in a small clearing, a patch of corn or vegetables, the dense forest but a few steps from the door. To the pioneer and his family, who had dreamed of creating here happiness and plenty, they proved death-traps. Over and over the same scene was enacted. The stealthy approach of the Indians, a sudden shot, the warwhoop, the braining of the wife and children, the cabin in flames, and then silence and desolation as the savages disappeared in the forest with four or five fresh scalps hanging from their belts.[100] As the news of these horrors spread throughout the settlements the people fled eastward, crowding every road and trail in a frantic effort to escape, until whole sections had been deserted.

And on all sides, from the Germans on the exposed northern

[100] S. G. Fisher, *Penna. Colony and Commonwealth,* pp. 162, 163.

frontier as well as from the Scotch-Irish, came urgent appeals to the Assembly for protection. Why did they not vote money for arms and ammunition, why not erect forts to which the people could flee, why not organize expeditions to invade the Indian country? Could it be that the Quakers, because of their principles of non-resistance, would do nothing to protect the people from butchery? The mutilated bodies of one family were packed in a wagon, exhibited in the streets of Philadelphia and finally laid out in front of the State House. Four hundred Germans marched on the city, crowded into the Assembly hall, talked face to face with the members and with rough bluntness demanded protection.

The Quakers themselves were now thoroughly aroused to the necessity of vigorous measures. Although their supply bills were repeatedly vetoed because they would not exempt the proprietary estates from taxation, they voted in all no less than £218,567 sterling, to carry on the war, built a series of forts over a two-hundred-mile front and provided them with garrisons, sent expeditions into the Indian country and tried to draw off the Delawares and Shawnees with a separate treaty. But all this was done with much sorrow and heart-burning, and only after nine of the stricter Quakers had resigned from the Assembly. With the coming of peace the Friends still retained their ascendency in the government, but with shaken confidence and diminished prestige.

But the severest test of their principles was still to come. Immediately after the Treaty of Paris the remarkable chieftain Pontiac, realizing that the advance of the English was rapidly dispossessing the Indians of their lands, organized the tribes from Lake Ontario to Georgia for a concerted effort to drive the white men into the ocean. Once more the warwhoop resounded on the frontier, the old sickening story of killings and burnings was told again, once more the people fled eastward in droves. Fort after fort fell before the Indian attacks, Le Boeuf, Venango, St. Joseph's, Miamis. Only a remarkable victory in a forest battle at Bushy Run, in August, 1763, won by the courageous and able Colonel Henry Bouquet, saved Fort Pitt itself.

The Scotch-Irish, urged on by their ministers, sought to revenge themselves on the Conestogas, the degenerate remnants of Penn's old friends and allies, now quite harmless and under the protection of the whites. Accepting literally the words of the Bible directing the faithful to smite the enemies of the Lord, a party, known as Paxton Boys, fell on a small group of Conestogas and cut them to pieces. The action of the Assembly in bringing to Philadelphia a number of Moravian Indians aroused the frontiersmen to fury. A band, estimated at from 500 to 1500, seized their rifles and set out for Philadelphia bent not only on putting an end to the poor Indians, but on bringing forcibly to the attention of the Assembly their many grievances.

For once the Quakers were thoroughly aroused. The dreaded Calvinists were upon them determined on blood and perhaps revolution. The Indian quarters were fortified, companies of foot and cavalry were organized, staid Quakers went through the streets with muskets in their hands.[101] When an alarm was sounded in the dead of the night the bells were rung, the houses lit up, and the people, seizing their arms, rushed into the street. Fortunately it proved to be only a party of Germans marching in from the country to assist their Quaker friends. As it turned out the backwoodsmen got no farther than Germantown, contenting themselves with a memorial demanding the removal of the Moravian Indians, a bounty on Indian scalps and a juster system of representation.

But bitterness long rankled in the breasts of the Scotch-Irish. The iniquity and hypocrisy of the Quakers were discussed in many an humble home and denounced from the pulpit of every log church in the frontier region. One backwoodsman put his thoughts into verse: Go on, good Quakers, he said:

> "Encourage ev'ry friendly savage,
> To murder, burn, destroy and ravage;
> Of Scotch and Irish let them kill
> As many thousands as they will
> That you may lord it o'er the land,
> And have the whole and sole command."[102]

[101]Hist. Soc. of Penna., *Collections,* Vol. I, p. 75.

[102]S. G. Fisher, *Penna. Colony and Commonwealth,* p. 249.

The time was not far distant when the Scotch-Irish, in concert with the Philadelphia populace and other discontented elements, were to overthrow forever the Quaker ascendency. No one in Pennsylvania suspected when the Sugar Act and the Stamp Act were passed, that these measures were the prelude, not only to independence but to a political revolution within the colony itself. The Quaker merchants, their trade with the foreign West Indies crippled, were among the first to protest and fifty of them signed the non-importation agreement.[103] Taxation of the colonies by Parliament threatened to undermine all the rights and liberties won by the Quaker Assembly during eight decades of political strife, and so long as resistance was confined to protests and peaceful coercion, they were foremost in the American cause.

But when matters took a more serious turn they began to draw back. The Quaker merchants of Philadelphia, like the merchants of other ports, shrank from a war which would drive their ships from the ocean and bring desolation to their wharves and warehouses. The Society as a whole now as always opposed armed resistance and pleaded for patience and compromise. Moreover, when they realized that independence would entail the overthrow of the provincial charter, and with it their own traditional ascendency, they became thoroughly alarmed. After all the rule of the British government, however reactionary, was better than handing over the province to Scotch-Irish Presbyterians and the Philadelphia populace.

The turn affairs were taking became apparent when Paul Revere arrived in Philadelphia in May, 1774, to plead with the Pennsylvanians to join in measures of resistance to the Boston Port Bill.[104] The popular party wished to give assurances of full sympathy to the Bostonians, the Quakers and other conservatives were for proceeding cautiously. A public meeting at the City Tavern expressed its sympathy with the people of Boston who were "suffering in the general cause," but a committee of the Assembly wrote somewhat coolly advising them to seek redress only through constitutional means. This in turn was offset by a

[103] R. M. Jones, *The Quakers in the Amer. Cols.*, p. 560.
[104] S. G. Fisher, *Penna. Colony and Commonwealth*, pp. 296, 297.

spontaneous demonstration on the day the Port Bill went into effect. "If we except the Friends, I believe nine-tenths of the citizens shut up their houses," wrote one observer. "The bells were rang muffled all day, and the ships in the port had their colors half hoisted."[105] A few days later 8000 persons gathered in the State House yard, and passed resolutions declaring the Port Bill unconstitutional and calling for a Continental Congress.[106]

The meetings of Congress at Philadelphia influenced the local situation profoundly, for the Pennsylvania liberals were encouraged by the presence and counsel of men of like views, while the Quakers, or Broad-brims, as John Adams called them, realized that they were in conflict with a movement continental in scope. If Congress led the colonies into war and perhaps independence Pennsylvania might find it difficult to hold back. The uneasiness of the Friends was increased by the growing power of the local committees of correspondence and the voluntary formation of armed bands, or Associators. With arms in the hands of the mechanics and artisans of Philadelphia and the discontented frontiersmen, the old régime had every reason for apprehension.

In this crisis the Assembly made wide concessions in the hope of stemming the tide. They ignored the Tory governor, John Penn, in passing laws, appropriated large sums for the defense of the province and added no less than seventeen new members. But this was offset by their instructions to the Pennsylvania delegation in Congress to oppose independence. "We strictly enjoin you that you, in behalf of the colony, dissent from and utterly reject any propositions . . . that may cause or lead to a separation from the mother country, or a change of the form of this government." "My God," exclaimed Charles Lee, "why does not your whole province arouse themselves, kick the Assembly from the seat of representation which they so horribly disgrace and set 'em to work German Town stockings for the army—an employment manly enough for 'em."[107]

[105]Peter Force, *American Archives,* Fourth Series, Vol. I, p. 365.
[106]J. P. Selsam, *The Penna. Const. of 1776,* p. 55.
[107]N. Y. Hist. Soc. *Collections,* "Lee Papers," Vol. I, p. 227.

Arouse themselves the Pennsylvanians did, but not until Congress itself had given them the cue. On May 15, 1776, a resolution was passed aimed especially at the Pennsylvania Assembly, recommending the overthrow of the royal and charter governments and the setting up of state constitutions under the authority of the people. The news of this important step spread like wildfire throughout the city and the province and at once became the subject of excited discussion in every coffee-house and tavern. The conservatives were dismayed. "I think the Assembly of this province will not consent to change their constitution," said James Allen, "and then heigh for a convention. A convention chosen by the people will consist of the most fiery Independents; they will have the whole executive and legislative authority in their hands."[108]

This prediction proved correct. On May 20, several thousand people assembled in the rain in the State House yard, and cheered lustily when the Resolution of May 15 was read. They then proceeded to vote resolutions of their own: that the Assembly was no longer competent to the exigences of affairs, and that "a provincial convention ought to be chosen by the people, for the express purpose of carrying the said resolve of Congress into execution."[109] Although the gazettes were filled with the protests of the conservatives, and an Address and Remonstrance, signed by 6000 people, demanded the continuance of their "birthright in the charter and wise laws of Pennsylvania," the liberals proceeded enthusiastically with this plan.

In the meanwhile the dying Assembly met once more in an attempt to maintain its authority. It probably was already too late to stem the tide of revolution even had it directed the Pennsylvania delegates in Congress to vote for independence and entered with a whole heart into the war. But they were not ready to go so far. All they would do was to rescind the instructions requiring the delegates to vote against independence, thus leaving them free to use their own judgment. Thereupon the ultra-Whigs ceased to attend, so that the Speaker was unable to

[108] *Penna. Magazine*, Vol. IX, p. 187.
[109] *Penna. Gazette*, May 22, 1776.

command a quorum. A rump continued to meet from time to time until September 30, when it quietly passed out of existence.[110]

On June 18, a Provincial Conference, representing the city and county committees, met in Carpenters Hall to prepare for the constitutional convention. With one brief resolution it swept the old rotten borough system into the discard, declaring that in "any question which may come before them the city and counties respectively have one vote."[111] With the franchise they were equally thorough. It was resolved that every Associator who paid either provincial or county taxes "should be admitted to vote for members of the convention." Having thus increased their own strength by many thousands of votes, they proceeded to weaken the conservatives by imposing a severe test oath or affirmation repudiating allegiance to George III.[112] It remained only for the convention, which opened its sessions in the West Room of the State House on July 15, to crown the work thus started and Quaker ascendency in Pennsylvania was at an end.

As one reviews the history of Penn's Holy Experiment he is tempted to compare it with the so-called Wilderness Zion of the Massachusetts Puritans. The two had many things in common. In Massachusetts as in Pennsylvania the civil government worked hand in hand with the Church, enacting into law many of its tenets and carrying out its policies; both demanded a severe code of moral conduct, although the Puritans were stricter than the Quakers in enforcing it; both suffered from interference by the British government; both were influenced profoundly by conditions in the New World; both had to meet the problem of newcomers unsympathetic with their purposes.

On the other hand, there were marked differences. The Wilderness Zion lasted nearly two centuries, the Holy Experiment practically came to an end in less than one; in Massachusetts heretics were ejected or if they insisted on remaining severely persecuted, Pennsylvania decreed religious freedom; the Puritans

110 *Votes and Proceedings of the House of Reps.*, etc., Vol. VI, p. 764.
111 *Penna. Archives*, Second Series, Vol. III, pp. 635–637.
112 *Ibid.*, p. 640.

believed it God's will that they should smite His enemies or the enemies of His Church, the Quakers emphasized peace and love for all mankind.

In each case, however, the causes of ultimate failure were similar. Even though each experiment entailed the segregating of men of like faith in a distant wilderness, in part at least to protect them from contact with error, in neither was even partial isolation attained. New England was inhospitable enough to newcomers, even to the Scotch-Irish Presbyterians, but the Puritan traders who visited every port from Virginia to Bristol and from Spain to Jamaica, could not help knowing and perhaps respecting the views of various nationalities and faiths. The Quakers, their province invaded by thousands of Lutherans, Reformed, Anglicans, Presbyterians, were early put on the defensive.

Both Puritans and Quakers found their severe moral codes a source of weakness, for it was difficult to uphold them in the face of human inclinations, especially after the passing of the first generation. It was comparatively easy for the persecuted Quaker or Congregationalist in England to live a life of austerity, for they were fired with the spirit of the zealot, felt themselves to be the discoverers of fundamental truth; but their sons, prosperous, protected, members of the ruling class, succumbed more easily to worldly temptations.

At first view the imprint of the Holy Experiment upon American civilization would seem to be small. Whereas the Wilderness Zion sent out its hordes to New York, New Jersey, northern Pennsylvania and the Great Lakes, the Friends failed to reach out even into western Pennsylvania. Their Society, because of its policy of defense rather than aggression, failed to become one of the great American denominations, numbering in 1926 but slightly over one hundred thousand as compared with the millions of Roman Catholics, Methodists, Baptists, Presbyterians.

Yet who can say that the Holy Experiment was a failure? Were William Penn to return to Philadelphia he would be perplexed at the towering skyscrapers, the bustling throngs in the streets, the thundering trains of the elevated; he would grieve at the boisterous crowds at Sunday baseball games, at the theatres, perhaps even at the art galleries and scientific museums; but he would find at least something in the spirit of the people—their freedom from religious hatreds and persecutions, their hospitals and correctional institutions, the absence of slavery—in keeping with his own views and with the hopes he entertained when he began his great venture two and a half centuries ago.

Chapter VII

THE QUAKER SPIRIT IN BRICK AND STONE

IN THE closing decades of the seventeenth century architecture in the older colonies had gotten out of step with developments in England. While Inigo Jones, Sir Christopher Wren, Sir Roger Pratt and other great architects were remodelling the mother country in the school of the Renaissance, the Virginians and New Englanders continued in the medieval tradition. Before William Penn plotted out the squares and streets of the city of Brotherly Love there stood few if any Renaissance buildings in all the region from Maine to South Carolina. But the Quakers were unacquainted with Virginia or Massachusetts and could not draw architectural inspiration from them. They came direct from England, most of them, and as a matter of course built their city in conformity with the English standards of their day. Philadelphia from the first was a Renaissance city.

The greatest influence upon urban architecture in England at the time of the Quaker migration was the rebuilding of London. Prior to the great fire of 1666 the city had been medieval, a maze of half-timbered houses, built in a network of narrow crooked streets and lanes. But when the flames had swept over this combustible mass, leaving blackened ruins and ashes, the city was rebuilt of brick in conformity with Renaissance ideas. In 1667 was passed the London Rebuilding Act, which by its restrictions and specifications brought a uniformity hitherto unknown, and gave birth to a new English urban architecture.[1]

The act recognized four types of houses, of two, three and four stories and "four story houses of the greatest bigness," classified according to by-lanes, streets and lanes of note, high and principal streets.[2] There were tables for each type which prescribed the thickness of walls, height of ceilings, size of beams and even

[1] Walter G. Bell, *The Great Fire of London*, pp. 290, 291. [2] *Ibid.*, p. 251.

exterior details. For houses on high streets two balconies were required "four feet broad, with rails and bars of iron," between them a "pent-house of the breadth of the balcony to be covered with lead, slate or tile."[3] So along Thames Street, Cannon, Cheapside and St. Michael's Lane appeared long rows of brick houses, their signs swinging over the footways, with decorated doorways, shop windows on the ground floor and casement windows above, here and there an iron balcony or a pent roof, all with roofs sloping back from the street.[4] It was a picturesque London, this new London of Wren and Webb, and totally different from the city to which Charles II had returned from his exile only six years before the fire (Plate 14).

The fame of the rebuilt city filled England. To the people of that day the new architecture seemed a tremendous advance, not only in safety and convenience but in beauty and correctness of design. So the builders who went over to Penn's new colony on the Delaware imitated it so far as local conditions permitted, in almost every detail. The houses of Philadelphia are "of brick, generally three stories high after the mode in London," wrote Gabriel Thomas in 1698.[5] "John Day (has built) a good house, after the London fashion, most of brick, with a large frame of wood in the front for shop windows," Robert Turner stated in 1685.[6] Along High Street, Second and Front arose one substantial house after another, some two, some three stories high, with iron balconies, pent roofs and casement windows (Plate 15).

Some of the houses were of timber, for wood was plentiful and cheap and the need of quick construction urgent. In one instance a log house was built in Chester County, floated up the river, and put up in Philadelphia.[7] It is probable that this was not the only log house in the city, for the Quaker immigrants when they first landed must have pressed into service some of the near-by Swedes to put up temporary shelters. The first Anglican church in Philadelphia, built in 1695, was a wooden structure with typically Swedish lines, erected no doubt by some of the Swedish members

[3]*Ibid.*, p. 291. [4]John Stow, *A Survey of the Cities of London and Westminster.*
[5]A. C. Myers, *Narratives of Early Pennsylvania*, p. 317.
[6]*Ibid.*, p. 271. [7]J. F. Watson, *Annals of Philadelphia*, pp. 150, 151.

Plate 14. LONDON, RESTORED AFTER THE FIRE OF 1666

Plate 15. HIGH STREET, PHILADELPHIA, IN 1799

PLATE 16. DUNSTER, ENGLAND, SHOWING PENTROOF

PLATE 17. *Left:* Wynnestey, Philadelphia, showing pentroof and door hood. *Right:* Eagle house, Germantown

PLATE 18. LETITIA HOUSE, PHILADELPHIA

of the congregation.[8] In a few cases the more permanent houses were "first framed of heavy timber and filled with bricks," the beams being concealed and showing only as lintels or as door and window frames."[9] The usual practice, however, was to build entirely of brick. So early as 1685 Robert Turner wrote that many were following his example in using brick and that some "that built wooden houses are sorry for it." It is as cheap to build of brick, he continued, since more brick makers have fallen in, and now "many brave brick houses are going up." The presence of limestone in abundance made it unnecessary to resort to oyster shells in making mortar.[10]

The business streets of early Philadelphia were closely built up. The visitor to the city as his boat came up the river and made fast to the wharf at the foot of Market Street, looked out on a mass of mercantile houses which must have reminded him of Thames Street, London. He saw the same regular brick fronts, the same shop windows with their little panes, the same swinging signs, iron balconies, simple cornices, gently sloping roofs pierced here and there by dormers, picturesque chimney-pots, stone posts separating the footpath from the roadway.[11]

From the first almost every Philadelphia house had its balcony[12] where it was the custom for the family to gather on hot summer evenings to catch every breath of air and to view the stream of passers-by in the street below. Watson tells us that the balconies "were a part of the social system of our forefathers."[13] In time most of them disappeared, some because they had become unsafe, others because the tenements to which they were attached had been pulled down to make room for warehouses. The roof balcony which became popular in mid-century, tended more to seclusion than the old type and afforded a wider prospect.

The most characteristic and interesting feature of Philadelphia architecture was the penthouse or roofed projection between the upper and lower tiers of windows. Sometimes it was found only

[8]H. M. Lippincott, *Early Philadelphia*, pp. 68, 69.
[9]J. F. Watson, *Annals of Philadelphia*, pp. 138 ff.
[10]A. C. Myers, *Narratives of Early Pennsylvania*, pp. 269, 271.
[11]See Birch Engravings.
[12]*Ibid.*, p. 271.
[13]J. F. Watson, *Annals of Philadelphia*, p. 217.

in the front, sometimes on three sides, sometimes on the gable ends as a continuation of the cornice. It seems to have been almost universal from the first, for we find it on the oldest houses—the Merion Meeting House, the London Coffee House, the Penny Pot House, etc. Although its popularity declined with the advent of the more ornate architecture of the mid-eighteenth century, it was by no means discarded. We glimpse many examples in a view of the market in the *Columbia Magazine* of 1787, in the famous Birch engravings and in numerous drawings and photographs made in the nineteenth century. Appearing frequently with the pent roof was the door hood, in some cases as a shed sloping away from the door, in others as a gable perhaps superimposed on the pent roof. Together these two interesting features are the distinguishing marks of early Quaker architecture (Plate 17).

Certain writers have assumed that the pent roof and the hood are German in origin and that the Philadelphia carpenters borrowed them from Germantown. But the hood is almost unknown in Germany while the pent roof of the middle Rhine provinces does not resemble that of Pennsylvania.[14] The Quaker builders did not have to borrow either the pent roof or the hood since they were well acquainted with both in England. As we have seen, the pent roof was common in the restored London, in some cases actually being required by law, and one might have seen examples so late as 1796 on the old buildings in Butchers' Row near Temple Bar.[15] It was common also in parts of Somerset and Devon, as some of the quaint old houses of Looe, Dunster and Exeter testify[16] (Plate 16).

Among the Quakers who founded Philadelphia were several men of means, who built substantial residences comparable in beauty and charm to those of the Virginia planters or the New England merchants. Their excellent proportions are explained by the presence in the city of James Porteus, a trained British architect. Porteus is said to have been a native of Dumfries, who

[14]H. Rebensburg, *Das Deutsche Dorf,* Plate 63.

[15]*Select Views of London* (London, 1804), Vol. I, Plate 18.

[16]Britton and Brayley, *Beauties of England and Wales,* Vol. IV; J. Crocker, *Sketches of Old Exeter.*

had lived in London before coming to Pennsylvania.[17] It was he who designed the residence of Samuel Carpenter at the corner of Second Street and Norris Alley known as the Slate Roof House, and famous as the abode of William Penn when he visited the town in 1699.[18] Built in the style of the E-shaped Tudor manor, with central pavilion and two projecting wings, it resembled the Lewis Burwell house in Virginia.

Equally conspicuous in the skyline of early Philadelphia were the Thomas Fairman house, built beside the Delaware almost in the shadow of the famous Penn treaty elm;[19] the Edward Shippen house, its great size and ornateness lending an atmosphere of elegance and luxury; the Joshua Carpenter house, conspicuous for its heavy cornice and pent roof; the famous London Coffee House at High and Second Streets, "where politicians, wits, military officers and merchants" met to discuss over their cups of coffee the latest news of war or politics or Court;[20] the Cross Keys Inn, the Dunlap house, the Anthony Benszet house.

These pretentious houses stood out, however, from the mass of humbler homes. The charming Letitia house, which has been restored and moved to the right bank of the Schuylkill in Fairmont Park, seems to have been typical of the homes of the smaller merchants, skilled artisans and professional men. As one views its simple lines, its lack of ostentation, the gleaming white of window and door frames, the solidity of the brick-work, the plainness of cornice and pent roof it seems to breathe the very spirit of Quakerism. It is easy to people in imagination the streets of a town made up of such little gems as this, with men in simple clothes and broad-brimmed hats who greet each other soberly with "thee" and "thou" as they go about their daily tasks (Plate 18).

It was the Letitia house, rather than the Slate Roof house or the Shippen house, which set the style for the region tributary to the Quaker capital. In the rural districts, where there was no reason to economize on building space, the houses usually had a wider frontage, but in other respects they adhered closely to

17He is said to have come under terms of indenture.
18Thompson Wescott, *The Historic Mansions of Philadelphia,* p. 43.
19H. M. Lippincott, *Early Philadelphia,* p. 58.
20Sherman Day, *Historical Collections,* p. 572.

the Philadelphia model. There is the same regularity in window spacing, the same wooden shutters, the same pent roof and door hood, the same roof lines, the same simple cornice, the same paucity of dormers, the same end chimneys. The building material differed according to locality, for the farmer could not afford to haul brick or stone long distances to the site he had chosen for his home. Where field stones or limestone quarries were close at hand he built of stone, where clay and lime were abundant, of brick. If we draw a line on the map from Princeton to Wilmington, we find that in the region east of it, including Philadelphia, both banks of the Delaware and southern New Jersey, the houses are generally of brick, whereas to the west they are almost invariably of stone. But differences in building material do not break the essential unity of the architecture on both sides of the line, do not conceal the fact that Washington's headquarters at Valley Forge, let us say, is merely a Letitia house in stone.

We find these quaint little homes in a radius of fifty miles of Philadelphia, perhaps nestling on the hillsides overlooking the Christiana River in Delaware, or on the marshy banks of Alloway creek in Salem County, New Jersey, or hidden far up some obscure lane in Burlington County. We trail them in the Oley valley, near Reading, or up the Schuylkill, or westward to Lancaster or even York. This uniformity no doubt was the result of the influence of the Quaker metropolis. Penn's land of promise drew settlers from many parts of England, so that there must have been widely divergent architectural traditions among the carpenters and masons scattered throughout the region. That the original tendency was toward diversity is indicated by the individual traits displayed in different localities, for instance by the brick diaper work in Salem. But the builder of New Castle, or Chester, or Burlington, or Reading, when he came to Philadelphia and viewed the latest styles in vogue there, could not resist the temptation to imitate them in his home town. So, just as England was the great source of architectural inspiration for the American colonies as a whole, Philadelphia fixed the styles for the region of which it was the economic and religious center.

Perhaps it was inevitable that the first place to feel the influence of the Philadelphia builders should be Germantown. No doubt there were carpenters and masons among the groups which came from Holland and Germany to the little settlement overlooking the Wissahickon, who thought only of erecting houses like those they were accustomed to in the homelands. But finding themselves in an English community and being unacquainted with conditions in Pennsylvania—the climate, building materials, etc., they turned to their friends the Quakers for guidance in architecture as in other matters.

The traveller who strolled through the quiet village in the early years of the eighteenth century was reminded not of Holland or Germany, but of England and especially of Philadelphia. Stretching out along one wide avenue was one little house after another, the Michlin-Sorber house, the Dannenhower house, the Christopher Sauer house, charming old Grumblethorpe, the Christian Lehman house and many others like them, all built of stone, two stories high, the gable ends at right angles to the street, the pent roof very prominent, the sashes of the windows divided into many tiny panes.[21] But the visitor would have noted that many of the doors were in upper and lower sections, in true German and Dutch style, that here and there were typical Dutch stoops where the owner sat in the evening smoking his pipe, and that many of the cellar windows were arched. Even though he were unacquainted with the history of the village, he might have guessed that he was in a community made up largely of Dutch and Germans who were rapidly being absorbed into the surrounding English population (Plate 17).

Turning south to the rolling hills and gentle valleys of Chester County, we constantly run upon the trail of Quaker architecture. Now it is a group of old houses in some secluded glen, now a lone farmhouse half hidden in a cluster of trees, now an inn beside the highway. There is no mistaking the familiar door hood, the pent roof between stories or as a continuation of the cornice, the gentle pitch of the roof, the position of the chimney. Only the rough stones of the walls woven into alligator skin

[21]Penna. German Society, *Proceedings*, Vol. XXIII.

patterns differentiate these houses from those of early Philadelphia, and lend a touch of individuality which is not lost even by an occasional coat of whitewash.[22] Chester is clearly the stone-house county, and when one runs upon a brick house, like the quaint old building on the Percy Chandler estate near Chadds Ford, or Primitive Hall, Chatham, he realizes that he is approaching the brick region of Delaware a few miles distant across the border.

But Delaware itself was not wedded to brick, for some of the old houses, near the famous arched boundary line are of stone, while at Lewes and elsewhere on the bay the almost universal use of shingles lends a New England flavor of salt water and fish. Yet diversity is what one would expect in a region where Swedes and Finns mingled with Dutch and Dutch with English. Nonetheless, in this medley of building materials and architectural traditions we detect the influence of Porteus and his fellow Philadelphia builders in the familiar pent roof, the simple interior woodwork, the fifteen light windows of old houses at Marshallton, Newport, Christiana and elsewhere.[23] Charming New Castle, nestling on the bank of the Delaware and long a center of Dutch and Swedish life, seems to have resisted the influence of Philadelphia during the first half of the century and to have succumbed only in the Georgian period. Strangely enough the early Delaware builders also turned their backs upon the striking houses of Salem across the river, some of them almost in sight of their workshops.

It is the unique character of the brickwork of the Salem houses which gives them such individuality and charm. The checkerboard effect which one notes everywhere in the country, produced by setting glazed headers in Flemish bond, is common enough in Maryland and Virginia, but the more intricate patterns can be matched nowhere else in America. One may surmise that a family of bricklayers trained in this kind of work, perhaps from one of the eastern shires of England, came to Salem where their zig-zags, diamonds, dates and initials worked into the gable ends

[22]Eleanor Raymond, *Early Domestic Architecture of Penna.*, Plates 34, 39, 57, 63, 69.
[23]Geo. F. Bennett, *Early Architecture of Delaware*, pp. 58, 59.

with vitrified brick, won them a reputation for skill and added distinction to the building.

No doubt they would have been surprised had they been told that many of their commonest patterns had been used in France in the late Middle Ages, and from there had made their way into England so early as the fifteenth century. Among the English buildings which furnish excellent examples are the Little Leez priory, Layer Marney Hall, and Sandon church, all in Essex. Diamond, zig-zag and checkerboard patterns predominate, their purple, blue or gray standing out in sharp contrast to the red background.[24]

The Salem County bricklayers not only used the old patterns but varied them with elaborate designs of their own. The Abel Nickolson house, Elsinboro, has the entire end covered with a diamond pattern with the date 1722 worked in under the gable (Plate 19); the William Hancock house, where a body of Americans were surprised and massacred by the British in March, 1778, is set off by a series of zig-zags surmounted by the initials W.S.H. and the date 1734. The John and Mary Dickinson house, Alloway township, and "Retreat," Pilesgrove township, are decorated with diamonds, triangles and ellipses[25] (Plate 20). Despite this unique brickwork, the old Salem houses, so far from escaping the influence of near-by Philadelphia to which the region was bound by close economic ties, are typical examples of Quaker architecture. Two stories high, wide of front, with interior end chimneys, pent roof in front but not at the ends, the door occasionally hooded, their kinship with the Letitia house, the Germantown houses and the Chester houses is obvious. One does not often run upon these old farmhouses by chance, for many of them are hidden up some secluded road or beside a creek once a by-lane of water transportation, but the motorist travelling north or south over the New Castle ferry would be richly repaid to pause long enough to hunt them out. He will find them not only distinc-

[24]Nathaniel Lloyd, *A History of English Brickwork*, pp. 129, 360, 437, 438.

[25]Joseph S. Sickler, *The Old Houses of Salem County* (Salem, N. J.). I am deeply indebted to Mr. Sickler for his courtesy in permitting me to make copies of several of the photographs reproduced in his book.

tive and interesting, but not less charming than the colonial cottages of Massachusetts or Maryland or Virginia.

Turning now to the Quaker meeting houses we find that their character was determined by Quakerism itself. They had to be like the people who worshipped in them, simple, unostentatious, devoid of ornament. For a meeting house to have stained glass windows, carved woodwork or candelabra would have been as improper as for the Quaker himself to wear a velvet coat and ruffled shirt, or for the Quakeress to bedeck herself with silks and jewelry. It was not enough to avoid all the features of the Roman Catholic or Anglican church building—the cruciform body, the buttresses, the spire, the altar, the choir, the figures of saints—it must not be a church at all. The Inner Light could manifest itself amid bare walls and plain benches as fully as in the magnificence of the medieval cathedral.

It was to be expected, then, that the meeting house should resemble a large dwelling house, built in the style which we have learned to associate with the early Philadelphia architects. Fortunately many have been preserved and the motorist runs upon them perhaps dominating a bit of rising ground, perhaps in the midst of a straggling village and set apart by an extensive church yard, perhaps half hidden in a grove of giant elms. We recognize them at a glance, for there is no mistaking the rectangular form, the roof which rises gently to a ridge without gambrel or hip, the single or double tiers of windows, the tiny panes, the shutters showing snow-white against the darker walls, the simple cornice extended across the gable ends, the pedimented hoods protruding out over the doors like old ladies' bonnets which have been set too far forward, the whole presenting a delightful picture of repose and simplicity.

The architecture of the meeting house was as unchanging as Quakerism itself. Although the early Friends probably had no intention of creating a distinct type when they planned their places of worship, once that type was clearly defined and had become hallowed by tradition, they clung to it with characteristic tenacity. The advent of the Georgian barely touched the meeting house, the classical revival came and went leaving it un-

PLATE 19.
ABEL NICKOLSON HOUSE, SALEM COUNTY, NEW JERSEY

ATE 20. JOHN AND MARY DICKINSON HOUSE

PLATE 21. BUCKINGHAM MEETING HOUSE

PLATE 22. CROSSWICKS MEETING HOUSE

PLATE 23. "OLD SWEDES," WILMINGTON

changed. The Providence meeting house at Media, built in 1814, differs in no essential detail from the one at Radnor erected in 1713. The pitch of the roof is not so steep, the hood is pedimented not sloping from the door, none of the windows is arched, yet one might step from one building into the other with no consciousness that they are separated by a full century.[26]

Nor does size any more than time destroy the unity existing between meeting houses. The tiny building at Odessa, Delaware, said to have been a station in the underground railway for runaway slaves, bears a striking resemblance to the rather extensive two-storied structure at Crosswicks; the little house at Chadds Ford is but the Buckingham meeting house at Lahaska, Pennsylvania, in miniature[27] (Plate 21). Stirring scenes took place around some of these old houses during the Revolution, and it must have grieved the peace-loving Quakers when a cannon ball struck the wall of the Crosswicks meeting house or when the floor of the Birmingham meeting house was stained with the blood of men wounded at the battle of the Brandywine[28] (Plate 22).

Since the Quakers turned their backs on the usual ecclesiastical architecture, it was left to the Swedes to build the first substantial real churches in the Delaware region. Holy Trinity, known as Old Swedes, erected at Wilmington in 1698–99, and Gloria Dei, put up a year later at Philadelphia, illustrate well the operation of the melting-pot (Plate 23). No doubt Eric Bjork, who came over to minister to the congregation at Wilmington, would have demanded a building in the Swedish style had he been able to secure the proper workmen, but when he was forced to employ men with such names as Joseph Yard, John Stuart, John Smart and John Harrison, he must have realized that it would be English in character, not Swedish.[29] The building, standing just on the line between the stone and brick regions, is of rough stone, whereas its sister church at Philadelphia is of brick. Fortunately both "Old Swedes" are standing, and one may see Holy Trinity

[26]Philip B. Wallace, *Colonial Churches and Meeting Houses,* pp. 119–126, 174, 175.
[27]B. J. Lossing, *Field Book of the Revolution,* Vol. II, p. 169. [28]*Ibid.,* pp. 12, 169.
[29]Geo. F. Bennett, *Early Architecture of Delaware,* pp. 23, 24.

from the Pennsylvania trains as they approach Wilmington from the north, the church yard holding the surrounding modern buildings at a sufficient distance to preserve the atmosphere of quiet dignity and repose.[30]

Gloria Dei is just as clearly English, the steep roof lines, the porches with pediment and pent roof, the quaint fenestration, the Flemish bond fitting perfectly into the Quaker architecture of the period[31] (Plate 24). Yet the rather squat, ornate pulpit, the baptismal font brought from Sweden, the two cherub heads on the organ loft and the rounded ceiling lend a touch of the Scandinavian. It is remarkable that the little structure should have such excellent proportions and perfection of detail in view of the fact that it was built in part by members of the congregation who contributed their labor in lieu of money, the minister himself serving as a hod carrier.[32] "Thus, with God's blessing we have completed the great work," wrote Mr. Bjork, "and built two fine churches superior to any built in this country . . . so that the English themselves, who now govern this province and are richer than we, wonder at what we have done."[33] It is indeed strange that the first churches on the Delaware in the English architectural style should have been erected for Swedish congregations probably none of whose members had ever seen an English church before save the little makeshift which was the forerunner of Christ Church.

A full decade was to pass before the Episcopal congregation at Oxford, north of Philadelphia, put up a building somewhat in the style of the Old Swedes. The steep roof lines, the porches, the quaint fenestration and the Flemish bond link it also with the small churches of Maryland and Virginia, while the bit of diaper work to the left of the west door leads to the surmise that the bricklayers may have been borrowed from Salem County.[34] St. David's church, Radnor, built in 1714, belongs to the same general class, although its rough stone walls, its very

30P. B. Wallace, *Colonial Churches and Meeting Houses,* p. 244.
31*Ibid.,* pp. 55–73.
32John F. Watson, *Annals of Philadelphia,* Vol. I, p. 148.
33Scharf and Wescott, *History of Philadelphia,* Vol. II, p. 1234.
34P. B. Wallace, *Colonial Churches and Meeting Houses,* pp. 74–77.

wide arched windows, its unique outside staircase to the gallery give it marked individuality.[35]

The history of early Quaker architecture is richly deserving of study, not only because it illustrates so well the principles of transit and development, but because it gives us an intimate insight into the lives, habits and thoughts of the people. Perhaps it is not too much to say that one cannot be thoroughly acquainted with the Quaker region which centered in Philadelphia until he knows its architecture. And though Philadelphia itself as Penn knew it has long ago vanished, in near-by Germantown and in the rural districts of the lower Delaware innumerable charming old houses remain to carry us back to the days of settlement. Those who take the trouble to hunt them out will be richly rewarded not only by the story they tell of a bygone age and of interesting men and events, but by their charm of proportion and detail.

Had Philadelphia been cut off completely from England the Quaker architecture might have persisted indefinitely, becoming more and more individual as local conditions brought modifications. But there was no interruption in the intercourse with the mother country. With the arrival of every ship from London the people scanned eagerly the gazettes and books it brought and questioned newcomers as to what was going on in England. Among the books consigned to the local dealers or to individual builders might be James Gibbs' *A Book of Architecture,* or Isaac Ware's *A Complete Body of Architecture,* or Abraham Swan's *The British Architect,* or Batty Langley's *City and Country Builder's and Workman's Treasury of Designs.* Even the most conservative architect after mulling over the designs in these volumes, must have had the urge to base his own work upon them. Even had he desired to cling to the old ideas his patrons would have deserted him for one versed in the new architectural fashions.

Not infrequently a builder or architect from the mother country would set up shop, announcing through the medium of the press that he was prepared to build "in the modern taste." Thus

[35] *Ibid.,* pp. 127–135.

Thomas Carstairs "architect and house carpenter, lately arrived in this city from London," informed the public that he intended "to follow his profession in all its various branches, being regularly bred to it, and well acquainted with all its modern improvements."[36] The native Philadelphia architect's only hope of competing with newcomers such as this was to make himself equally conversant with the English styles. We can imagine, then, with what assurance William Williams, "a native of this city," announced to his friends and the public "that having lately returned from London, where he has for some time studied architecture in its various branches, proposes carrying on the business of house carpentry."[37]

In this way the early Quaker architecture gradually fell under the spell of the Georgian. It must not be supposed that the Philadelphia builders of the mid-eighteenth century were slavish imitators, for their buildings express their own ideas both individually and as a group. Conforming strictly to the rules laid down in the English builders' guides, now and then even taking from them without modification a door or a dormer or a mantel or even an entire façade, they nonetheless established a distinct architecture of their own which we may call the Philadelphia Georgian. It bears always the stamp of its parentage and its kinship with the New England Georgian, the Maryland Georgian, the South Carolina Georgian, but it has its own individuality, is different from them all.

All important in fixing the character of Georgian architecture in the Philadelphia region was the Carpenters Company. This organization, founded in 1724 by the leading architects and builders of the city, was modelled upon The Worshipful Company of Carpenters of London. Among the original associates were James Porteus, Joseph Henmarsh, Samuel Powell, Jacob Usher, Edmund Woolley, John Harrison and Isaac Zane.[38] They put out a *Book of Prices,* so "that the workmen should have a fair recompense for their labour and the owners receive the worth of their money," stimulated the study of the best models, collected

[36]*Penna. Packet,* Feb. 5, 1784. [37]*Ibid.,* Jan. 4, 1773.

[38]Joseph Jackson, *Early Philadelphia Architects,* pp. 39, 40.

a fine architectural library, encouraged interchange of ideas and maintained high standards. In 1770 the Company set an excellent example by erecting for its own use the beautiful hall which four years later won fame as the meeting place of the First Continental Congress.[39]

The individuality of the Philadelphia Georgian does not lie in the outward form of the buildings. The counterpart of almost every church, public building or residence may be found in England or the other colonies. Christ Church is largely a replica of St. Andrew by the Wardrobe, charming Mount Pleasant reminds us of Eaton Hall and other English country residences, the George Read house, New Castle, would be quite at home among the Georgian houses of Alexandria, Virginia. But the architecture of the Philadelphia region has its own flavor because of the constant repetition of certain decorative details, the Doric doorway, the Palladian window, a distinctive mantel, a graceful dormer.

This uniformity was in part the result of the publication by the Carpenters Company of a *Manual* with plans, elevations, house-frames, roof-trusses, windows, transoms, doors, mantels, dormers. The little volume became the standard work for the entire region, and every carpenter from New Castle to Princeton must have carried a copy in his pocket. One has only to compare the *Manual* with the Georgian buildings within a fifty-mile radius of Philadelphia to appreciate the influence it exerted. The Doric doorway with simple pediment shown in the *Manual* (Fig. 15) appears with the addition of fluting in the columns in the front door of historic old Cliveden, with the substitution of Ionic capitals in Solitude, at Woodford, and with certain elaborations at Mount Pleasant. The mantel selected for publication in the *Manual* is strongly suggestive of the beautiful mantels at Belmont, the Powel house, Woodford, the Corbit house at Odessa, and elsewhere (Fig. 14). The pedimented dormers of the *Manual,* distinctive for their interlocking mullions within the rounded top and their flanking ornaments have their counterparts in innumerable old houses, the most perfect examples perhaps being

[39]Horace M. Lippincott, *Early Philadelphia,* pp. 331–335.

those at Cliveden, Mount Pleasant and the Corbit house (Plate 27).

The Carpenters Company was largely responsible, also, for the development of a group of architects second to none in the colonies. Most of them were members of the Company itself, others were influential amateurs whose interest in architecture it stimulated and guided. It was an efficient combination, this teamwork of professional and amateur. It required the vision, good taste and political influence of Attorney General Andrew Hamilton to plan the group of public buildings in the civic center of Philadelphia, the technical skill of Robert Smith, Edward Woolley and other professionals to give them perfection of detail.

FIGURE 14. MANTEL FROM MANUAL OF CARPENTERS COMPANY

Equally fortunate was the association of Doctor John Kearsley,[40] a practising physician, and a professional builder, apparently John Harrison,[41] in the erection of beautiful Christ Church (Plate 24). Although the exterior is very similar to St. Andrew by the Wardrobe and although numerous details are taken from English books of architecture, the building has a character, a charm of its own. The well-balanced tower, topped by a graceful steeple,[42] the Palladian window, the elaborate cornice, the arched windows set with small panes, the roof balustrade topped by urns, the brick pilasters, the east pediment, the interior with its

[40]Dr. Kearsley's obituary notice stated that "he was well acquainted with the principles of architecture, a monument of which we have in Christ Church." P. B. Wallace, *Colonial Churches and Meeting Houses,* p. x.

[41]Joseph Jackson, *Early Philadelphia Architects,* p. 42.

[42]Said to have been added by Robert Smith.

PLATE 24. *Left:* "Gloria Dei," Philadelphia. *Center:* St. Peter's, Philadelphia. *Right:* Christ Church, Philadelphia

rich Georgian detail—fluted columns, delicately carved pulpit and reading desk, the fan light over the gallery door—combine to make an architectural gem of which any city might be proud. Doctor Kearsley, although he complains that he "toiled hard, neglected his own business and received no recompense but calumny and ill-treatment," had the satisfaction of producing perhaps the most exquisite building in the colonies. That the congregation eventually appreciated his great efforts is shown by a vote of the vestry for "forty pounds for a piece of plate, as a lasting memorial of his services."[43]

FIGURE 15. DOOR—FROM MANUAL OF CARPENTERS COMPANY

It might have been expected that Christ Church, because of its influential congregation and its perfection of form and detail, would have served as a model for other churches in the surrounding region. But the congregations in small towns and in the rural districts could not make the necessary outlay for so elaborate a structure, while in England, to which the colonial builders looked for inspiration in ecclesiastical as in domestic architecture, the Wren type of church was going out of style. On the other hand, the tower of Christ Church seems to have been widely imitated with very happy effect—in Trinity Lutheran church, Lancaster,[44] the German Reformed church, York,[45] and elsewhere. In many cases the tower was omitted, in others builders departed from the accepted standards with unhappy results, as in the overgrown tower of St. Peter's, Philadelphia, and the ill-proportioned tower and box-like cupola of Trinity, Swedesboro.

[43]Scharf and Wescott, *History of Philadelphia,* Vol. II, p. 1344.
[44]Built in 1761. [45]Built in 1799.

The accepted model of the church body seems to have come directly from England. One finds it so early as 1745 in St. James', Lancaster, and it persisted into the nineteenth century as is evidenced by St. Michael's, Strasburg; it occurs not only in Episcopal and Lutheran churches, but in Presbyterian and even Baptist churches. Perhaps the widest known example is St. Peter's, Philadelphia, designed by Robert Smith and completed in 1761 (Plate 24). The simple rectangular body of this building, the low roof, gable end set off by a circular window and a continuation of the cornice, Palladian window at one end, two doors on each side and two tiers of arched windows are repeated over and over in churches throughout the lower Delaware region.[46] The Philadelphia Georgian church lacks the simplicity and plainness of the Quaker meeting house, the ornateness of the Wren model, the grace of the Gothic church, but its excellent proportions set off by a few classic details give it an atmosphere of dignfied repose.

It might have been anticipated that a city which possessed so able a group of architects as were gathered within the Carpenters Company would have a group of public buildings second to none in the colonies. But it was an amateur, Attorney General Andrew Hamilton, who conceived the idea of a civic center, who had the influence, persistence and private resources to carry it through, and the good taste to select a beautiful design, perhaps actually to draw it himself. Out of his own pocket he not only paid for the completion of the State House, afterwards known as Independence Hall, when the funds appropriated proved insufficient, but purchased the adjacent properties on which Congress Hall and the City Hall were later erected.[47] It was by the narrowest margin that his plan was accepted, for Doctor Kearsley, who was on the building committee with him, came forward with a design of his own which was rejected by the casting vote of the third member. One wishes that Kearsley's drawings had come down to us so that we could know what manner of building the architect of Christ Church had in mind for the structure which fate

[46]P. B. Wallace, *Colonial Churches and Meeting Houses*, pp. 31–54.
[47]Joseph Jackson, *Early Philadelphia Architects*, pp. 58, 59.

had decreed should be the cradle of American independence. Long before the work was completed Hamilton, disgusted with Kearsley's opposition, with labor troubles and "the unjust reproaches of malicious persons," requested the Assembly to "discharge him from having any further concern" with it. Fortunately the legislators refused to do so, and Hamilton brought to completion the building which became as he had predicted "a credit to the whole province."[48]

Independence Hall consists of a large central building and tower to which open arched loggias connect two small hip-roofed wings (Plate 25). The architecture conforms neither to the early Quaker nor the Philadelphia Georgian schools, lacking the pent roof, the door hood and other features of the former, as well as the distinctive ornateness of the latter. But the long sweep of the two rows of windows each with twenty-four little panes and topped by flat brick arches, the simple almost plain door, the marble quoins, horizontal bands and oblong slabs of the street front, the balustraded roof flanked by large arched chimney stacks combine to give an impression of balance, dignity and repose.[49] The tower, which was completed in 1751, sixteen years later than the building itself, is Philadelphia Georgian, the Doric door, the Palladian window, the Ionic pilasters of the second and third sections, the Corinthian pilasters of the wooden superstructure, the octagonal arched belfry all link it with the work of Robert Smith and his associates.[50]

Perhaps the tower would seem too large were it not for the fact that it dominates not only Independence Hall, but the entire civic group. Congress Hall, which flanks Independence Hall on the right, with its arched windows, its classic doors, its pedimented front, its cupola, is clearly of the Philadelphia Georgian school. It is balanced on the left by the City Hall, finished in 1791, which conforms to the same style. That the civic group harmonized so perfectly was not a fortunate stroke of chance, but the result of Hamilton's foresight. When he conveyed the

[48]Scharf and Wescott, *History of Philadelphia,* Vol. III, p. 1733.

[49]Cousins and Riley, *The Colonial Architecture of Philadelphia,* pp. 196–200.

[50]Frank M. Etting, *The Old State House,* p. 26.

two corner lots to the city and county, he secured a resolution that any buildings erected on them should be "of the like outward form, structure and dimensions." The unique civic group was completed by the erection in the immediate vicinity of the Episcopal Academy, the Philosophical Hall, the Philadelphia Library and Carpenters Hall.[51]

The Philadelphia public buildings won the admiration of architects in all the surrounding region and influenced strongly the style of county and town halls. Perhaps the most charming example, fortunately still standing almost unchanged, is the Burlington County court house at Mount Holly, built a few years after Congress Hall and undoubtedly patterned after it.[52] Dating to the same decade and even more like Congress Hall is old Town Hall, Wilmington.[53] The old State Capitol, at Trenton, built in 1794, shows the influence of the Philadelphia Georgian, and may be compared with the State House at Reading, and with the court houses at Lancaster and York.[54]

It was a tribute to the Carpenters Company that the Trustees of the College of New Jersey should have selected one of their members as the architect of Nassau Hall. When the building committee came to Robert Smith he must have been somewhat perplexed, since there were no college buildings nearby from which to draw inspiration. So he seems to have turned to Gibbs' *A Book of Architecture,* and selecting a drawing of King's College, Cambridge, modelled the building in outline after it. Nassau Hall was a rectangular building of rough stone, with three front entrances, central pediment, and low hipped roof set off by urns and surmounted by a small cupola. So admirably was it suited for its purpose that it became the model for University Hall, Brown; Dartmouth Hall and other college structures.

The transition from early Quaker to Georgian affected domestic architecture not less profoundly than ecclesiastical and public architecture. As Philadelphia grew prosperous, many families acquired wealth and there was a relaxation of Quaker austerity,

[51]Joseph Jackson, *Early Philadelphia Architects,* p. 58.
[52]*The White Pine Series,* Vol. XII, p. 3.
[53]Geo. F. Bennett, *Early Architecture of Delaware,* p. 42.
[54]Lancaster County Hist. Soc., *Papers and Addresses,* Vol. XXIV, pp. 98, 99.

the new style with its elegance and ornateness received a hearty welcome. Houses which in Penn's day had been considered stately and beautiful now seemed homely, plain and insignificant. So, along High Street, Arch, Chestnut and Walnut new houses arose, built after the fashion of Gibbs, or Swan or Halfpenny. The old pent roof and gallery gave way to brick or marble belts, the hood to the classic pediment, the simple cornice to molded wood cornices often with hand-tooled modillions, the simple doorways to recessed entrances with fluted columns or pilasters, the watershed dormer to the pediment dormer flanked by elaborate scroll work (Plate 26).

The change takes place as it were before our eyes as we view the city across the Delaware from the New Jersey shore, in the Nicholas Scull view of Philadelphia. Overlooking the river, with its little wherries and larger merchant vessels proudly displaying the English flag, is a jumble of warehouses, stores, residences and churches, with a wooded elevation fading into the distance behind Sassafras and Vine Streets. Most of the smaller houses seem to be in the old style, for we easily detect the rows of pent roofs, the front galleries and low roofs, but here and there are larger buildings whose steeper roof lines, roof balconies and high chimneys proclaim their more recent origin. And standing out over the mass is the State House tower, the cupola of the Reformed church, the spire of the Presbyterian church and the tower of Christ Church so exaggerated in size by the artist as almost to rival a modern skyscraper. Had Penn been able to stand beside Scull as he made his drawing he would have noted many familiar landmarks—the London Coffee House, the Benezet house, the old Court House, the Shippen house—but the changes that had taken place since his day were so great that he would have wondered whether this could really be his own City of Brotherly Love.

Had the founder crossed the river to examine the interiors of some of the stately new residences, he would have been startled and perhaps shocked by the scene of almost palatial elegance. The rich panelling of the rooms, the cornice and frieze beautifully moulded or perhaps hand carved, the fluted pilasters, the graceful trim of windows and doors, the carved mantels with broken pediments (Plate 27), the Chippendale furniture would all have seemed bewildering and inconsistent with Quaker ideals. He would have excused the elaborate beauty of Christ church as the expression of Episcopal worldliness, would have rejoiced to find the meeting houses as simple and unadorned as ever, would have approved of the State House while frowning upon the tower as over ornate and lacking in utility.

The Philadelphia merchants, like other Englishmen, loved the countryside, the woods, the fields, the meadows, and many were not satisfied to be cooped up in the city, however elegant their homes and charming the little gardens which they had laid out in the back yards. So some of them sold their homes on Chestnut or High Street and built stately seats along the high wooded banks of the Schuylkill or the Wissahickon to live there like country squires. A few even kept two establishments, a town house for winter and a country seat to which to retreat in the summer. Today some of these estates have been swallowed up by the city or encroached upon by the spread of suburbs, yet enough have been preserved, their original architecture almost unchanged, to constitute a group of colonial mansions rivalled only by those of Annapolis and the lower James. In them we find the Philadelphia Georgian at its best.

In 1761 John Macpherson, a Scotch sea captain who had won a fortune and lost an arm at privateering, built a beautiful mansion in what is now Fairmount Park (Plate 28). Here he lived sumptuously, entertaining many prominent persons and employing his time with ingenious inventions, philosophy and astronomy. At last, when financial reverses overtook him, he sold the property to General Benedict Arnold, who bestowed it upon his bride, the beautiful Margaret Shippen. One wonders whether Arnold could really have enjoyed Mount Pleasant, could have felt the repose which its gardens offered or appreciated the beauties of its architecture, with his mind alternating between the happiness of his honeymoon and the dark plot which he was forming against his country and the great commander who had befriended him and who trusted him so implicitly. However, he

26. *Left:* Read House, New Castle, Delaware. *Right:* Powel House, Philadelphia

27. *Left:* Cliveden, Germantown. *Right:* Mantel at Belmont

PLATE 28.

MOUNT PLEASANT, PHILADELPHIA

could hardly have failed to experience some satisfaction in an estate which was the gem of the Philadelphia region and one of the most beautiful in America. The house is of cut stone with heavy brick quoins, great quadruple arched chimney stacks at each end, a broad flight of stone steps leading to a pedimented Doric doorway, a Palladian window above setting off the front projection, hipped roof pierced by dormers and crowned by a ballustrade. Two flanking buildings add a manorial air reminiscent of the South.[55]

Hardly less beautiful, and even more famous, is Cliveden, the seat of the Chew family (Plate 27). Here it was that the British took refuge during the battle of Germantown, and by their stubborn resistance to the attacks of Washington's men held up the advance and gave Howe a chance to rally his forces and turn the tide of victory. Although the building suffered greatly from the discharges of the American cannon, the damage was soon repaired, and it stands today much as it was when Benjamin Chew built it in 1761. It is a two-and-a-half-story mansion of heavy cut stone. The doorway with its stone steps, fluted Doric columns, and pediment, the block cornice, the roof urns, the dormers are all typical of the Philadelphia Georgian. In the rear are two wings used for servants' quarters, kitchen and laundry.[56]

Other Georgian residences in the Philadelphia area are Laurel Hill, on the Schuylkill; Woodford, Fairmont Park; Lemon Hill, famous for its gardens overlooking the Schuylkill; Landowne, the home of John Penn, grandson of William Penn; Walnut Grove, the home of Joseph Wharton, Upsola, on the Germantown road; Carlton and Spring Bank, Germantown; Hope Lodge and the Highlands, Whitemarsh; Chalkley Hall and Port Royal House, Frankfort.

Nowhere was the influence of the Philadelphia Georgian stronger than in the little river town of New Castle, and nowhere have more of the houses been preserved. The Strand, the narrow street paralleling the Delaware, retains its eighteenth-century

[55]Eberlein and Lippincott, *The Colonial Homes of Philadelphia,* pp. 113–121; Cousins and Riley, *The Colonial Architecture of Philadelphia,* pp. 72–76.

[56]Wallace and Miller, *Colonial Homes,* pp. 166–172.

flavor almost unchanged. Of its houses the most stately and beautiful is the George Read house[57] (Plate 26). Built of bricks purchased of the Philadelphia burner, Jeremiah Hornkett, and of Philadelphia lumber brought down the river on shallops, and unquestionably designed by the Philadelphia architect Peter Crowding, who served as head carpenter, the building was as much the product of the Philadelphia school as though it had been erected in Fairmont Park. Even had we no information as to the builders the charming Palladian window and balcony, the roof balustrade set off by urns, the block cornice, the dormers, the flat window arches of marble, the delicately moulded interior woodwork, the exquisite Adam mantels, the fluted pilasters, the elaborate transoms would have betrayed its origin.[58]

The story of architecture in the Philadelphia region illustrates clearly the principles of transit and development so fundamental in the creation of American civilization. Like the settlers on the James and the Puritans of Massachusetts the Quakers brought with them a distinct type of English architecture. Their capital city was to be so far as they could make it so, a replica of the restored London, their country houses were to be built in the current English style. Thus the London Coffee House, the Letitia house, old Wynnestay were essentially English houses transferred to America, and even the little meeting houses, distinctive though they were, were but the embodiment in American brick and stone of English ideas.

Yet in its new environment Quaker architecture immediately felt the influence of local conditions—building materials, climate, labor costs, isolation. It was as though America gripped the English houses and slowly but irresistibly remoulded them into American houses. And when, out of the force of inheritance and the force of local conditions, a distinctive architecture developed, it began, under the operation of the melting-pot, to impress itself upon neighboring foreign groups—Germans, Dutch, Swedes, Welsh. Later the continued contact with England brought new

[57]Begun 1791 and completed in 1801.

[58]*White Pine Series,* Vol. XI, No. 6; Geo. F. Bennett, *Early Architecture of Delaware,* pp. 111–129.

architectural ideas, and sweeping aside the early Quaker, conquered the lower Delaware for the Georgian. But the Georgian could no more escape the force of American conditions than the Quaker, so that it in turn eventually took on its own individuality, became the Philadelphia Georgian.

The use of rough stone to carry out the ideas of Gibbs, Ware and Swan is so instructive that it deserves more than passing mention. For Georgian houses brick or dressed stone was the accepted medium, and rough stone was considered unsuited to the sophisticated façade with its delicate ornamentation, its Palladian windows and classic doors. Yet the local architects of the stone region of Pennsylvania, instead of discarding their accustomed material, made the new architectural ideas conform to it. It is true that whenever possible they cut the stones into something like rectangular blocks, but more frequently they were laid in the rough. Thus there developed that unique type of house, the rough stone Georgian, which like the wooden Georgian house of New England marked what one may call a qualified declaration of independence by local builders.

As the architectural history of the lower Delaware region passes in review before us we see in the space of a century the transit from England of a distinct architecture, its modification by American conditions, its conquest of near-by groups, its overthrow by the invasion of the English Georgian and the modification of the latter to form the Philadelphia Georgian.

Chapter VIII

FROM RHINE TO SUSQUEHANNA

THE traveller who takes boat on the upper Rhine in northern Alsace to glide downstream to Mainz or Bingen views a fair and fertile region. On either side are mountain ranges covered with forests, cut here and there with clearings; to the right the picturesque Black Forest and Odenwald, to the left the Hardt and the hills of the Westrich. The slopes from the mountains to the river are covered with fields of wheat or potatoes like an unending crazy-quilt, interspersed at amazingly close intervals with little villages, whose red-tiled roofs cluster around a lone church tower, connected one with the other by thread-like roads lined with fruit trees. Through this beautiful scene runs the Rhine, its banks dotted with villages and cities, upon its surface an occasional steamer or tug with a trailing line of barges.

But the Rhine Palatinate, the homeland of many thousands of emigrants to the American colonies in the eighteenth century, was not confined to the prosperous, thickly populated Rhine valley. It included also the Hardt mountain region, that backbone of the Palatinate; the fruitful southwest highlands, a part of the Westrich, with its village-covered heights and the gentle hill country around Zweibrücken; the gloomy marsh lowlands of the west; the multiform north Palatinate mountain land. The whole presents an impression of geographic diversity, a diversity which is reflected in the agriculture, industry, customs and culture of the people.

The Palatinate Rhine valley, which is protected from the piercing winter winds by the bordering uplands and mountains, enjoys an exceptionally mild climate. Spring comes early and autumn lingers long. The mean temperature for January is from thirty degrees to thirty-two degrees Fahrenheit, sixty-three degrees for July, and over fifty degrees for April and October.[1] The duration of the snowfall is usually only twenty days. In the Palatinate uplands, however, the average temperature is lower and the duration of the snowfall longer.

Since the soil, for the most part, is as favored as the climate, the Rhine Valley is one of the richest agricultural regions in Germany. The river meanders through lowlands of alluvial soil, damp and often boggy, while on either side rise slopes of loess, or calcareous clays containing organic remains—land shells and bones of mammals.[2] Geologists have long wrangled over the origin of this vast loess layer, but there is no disagreement as to its richness for agricultural purposes. For centuries it has continued to yield its abundant harvests—wheat, barley, rye; fruits such as grapes, apples, pears, plums, cherries; many kinds of vegetables, and in more recent times, sugar beets, tobacco, and potatoes. The uplands, above the loess layer, covered as they are with pines and other soft woods, have become centers for lumbering and for the manufacture of wooden toys, clocks, and musical instruments.

In the fourth century of the Christian era, this fair region was the prize contended for by Romans and Alemanni from the middle Elba region. In 347 the Emperor Julian fought a terrible battle with these fierce foes, and the struggle was continued by Valentinian I. In the end the Alemanni prevailed and took possession of both banks of the Rhine. In the next century, however, they in turn became the object of a fierce assault by the Franks under the mighty Clovis. At the battle of Tolbiac in 496, the Alemanni were conquered. The more unyielding of the nation retired to Switzerland, while those who remained on the Rhine mingled with the Franks to form a new Frankish-Alemannic racial group. Thus the "Palatines," who for twelve centuries have retained possession of the Rhine Valley and Palatinate uplands, were the product of two of the most warlike of the ancient Germanic tribes.[3] The Palatine of today, gay, alert, op-

[1] *Forschungen zur Deutschen Landes- und Volkskunde,* Vol. XXVI, p. 166.

[2] James Geikie, *Prehistoric Europe* (London, 1881), pp. 145, 146; Gustav Braun, *Deutschland,* pp. 236–254.

[3] Oscar Kuhns, in *Penna.-German,* XII, p. 82.

timistic, impetuous, brave, betrays more the Frankish than the Alemannic nature. But he is the product not only of his racial ancestry but of the land in which he lives, with its sunny skies, its fertile soil and its mild climate.[4]

The basic unit of economic and social organization in the Palatinate, as in other parts of Germany, was the agricultural village. Save in rare cases, the residences, stables, and barns of the peasants were clustered in the village proper, under the shadow of the church tower, while the arable lands or meadows lay round about. Each holder had his parcel or strip of arable field, and at dawn, shouldering his hoe or his scythe, went out to plant or till or reap. Albert Becker warns us against grouping the Palatinate villages under such usual middle German types as *Gruppen, Haufen, Strassen,* or *Streulage* villages, as each had its own individuality, was the product of history, or soil, or topography.[5] Here we see a village with the houses nestling close together around the church, here they are stretched out on both sides of a long street.[6] In the east some of the villages are so large as to assume the appearance of little cities; in the forest areas they often seem mere hamlets, straggling along creeks or narrow vales.[7] The Palatinate, although so distinctly the home of the agricultural village, was not without its isolated farms. In some of the other regions which contributed to the migrations to America, especially in parts of Baden, in upper Württemberg, Upper Bavaria and Switzerland, the farm was the usual agricultural unit.

Whatever the character of the village proper, the holdings of the peasant were staked off in the fields near-by. Sometimes they lay in narrow strips, sometimes in more compact units, distributed in the arable lands, the meadows and gardens. Had the peasant held his land in fee simple, free of feudal impediments, personal services or fees due the landlord, he would have attained a position of prosperity and contentment, especially in the rich region overlooking the Rhine. But for centuries the peasant had been

[4]J. F. L. Raschen, in *Penna.-German,* IX, p. 392; Albert Becker, *Pfälzer Volkskunde* (Bonn, 1925), p. 91.

[5]Albert Becker, *Pfälzer Volkskunde,* p. 51.

[6]*Penna.-German,* IX, p. 393.

[7]Albert Becker, *Pfälzer Volkskunde,* p. 47.

but a sponge from which the landlord squeezed the last penny. As Goethe remarked, "It was always the peasant who had to carry the burden."

In some parts of Germany the peasants were in a condition bordering on slavery. In the east, especially, where the landlord was usually sheriff, magistrate and police chief, all in one, they had few rights which were respected. They were bound to the soil, could not marry without permission, and were burdened with all kinds of services to the landlord. Often they were forced to work three days a week or even more under the lash of an overseer on the lord's land; to pay the best horse or best cow as an inheritance tax; to lend their children for compulsory service. In the west, however, including the Palatinate, services and dues of this kind had as a rule been commuted to money payments. There the landlord and the *Gerichtsherr* were not always the same person, and the peasant could appeal to the prince for protection. The corvée was usually narrowly limited, in some places to only a few days a year, hereditary leases were the rule, the peasant could dispose of his holdings and owned his tools and buildings.[8] Feudal dues were still burdensome, and left the peasant little more than a bare existence, but they fell more on the land than upon his person. It was only with the French Revolution that many of these burdens were swept away. When Crabb Robinson, in the opening years of the nineteenth century, visited northern Baden, he found the peasants there envying their fellows of the Palatinate because "on the left bank of the Rhine they pay no more tithes . . . we are squeezed most sadly here."[9] Yet in the eighteenth century at the time of the migrations, in the Palatinate as in other parts of Germany, the tenant was left little more than a bare subsistence.

The capacity for unremitting toil of the "Palatine," his readiness to expend the greatest labor and time upon his little holding, made him a successful agriculturist. At the break of dawn he was at work in the fields, his barefoot wife often at his side, and

[8] W. H. Bruford, *Germany in the Eighteenth Century* (Camb., Eng., 1935), pp. 106–111; Gustav Freitag, *Bilder aus der Deutschen Vergangenheit,* III, 427–435.

[9] E. J. Morley, *Crabb Robinson in Germany,* p. 20.

only with the failing of daylight, perhaps at nine or nine-thirty, would he return to his home. But in his agricultural methods he was chained to the medieval routine of community cultivation. There was no room for individual experiment; each peasant in a certain field must plant on his little strip the same crop at the same time as every other peasant. There was an unvarying succession of spring-sown grain, usually barley and oats, autumn-sown grain, or wheat and rye, and fallow. Only in his garden patch, with its vegetables, fruit and fodder, was he free from the restraint of the community routine.[10] The Palatinate was more progressive in the agricultural methods than some of the regions of east Germany, but it was far behind the famous farmers of the Netherlands.

Yet the great fertility of the Rhine Valley made the eastern part of the Palatinate one of the garden spots of Europe. Here the eye of the traveller was struck by the waving fields of wheat, rye, oats, barley and buckwheat; here were vineyards stretching up the slopes towards the wooded summit of the Hardt mountains; here were fruit trees breaking under their burden of apples, or pears, or plums or cherries; here luxuriant vegetable gardens. The potato, which has since become a principal crop of the Palatinate as of other parts of Germany,[11] was introduced in the early years of the eighteenth century and was gaining rapid favor in the decades which saw the chief migrations to America. The peasant had usually his own cows, which yielded milk for his table and for making cheese and butter; his hogs afforded him meat; his poultry supplied him with eggs; he often had his bee-hive with its abundant yield of honey.[12]

The peasant was as conservative in his farm implements as in his agricultural methods. His plow, if he had one, was a clumsy implement identical with that in use by his ancestors of the Middle Ages. It consisted of a rounded pole forked at one end to form handles, a wooden mould board, and a simple flat share,

[10] W. H. Bruford, *Germany in the Eighteenth Century,* pp. 112–114.

[11] In a village near Göttingen there stands a monument erected in grateful memory by the peasants to the year of the abundant potato crop.

[12] Adolf Bartels, *Der Bauer in der Deutschen Vergangenheit,* Vol. VI, pp. 20, 21.

the whole mounted on a pair of little wheels.[13] The harrow, which was of wood, teeth and all, might have seen service in the days of Frederick Barbarossa. In the eighteenth century, when so many peasants were leaving for America, the flail, the wooden rake, the scythe, the sickle, the spade, the hoe, were the everyday accompaniment of peasant life.[14]

Each village, to a large extent, was a self-contained economic unit. Hardware, a few spices, and salt had to be imported from the nearest city, while occasional purchases were made from peddlers, or craftwork done by travelling artisans. But the grain was ground in the local mill, iron work was forged in the nearby smithy, the local masons and carpenters did the building and repairing, fuel and building material came from the village woods. Within the house the long winter months were spent in making or repairing all kinds of useful articles. The men carved wooden spoons, platters and bowls, plaited wicker baskets, repaired scythes, rakes, flails, ox yokes. Women plaited straw for neck collars, stitched and stuffed sheep-skin bags for cart saddles, wove stirrups and halters from hemp or straw. "Spinning wheels, distaffs, needles were never idle. Coarse, home-made cloth and linen supplied all wants. . . . Women spun, wove, cut out and dyed cloth, as well as brewed and baked for the household."[15]

With the disintegration of the manorial system the community artisan became an independent worker—the blacksmith, the wainwright, the tailor, the shoemaker, the butcher, the baker. The village artisan, trained from early youth to his trade, often acquired great skill, but he was handicapped by centuries of conservative tradition. Like his fellow villager, the agriculturist, his tools and his methods alike went back to medieval times.[16] Moreover, he was forced to face the competition of the itinerant

[13]Wm. Howett, *Rural and Domestic Life in Germany* (London, 1842), p. 26; compare with plows shown in Adolf Bartels, *Der Bauer in der Deutschen Vergangenheit,* Vol. VI, pp. 20, 21.

[14]Albert Becker, *Pfälzer Volkskunde,* p. 242. The German agricultural tools are still often primitive. See Bulletin 213, Farmers' Annual Normal Institute, *Proceedings,* p. 77.

[15]W. H. Bruford, *Germany in the Eighteenth Century* (Camb., Eng., 1935), pp. 118, 119.

[16]Albert Becker, *Pfälzer Volkskunde,* p. 276.

journeyman, who went from village to village, house to house, seeking work. If he found a patron, unslinging his knapsack and taking out his tools he went to work making shoes, or clothes, or repairing clocks or kitchen utensils. In the Palatinate, especially, the itinerant worker and salesman early played an important part in the life of the people, and the Pirmasens shoemakers, the Ramberger brush-makers, the broom traders and wood-carvers from Busenberg, the Glöcklinger liquor traders, acquired a well-deserved reputation for the excellence of their wares.[17]

The commerce of the Rhine, handicapped as it was during the Middle Ages and even in the eighteenth century by restrictions and duties, gave rise to Speyer, Kaiserslautern, and other important cities. Speyer was founded about 1240, and first gaining prosperity through the wine trade, later developed the manufacture of woolens and linens. The town of Lambrecht, with its Walloon population, acquired early and still retains its thriving cloth industry.[18] Many of the industries of the old Palatinate have now disappeared, the victims of devastating wars or unwise restrictions, or the competition of modern industry. But the iron trade at Donnersberg, the potters and tilers of Jockgrim and Rheinzabern, the quarries and lime-pits, charcoal burning, the making of pitch and potash, continue active.[19] Thus, although the Palatinate of the eighteenth century was chiefly agricultural, it had its share of trade and industry, developed thousands of artisans, many of whom brought their technical skill to the forests of Pennsylvania.

Industry in the Palatinate owed much to the skill and technical knowledge of the many foreigners who fled to the province as a refuge from religious persecution. Charles Louis, who became elector in 1632, discarding the idea that a prince should force his subjects to be of the same confession as himself, opened his doors to the persecuted of other lands. So from France came groups of Huguenots, from Switzerland oppressed Mennonites; many Dutch families settled at Kriegsheim, near Worms, fleeing

[17] *Ibid.*, p. 273; William Howett, *Germany*, pp. 122–140.

[18] Albert Becker, *Pfälzer Volkskunde*, p. 272. [19] *Ibid.*

Walloons made their home at Mannheim.[20] These hapless people, many of them among the most skilled workers of Europe, introduced new industrial methods, and in some cases new industries. The cloth trade of the Walloon town of Lambrecht in the Hardt region still endures.[21]

Travellers to Germany in the eighteenth century often remarked on the submissive spirit of the German peasant. "The German peasantry, though their comforts do not seem to me to be less than those of the British, have less public spirit," remarked Crabb Robinson, in 1801, "less the habit which teaches them 'their rights to scan—and learn to venerate themselves as man.' The corvée and other vassalage services which the prince can demand from his peasants in most parts of Germany tend to degrade the mind by making it constantly feel its dependence and subjection to the will of another."[22]

The peasant had been taught by centuries of experience that his task in life was to labor early and late for a bare existence, that matters of state were beyond his knowledge and his sphere, that he must accept wars, robbery, pillage, oppressions, crushing taxes, as he accepted drought or pestilence. He was not dissatisfied with his lot in normal times, his wants were few, his tastes simple, he loved his home and his fields, felt himself as much a part of the province as its plains and hills and forests, was steeped in its customs, traditions, superstitions, native art. But when heartless landlords and princes took the food from his mouth, when foreign soldiers laid his home in ashes and slaughtered his cattle, when he was subjected to religious persecution, he might gather up a few meager belongings, and turning his back on the homeland seek his fortune elsewhere, even in a wilderness three thousand miles away across the Atlantic.

For the Palatinate the seventeenth century was a century of horrors. It was the Elector Palatine Frederick V himself who, by accepting the crown of Bohemia, precipitated the Thirty Years' War, and his Rhine territories paid the penalty. When

20*Penna.-German,* Vol. I, pp. 293, 295; Vol. IX, pp. 390, 391.

21Albert Becker, *Pfälzer Volkskunde,* p. 272.

22E. J. Morley, *Crabb Robinson in Germany,* p. 69.

Tilly swept through the region in 1622, his soldiers were guilty of atrocities which would have put to shame a band of Iroquois on the warpath. At the capture of Heidelberg they "murdered and tortured without regard to age or sex; they drove nails through their hands and feet, or burnt the soles of their feet with hot irons."[23] Hardly had the land begun to recover from this dreadful blow when, in 1634, the savage cavalry of Horn and Bernard of Weimar, spreading over the province, left a trail of burning villages, devastated fields, and suffering, homeless people.[24] In the years from 1635 to 1638 famine and pestilence settled down upon the land, and the once flourishing fields and vineyards were given over to roving bands of wolves.

With the return of peace, the province slowly recovered from these disasters; the wretched people crept out of their hiding places in cellars, woods and caves, towns and villages were rebuilt, the fields were put again under cultivation, orchards were planted. But twenty-six years after the Peace of Westphalia the region was again devastated, this time by the brutal soldiers of Turenne. Once more we hear the monotonous tale of horrors—townsman and peasant plundered, fields devastated, cattle carried off, cities and villages burned, homes robbed.[25] And this was merely the prelude to the atrocities committed by the French invaders in 1689 under General Montclas. The unfortunate Elector Philip William stood on the walls of his castle at Mannheim, and counted in one day twenty-three towns and villages in flames. "The fields where the corn had been sowed were plowed up. The orchards were cut down. . . . Not a vine, not an almond-tree was to be seen on the sunny hills." Worms was reduced to ashes, its prosperous citizenry forced to flee or to hide in pest-ridden cellars.[26] Even this was not the end, for in 1707, during the war of the Spanish Succession, Marshal Villars led an army through the Palatinate and once more we hear the old story of burning villages and ruined peasants.

In the years of peace which followed, the thrift and energy

[23]Ludwig Häusser, *Geschichte der rheinischen Pfalz* (Heidelberg, 1845), Vol. II, p. 399.
[24]*Ibid.*, pp. 519–542. [25]*Ibid.*, pp. 626–638.
[26]Macaulay, *History of England*, Vol. III, p. 112; Heinrich Boos, *Geschichte der rheinischen Stadtkultur*, Vol. IV, p. 469.

of the people, together with the richness of the soil, would have brought a return of prosperity had it not been for the heartless oppressions of the princes. The Electors John William (1690–1716) and Charles Philip (1716–42), dazzled by the glory of Louis XIV, were intent only on aping the splendors of Versailles. Charles Philip, especially, although a religious zealot who on occasion scourged his own body or washed the feet of old people, was pitiless in squeezing the last penny from his ruined subjects. His court retinue vied in numbers and in costly clothing with those of the greatest monarchies of Europe, for the staff of the Chief Steward numbered fifty-eight officers and of the Chief Chamberlain eighty officers, while other departments were on the same footing. When distinguished visitors came to the Palatinate, the whole army of parasites was paraded in public, so that the people were compensated for their poverty with empty pomp.[27]

The Elector was very fond of hunting and indulged in the sport upon such a magnificent scale that it bore heavily upon his exchequer. It is said that during the wars he repined over the loss of his game more than over the agony of the peasantry. The magnificent buildings which he erected were enduring monuments of his rule. His great palace, begun in 1720 and completed in 1729, created astonishment in visitors, not because of its beauty but its vast proportions and its heavy masonry. Bigoted, pleasure-loving, frivolous, intolerant, with no talent for administration, dazzled by the tinsel of court display, Charles Philip was blind to the sufferings of his subjects. His taxes bore with killing force on the backs of his subjects, stifled trade, crushed industry, beggared the peasantry and threatened to depopulate the country.[28]

Despite all, it is probable that the exodus from the Palatinate would not have assumed very large proportions had not religious persecution added its share to the woes of the people. The Palatinate was chiefly Calvinistic with many Lutheran churches, and had long enjoyed a large degree of religious toler-

[27]Ludwig Häusser, *Geschichte der rheinischen Pfalz,* Vol. II, p. 899.
[28]*Ibid.,* pp. 893–905.

ation under a succession of Lutheran and Calvinist princes. But all was changed under John William, the second ruler of the Roman Catholic Neuberg line, who was under the influence of the Jesuits. In some places the Protestants were ordered to share their church property with the Catholics, in others they were ousted completely. We may judge the spirit of John William by his statement that he considered it "an inconceivable mark of divine favor . . . that the electorate of the Palatinate . . . had fallen again into Catholic hands." Protestants were ordered to bend the knee at the passing of the Host, to furnish flowers for Catholic church festivals and to submit to the proselyting of the Jesuits. Their pastors were deprived of their livings, and many imprisoned.[29]

Bending beneath the weight of so many disasters, thousands gathered up what they could of their belongings, and set out for a new world, there to begin life over again. "In this way a part of the riddle is explained which seemed so mysterious to the statisticians of that time; *i.e.,* why precisely in these years of peace the population of the Palatinate diminished so surprisingly," says Häusser. "Schlözer was astonished that from no land in the world relatively so many people emigrated as from this paradise of Germany, the Palatinate. . . . By the way of England so many were shipped to America that for a long time the name of Palatinate was used as a general term for all German emigrants."[30] It is stated that out of three districts (Oberämtern) alone over four hundred well-to-do families emigrated.

The causes of the migration of Swiss to America, a movement which assumed large proportions, differed only in that their mountain country had in large part escaped the scourge of war. The lower classes were burdened by feudal dues—the tithe, the land-tax, and body services—while certain religious sects, especially the Mennonites, were bitterly persecuted. So early as the seventeenth century the members of this sect, attracted by the tolerant rule of Charles Louis, began to move down into the

[29]Oscar Kuhns, in *Penna.-German,* N.S. Vol. I, pp. 294–296; Ludwig Häusser, *Geschichte der rheinischen Pfalz,* Vol. II, pp. 805–830.

[30]Ludwig Häusser, *Geschichte der rheinischen Pfalz,* Vol. II, p. 900.

Palatinate.[31] But when later they found themselves exposed in their new home to wars, oppression and renewed persecution, many joined the movement to America. Their example was soon followed by thousands of their brethren in Switzerland. Before the middle of the eighteenth century the exodus had assumed such proportions that both Zürich and Bern issued decrees intended to check it.[32]

The stream of Palatinates and Swiss was joined by Germans of other provinces—Alsatians, Hessians, Bavarians—with isolated groups of foreigners—Walloons, Dutch, French Huguenots.[33] They were inspired with hope in the promised land across the ocean by the visits of William Penn to the Rhine region in 1677, and by his various letters and pamphlets, many of which were translated into German and widely circulated. "Along the Rhine a number of families have banded together to accept the invitation of an Englishman named William Penn, who recently visited that community, to settle in that beautiful land" (America), wrote a resident of Heilbron to his son in New York in 1681. "We, as also the Platenbach family, are only waiting a good opportunity when the dear Lord will take us to you. Your brother Peter is learning shoe-making and will soon be free. America is the only dream of Elizabeth. Catherine, only six years old, asks us daily, 'Will we soon be going to our brother in America?' "[34]

Some of the first settlers wrote back glowing descriptions of the land of plenty, and their letters were printed and widely circulated. "The farmers or husbandmen live better than lords," declared Georg Wertmüller. "If a workman will only work four or five days in a week, he can live grandly. The farmers here pay no tithes nor contributions. . . . Handicraftmen earn here much money."[35] Christopher Sauer tells us that when he first came to Pennsylvania and found conditions there in striking contrast to those in Germany, he wrote to all his friends "of the civil and

[31] W. D. Hull, *William Penn,* etc. (Swarthmore, 1935), pp. 161, 162.

[32] Oscar Kuhns, in *Penna.-German,* N.S. Vol. I, pp. 297–299.

[33] Benjamin Rush, *Manners of the German Inhabitants of Pennsylvania* (I. S. Rupp, Philadelphia, 1875), p. 5.

[34] W. D. Hull, *William Penn,* pp. 316–318.

[35] *Ibid.,* p. 319.

religious liberty, privileges, etc.," and his letters, printed and reprinted, induced "many thousands" to come over.[36]

So the tide of emigration set in. Bringing with them a few personal belongings, packed perhaps in the decorated family *sockeltruhe,* they took boat on the Rhine for Rotterdam, where passage could be had for Philadelphia. We gain a vivid impression of the vast tragedy of the movement from Müller's account of the departure of a group of Bernese Mennonites in 1711. "Sitting on boxes and bundles, which were piled high in the middle of the boat, could be seen gray-haired men and women, old and feeble; yonder stood the young gazing in wonder at the shores as they slipped by. At times they were hopeful, at others sad, and their glances would alternate, now to the north, now to the south toward their abandoned home, which had driven them out so unfeelingly, and yet whose green hills and snow-capped mountains they cannot forget."[37]

Only too often the voyage was even more tragic than the departure. There was overcrowding on the ships, food often ran short, smallpox and other diseases took a terrible toll, there was always danger of shipwreck, many were cheated and robbed by unscrupulous ship-masters, some were actually sold into temporary bondage. Caspar Wistar tells us: "One ship among the others sailed about the sea twenty-four weeks, and of the 150 persons who were thereon, more than 100 miserably languished and died of hunger." On another ship 250 passengers out of 312 died during the voyage. Thus the introduction of these unfortunate people to the New World was accompanied by injustice and suffering as great as those which drove them from the Old.[38]

As the newcomer, passing through Philadelphia and out into Lancaster or Berks or Dauphin, gazed upon the great forests of Lancaster or the blue hills of Dauphin, he could have had but a vague conception of how his new homeland would change his life and the life of his descendants. He hoped to swap poverty,

[36] *Penna.-German,* N.S. Vol I, p. 299. [37] *Penna.-German,* N.S. Vol. I, p. 314.

[38] Gottlieb Mittelberger's *Journey to Pennsylvania, 1756* (C. T. Eben, Phila., 1898); Oscar Kuhns, in *Penna.-German,* N.S. Vol. I, pp. 316–320; A. B. Faust, *German Element in the U. S.,* Vol. I, pp. 67–72; G. L. Omwake, in *Penna.-German,* N.S. Vol. I, pp. 718–724.

persecution and oppression for prosperity and freedom, but he expected as a matter of course to retain his language, his religion, his architecture, his agricultural methods, his mechanical crafts, his peasant art, his folklore, his simple customs, his accustomed food, his music, his farm implements, his costume, his furniture. These things had come down to him through the centuries, he could see no reason why they should not persist on the soil of Pennsylvania as well as in the Rhine Valley or in the mountains of Switzerland.

In fact there are many points of similarity between the region selected by most of the newcomers and the Rhine Palatinate. Although branches of the great stream of German immigration flowed into New York, New Jersey, Virginia, and the Carolinas, the main current was directed toward Pennsylvania. The settlers planted themselves in the immediate vicinity of Philadelphia, spread up the Schuylkill, out to Lancaster and York counties, swarmed into Bucks, Dauphin, and Berks, ascended the Lehigh valley and planted outposts as far north as the Delaware Water Gap. At the end of the colonial period their settlements spread in a fairly compact array of farms and towns from Easton, on the Delaware, westward to Broad Mountain, and southwest to York.

It is a fair and fertile region which the Germans selected for their new home. Between the line of the Blue Mountains, which stretches northeast and southwest, and the Delaware River and Mason and Dixon Line, lies a broad expanse of comparatively level country. In this lowland one finds various soils—transported soils, crystalline soils, shale soils, triassic sandstone soils, etc. But richest of all are three limestone belts, one extending from the northern suburbs of Philadelphia westward to Lancaster County, the second occupying northern Lancaster, and the third bending in a broad arc from Easton, through Bethlehem, Reading and Carlisle to Chambersburg.[39] Although quite different in origin from the loess of the Rhine Valley, its contents are so similar that the Palatine felt himself immediately at home with it. As he had left behind one of the richest calcareous soils of

[39] A. B. Hulbert, *Soil*, pp. 129–131.

Europe, so he now found himself planted in one of the richest limestone regions of America.

The climate, too, is similar. Although the summers are hotter than in the Palatinate, and the winters colder, the mean temperatures differ little. Between 1874 and 1924 there were only twenty-four days in which a temperature below zero was recorded at Philadelphia. In the southern counties there is an average growing season of 207 days, a precipitation of forty-six inches a year, a freedom from droughts, tornadoes, and prolonged snowstorms.[40] There were few adjustments indeed in the life and economy of the Palatine necessitated by different climatic conditions.

Even the topography is similar. The gently rolling limestone and sandstone regions must have reminded him of the *Vorderpfalz,* the Blue Mountains of his Hardt, the rough borderlands of his Westrich. As a substitute for his Rhine, Neckar and Main, he found the Delaware, the Lehigh, the Schuylkill, and the Susquehanna. In agriculture, commerce, and industry there would seem to be no reason why the Palatine should not establish essentially the same system to which he had been accustomed. For the Swiss or the Bavarian, of course, the change was more pronounced, for there was little similarity between southeastern Pennsylvania and the mountains and valleys of Bern or Zurich or Oberbayern.

The newcomer perhaps did not at first realize that the cheapness of land, that distinguishing feature of the New World, made a duplication of the agricultural systems of either Germany or Switzerland impracticable. To the German peasant the possession of land was the most important temporal concern in life—the land gave him his daily bread, upon it he toiled and had his everyday existence. When he found that in Pennsylvania 100 or perhaps 300 acres could be had for the price of a dozen acres in the Vorderpfalz, he stretched his means to the limit to purchase. We find Gabriel Schuler buying first a tract of 450 acres, and later investing in 700 acres at Franconia, Montgomery

[40]Henry F. James, *The Agricultural Industry of Southeastern Pennsylvania* (Phila., 1928), pp. 10–20.

County.[41] When Gerhard Brumbach settled in Vincent township he leased 600 acres with the privilege of buying.[42] The average holdings of farmland of the Pennsylvania German in the colonial period was many times as great as that which his father had relinquished when he left the Palatinate.

This fact made the establishing of the agricultural village, that foundation stone of German rural economy, impossible. It was no great matter for the people of Kriegsheim to go out from the village each morning for work on their tiny holdings, for it might entail a walk of but five or more minutes, but in Pennsylvania, had agricultural villages been established, the workers might have had to walk a mile, perhaps five miles. In other words, it was impracticable to have village communities with individual holdings averaging hundreds of acres, and the total area fifty or a hundred square miles.

Moreover, the legal background of the community village, the mass of rights and restrictions and dues which in Germany had come down through the centuries, was lacking in America. Unless the newcomers created it out of the whole cloth, fitting it into the pattern of the provincial law, some other form of rural life would develop. Presumably they had little desire to duplicate a system which was associated in their minds with poverty, oppression and injustice. Had their religious life, like that of the New Englanders, been closely intertwined with civil affairs, the congregation could have provided a unit around which to organize the village. But the German peasant knew little or nothing about governmental matters, even in his fatherland, so that when he found himself in an English province, it seems not to have occurred to him that he might take the initiative in organizing a distinct type of religious and civil community.

So the basis of agricultural life became, not the village or manor, but the independent farm. The Teuton immigrants were not unacquainted with farm life, for the *Einzelhof* existed in parts of Baden, in the mountain region from Rastatt to Harnberg, in south Bavaria, in upper Württemberg, in Switzerland,

41 *Penna.-German*, N.S. Vol. XII, p. 216.
42 *Ibid.*, N.S. Vol. XI, p. 165.

and here and there in the Palatinate.[43] Yet the overwhelming majority had been accustomed to the village, and the change to the farm affected their lives profoundly.[44] Whereas before they had a compact community life, almost touching elbows with their neighbors on either side, with the church, the mill, the blacksmith shop, the baker, all within easy walking distance, they now lived in comparative isolation.

The village well, in the Palatinate a place for neighborly gossip, gave way to the spring or farm well, the community bakehouse to the private oven. The farmer could no longer sit behind his double door conversing with passers-by. Household industry—spinning, weaving, shoemaking, tailoring—became more important than ever, when there was no village smithy or shoemaker or tailor close at hand. It was difficult to foster religion and to establish efficient schools, when the distances were so great. It must have been a severe hardship upon the pious German to hitch up his horse on Sunday morning for a journey perhaps of five miles over the rough roads to attend worship. Had the settlers not been fired with religious zeal, the change from the village to the farm would have had the most serious effect upon the congregations.

Although the German could not duplicate in his new home the system of the old, his knowledge of agriculture was of inestimable value to him. His infallible judgment in picking the most fertile soil is no doubt explained by his long acquaintance with the Rhine valley loess. It is said that he was guided by the trees, taking it for granted that where the growth was luxuriant and tall, the soil must be fertile.[45] In clearing the land, his training in thrift and hard work made him scorn the slovenly method of girdling the trees and leaving them to die. He chopped down the trees, split the large limbs and trunks into firewood or fence rails, and grubbed up the underbrush and saplings. His field was thus so thoroughly cleared that it could be put under cul-

[43]Gustav Braun, *Deutschland,* Vol. II, Chart 7 (Berlin, 1916); Albert Becker, *Pfälzer Volkskunde,* p. 47.

[44]William Beidelman, *The Story of the Pennsylvania Germans* (Easton, 1898), p. 141.

[45]Benjamin Rush, *Manners of the German Inhabitants of Pennsylvania,* p. 13; S. G. Fisher, *The Making of Pennsylvania* (Philadelphia, 1896), p. 110.

tivation at once without fear of breaking plows and harrows.[46]

On the other hand, the cheapness of land and the dearness of labor tempted him, as well as his English neighbor, to abandon the three field system with its accompanying rotation of crops. It was in 1748 that Peter Kalm remarked on the wasteful system of agriculture in vogue in Pennsylvania. When a bit of land had been cleared, he tells us, it was tilled for several years successively, without being manured, until it lost its fertility, and then left fallow while the owner made a new clearing. After a number of years the original field, which by that time had recovered much of its fertility, was again put under cultivation, and the process was repeated.[47]

That methods were the same at the end of the colonial period is pointed out by a writer who published a book on American husbandry in 1775. The system used on a typical farm at Durham was to plant a new field for fourteen years successively with wheat, Indian corn, wheat again, barley, oats, barley again, buckwheat, oats, and peas. After this the land was left fallow for seven years. This bad husbandry, we are told, "is owing to plenty of land, for new settlers always take up as much as they possibly can, and far more than they know how to stock or cultivate. They can afford no care for manuring, nor yet to clear two pieces of ground for corn as long as one will bear it. They clear a field and have not strength of ploughs or cattle and men to crop more than that; they therefore stick to it as long as they can get any" grain.[48]

During the Revolution there came a change in agricultural practice, a few of the most enterprising abandoning the old wasteful methods for crop rotation. They usually planted Indian corn the first year and wheat together with grass seed the second, after which the field was left for pasture for several years.[49] But

46Benjamin Rush, *Manners of the German Inhabitants of Pennsylvania,* p. 15.

47Peter Kalm, *Travels into North America* (London, 1772), Vol. I, pp. 144–145.

48*American Husbandry* (London, 1772), Vol. I, pp. 171–173. Neither Kalm nor the author of *American Husbandry* is referring specifically in these statements to the German farmers. But the facts that they do not except the Germans, and that both must have seen at least some German farms lead us to conclude that their descriptions were applicable to Germans as well as English.

49W. F. Dunaway, *A History of Pennsylvania* (New York, 1935), p. 259.

this improvement, as well as the earlier practice, was dictated by local conditions rather than by inheritance, for land had risen in value as the population became denser, and it no longer paid to exploit it in order to save labor. In other words, as it was the cheapness of rich land which caused the Germans to abandon the agricultural practices of centuries, so it was the increasing cost of land which dictated a return to them.

On the other hand, the German immigrant clung tenaciously to the tools of his ancestors. He cut his grain with the ancient sickle, his grass with the scythe; his threshing was done with the flail or by trampling the wheat on the barn floor by horses; he used cumbersome plows with wooden mould-boards, wooden-toothed harrows and rakes, antiquated hoes, spades, pitchforks and mattocks.[50] It was only with the end of the colonial period that the cradle began to supplant the sickle. Plows and harrows, drawn often by oxen, were guided by boys, with ropes and chains for harness.[51]

The farmers' most important crop was wheat. "They sow immense quantities, about the latter end of September generally; using from two to three bushels of seed an acre, which on good lands yield from 25 to 32 bushels per acre. . . . Wheat thriving so well in Pennsylvania makes them neglect maize, which is a much less valuable grain." Rye was a common crop on sandy soils and on fields exhausted by successive crops of wheat. Barley and oats were sown usually in April and gathered in July. The culture of hemp and flax was of major importance, not only to supply the needs of the housewife, but for the Philadelphia market.[52]

Among the immigrants were many vintners from the great grape-growing regions of the Palatinate. Rush tells us that of the arrivals at Philadelphia from April to July, 1709, there were 1838 husbandmen and vine-dressers. It was natural that the latter should seek to continue in Pennsylvania the husbandry to which

[50] *Penna.-German,* Vol. XII, pp. 213, 291; Jesse L. Rosenberger, *The Pennsylvania Germans,* p. 36.

[51] W. F. Dunaway, *A History of Pennsylvania,* p. 258.

[52] *American Husbandry,* Vol. I, pp. 157–164; Benjamin Rush, *Manners of the German Inhabitants of Pennsylvania,* p. 20.

they had been accustomed. But vine-growing met with very little success. It has been stated that the soil did not contain the proper amount of moisture, and that insect pests appeared which the Germans did not know how to cope with.[53] It must have been with great reluctance that hundreds of settlers, whose whole economic life, traditions, and even art in Germany had centered around the cultivation of the vine and the production of wine, converted their vineyards into wheat fields. It meant the severing at one stroke of one of the strongest ties with Germanic culture.

Indispensable adjuncts of every German farm were the garden and the orchard. It was often the very first step of the new settler to "get ready a field for an orchard, planting it immediately with apples chiefly, and some pears, cherries and peaches. This they secure by an enclosure, then they plant a piece for a garden." Here thrived the cabbage and the turnip, which grew to such enormous sizes as to astonish visitors from Europe, as well as onions and carrots, gooseberries, currants, strawberries, and raspberries.[54] Advertisements in the *Pennsylvanische Berichte* of farms for sale frequently emphasized the *Baum-Garten,* with fifty or more young *Apffelbäumen* all bearing profusely.[55]

Since the German farmer was dependent upon his own efforts for his linen for table and clothes, and tow for bags and wagon covers, he usually planted a part of his land with flax. The multiform tasks which he or his wife had to perform from the day the ground was prepared until the yarn was handed over to the weaver were arduous indeed. They must plant the seed, harvest the crop, not with sickle or scythe, but by pulling up the stalks, thresh it in the barn with a home-made bat, ret it in the sun, subject it to *flachsbrecha* or breaking, swinging, hatcheling and spinning.[56] When the German farmer retired at night under his bed linen, or drew on his undershirt in the morning, or wiped his

[53]*Penna.-German,* N.S. Vol. XII, p. 533. Pennsylvania vine growers have to contend with the Grape Root Worm, Grape Berry Moth, Grape Curculio, Grape Leaf Hopper, etc., *Pennsylvania Dept. of Agriculture Bulletin, No. 217,* p. 48.

[54]Benjamin Rush, *Manners of the German Inhabitants of Pennsylvania,* p. 23; R. W. Kelsey, *Cazanove Journal* (Haverford, 1922), p. 34; Peter Kalm, Vol. I, p. 69. Lewis Miller states that Christian Lehman of York, raised a pumpkin "as large as a barrel."

[55]*Pennsylvanische Berichte,* Sept. 16, 1750; Jan. 16, 1750.

[56]*Penna.-German,* Vol. IX, pp. 266–273.

hands on his towel, he had the satisfaction of realizing that he was enjoying the fruits of his own arduous labor.[57]

Every German farmer had his herd of cattle, not usually to supply the demands of the Philadelphia or Lancaster markets, but as an integral part of his farm economy.[58] His cattle supplied him with meat and milk for his table, hides for shoes and harness, manure for his gardens and fields, even with draft animals for his plow and his wagon. The inventory of the estate of Daniel Rosenberger, in 1771, shows four horses, one colt, nine cows, four heifers, two calves, one bull, ten sheep and four hogs.[59] A prime consideration in the value of any farm was the extent and richness of the meadow, and when it was advertised for sale the owner was sure to point out that it had fifteen or twenty acres of *Wiesen* cleared.[60] Not infrequently the Germans saved their grass from the withering rays of the summer's sun by irrigation. "Here I found the splendid method of irrigating meadows by canals, into which the springs flowed," wrote Governor Pawnall in 1754. "The water runs down the hill and waters the entire meadow."[61] Benjamin Rush stated that the Germans fed their horses and cows well, so that the horses did twice the work and the cows yielded three times as much milk as "those less plentifully fed."[62] While farmers of other nationalities often gave their cattle no shelter in the winter, the Germans kept them warm in their great combination barn and stables, and so saved both the animal and hay.[63]

In addition to his cattle the farmer had his work horses, his flock of sheep to provide him with wool and meat, his swine and his poultry. Christopher Wiegner writes in one of his letters that one day he was summoned home from church by the

[57]Penna. German Society *Proceedings,* Vol. X, pp. 25–29.

[58]See inventory of estate of George Hollenbach, Aug. 13, 1736, *Penna.-German,* Vol. XII, p. 679.

[59]J. L. Rosenberger, *The Penna. Germans,* pp. 145, 146.

[60]*Pennsylvanische Berichte,* April 2, 1757, Sept. 16, 1750, Jan. 16, 1750.

[61]*Penna.-German,* Vol. XII, p. 534. "They are very well acquainted with the husbandry of watering meadow lands, by conducting brooks over them . . . bringing the water in little streams along the sides of the hills."—*American Husbandry,* Vol. I, p. 166.

[62]Benj. Rush, *Manners of the German Inhabitants of Penna.,* p. 16.

[63]*Ibid.,* p. 20.

"swarming of his bees."[64] The Germans brought bee culture with them from the Palatinate and continued to pursue it throughout the colonial period. Cazenove remarked upon it when he travelled through Pennsylvania at the end of the eighteenth century.[65]

The Germans and Swiss brought their system of household manufactures to Pennsylvania almost unchanged. In Lancaster or Dauphin as in the Palatinate the family congregated on winter evenings around the five-plate stove to knit, or spin, or mend the farm implements. Save for their best suits, brought from Germany or purchased at the nearest town, they made their own clothes.[66] The flax field and the sheep furnished flax and wool for the spinning wheels, and the spinning wheel in turn the thread for the family loom. So large were the looms that an especial shed was provided for them, but in time it became customary to turn the thread over to professional weavers. The mother and daughters often busied themselves with knitting, for there was constant need of stockings, socks, mittens, and caps. "In many a home a half-dozen spinning-wheels were kept buzzing. The daughters spun their own marriage dower. There was plenty of noise when the wheels were humming and droning and plenty of dust too, especially when flax was spun."[67]

Some farmers were skilled shoemakers, but with the advent of the travelling artisan many resigned this difficult task into his hands.[68] In the summer shoes were seldom worn by either sex, and it is said that many took their shoes to church in their hands so that the discomfort of wearing them need be endured only during services.[69] The father and sons must be not only husbandmen but skilled mechanics, for today they might have to build a shed, tomorrow repair a broken plow, the next day construct a cider-press, the next forge a skimmer or ladle, the next tan a cowhide for the shoemaker.

The work of the women was even more varied and unrelent-

[64] *Penna.-German,* Vol. VII, p. 5.
[65] *Cazenove Journal,* p. 34.
[66] *Ibid.,* p. 34.
[67] *Penna.-German,* Vol. IX, p. 83.
[68] J. L. Rosenberger, *The Penna.-Germans,* p. 39.
[69] Penna.-German Society, *Proceedings,* Vol. X, p. 31.

ing. Not only must they clean the house, do the family washing, prepare the meals, dry apples and peaches for pies, milk the cows, make cheese, churn, spin, dip candles, and knit; often they had to work in the fields, bare of foot, cutting or gathering in the crops.[70] Travellers in the Palatinate who spoke pityingly of the hard labor of women there, would have been surprised to find conditions little changed in Pennsylvania, the land of plenty. The maiden was valued by her suitor, not so much because of beauty or quickness of wit, as for her ability as a housewife.

> "All die Mädche misse lerne
> Gut zu schpinne un zu zwerne;
> Die wu scheene Kleeder welle,
> Misse sich ans Schpinnrad schtelle."

Every farmer had his apple-press. In the early days the press consisted of two solid cylinders fifteen inches in diameter and twenty inches long, cut from the trunk of a tree, notched to fit into each other, and set upright side by side in a stout wooden frame. A long pole or sweep, drawn by a horse, set the cylinders in motion, while a hopper fed in the apples. Lewis Miller describes for us a tragedy caused by one of these presses near York. David Miller was standing beside the press when a young woman momentarily distracted his attention by throwing an apple at him. His hand was caught by the cylinder and badly mangled. Apparently infection followed, for, despite the amputation of the hand, the young man died two weeks after the accident[71] (Plate 29).

The large degree of economic independence enjoyed by the Pennsylvania German farmers is illustrated by the husbandry of the Geiger brothers, three bachelors, Conrad, Paul, and Peter, who lived near York. "They do all the work what belong to housekeeping," Lewis Miller relates in his imperfect English, "their own kooking and washing, spining thread and weave on the loom, make clothing to dress. And do their own smith

[70]Benjamin Rush, *Manners of the German Inhabitants of Penna.*, p. 25; *Penna.-German*, Vol. XII, pp. 74–75.

[71]Ludwig Miller, *Chronicle of York, Pennsylvania* (York Historical Society).

ATE 29. DAVID MILLER'S HAND CAUGHT IN THE APPLE PRESS

ATE 30. LEWIS MILLER VISITS THE FARM OF THE GEIGER BROTHERS

PLATE 31. A GROUP OF YORK, PENNSYLVANIA, CITIZENS SHOWING EARLY NINETEENTH-CENTURY COSTUMES

work. And farm a few acres of land in wheat and corn for bread. . . . And have a fine garden, and orchard of all kinds of good fruit trees, and a stand of beehives where bees are kept for the honey. And to make a little money they make and burn charcoal and sell them in town. They have horses, cows, sheep, hogs, chickens and turkeys"[72] (Plate 30).

Benjamin Rush praised the Germans as the most successful farmers in Pennsylvania. Their farms are distinguished by the "superior size of their barns," he says, "the height of their enclosures (fences), the extent of their orchards, the fertility of their fields, the luxuriance of their meadows and a general appearance of plenty and neatness in everything that belongs to them."[73] This success must be attributed in part to their training in husbandry, in part to their thrift, in part to their capacity for hard and unremitting labor. One writer explains the German's capacity for slaving and saving by the fact that in the fatherland he had been compelled to utilize every inch of soil, to expend the last bit of strength in order to keep body and soul together. "Their severe training more than their greed compelled them for the first few generations at least to follow the same methods and practice the same rigid economy as their fathers."[74]

All in all the husbandry of the German peasant was profoundly altered by the transit to America. Despite the similarity of the soil and climate of southeastern Pennsylvania to those of the Palatinate, despite his desire to do all things in the old German manner, he could not escape the influences of the New World. With fertile acres so cheap as to be within his grasp in what seemed to him princely amounts, with the old burdens of dues and services non-existent, and taxes vastly lightened, the old economy of the manor, the agricultural villages, and the compulsory rotation of crops, could not be duplicated. He came from one of the oldest and most highly developed agricultural regions of Europe into a wilderness; for him to transform this wilderness into another Palatinate was impossible. But the greatest change

[72]Ludwig Miller, *Chronicle of York, Pennsylvania.*

[73]Benjamin Rush, *Manners of the German Inhabitants of Penna.*, p. 32.

[74]Dr. George Mays, in *Penna.-German*, Vol. VII, p. 151.

lay in the matter of his personal status, the transformation of the German peasant into the American farmer.

The character of the food served in the home of the German was not greatly altered by the transit to America. His table was more bountifully provided, there were never times of stint and hunger, he could enjoy certain dishes prepared from products indigenous to America, such as maize or pumpkin, but in the main he ate what he had learned to love as a child in the fatherland. Rush states that he ate sparingly of boiled animal food, with much vegetables, especially salad, turnips, onions and cabbage, together with much cheese. He drank milk, and also on occasion cider, beer and wine;[75] seldom distilled spirits, tea or coffee. It was customary for the wife to cut up apples and other fruit and permit them to dry, thus preserving them for use during the winter. Favorite dishes were potato soup, meal soup, sauerkraut, fat pork, dried apples, dough buttons, filled pig stomach, souse, sausage, liver pudding, turkey, goose, duck, chicken, beef, veal, apple fritters, funnel cakes, dried-apple pies, gingerbread, and vinegar punch.[76]

Many of the immigrants brought several suits of clothes with them from Germany or Switzerland, stored away in the ornate family chest, and these no doubt lasted for a generation or two for holiday or Sunday dress. When Cazenove was at Myerstown he was surprised to see people coming out of church dressed in the manner of Westphalia. The green or blue coats, the pulled-down hats, the high boots extending above the knee, even the bearing and general appearance of the men seemed to him European, not American. Only the young had given up some of the old German dress under the influence of the new country.[77]

In the days when the German settlements were just emerging from the frontier stage, men wore clothes made, at times, of linsey-woolsey; at times of leather or bucksin (Plate 33). The women wore short gowns with kerchiefs, small shawls or hoods as head covering. Fashions seemed to have changed in keeping with the trend in Philadelphia, although lagging some years

[75]Benjamin Rush, *Manners of the German Inhabitants of Penna.*, p. 20.

[76]F. J. F. Schantz, in Penna.-German Society *Proceedings*, Vol. X, "Domestic Life," etc., p. 18.

[77]*Cazenove Journal*, p. 45.

behind. We find certain old men, especially ministers and school teachers, clinging to their knickerbockers, long frock coats, and broad-brimmed hats, until far into the nineteenth century[78] (Plate 31). The Old Order Amish, a type of Mennonites, continue today to wear a distinct costume of their own, the men with a sort of jacket, fastened with hook and eye, long black trousers and round-crowned, wide-brimmed hats, the women with black shoulder-capes, and little black bonnets stuck on the back of their heads. The married men all have beards, the unmarried men are clean-shaven.[79]

No doubt the first Mennonite immigrants wore beards, knee breeches, and the hook-and-eye coats, for that was the prescribed costume of their brethren in Switzerland. But in time the Mennonite styles in America changed. The so-called plain or collarless coat became universal at the time of the Revolution, and is still worn by ministers and a few old laymen. The "shad-belly" coat, or cutaway without collar, was regarded as the prescribed uniform for Mennonites of good standing during the early part of the nineteenth century. It was in 1847 that John H. Oberholtzer was excluded from the Council of his church, because some of the brethren held it wrong of him "to wear a collar on the coat or buttons on both breasts."[80] Today the Mennonites wear dark suits, the coats with standing clerical collars, with no buttons on sleeves or back, and black felt hats with narrow brims.[81]

Not all of the German immigrants were peasants; many were skilled craftsmen. Of 1838 new arrivals at Philadelphia in April, June and July, 1709, 56 were bakers, 87 masons, 124 carpenters, 68 shoemakers, 99 tailors, 29 butchers, 45 millers, 14 tanners, 7 stocking weavers, 6 barbers, 4 locksmiths, 95 cloth and linen weavers, 82 coopers, 13 saddlers, 2 glass blowers, 3 hatters, 8 lime-burners, 2 engravers, 3 brickmakers, 2 silversmiths, 48 blacksmiths, 3 potters, 6 turners.[82]

[78]Ludwig Miller, *A Chronicle of York.*

[79]J. L. Rosenberger, *The Penna.-Germans,* pp. 123, 124.

[80]Penna.-German Society *Proceedings,* Vol. XXXV, pp. 392, 393.

[81]J. L. Rosenberger, *The Penna.-Germans,* p. 111.

[82]Benjamin Rush, *Manners of the German Inhabitants of Penna.,* p. 10.

The German artisan upon his arrival, or at the expiration of his term of indenture, must have looked around for an opportunity to pursue his old vocation. Some no doubt set up shop in Philadelphia or Lancaster or York, some may have shouldered their journeyman's kit and set out as travelling workers. Thousands must have deserted the forge, the last, or the loom, to purchase land and begin life over again as farmers. Of these many made use of their skill as artisans in the multiform tasks of the farm, while some converted one room of their homes into a workshop and combined shoemaking, weaving or tanning with husbandry. But the artisan, as well as the farmer had to adjust himself to new conditions. In some cases he found that there was little or no demand for the products he had turned out in Germany, in others the raw materials were different in character, in still others, as in the making of rifles, a higher degree of skill was necessary. "Since their settlement in Pennsylvania many of them have acquired the knowledge of the mechanical arts, which are more immediately necessary and useful in a new country," says Benjamin Rush, "while they continue . . . the arts they imported from Germany with vigor and success."[83]

The extent to which the mechanical arts were combined with husbandry is revealed in the advertisements in the Pennsylvania German newspapers. We find Henrich Lora, in 1750, seeking to rent his farm of 200 acres, including a large tannery;[84] another farmer a few years later offering for sale his *Plantasche* on which was a well-equipped malt-house and a malt-mill;[85] Nicolaus Seitzinger advertising for rent his farm with a smithy and smith's tools;[86] Jacob Bayerle explaining that he had on his place an oil-mill and a sawmill.[87] Thus German Pennsylvania was not only the richest agricultural region in the colonies, but a beehive of small industries.

As the population increased in density, many artisans settled in villages, rented or built a house, and opened shop in one of the lower rooms. Thus when the near-by farmer went to town to sell his vegetables, fruit, butter and cheese, he found it also a

[83]*Ibid.*, p. 33. [84]*Pennsylvanische Berichte*, Sept. 16, 1750.
[85]*Ibid.*, March 4, 1758. [86]*Ibid.*, Nov. 1, 1750. [87]*Ibid.*, Feb. 1, 1750.

convenient place to purchase articles which it was impracticable for him to manufacture at home. He might buy shoes from the local shoemaker, clothes from the tailor, beer from the brewer, barrels in which to ship his crops, chairs and tables from the cabinet-maker, bridles and harness from the saddler, a new wheel for his wagon from the wheelwright, a kettle from the coppersmith, perhaps a grandfather clock from the watchmaker.[88] And here and there in the country districts, where there was water-power, or raw materials, or a ready market near at hand, one might see iron furnaces, or potteries, or smithies, or picturesque stone grist mills. This explains why certain counties became noted as the center of especial industries—Franklin for scythes and sickles, Northampton for rifles, Bucks for pottery, Lancaster for glassware.

When Cazanove stopped at Kutztown, he found there a carpenter, a turner, a joiner, two hatters, a saddler, a baker, a shoemaker, two tailors, a locksmith, a wheelwright, a weaver, a potter, a tobacco factory, a tan-yard, and five women spinners.[89] This was probably typical of the small Pennsylvania German town. The work done in larger places was, of course, far more extensive. In the town of Lancaster from May, 1769, to May, 1770, the looms turned off no less than 27,793 yards of cloth.[90] Among the picturesque characters in York depicted by Lewis Miller were George Adam Gosler,[91] cabinet-maker (Fig. 27); Christopher Stocker, potter; William Schröder, spinning-wheel-maker; Betty Hauser, linen weaver; Gorgiens, parchment-marker; Fackler, Schreck, Weber, and Platz, stocking weavers; Grumb, violin-maker; Frederick Zorchger, chemist; Joseph Wampler, carpenter; the former Hessian, David Cranmer, house-painter; Worley, sickle-maker (Plate 31); Henry Epply, mason; John G. Stoll, cooper (Plate 33); and Weaver, wagon-maker.[92]

In certain crafts the Germans were undisputed leaders in the colonies. Noted as lovers of music, they became the chief, almost

[88]Daniel Rupp, *History of Lancaster County,* pp. 329–330.

[89]*Cazanove Journal,* pp. 29–30.

[90]J. O. Knauss, *Social Conditions Among the Penna-Germans,* p. 132.

[91]See p. 344.

[92]Ludwig Miller, *A Chronicle of York.*

the only makers of musical instruments. The zithers of Bucks County, and the organs, pianos, spinets, and hand-organs of Lancaster found their way into church and home in all parts of Pennsylvania. David Tanneberg, of Lititz, built organs for the Reformed Church of Lancaster, Zion's Lutheran Church, Philadelphia, and the Moravian Church, Lancaster, which for tone quality were declared to be the equal of the best in Europe.[93] He died at York in 1807 while working on the organ for the old Lutheran Church[94] (Plate 32). Of the highest quality, also, was the work of Philip Fyring, who built the organ for Saint Paul's Church, Philadelphia. The center of this industry was the little town of New Holland, near Lancaster.[95]

There was one product of German craftsmanship which found a ready market on the expanding frontier region. The pioneer in the backwoods of Pennsylvania, in the Shenandoah valley, and across the mountains in the beautiful Kentucky region, found it impossible to bring over the hundreds of intervening mountains and through the forest to his home many of the wares of the older regions. But though he might deny himself manufactured furniture, or "store clothes," or earthen ware, or even farm implements, he dared not be without his rifle. To it he looked not only for the protection of his family from Indians and wild animals, but in large part for his daily food. And though it came to be known as the Kentucky rifle, it was chiefly the invention of the German gunsmiths, and for decades was turned out from the shops of Lancaster.

The evolution of this weapon can be traced by successive steps from the German wheel-lock rifle of 1600, through the heavy stock and short-barrelled flint-lock, popular six decades later, to the long-barrelled rifle of Pennsylvania.[96] The smooth-bore fowling pieces and short rifles brought over by the German immigrants were unsuited to a country where life and death hung on their accuracy and the rapidity with which they could be fired. Gradually the local gunsmiths lengthened the barrel, which made

[93]J. O. Knauss, *Social Conditions Among the Penna.-Germans,* pp. 135–137. Also for the Lutheran Church, Lancaster. Zook, *Historical and Pictorial Lititz.*

[94]Ludwig Miller, *A Chronicle of York,* p. 98. The organ was finished by one Hall.

[95]Zook, *Historical and Pictorial Lititz.*

[96]G. W. Dillin, *Captain John.*

32. DAVID TANNEBERG, WORKING ON ORGAN AT YORK

33. *Left:* Old Kreitler, making buckskin suits at York, Pennsylvania. *Right:* John G. Stoll, cooper of York, Pennsylvania

PLATE 34. CHRISTIAN HERR HOUSE, NEAR LANCASTER

PLATE 35. TYPICAL PALATINATE COURT

them better suited to the slow-burning powder of America, and added to precision of aim.[97] At the same time they reduced the bore from the European standards of .40 to .50 to .50 to 1.00, thus saving precious powder and lead, and eliminating unnecessary weight.

Important also was the invention by a Pennsylvania gunsmith of the greased patch—a small piece of cloth or buckskin soaked in grease, which was used for wadding. It was placed over the muzzle, the bullet was set on it, and both rammed down together. This permitted the use of smaller bullets, since the patch fitted tightly enough to give the rotary motion on firing; it made the loading easier and more rapid, and cleared the barrel of burned powder.[98] With a "Kentucky rifle" one could fire far more rapidly than with a European rifle, for it was not necessary to stop after a few shots to clean out the fouled barrel. This, together with its accuracy, made it one of the most deadly weapons in the world, and gave to it a rôle of vital importance in the making of the United States.

During the Revolution the British early learned to dread the rifle of the backwoodsmen. It was at the battle of Long Bridge, near Norfolk, Virginia, that they first encountered a force armed with this weapon, and their bloody defeat may in large part be attributed to it, for when they attempted to charge in the face of the Virginia frontiersmen, they were picked off with deadly accuracy.[99] On June 14, 1775, Congress called for ten companies "of expert riflemen," to be used in the siege of Boston, and soon after the men were on their way to Cambridge. Here their feats of marksmanship aroused the admiration of their comrades, and the deadly execution of their fire the dread of the British. At the battle of Long Island the enemy singled out the frontiersmen for especial revenge, their officers pointing out the position of "the dread greencoated riflemen of Pennsylvania," and urging their men on to the attack.[100] The rifle also was all-important

[97]The best rifles were from four to five feet long and the barrels from 40 inches to 50 inches.

[98]Edwin Lefèvre, "The Meaning of Penna. Dutch Antiques," *Saturday Evening Post*, Aug. 20, 1935.

[99]T. J. Wertenbaker, *Norfolk—Historic Southern Port*, pp. 63, 64.

[100]*The Penna.-German*, Vol. IX, pp. 113–114.

in the winning of the West, in Andrew Lewis's great victory at Point Pleasant, and at Kaskaskia and Vincennes. It was in part responsible for one of the most crushing defeats ever suffered by a British army, for it was the Kentucky rifle which made it possible for Andrew Jackson's frontiersmen to pick off the enemy as they charged up to his breastworks in the battle of New Orleans, until they broke before the deadly blast.

The men who made the Kentucky rifle were more than skilled artisans, they were artistic craftsmen, bestowing upon their work the loving care of a silversmith or a cabinet-maker.[101] Their rifles were not only durable, accurate, correctly proportioned; they were also decorated with carving, and inlaid with silver or brass (Fig. 16). On one we see a lion rampant, on another an eagle, on still another a star or a crescent. The patch box in the butt of the stock, where the rifleman kept his grease, had a hinged cover of brass, which also was often delicately engraved. The beautiful graining of the stock itself, which was made of curly maple, and not of walnut as in Europe, harmonized perfectly with the silver, brass or ivory decorations.[102] These old rifles were as far removed as possible from the standardized products of today, for each was different from the other, each had its own individuality.

The history of the rifle in America runs counter to the usual course for transplanted crafts and arts. In place of the deterioration which so often was the accompaniment of frontier conditions, one finds a steady advance, which eventually made the American rifle the best in the world. After all, it was necessity which was the moulding influence. There was no vital demand for paintings, or literature, or science, but there was an urgent demand for an efficient weapon. In rising to this emergency the gunsmiths of Lancaster and Northampton proved that under certain conditions the New World could surpass the Old.

The Pennsylvania artisan was protected from ruinous competi-

[101]Among the leading gunsmiths were J. Kassler, John Moll, Frederick Zorger, John Armstrong, Peter Brong, L. Haeffer, John Tyler, Jacob Newhardt, Daniel Kleist, and John Young. It will be noted that some of the names are English.

[102]Joseph Downs, *The House of the Miller at Millbach* (Pennsylvania Museum of Art, 1929).

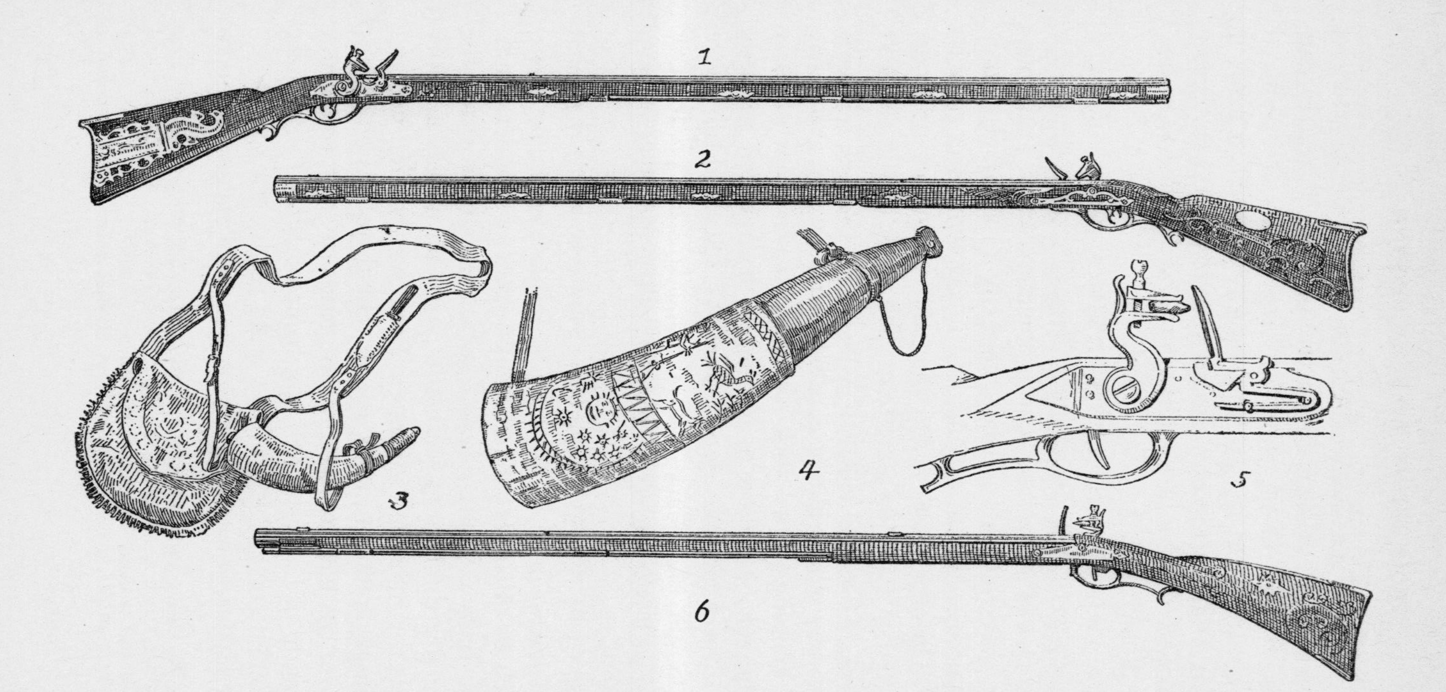

FIGURE 16. 1–2 EARLY PENNSYLVANIA FLINT-LOCK RIFLE. 3. HUNTING BAG AND POWDER-HORN. 4. PENNSYLVANIA INDIAN POWDER-HORN. 5. MECHANISM OF A FLINT-LOCK RIFLE. 6. A 1729 PENNSYLVANIA RIFLE

tion from England by the fact that the English did not require flour, the only product which the province could send in payment for manufactured goods. Nonetheless, the stores of Philadelphia, and even of Lancaster and Easton, always had on hand a supply of English goods, especially articles of finer workmanship which the local artisans found it difficult to turn out. Wilhelm Klampffer advertised in 1756 that he had for sale in his store on Second Street, Philadelphia, red, blue, and black cloth of various kinds, knives, files, buckles, powder, etc.[103] At Bethlehem, Cazenove saw a store filled with all kinds of goods from England and Germany.[104] But Pennsylvania enjoyed a far greater degree of economic independence than the tobacco or the sugar colonies, since her exports and imports amounted to but a fraction of the production of her farms and shops.

Commerce, both foreign and internal, was handicapped by the difficulties of transportation. It is true that the Delaware offered a magnificent highway for trade from the ocean to Philadelphia, but connection with the back country was far less favored. It was no easy matter for the farmer of Bucks or Montgomery or Berks to get his wheat or flour to Philadelphia, and bring back English cloth or farm implements or household furniture. The Delaware was convenient indeed for those fortunate enough to have their farms near it below the Trenton falls, but there were serious impediments above. The shallowness of the water in some places, the swiftness of the current which eddied through rocky channels in others, rendered the stream unfit for navigation by ordinary sailboats. In time a vessel made its appearance, the celebrated Durham boat, especially designed for the upper Delaware. About sixty feet long and eight feet wide, drawing only two feet when loaded, the center open but with decks on either end, the vessel resembled an enormous canoe. The Durham boat could take downstream as many barrels of flour as fifteen Conestoga wagons, and the voyage was inexpensive, since the current of the stream provided most of the propulsion.

[103] *Pennsylvanische Berichte,* Feb. 16, 1756.

[104] This was during the national period when American trade was no longer subject to the British Navigation Acts.

On the other hand, the return trip was tedious indeed, the crew forcing the vessel slowly upstream by means of long "setting poles."[105] Between Easton and Philadelphia transportation costs at the end of the eighteenth century were twenty-five cents a barrel downstream, and fifty cents for a hundred pounds upstream.[106]

The Schuylkill was a similar highway of commerce although the difficulties were even greater. When Colbert-Maulevrier visited Reading in 1798, he found there several storehouses where grain from the surrounding country could await until highwater made it possible to ship it downstream. There was then a fleet of about fifty boats employed in the trade,[107] each about sixty feet by eight feet, with a capacity of twelve tons. On the other hand, the Susquehanna tended to divert the trade of Lancaster and York away from Philadelphia to Havre de Grace or Baltimore.[108] But the Susquehanna is shallow and in many places obstructed by rocks, so that frequently navigation was interrupted for weeks.

Dissatisfaction with river transportation early brought about a demand for adequate highways. It was in 1731 that the people of Lancaster County petitioned the Assembly for a serviceable road to Philadelphia that they might bring "the produce of their labors" to that city. So surveyors were soon at work laying out the route, trees were felled, underbrush cleared away, bridges built and the stream of traffic started on what became known as the King's Highway.[109] In time other roads began to spread out from Philadelphia, like spokes from the hub, and though rough and ill-kept, did service for an ever-increasing traffic.

To convey his produce to market over these roads the German used the celebrated Conestoga wagon (Fig. 17). These "ships of inland commerce" had long, sturdy bodies slightly curved and painted blue, with linen or hempen covers drawn tightly over

[105]Anderson, *Navigation on the Delaware and Lehigh Rivers*, Bucks Co. Hist. Soc., Vol. IV, pp. 282 ff.

[106]*Cazenove Journal*, p. 19.

[107]G. Chinard, *Voyage dans L'Intérieur des États-Unis et au Canada* (Baltimore, 1935), p. 3.

[108]*Ibid.*, p. 20.

[109]I. D. Rupp, *History of Lancaster County*, pp. 262–263.

strong hoops, projecting like bonnets in front and behind. In September and October one might see in one day on the Lancaster or Reading road from fifty to a hundred such wagons, each drawn by four or six heavy horses often adorned by bows of bells.[110] In Philadelphia the wagons were backed up in long rows before the shops in Market Street or the warehouses on

FIGURE 17. THE CONESTOGA WAGON

Front, the horses tied behind peacefully munching their food after the long haul.[111]

If the Conestoga wagon was the "through freight truck" of the German, his market wagon corresponded to the light station car of today. In it he took his farm produce to the nearest town for sale to the local market, or perhaps at the curb market. The market at Lancaster resembled closely the markets of the German city. Here one could see the little wagons of the Mennonites, Amish and other groups, along the curb on Duke, Vine and Prince streets, their horses stabled at the inn near by. In boxes or on little trestles the farmers, picturesque in their broad-brimmed hats, displayed their wares—fowls, butter, eggs, apples,

110Benjamin Rush, *Manners of the German Inhabitants of Penna.*, p. 26.
111See W. Birch and Sons' engravings of Philadelphia.

cider, apple-butter, sausage, beans, beets, corn, carrots, turnips, lettuce, *snits*. When the day waned and most of their produce had been disposed of, they hitched their woolly horses to the wagons, and plodded off along the road to Ephrata, or Manheim, or Mount Joy.[112]

Despite the tenacity with which the German clung to old ways, before the end of the eighteenth century German Pennsylvania had developed a distinct life of its own, different not only from English Pennsylvania, but also from the Palatinate or any other part of Germany. The statement of a Buffalo newspaper in 1856 that the immigrants came as "a fragment of the Middle Ages," and perpetuated in America that "dark and gloomy" state of society, is entirely without foundation in fact. A full half century before this accusation was made, the Germans had developed an agricultural economy different from that of Germany, had surpassed their cousins of the fatherland in certain crafts such as rifle-making and wagon-making, had acquired a distinct dialect of their own, were enjoying political and civil privileges unknown in Germany, were becoming educated to their duties as citizens of a free country, were even wearing different clothes, building their houses and barns in accord with conditions in their new homeland.

They had no sooner put foot on American soil than they began to experience the force not only of local conditions, but of the melting-pot. Those who came first were thrown into contact with the medley of English, Welsh and Dutch Quakers whom Penn had called to his province. Those who, coming later, passed out to the western parts of the German settlements had to rub elbows with the Scotch-Irish. The process of assimilation, although slower for the Germans than for the Dutch, the Huguenots and other groups, has been equally inescapable, the ultimate outcome is just as inevitable. Not less important was the contact of one Teuton group with another—Palatine with Swiss, Swiss with Bavarian, Mennonite with Moravian, Lutheran with Reformed.

[112]Cornelius Weygandt, *The Red Hills*, pp. 17–22. The author has often watched with interest an almost identical scene at the curb market around the Rathaus at Göttingen, Germany.

The Pennsylvania German may have derived his early residence from the Palatinate, his barn from Switzerland, his decorated clothes-chest from Bavaria, his public buildings from England.

The Germans might have had even greater success in retarding assimilation had there been closer contact with the fatherland. But the German of Lancaster or Bethlehem or Reading was cut off from his old home, even more than were the Dutch on the Hudson from Holland after the English conquest. He found himself under the jurisdiction of the English government at Philadelphia, and subject to the British Navigation Acts. Even though he might import German wares by way of England, even though he might purchase German books, even though he kept up a correspondence with friends at home, the changing course of German culture could have but a weakened influence on his life. During the colonial period the continuing tide of newcomers kept fresh the memories of the homeland, introduced new ideas, new styles, but with the drying up of migration, the Pennsylvania German was left almost entirely to the moulding influences of the New World.

The migration of so many thousands of Germans and Swiss to Pennsylvania was a matter of grave concern to some of the leaders of public opinion. Even Benjamin Franklin, broad-minded liberal that he was, expressed the fear that they might impose their culture upon the entire colony. "Few of their children in the country know English," he said. "They import many books from Germany, and of the six printing houses in the province, two are entirely German, two half German half English, and but two are entirely English . . . The signs in our streets (Philadelphia) have inscriptions in both languages, and some places only in German . . . Unless the stream of importation could be turned from this to other colonies . . . they will soon [so] outnumber us that all the advantages we will have, will in my opinion, not be able to preserve our language."[113]

Perhaps Franklin's apprehensions might have been realized, had not the German immigration been offset by the great influx of Scotch-Irish, the increase of the English population, and the

[113]Sparks, *Works of Franklin,* Vol. VIII, pp. 71–73.

flow of Germans from Pennsylvania into Maryland and Virginia. At the end of the colonial period, the Germans and Swiss constituted about one-third of the population of the province. Since they were settled chiefly in a few counties, where they formed an overwhelming majority, they were not in a position to impose their culture on other regions. This very fact, however, made it possible for them to preserve the longer their own civilization—their distinct religious sects, their language, their social customs, their peasant art, their crafts, their folklore, to some extent their architecture and their husbandry. Even today, after the lapse of two and a half centuries, the Teuton inheritance is a powerful and living force in the region between the Lehigh and the Susquehanna.

Chapter IX

VOLKSKUNST

IT HAS been suggested by German scholars that the art of the European peasant was no more than medieval art in a degenerate form. When the noble ship of medieval art went ashore, they say, and the cargo was strewn about on the sands, the peasants rescued and preserved it, at the same time distorting and misinterpreting it.[1] Whatever of truth there may be in this, peasant art was not a mere imitation, but a living art, the product of his own character and mind, his fertile fields and his forest-covered mountains. If he worked into his pottery designs of flowers and birds, it was because he loved flowers and birds, or because he accepted them as religious symbols; if his stove plates told the story of Adam and Eve, or of Samson and Delilah, it was because the Bible was his daily food.

Peasant architecture especially was vigorous, natural, expressive; reflecting traditions, but adapted to his surroundings, needs and economy. One finds in the Palatinate building forms suggestive of the ancient Franks, but modified to suit the climate, soil, agriculture, building materials of the region. The homes of the lower Palatinate differ from those of the Hardt mountains; those of the Westrich from those of the vintners of the south Palatinate. The Swiss houses, also, although having a marked individuality of their own, differ widely in different regions. The Bernese peasant house has a greater kinship with that of the Black Forest than with the architecture of Valais or of Fribourg; the Appenzell house is very similar to that of upper Bavaria. In one place it is the presence of wood in abundance which determines the architectural style, in another the bitter winter winds, in still another the slope of the land, in another the necessity for protection from robbers, in another the needs of the wine industry.

[1]Konrad Hahm, *Deutsche Volkskunst,* p. 15.

Thus there are many architectures within the regions whence the Germans of colonial America came, with variations in each—variations of districts, villages, individual houses.

If we select for consideration first the Palatinate, as the province which sent out so many settlers to America, and in the Palatinate select the Rhine valley, we discover that the predominating type of architecture shapes itself to the needs of the so-called Frankish court.[2] Here the entire group of buildings essential to the husbandman's life—residence, barn, stable, sheds, wine press, bake house, distillery—are set around three sides of a court, while the fourth side is closed by a high wall. The Frankish court presents a striking contrast with both the lower Saxon peasant house of the north and the great farm buildings of the Black Forest, Upper Bavaria and Switzerland, each of which includes under one roof residence, barn and stables. Although the court plan seems to have had its origin in the middle Rhine cloister, its development was shaped by local conditions, especially by climate and topography. Both the north German and the southern mountaineer needed a roof to protect him in his work from the cold and the snow of winter, but the farmer of the middle Rhine valley preferred to work in the open under the warm rays of the sun. Moreover, since he lived in a comparatively level country, he saw no reason why he should imitate the "banked" peasant house with its two, three or even four floors. He could boast also of the greater safety of his own plan, for it protected him from the danger of fire on the one hand and of robbery on the other.

One enters the court through the great arched gate, which is large enough to admit wagons piled high with hay, or perhaps through the little side gate for pedestrians[3] (Plate 35). Before us lies a rectangular space, paved with stone, the manure pile on one side, the well on the other.[4] To the left is the residence, one gable end facing the street, the front looking out on the court, the other gable end connected with a shed or perhaps the stable. The barn, with its threshing floor, its storage rooms for hay

[2]Albert Becker, *Pfälzer Volkskunde,* p. 52.

[3]*Das Läuferle,* of Alsace.

[4]Klaus Thiede, *Deutsche Bauernhäuser,* p. 45.

or wheat or rye, usually occupies the entire rear of the court, while on the right are the wine press, the wine cellar, the bake house, the distillery. There is something snug, inviting, homelike, safe about the Frankish court. In its practical application it is adaptable to all kinds of farm life, for the cattle raiser, the vintner, even the blacksmith, as well as the husbandman,[5] while its compactness would be the envy of the designers of the American modern kitchen. To this safe haven came the peasant after his hard labors in the outlying fields; here he housed his horses and cattle, stored his grain or his vintage; here he repaired broken wheels, tools, or casks; here his wife and daughters cooked his food, wove his clothes, cleaned, washed clothes, milked and performed the other thousand tasks which in all lands fall to the lot of the farm woman.

Despite the fact that it is Alemannic in origin and not Frankish,[6] the middle Rhine residence is in perfect keeping with the court ensemble (Plate 35). In former times built usually in picturesque half-timber patterns, it is now more frequently of stone.[7] The front door in some cases is upon the ground level, in others five or six feet above the court with single or double stairs leading up to a platform or porch covered by a projection of the roof.[8] The door itself fits perfectly into the scene, with its heavy oak panelling cut in diagonal lines or boldly outlined diamonds, and its artistic hand-wrought hardware. Since the door is usually in two parts, the peasant may open the upper section, and, leaning upon the lower with his little pipe in his mouth, look out complacently over the courtyard.[9]

The roof, which is usually devoid of dormers, descends sharply, its lines broken by graceful undulations and the bell-like flare at the eaves. The picturesque thatch, which makes a house so cool in summer and so warm in winter, has given way in some

[5]Albert Becker, *Pfälzer Volkskunde,* pp. 52, 53.

[6]Heinrich Rebensburg, *Das Deutsche Dorf,* p. 83.

[7]Many of the buildings which were destroyed in the wars of Louis XIV were replaced with stone, because of the increasing scarcity of timber.

[8]Albert Becker, *Pfälzer Volkskunde,* Figs. 87, 95, 105; *Das Bauernhaus in Deutschland, Elsass,* Nr. 3, Abb. 2; *Baden,* Nr. 3.

[9]Albert Becker, *Pfälzer Volkskunde,* p. 59.

cases to tile, whose brick-red coloring may be regarded as a token of insurance against the glaring red of conflagrations.[10] The chimney is almost invariably in the center. In the half-timber houses the beams lend themselves not only to structural utility, but to artistic expression, the usual upright, diagonal and horizontal timber being varied with richly carved squares, crosses, circles and diamonds. The appearance here and there of baroque cornices and ornaments betrays the fact that many of the houses were built after the great wars of the seventeenth century. The spaces between the beams are filled in with wattle covered with clay, mixed with straw and lime, but brick filling, perhaps worked out in complicated designs, is not unknown. To provide a measure of protection for the walls, the upper stories often project slightly over the lower, or on the gable ends tiled pent roofs project for a foot or so between stories. A characteristic touch are the inscriptions upon the cross timbers—the name of the builder, a Bible verse, or mottoes in Latin or in German (Plate 38).

On stepping through the front door one finds oneself in a hallway, with the stairs at the rear, the living-room to the left and the kitchen to the right, with the little spare room behind it. If we turn into the *Zimmer,* we find ourselves in a roomy apartment, with two windows looking out over the court and two over the street, the floor planked and covered with sand. In one corner is the cupboard laden with mugs and plates, in another the stove; against the wall is the dower chest and in the center of the room the family table. A curtained alcove contains the four-poster bed, so high that one must use a ladder for retiring, whose massiveness is accepted as a mark of the more substantial man. The peasant sleeps upon a mattress of straw, and under the *plumeau,* a heavy comforter filled with goose, duck or chicken feathers, which takes the place of blankets.[11]

In the kitchen the center of interest is either the great hearth, with its suspended cauldron, or, in case there is no bake-house

[10] A few years ago thatched houses could still be seen at Nanzweiler, Börsborn, and elsewhere in the Palatinate.

[11] Albert Becker, *Pfälzer Volkskunde,* pp. 60, 61; Robert Wuttke, *Sächsische Volkskunde* (Leipsig, 1903), pp. 415, 416.

in the court, a bake-oven built through the wall. Here are the usual assemblage of household utensils—decorated earthen plates and jars, pewter dishes, the griddle iron, lamps, skimmers, dough trough, etc. In the basement below is a little pantry, perhaps with a well or running spring. Outside, all opening upon the court, are servants' quarters, a store-room redolent of drying apples, the horse and cattle stalls, bins for storing fodder in summer and turnips in winter, the hay loft, threshing floor, pig sties, dovecote, scales, fruit press, perhaps the wine cellar.[12] Of great importance in the economy of the household is the bake-house, situated usually across the court from the residence.[13]

Had the emigration to America in the eighteenth century been confined to the Palatinate lowlands, the transit of architecture would have been comparatively easy to trace. But the emigrants from Switzerland introduced certain features of Swiss architecture, from Baden something reminiscent of the great farmhouses of the Black Forest, from Upper Bavaria perhaps a distinctive ornament, from Saxony a peculiar method of log construction, from Hanover the brick filler for half-timbering. Of especial importance is the log house, since the Germans took this type of building to America, where for decades it was their main dependence. In former centuries, before the forests were so greatly reduced in size and when wood was cheap, the peasants made wide use of logs in their homes. And though later generations turned more and more to half-timbering or to stone, the existence today of thousands of log houses, especially in the heavily wooded mountain districts, proves that the transition is by no means complete.

The German log house not only is quite different from the Swedish log house, but varies greatly in different parts of Germany itself. Especially attractive is the type, common in Saxony and northern Bohemia, in which the upper story rests, not on the logs of the lower story, but upon wooden columns, often turned and richly carved (Fig. 18). Distinctive also are the Swiss

[12] *Das Bauernhaus im Deutsche Reich,* Text, p. 256.

[13] Heinrich Rebensburg, *Das Deutsche Dorf,* Fig. 87; Albert Becker, *Pfälzer Volkskunde,* p. 61.

FIGURE 18. LOG HOUSE NEAR GROSGSCHONAN

FIGURE 19. LOG HOUSE NEAR LANDIS' STORE, PA.

houses, where the logs are carried out several feet beyond the walls to support the overhanging eaves of the roof, the pent roofs, or the balconies. The Germans, unlike the Swedes, usually squared the logs, and fitted them one into the other at the corners with an exact and peculiar notching, which lends strength to the walls, reduces the space between logs, and sheds the water outward.[14] The German log house, unlike the typical American log cabin, was not intended to save labor, and is often a marvel of painstaking and skillful workmanship.

The large expanse of roof so typical of German houses gave the builders an opportunity to display their skill and artistic sense in the laying of tiles. Just as the little boy in his nursery delights in making fancy figures with his colored blocks, so the tiler worked out in infinite variety on his roofs squares, pointed arches, diamonds, etc. Sometimes, however, he contented himself merely with laying each tile below and under its fellow above, so that they look like the backs of worshippers in church all bent in prayer. Since the vertical lines run through, the joint between two tiles always coinciding with the joint between the next two above, one wonders why the water does not find its way through to the room below. The secret lies in the grooving of each tile, which is contrived to divert the water away from the joint and deposit it in the center of the tile below. The tiles are not nailed to the roof after the manner of slate in America, but are held in place by lugs, or small projections on the under side, hooked over horizontal laths[15] (Fig. 20).

Weather-boarding in former centuries was not popular among the peasant builders, for before the mills had lowered the cost of sawing out planks, the shrinking of the forest areas had run up the price of timber. But when weather-boarding was used the planks were laid vertically, not horizontally. This rule holds even

[14]*Das Bauernhaus in Deutschland, Elsass,* Nr. 2; see also Bruno Schmidt, *Das Sächsische Bauernhaus,* p. 39; *Das Bauernhaus in Deutschland, S. Meiningen,* Nr. 1, Abb. 2; *Forschungen zur Deutschen Landes-und Volkskunde,* Vol. XXIX, "Das Bauernhaus in Oberösterreich," p. 47.

[15]Klaus Thiede, *Deutsche Bauernhäuser,* p. 60. An excellent example is shown in Heinrich Rebensburg's *Das Deutsche Dorf,* Fig. 154; Bruno Schmidt, *Das Sächsische Bauernhaus,* etc. (Dresden), pp. 26, 27.

for the boarding on the gable end under the eaves so common in stone and half-timber houses.[16] Possibly the Germans preferred the vertical planking because it gave an appearance of height to their houses in keeping with their towering roofs. On the other hand, their fondness for solidity found expression in the rounded arch, which they used not only in their gateways, but in house and basement doors, especially when the walls were of stone. In the same spirit they vaulted their wine cellars and their basements with masonry far heavier than was structurally necessary,

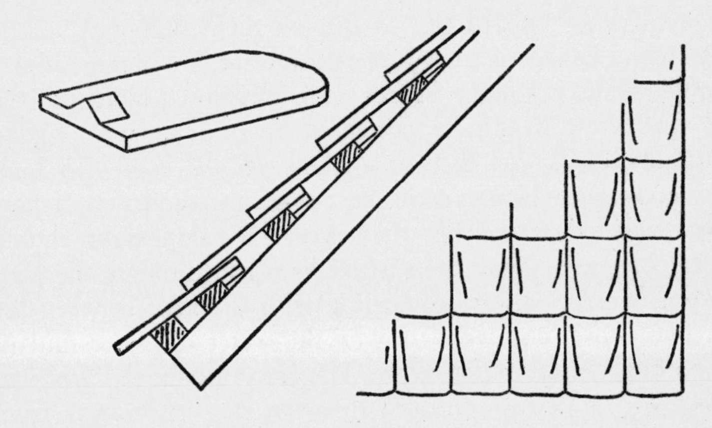

FIGURE 20. GERMAN TILES AND MANNER OF LAYING

lending them at the same time that air of mystery which has tempted poets and story-tellers to people them with elves and fairies.

In the eighteenth century, when Germans and Swiss were pouring down the Rhine and across the Atlantic to America, peasant architecture both in Germany and Switzerland was essentially medieval. German writers have pointed out that many of the farmhouses of that time resembled so closely the houses shown in Albrecht Dürer's engraving made four hundred years ago that their descent from them can hardly be questioned.[17] When pillaging soldiery burnt the peasant's home, he usually

[16] Klaus Thiede, *Deutsche Bauernhäuser,* pp. 15, 16, 17, 18, 20, 22, 46.
[17] Heinrich Rebensburg, *Das Deutsche Dorf,* p. 71.

rebuilt on the old foundations in the time-honored style, so that today thousands of villages in Germany are almost untouched by the coming and going of the architectural styles which have left so deep an imprint on the cities. If we visit Göttingen, one of the quaint old cities of Hanover, we find the old section centering around the Rathaus and St. Johannes Kirche quite medieval; the university buildings are in the Renaissance style; beyond the circle of the walls are many dignified residences which speak unmistakably of the age of Wilhelm I; while in recent years modernistic apartment houses have been springing up in the suburbs. But walk a few miles out to Geismar, and you find yourself in a medieval village.

The peasant's home was an expression of the peasant himself. A street in Hassloch, in the Rhine plain, with its high stone walls pierced by arched gates, its picturesque half-timbered gable-ends, its tiled roofs, is as German as the costume or the speech of the people themselves. There could be no mistaking it for a French village street or an English street. So the Palatine, when he turned his back on his homeland to settle in far-away America must have expected as a matter of course to build in the manner of his ancestors. He envisaged in this strange land of promise to which William Penn had invited him a Frankish court, or a Westricher *Einfirsthaus,* or an Edenkoben vintner's house.

But when he found himself in Pennsylvania where everything was so different, these visions must have grown dim. Instead of the populous cities, busy villages, cultivated fields to which he had been accustomed, he found unbroken forests, vast solitudes, nature in all its untamed strength. As he looked out over his leafy domain, which it was his task to convert into a farm, a domain perhaps as large as his native village, he realized that matters of more immediate concern than building a substantial residence must claim his attention—cutting down trees, clearing away stumps and underbrush, preparing the soil, laying out crops, building fences, making a shelter for the cattle. He was fortunate if he could find time for the crudest log cabin for his family, a makeshift until the time when the first pioneer tasks had been accomplished.

Even then he had to build in the simplest manner, availing himself of the materials at hand and adapting building methods which would economize in labor. He could not lavish upon his new home the infinite care given to the construction of the village house of Germany with its nicely jointed masonry, its ornamental beams, its carved doorways. So his thoughts turned to the log houses of the German forest regions. As he felled the great trees to make room for fields of wheat and rye, he must have realized that here before him lay the proper material for his home and his barn. If he happened to be ignorant of the details of log construction he could consult his neighbor, a native perhaps of the Odenwald or the Black Forest. From him he could get the proper method of squaring the logs, of notching the ends, of fitting in the door or the windows, of putting on the roof. Certain writers have assumed that the Pennsylvania Germans learned to build log houses from the Swedish settlers on the lower Delaware, but the most cursory examination of these old structures shows them to be German, not Swedish, in their antecedents.

If one will wander through the German districts of Pennsylvania, up the Lehigh, or through Lancaster County or up the Oley valley, he will find many time-honored relics of these primitive houses, some still occupied, others mere shells falling into rapid decay. From them we learn that the Germans made use of several distinct methods of log construction. When haste was the prime consideration, they neglected alike tradition and habits of exactness to build in the crudest way with logs roughly squared or left in the round, simple notching a few inches from the end, and wide crevices filled with clay and stone[18] (Fig. 21a). The skilled carpenters of Upper Bavaria or the Black Forest would have scorned this crude structure, but the Pennsylvanian prized it as a shelter for his family in the hard pioneer days.

Much neater and also more frequent was the notching in which the upper end of the log was cut on an obtuse angle like

[18]Compare with log houses at Serfans, near Prutz-Landeck (H. Rebensburg, *Das Deutsche Dorf*, Fig. 113). Of this type was the Yeakel cottage, Chestnut Hill, Philadelphia.

the roof of a house and fitted into a niche in the log above (Fig. 21b). This type required more careful workmanship, the logs always being "dressed" with an ax on the two vertical faces, but it left very wide spaces to be filled with "chinking."[19]

When time permitted, or perhaps when the immigrant was

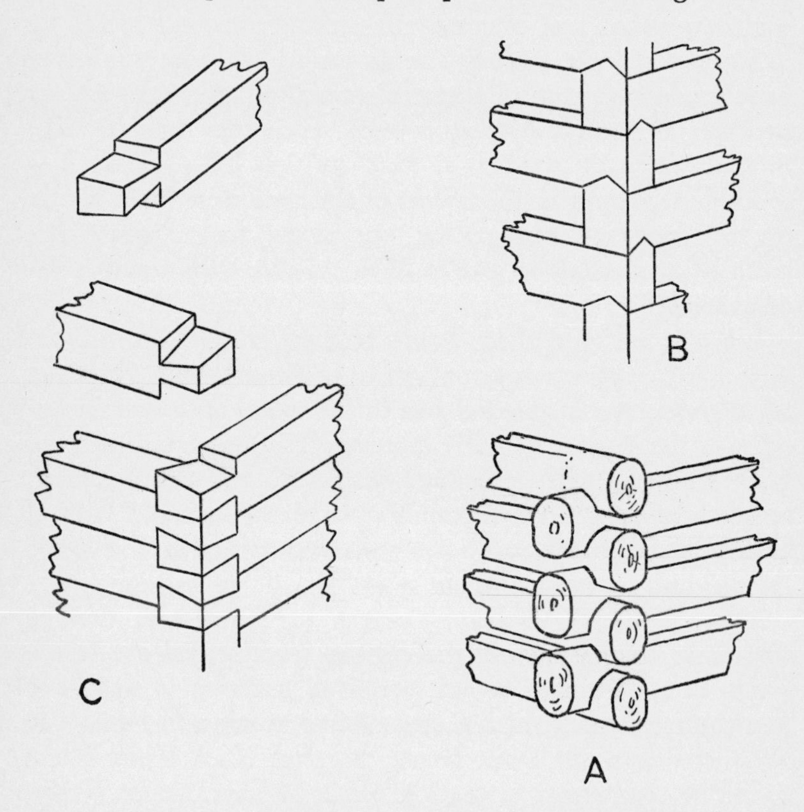

FIGURE 21. NOTCHING OF PENNSYLVANIA LOG HOUSES

skilled in carpentry, the logs were laid in the usual careful German fashion, with the so-called *schwalbenschwanz* notching. This required such exactness and nicety of work that it was done, not with the broad-ax, but the hatchet. Each surface of this

[19]G. Edwin Brumbaugh, "Colonial Architecture of the Pennsylvania-Germans" in Penna.-German Society *Proceedings,* Vol. XLI (1931). We have an excellent example of this type in the Indian Ridge House, Bucks County.

notching was made to slope in such a way as to drain outward, and so protect the inside from dampness on rainy days (Fig. 21c). The four sides of the log itself were first dressed with the broad-ax or the *Bundhacke,* and the inner side smoothed with the hatchet. The under and upper sides of the logs were often slightly grooved and the resulting shallow opening niched to make the wall weatherproof. The dovetailed log house is in many ways superior to that of frame construction; the walls are far stronger, as persons have discovered when they tried to take them down, more resistant to heat, and less inflammable. It is probable that most of the houses of this type were built, not in the first years of immigration, but in the second generation when it was possible to give to them the care their construction demanded.[20]

Still a fourth type of log house, brought probably from Saxe-Meiningen,[21] appears here and there in Pennsylvania. In it the builder sets up a frame and fills in the spaces with logs, somewhat in the manner of half-timbering. The logs are usually set horizontally, though sometimes vertically, and are mortised, tenoned and pegged into the uprights or plates and sills. Diagonal braces, notched in flush with the walls, add strength and enhance the resemblance to half-timber work.[22]

Although the Pennsylvania-German log house was thus as diverse in construction as the regions from which the immigrants came, the necessity of sacrificing tradition to simplicity and cheapness made them quite uniform in outward form. The Westrich house, the Swiss house, the great Black Forest house found no counterpart in the log houses of Lancaster or Northampton. Instead we find a rectangular structure, about thirty feet by twenty feet, sometimes two stories in height, sometimes only one with a loft, without dormers but with windows in each gable end, the chimney invariably in the center. The traveller Schöpf tells us that when he saw a house with a chimney at

[20]Of this type are the Balzer Kraus house, near East Greenville; the Gillam house, Newtown, Bucks County; an old house, Hinkletown; and houses in many other places.

[21]*Das Bauernhaus in Deutschland, Sachsen-Meiningen,* Nr. 1, Abb. 2.

[22]Examples of this type are found in Schaefferstown, Plainfield, and elsewhere.

either end he knew it was the home of an Englishman; if the chimney was in the middle, of a German[23] (Fig. 19).

It has been suggested that the pent roof, or shed, which appears so frequently in Pennsylvania-German log houses between stories or at the gable ends between the loft and the story below, was borrowed from the English. No doubt the immigrants, as they poured through Philadelphia, and noted house after house with pent roofs, gathered the impression that in America they were necessary as a protection to the walls. But it must be remembered that the pent roof was common in their native Germany. The settler who added it to his home in the American forest probably was thinking, not of Philadelphia, but of Neuburg, or Münsterappel, or Barbelroth, in his own Palatinate.[24]

Perhaps the most interesting German log house in America was the Miller homestead, two miles south of Harrisonburg, in the Valley of Virginia (Plate 36). This structure speaks vividly of the conflict of forces which created American civilization. The crudeness of the workmanship, the rough beams which support the porch, the hasty notching of the logs, the lack of balusters, carvings and other ornaments tell the story of pioneer conditions, of the owner's struggle with the forests, high labor costs and lack of transportation facilities. But the form, plan, structure and details are European, are based on the traditions of centuries of life in Switzerland or the mountain regions of south Germany. The stone basement, which was no doubt used for horses and cattle, the double porch resting on ceiling beams projecting beyond the walls, the two-story log superstructure, the long sweep of the steeply rising roof, the loft obviously used for storing grain, the central chimney, the roof bell all tell us that here we have a crude attempt to duplicate the peasant house of the Black Forest or the Jura. Fortunately, although only the foundation is standing, we are able to reproduce a photograph of this remarkable structure through the efforts of Doctor John Walter Wayland and the courtesy of the Miller family.[25]

[23]Schöpf, *Travels in the Confederation,* Vol. I, p. 125.

[24]Theodor Zink, *Deutsche Volkskunst, Die Pfalz,* Figs. 12, 13, 16, 22.

[25]Compare with Klaus Thiede, *Deutsche Bauernhäuser,* pp. 62, 63, 66.

PLATE 36. MILLER HOUSE, NEAR HARRISONBURG, VIRGINIA

PLATE 37. ELIE PFLIEGER VISITS THE HOMESTEAD AT YORK

PLATE 38. *Left:* Palatinate half-timbered house. *Right:* Spangler house, near York

In the early days of German Pennsylvania, the log house was almost universal. Philip Fithian, the itinerant Presbyterian preacher, when he visited Abbottstown, just prior to the Revolution, found "all the houses built with square logs."[26] Hagerstown he described as a place of two hundred homes, the greater part "built with logs neatly squared, which indeed make a good house."[27] Some years later, the French exile Colbert-Maulevrier spoke of Womeldorf as a little town, almost all of whose houses were built of squared logs with the intervals filled with stone, while Myerstown had one hundred houses, all of logs.[28] The log house, according to Benjamin Rush, lasted the lifetime of the first settlers, when it was displaced by a larger residence, usually of stone. Before the middle of the nineteenth century, many of the old log houses had been torn down, while others had become the objects of veneration to the sons and grandsons of the settlers who built them. It was in 1837, Lewis Miller tells us, that he took Elie Pflieger, who was on a visit to York, to see the two-story log house in which his father and uncles were born[29] (Plate 37).

One is inclined to wonder why the second generation of Germans, when they planned their larger residence to supersede the log cabin, so seldom made use of the old familiar half-timber construction. Beams could be had for the labor of cutting, lime was abundant, the climate was not so cold in winter nor hot in summer as to require thicker walls. True this type of construction had long been giving way to stone in the Palatinate, but many thousands who came to Pennsylvania had been born and reared in the quaint half-timber houses of Landau or Schifferstadt or Rohrbach. Apparently the German settlers discovered that with an abundance of timber, stone and lime it was economical to build either entirely of wood or of stone, so that the succession was from log to stone construction, not from logs to half-timbering.

Yet the custom of centuries was not lightly to be thrown aside,

[26]Albion and Dodson, *Fithian Journal*, p. 8. [27]*Ibid.*, p. 10.

[28]Gilbert Chinard, *Voyage dans L'Interieur des États-Unis*, etc., p. 4.

[29]Ludwig Miller, *Chronicle of York, Pennsylvania, 1799–1850*.

and here and there amid the usual log or stone houses, one found half-timber buildings, put up perhaps by newcomers not thoroughly acquainted with conditions in Pennsylvania. Lewis Miller gives us a fascinating picture of a half-timbered house near York which he visited in 1802, the home of two old people, Yargle and Susanna Spangler, whose curious dress and strange manners, as well as the sturdy uprights, plates, sills and diagonal braces of the house, reveal them as newcomers from Germany[30] (Plate 38).

On the southwest slope of Oley valley, hidden in the hills, stands an old Moravian meeting house, perhaps the sole surviving example of German half-timbering in Pennsylvania (Plate 39). The fact that this building, now used as a residence, has withstood the hand of time for nearly two centuries, shows that the unpopularity of half-timber construction among the settlers was not because of a lack of sturdiness or durability.[31] It is interesting to note that brick filling for the spaces between timbers, still popular in parts of Germany, was frequently employed in Pennsylvania. Had one wandered some years ago through Middle Street, Lancaster, he would have found several brick-filled half-timbered houses,[32] while we know that a house of the same type stood a century ago at No. 26 East Market Street, York[33] (Plate 40).

It was inevitable that the Germans, when they emerged from the period of the log house, should turn to stone for their chief building material. There is something substantial, enduring, about stone, which is in keeping with the German nature, the thing perhaps which makes him insist on solid foundations and thick walls, which is behind his love of massive furniture. Moreover, he was not only well acquainted with stone masonry in his native Germany, but he found abundant stores of building stone directly at hand. The earliest stone houses, often mere cabins, adhered more closely than those of later date to German models,

[30] Ludwig Miller, *Chronicle of York*.

[31] G. E. Brombaugh, Penna.-German *Proceedings,* Vol. XLI.

[32] J. M. Howells, *Lost Examples of Colonial Architecture,* Plate 53 (N. Y., 1931).

[33] York County Historical Society, 3–356.

and today when one wanders through the Oley valley or certain parts of Lancaster County, he will find here and there venerable reminders of the sixteenth- and seventeenth-century stone houses of the middle Rhine valley.

One of the most perfect examples is the Christian Herr house near Lancaster, said to have been built in 1719 (Plate 34). The sharply rising roof, the absence of dormers, the small windows, the central chimney, the character of the masonry take us in fancy to those quiet villages under the shadows of the Hardt mountains. Equally fascinating is the Heinrich Zeller house, near Womeldorf, with its projecting eaves supported by extended ceiling beams, its sheathed upper gable-ends, its heavy doors, its central chimney, its basement spring house.[34]

In nearly all of these early stone cabins there is a vaulted room in the basement built over a spring of water. The romantic tradition that the settlers thus sought an independent water supply in case of Indian attack, which has gained such wide credence, unfortunately will not bear close scrutiny. The spring room has no connection with the living quarters, so that the hapless member of the family sent to secure water during a siege would have been riddled before he could make the outside circuit from door to door. The spring room was built into these old houses because their owners were accustomed to spring rooms in their homes in Germany.

The European aspect of the early houses must have been enhanced by the thatched roofs which we have good reason to believe covered many of them. The pioneer farmer, perhaps many miles from the nearest tile burner, and himself too absorbed in the struggle for existence to spend his time in splitting shingles, frequently must have followed the example of Johannes Moelich in thatching his log cabin "with leaves or straw."[35] And later, when he had found other and perhaps better roof coverings for his

[34]In the same category are the stone cabin on the Moravian Seminary grounds, Bethlehem; the Bertolet cabin, Oley valley; the old cabin near Richlandtown; the cabin on the Shoemaker farm, Lancaster County; and many others. G. E. Brombaugh, in Penna.-Ger. Soc. *Proceedings,* Vol. XLI, Plates 16, 17, 20, 21, 23, 24, 25; Lancaster Co. Hist. Soc. *Papers and Addresses,* Vol. XXV, No. 8, p. 10.

[35]A. D. Mellich, Jr., *The Story of an Old Farm,* p. 146.

residence, he still clung to thatch for his barn. Jedidiah Morse tells us in 1789 that the barns were "commonly thatched with rye straw,"[36] and that the custom had not entirely died out in the middle decades of the nineteenth century we know from the statement of Benson Lossing that during his wandering over Revolutionary battlefields he came across "an old thatched barn" at Whitemarsh, near Germantown.[37]

But visions of the bright red roofs of the picturesque villages of the Rhine valley must have come frequently to the settler, so that when the burning of tiles was undertaken in conjunction with brick kilns or pottery works,[38] he was quick to make purchases. The Pennsylvania tiles, although less ornate than the German flat rectangular tile, in other respects duplicated them exactly. There was the same grooving, the same lug beneath, the same color, the same slight rounding at the end. They were laid, also, in the same simple pattern, with the joints carried through both vertically and horizontally (Plate 41). The author had imagined that the last Pennsylvania tile roof had long ago succumbed to neglect or to winds and storms, so that on a recent visit to Berks County he was greatly surprised to find a number still doing duty on outhouses. He has been informed by a friend who went to school as a boy in a tile-covered house that although one could look up and see sky between the joints, the rain never came through on the children. But tiles in Pennsylvania as in other parts of the Middle Colonies were susceptible to breakage, and the temptation to boys to bombard them with stones was sometimes too great to be resisted, as Jacob Busser, of New York, once found to his cost.

If the German farmer, turning his back upon both thatch and tiles, covered his roof with the cheaper wooden shingles, he still adhered to the traditions of the homeland in his method of laying them on, for each shingle was placed, not only under the row above, but under its neighbor to right or left. This practice gives

[36]Jedidiah Morse, *The American Geography* (Eliz. Town, 1789), p. 315.

[37]B. J. Lossing, *Pictorical Field-Book of the Revolution*, Vol. II, p. 115.

[38]Tiles were made by one Hülster, Upper Salford, Montgomery Co., so early as 1735; by the Moravians at Bethlehem about 1740, and at various places in Lancaster and Bucks.—E. A. Barber, *Tulip Ware of the Penna.-German Potters*, p. 107.

PLATE 39. MORAVIAN MEETING HOUSE, OLEY VALLEY

PLATE 40. HALF-TIMBERED HOUSE, YORK, PENNSYLVANIA

PLATE 41. TILE ROOF, OLEY VALLEY

PLATE 42. LUTHERAN CHURCH AT TRAPPE

the roofs of the Miller house, near Harrisonburg, the old Shoemaker stone cottage, Lancaster County, and other buildings where it is employed a ruffled or billowy effect, quite different from the shingled roof of an English house.[39]

Whenever time and means afforded, the German settlers made their doors with the same solidity and heaviness, equipped them with the same wrought-iron hinges as in Germany. In strict Palatinate style, the doors were often in upper and lower sections, so that one could remain shut while the other swung open (Plate 40). The John Richards drawings of old Germantown houses, made sixty or seventy years ago, when in most respects they had become distinctly English, show the double door in almost every other house.[40] Even when the door was not divided, the carpenters could not resist the temptation to make them as nearly as possible like those of Germany. So today when we stand before the door of the spring room at Fort Zeller or of a Berks County mill, or of the *Gemeinhaus* at Bethlehem, with their massive diagonal panelling, in fancy we are transported across the Atlantic to the Palatinate or Alsace or Bavaria.[41] Even the approach is almost identical with those of the Palatinate, for when it rises a few feet above the ground the door is reached, as in Germany, by steps built against the wall and rising on one or both sides to a platform.

If now we return to the early log cabins to examine their interiors, we find them as we would suspect, severely plain. The floor of spliced logs, clay or stone, the ladder or the crude steps leading to the loft, the rough table, benches, beds, and shelves, combine to give an impression of gloom which is only partly relieved by the dim light which comes in through the small casement windows. But the fire on the hearth or the glowing

[39]Lancaster Co. Hist. Soc. *Papers,* Vol. XXV, No. 8, p. 10. This method of laying shingles and slate is still in use in Germany. P. Schultze-Naumburg, *Der Bau des Wohnhäuser,* Vol. I, Figs. 20, 21.

[40]J. F. Sachse, "Quaint Old Germantown," Penna.-Ger. Soc. *Proceedings,* Vol. XXII. The door of the Jacob Heckert house, York, and that of Georg Müller, at Illig's Mill, each had two heavily panelled sections.

[41]The architects' drawings of the Moravian community houses almost invariably show doors with diagonal panelling.

stove lends a touch of cheer, which is heightened by the savory smell of *sauerkraut* and *speck*, or of *schnitz* and *knöpf*. And here and there the painted dower chest or a decorated trammel, or a carved spoon rack, lends a faint flavor of the fatherland.

The larger houses of the second generation afforded more comfort. One entered a front hall, and from it turned to one side into the living-room. Here was "the big fire hearth, in which was the iron crane and tripod with the steaming kettles hanging on them. . . . In one corner of the room stood the table with the benches running along its sides, and on it zinc dishes, pewter spoons and tin cups. In another corner stood the spinning wheel with bundles of flax, tow or wool. On the other side of the hall was the best room with plain but neat furniture, and back of it the *Kammer*, with the bed and crib. . . . In the attic were several beds for the boys, and hanging along the rafters were rows of smoked sausages and hams with bundles of flax and wool."[42] An inevitable accompaniment of the bed was the *plumeau*. "They cover themselves in winter with light feather beds, instead of blankets," says Benjamin Rush, which tends "both to convenience and economy, for the beds are warmer than blankets, and are made by themselves." One can but wonder, however, whether Rush ever slept under a *plumeau*. Had he done so he probably would have agreed with a New Englander who had an uncomfortable and sleepless night, and a Virginian who became so hot that he threw the thing off and so caught a severe cold, that it was an invention of Satan.

More pretentious was the interior of the type of house represented by the residence of Georg Müller, now preserved in the Pennsylvania Museum of Art. We can imagine the family at dinner in the hall seated around the long oak table, while the servant served the food from the cauldron or pots suspended in the great fireplace. On one side is a cupboard, laden with decorated pottery, on another a grandfather clock, here a stiff chair with a carved back, here the ornate double door, there the staircase with its distinctly German newel post and balusters. In the bedroom is a decorated chest of drawers, a dower chest, a corner

[42]*The Penna.-German*, Vol. VII, p. 388.

PLATE 43. THE HALL, GEORG MÜLLER HOUSE

PLATE 44. GEORG MÜLLER HOUSE

PLATE 45. TYPICAL PENNSYLVANIA–GERMAN GEORGIAN HOUSE

PLATE 46. GERMAN BARN, BERKS COUNTY, PENNSYLVANIA

PLATE 47. GERMAN BARN, BERKS COUNTY, PENNSYLVANIA

closet, the bed; on the walls is a fractur birth certificate, on the table the great family Bible[43] (Plate 43).

In Pennsylvania as in Germany the settlers had to have their delicious bread, and when the fireplace was not equipped with an oven, the baking was done, as in the fatherland, in an outside bake-house. This little structure was of stone, protected from the weather by a shingled or tiled roof, and provided with shelves for cooking utensils. Many stories are still told among the old families of the number of loaves one oven could turn out.[44] The use of the outside oven was gradually discontinued after the introduction in the nineteenth century of cook-stoves and kitchen ranges, and most of them have been torn down.[45]

As the early domestic architecture of the Pennsylvania Germans, whether expressed in log cabins, half-timbering, or stone, was determined by European inheritance and the frontier, so their houses in the second half of the eighteenth century showed the mingled influence of English ideas, continued contact with Germany, and local conditions. The proximity of the English, the example of their Georgian stone houses, the influence of the Carpenters Company of Philadelphia, and the importation of English books on architecture gradually won the Germans to English architectural designs. The regions nearest Philadelphia were the first to succumb. As we have seen, Germantown, even early in the eighteenth century, patterned itself after the Quaker capital of which it was a suburb, so that travellers on going from one to the other had no impression of contrast. The Wistar house, the Michlin-Sorber house, the Christopher Sauer house, the Daniel Pastorius house, and many others are typical examples of early Quaker architecture. Later in the century, when Philadelphia fell under the spell of the Georgian, Germantown was quick to follow suit. In time the contagion spread out to the remoter towns and farms, until all German Pennsylvania was dotted with stone Georgian houses[46] (Plate 45).

[43]Joseph Downs, *The House of the Miller at Millbach.*

[44]J. L. Rosenberger, *The Penna.-Germans,* pp. 52, 53.

[45]Interesting illustrations of bake-houses are shown in Eleanor Raymond's *Early Domestic Architecture of Penna.,* Plate 93, and in Penna. Ger. Soc. *Proceedings,* Vol. X, Part VII, p. 120.

[46]*The White Pine Series,* Vol. XIII, No. 4, Pls. XLV, XLVI.

But this English influence had to battle with a fresh stream of German ideas brought not only by continuing immigration, but by the importation of German books on architecture. The carpenter or the mason who had gone through his apprenticeship in the Rhine valley was not apt to discard what he had learned in favor of English ideas. The well-to-do business man or farmer might not care to build his house from plans from the books of Gibbs or Langley, when he could import books of designs from Germany. "Baron" Stiegel, famous for his glassware, owned Paul Heineken's *Lucidum Prospective Speculum,* published in 1727, which eventually came into the possession of the Moravian library at Bethlehem.[47] J. J. Schübler's *Synopsis Architecturæ,* published in Nürnberg in 1732, with plans and drawings of architectural details, M. Albert Daniel Mechlein's *Mathematischer Anfang,* a pocket-sized builder's manual, and other architectural volumes are also found in the Moravian archives.

Whereas the early Pennsylvania-German style was essentially medieval, these books emphasized the German Renaissance type. The German builders were late in falling under the influence of Palladio and his followers, and when at last Renaissance buildings began to arise in Germany, they were confined chiefly to public structures or to the residences of the rich. In the eighteenth century, however, the new vogue began to affect also humbler houses, even invading some of the rural villages of the Rhine valley. In Germany as elsewhere, the movement was marked by classical decorations, pilasters, ornate windows and doors, by the balanced façade, quoins and elaborate cornices. Distinctive of Germany itself, however, was the modified form of the mansard roof, the gambrel with the lower slope often bell-shaped, the upper overlapping to form upper eaves.

Had many of the later immigrants been persons of means, capable of erecting substantial residences, it is probable that the new vogue would have been strong in German Pennsylvania. But it was the sons or grandsons of the early comers who built

[47]Stiegel sold the book to Francis Thomas in 1774, who presented it to "Bethlehem Library" in 1818. Apparently Stiegel acquired the volume in 1767, too late to influence the plans for his "castle" in Mannheim.

the stone farmhouses which dot the countryside, men born in America, or who had left Germany in childhood and who perhaps had never seen a Renaissance house. So it was only occasionally, lost amid the usual English Georgian farmhouses, that one found a quaint limestone structure, whose gambrel roof with overhanging cornices, rounded windows, stringcourses, and perhaps quoins, proclaimed it as a bit of transplanted German Renaissance architecture. Perhaps the best-known example is the Georg Müller house, which might well have been patterned after the Wirtshaus zum Stern in Rheinzabern, South Palatinate[48] (Plate 44).

The transition from medieval to Renaissance architecture left the Seventh Day Dunkers at Ephrata untouched. When the brothers laid aside their long white cowls for the saw and the hammer to erect their *saal,* the Sisters' House, the Brothers' House and other smaller buildings, they built entirely after the manner of the Middle Ages. The entire group, despite the inevitable frontier crudeness, was suggestive of the Germany of Albrecht Dürer (Plate 48). The steep pitch of the roofs, the rows of watershed dormers, the small casement windows, the central chimney, the long narrow passageways, the tiny cells, the low pitch of the ceilings, the winding stairways all bespeak the Germany of old. The Brothers' House, which is no longer standing, with its lofty nave and its aisles beneath the sloping side roofs, was the only building in German America which suggested the aisled basilicas of Romanesque Germany. The Sisters' House is done in what amounts to half-timbering with heavy upright and cross beams filled with stone and covered on the outside with planks laid over with shingles in some places, with stucco in others, and with weatherboards in still others.[49]

If the Dunker builders were unaffected by the Renaissance, the Moravian brothers fell largely under its influence. The history of this sect is unique. Persecuted in Moravia and Bohemia, a group led by one Christian David took refuge in Saxony, where they were welcomed by Ludwig von Thurnstein, Count Zinzen-

[48]Albert Becker, *Pfälzer Volkskunde,* Fig. 106.
[49]Eleanor Raymond, *Early Domestic Architecture of Penna.,* Plate 9.

dorf. Here they founded the town of Herrnhut in 1722 on land donated by the Count, and erected their *Gemeinhaus,* Brothers' House, Sisters' House, Widows' House and other buildings. From this center the United Brothers, as they called themselves, went out to the world as zealots and missionaries, and wherever they

FIGURE 22. REAR VIEW OF MORAVIAN SEMINARY BUILDINGS, BETHLEHEM, PA.

established themselves and built their community houses, at Bethlehem, Nazareth, Lititz, Winston-Salem, one sees the architectural influence of the little town in far-away Saxony.

Herrnhut itself typifies the transition from the medieval to the Renaissance German architecture. If one had stood on a near-by eminence a century and a half ago and looked out over the Herrschaft garden toward the town, he would have seen a medley of steep roofs, some of them following the sharp lines of the

Middle Ages, others showing the distinctive German gambrel, pierced with ornate semi-circular dormers. As it was in Herrnhut, so it was with the Moravian communities in America. The visitor to Bethlehem, when he mounts the steep hill past the Seminary and emerges on the quaint sloping courtyard in the center of the Moravian group, is transported to another age and another country (Fig. 22). The sharply rising roof lines, the rows of quaint dormers, the central chimneys, the diagonal board

FIGURE 23. PROPOSED GEMEIN HAUS, BETHLEHEM

doors, the scrolled ends of the cornices, the stone buttresses, the entrance platform approached by stairs along the front walls, all blend in a harmonious picture that one easily peoples in imagination with pious Brothers in dark coats without lapels, broad-brimmed hats and knickerbockers, and Sisters in light blue or white, with "snipe bill" caps and bands of lace around the forehead.[50] Despite this medieval atmosphere, there is a clear reminder also of the Renaissance in the arched windows and the German gambrel roofs of the Bell House and a part of the Sisters' House.

While rummaging through some of the Moravian archives at

[50]Jacob J. Sessler, *Communal Pietism among Early American Moravians* (N. Y.), pp. 78–99.

Bethlehem several years ago, the author ran across many of the original plans for the Moravian buildings, among them the drawings for a *Gemeinhaus* which apparently was never erected. Its interest lies in the fact that it is more clearly Renaissance in style than any existing German building in America. The lofty central *saal,* with a balcony for musicians, the gambrel roof, the ornate central dormer, the elaborate cupola set off by pilasters, balustrade and bell-shaped cap, breaks so sharply with the old traditions that one suspects that the pious Brothers could not bring themselves to accept the plans (Fig. 23).

Bethlehem was not the only Moravian settlement which shows a mingling of the old and the new. At Nazareth the manor house, the stately building intended as a residence for Count Zinzendorf, with its simple but prominent cornices, its German mansard roof, its rows of rounded dormers, its roof balcony and cupola, is clearly in the spirit of the Renaissance[51] (Plate 49). Even the Whitefield house, despite its rough stone walls, departs from the old style in its roof lines, its windows and its string course under the second story windows. The architect's drawings for the Moravian buildings at Lititz show the same deference toward the Hernnhut models, the same yielding to the newer influences, but at Winston-Salem, North Carolina, both the Brothers' House and the Sisters' House are moulded almost entirely in the spirit of the Middle Ages.[52]

It is regrettable that the Pennsylvania Germans gave us no government buildings. How greatly it would have added to the charm of the region had they erected here and there in the county seats court houses patterned after the *Rathäuser* of the mother country. But the Germans, who at first were content to be governed by others in America as in Germany, seem to have had little voice in designing or building the court houses, even in counties where they constituted an overwhelming majority. At Lancaster, York, Reading, Allentown, the government buildings were Georgian in design, modelled closely upon Carpenters' Hall, or the Philadelphia City Hall, or the Mount Holly court house.

[51] W. C. Reichel, *Nazareth Hall* (Phila., 1869), p. 13.
[52] *Monograph Series,* Vol. XV, Pls. 22, 26.

Nor did the Germans produce a distinctive church architecture. When a group of settlers staked off their possessions in the wilderness, they usually gathered in some little clearing to sing hymns and pray and listen with reverent attention to the words of the *Prediger*. If some one had preceded them to the neighborhood he might invite them to worship temporarily in his humble cabin. Later, when the time came to erect a church it was usually of logs, often without belfry, fireplace, or floor. Only with the passing of years, when fields had been cleared, fences built, barns erected and filled with wheat or barley, did the settlers turn their thoughts to more pretentious structures. Even then they had no desire to duplicate the church buildings of their ancestors, which in their minds were associated with their persecution, the "synagogues" from which they had been driven. So one looks in vain for anything similar to the quaint old stone churches of the Rhine valley, with their Gothic arches and buttresses, their massive square towers surmounted by soaring dunce-cap spires. The Lutheran church at Trappe, the most distinctly Germanic church in Pennsylvania, is reminiscent rather of the little country chapels of Upper Bavaria or of the Black Forest than of the Palatinate (Plate 42). The Moravian church at Winston-Salem, the original Moravian church at Emaus, the New Jerusalem church, Berks, and others, while German in atmosphere and in certain details, break sharply with the models of the mother country. Before the end of the eighteenth century, Pennsylvania-German churches were modelled for the most part either upon the Quaker meeting houses or upon the Philadelphia Georgian. Saint Michael's at Strasburg; the old Lutheran church at York;[53] the beautiful Trinity church, Lancaster;[54] the Reformed church, Reading, were all in the spirit of Robert Smith and the other Philadelphia builders.

To understand this lack of a distinct church architecture, we must remember that although the religious beliefs of the Pennsylvania Germans are rooted in the traditions of centuries, and so have proved enduring in America, they are not rooted in the esthetic spirit which produced German ecclesiastical architecture.

[53]Built 1753.

[54]Built 1761.

Had the settlers been of only one religious denomination, it is probable that they would have developed a style of their own, born of their distinctive beliefs and of conditions in America, as New England Congregationalism and Virginia Anglicanism developed styles of their own. But the Germans were not only divided into numerous sects, but some of these sects had much more in common with the English or the Scotch-Irish than with their fellow Germans. So they fell under the influence of their neighbors, the Mennonites building Quaker meeting houses, the Lutherans, Anglican churches, the Reformed, Presbyterian churches.

In the grouping of the Pennsylvania-German farm buildings there was apparently no attempt to imitate the Frankish court. There were barnyards, of course, but one never finds the cobbled court shut in by residence, stables, barn, and the high wall with its arched gateway. Perhaps the abundance of space, as contrasted with the cramped conditions in the Palatinate village, suggested an arrangement in which the residence would be apart from the cows, horses, swine, and poultry. The farmer put his home within a stone's throw of his barnyard, but his bedroom no longer immediately overlooked the pig sty and the manure heap.

Nor were the Pennsylvania-German barns similar to the typical barn of the Frankish court. We are told that the first ambition of every settler after he had established himself in his new home, was to build a large and durable barn, perhaps of stone. No doubt these early structures were of various types, imitating so far as possible the barns and stables of the regions from which the settler came. But in time, most of these types passed out of use, and one only, selected from the others because of its suitability to America, remained to become almost universal. Retaining its European form, structure and interior arrangement, it underwent many modifications to conform to climate, building materials and other local conditions. If the Germans, in building residences and churches, fell completely under the influence of the English, in their barns, which are so individualistic as to be recognizable at a glance, they borrowed nothing. As the late Professor M. D. Learned has said, the chief routes followed in the expansion of German Pennsylvania "into Maryland, Virginia, or into the far West or even New York and Canada," may be traced by these interesting structures.[55]

We must seek the ancestry of the Pennsylvania-German barn in the wooded highlands of Upper Bavaria, the southern spurs of the Black Forest mountains, in the Jura region and elsewhere in Switzerland. The great peasant houses of these districts, despite

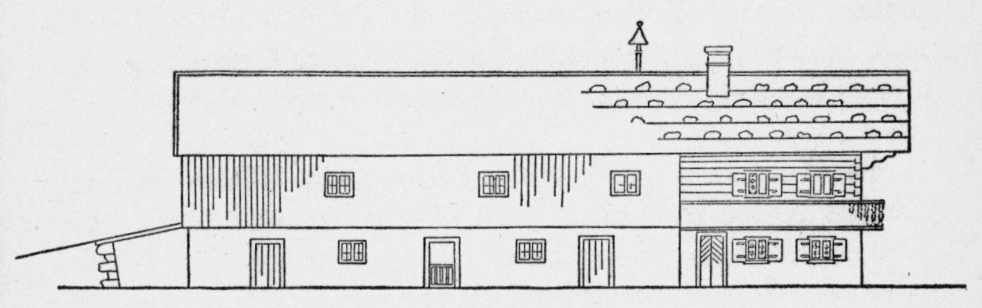

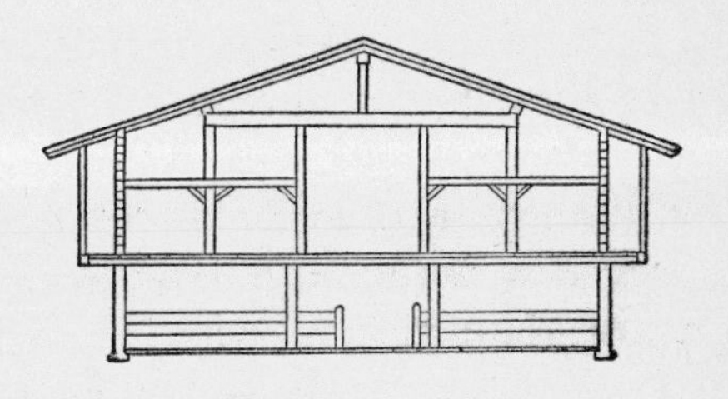

FIGURE 24. UPPER BAVARIAN PEASANT HOUSE

certain obvious differences, have much in common. They are mountain houses suited to the steep slopes, the biting winds, the heavy snows of the uplands, and so are to be contrasted alike with the Frankish court of the sunny Rhine valley, and with the one-story lower-Saxon peasant house of the northern plains.

In the Upper Bavarian house, which has the closest affinity of all to the Pennsylvania barn, the residence, barn and stable are found under one roof (Fig. 24). In front is the residence, rising two stories to the loft under the projecting eaves of the roof, its quaint casement windows, its long balcony protected by turned

[55] "The German Barn in America," *University Lectures,* University of Pennsylvania, 1913–1914, pp. 338–349.

banisters, its heavily panelled doors, its arched chimneys, its quaint designs carved in the gable end, its roof bell, all suggestive of the mountains and of Switzerland. The lower floor is usually of stone, the superstructure of hewn logs. Stretching out behind, sometimes for eighty to a hundred feet, is the combined stable and barn. The lower floor is assigned to the horses, cattle and oxen, the stalls being laid out along aisles entered from doors in the long side of the structure. Above is the barn, with hay loft and threshing-floor, the entrance for wagons being usually at one side rather than at the rear, and approached, if the ground is level, by a ramp, if hilly, directly from the upper level. In very large barns, as in the "Bauer in der Au," wagons enter from the rear and leave over a ramp on one side. Of special interest is the *Laube* or *forebay,* an overshoot of the barn floor, affording an enclosed gallery above and a protection to the walls, windows and doors of the stable below. The low roof, weighted with heavy stones to protect it from the fierce mountain winds, is supported not only by the log walls, but by numerous wooden uprights tied by horizontal beams and diagonal props.[56]

"We could follow this house far through the Alps," declares one distinguished student; from Upper Bavaria to the valley of the Inn, thence through Vorarlberg to Bern.[57] The Swiss peasant house in former times was usually made throughout of logs, but now the basement is often of stone. The roof lines are rather high and narrow and are hipped at the front end, but in other respects they resemble closely the Upper Bavarian house. There is the same residential section in front, with its balconies, windows, and ornaments, the same basement stable beneath the barn behind, the same approach to the threshing-floor directly from the hillside or over a ramp or bridge.[58] There are, of course, many and wide variations in the Swiss houses. Here one finds the barn and other buildings detached from the residence,[59] here

[56]*Das Bauernhaus in Deutschland,* Pls., Bayern Nr. 4 and 5; Klaus Thiede, *Deutsche Bauernhäuser,* Pls. 69, 71, 72; *Zeitschrift für Ethnologie,* Vol. XIX, pp. 578, 579, 580.

[57]*Ibid.,* Vol. XIX, p. 580.

[58]*Ibid.,* p. 582; *Schweizerisches Archiv für Volkskunde,* Vol. I, p. 586; Vol. XXXI, p. 172; Vol. XXIII, p. 64, Figs. 8, 10. *Das Bauernhaus in der Schweiz,* p. 6.

[59]*Schweizerisches Archiv für Volkskunde,* Vol. XXXI, p. 172.

the barn and stables are on the same level and attached to the residence with the roof axis at right angles to it;[60] here the arrangement of stalls and threshing-floor is different, here the forebay is concealed by vertical planking reaching to the ground. But the kinship of many Swiss peasant houses with the Upper Bavarian house is obvious.

If now we descend from the Swiss highlands and, crossing the upper Rhine, make our way into the Black Forest, we find still another variation of the peasant house. In outward appearance the Black Forest house resembles more closely the Swiss house than the Upper Bavarian house. Its huge hipped roof falling on either side often forty or fifty feet, unbroken by dormers, gives to it the appearance of a Noah's ark grounded on the side of a hill, its prow looking out over the valley. In interior arrangement it differs from the other highland peasant houses, in that the basement, which houses the horses and cattle, extends through the front part of the structure under the two residential floors, while the entire loft from gable end to gable end is used for the barn. Wagons are driven into this great room usually directly from the rising ground in the rear.[61] One looks in vain for a chimney. The smoke from the hearth in the *Küche* is permitted to rise into the loft under the roof, where it is supposed to protect the beams from destruction by worms, to cure the corn and fodder, and finally to filter through the thatch or out through a ventilator.[62]

The Swiss and south German immigrants, like other European peasants who were accustomed to the combined residence, barn, and stable, in America seem from the first to have detached the residence. The Miller house, near Harrisonburg, built in imitation of the Black Forest peasant home, is a very rare exception. The Swiss may have taken their cue from their neighbors from the Palatinate or they may have realized that the combination peasant house of their ancestors was not suited to conditions in Pennsylvania, where the need for hot fires in the residence in winter

[60] *Das Bauernhaus in der Schweiz,* Appenzell, Nr. 1, 2.

[61] *Das Bauernhaus in Deutschland;* Klaus Thiede, *Deutsche Bauernhäuser,* pp. 62, 63, 64.

[62] Heinrich Rebensburg, *Das Deutsche Dorf,* p. 77, Fig. 71.

and the discomfort of being housed with horses and cattle in the summer pointed out the desirability of separating the residence entirely from the stable and barn.

Having done this, the immigrant retained the remaining features of the highland peasant house almost unchanged in the barn and stable. The Pennsylvania-German barns are often of great size, perhaps one hundred feet by forty and rising forty or forty-five feet to the roof ridge. In some cases they are built entirely of stone, in others the basement is of stone. Many are throughout or in part of timber, while a few are of brick. The basement is used for housing the livestock, a series of doors in the front or long side leading directly to the stalls. Above is the barn proper, with its great hay lofts and threshing floor, with the entrance for wagons usually in the rear (Plate 46). This entrance is approached over a banked causeway, or directly from the hillside; more rarely over a bridge. Distinctive and almost universal is the forebay, or projection of the barn for five to ten feet over the stable below to form a covered space for farm implements and wagons. The forebay in many cases seems to have been an afterthought, for it is common to see it as a wooden addition built on to a stone barn. Frequently, however, it is sunk in the front of the building, in which case it may be supported, not by pillars, but by the side walls and by projecting ceiling beams of the stable[63] (Plate 47).

The Pennsylvania-German barn follows the Swiss and Upper Bavarian roof lines, rather than those of the Black Forest. The early thatch has now given way to wooden shingles, and these in turn in some cases to disfiguring asbestos shingles. The hay loft is very high, and is lighted often by two tiers of windows in front or behind and three or four in the gable ends. The boarding, where there is boarding, is almost always vertical in keeping with Swiss and German precedent. The ventilators, which in Europe served as outlets for the smoke from the hearth fire, have survived, either in deference to precedent, or to insure a change of air in the hay loft. In their later form the ventilators are made

[63]M. D. Learned, "The German Barn in America," *University Lectures,* Univ. of Penna. 1913–14, pp. 338–349.

to imitate spires or cupolas, or perhaps appear merely as apertures or slits in the gable end of the wall.

Though German architecture in Pennsylvania at a very early stage began to yield before English influences, and though the Palatine farmers discarded the Frankish farm court in favor of the south German and Swiss barn, the immigrants clung tenaciously to their peasant art. Perhaps this is so because German *Volkskunst* is the reflection of the peasant soul, the medium through which is expressed his beliefs, fears, superstitions, joys, hopes, his daily life. When we enter the living room of a south German peasant house, we find it a mirror of the man himself. The painting on the dower chest expresses his love for his wife; the image of Christ on the cross suspended in the corner, his religious devotion; the tulip on his pie plate, his love of flowers; the cross on his door latch, his fear of witches. Were a village of the Palatinate to be buried like Pompeii under volcanic ashes, the future archæologist could reconstruct not only the houses, but the very thoughts, the very souls of the people who lived in them.

Today our furniture, clothing, implements, utensils have lost the significance which once they possessed. The chair in which we sit, the bed in which we sleep, the coat on our back, the plate out of which we eat are soulless things, stamped off by the thousand or the million, in whose creation we have had no part and which are really strangers in our home. In the days before the advent of machine-made goods, it was otherwise. The home craftsman or the shop worker was in a very real sense an artist, and his creation the expression of himself, his homeland, and his age. The images which he created may be crude, the perspective false, the proportions awry, but they constitute art, in a sense as real as that of Michelangelo or Rembrandt. We may differ as to the meaning in the subtle smile of Mona Lisa, but the message of a German peasant painted cupboard, or carved spoon rack, or decorated vase is as clear as day. The peasant was never alone, for around him on all sides were creations which spoke to him of life, were for him alive—his clock, chest, cupboard, chairs, tables, pottery, bridal box, kettle-holder, bread pan, tiles, linen, embroidery, glass, stove, birth certificate, even his wine cask and his hoe.

German peasant art, like the peasant himself, is at one with nature, with the inevitable return of the yearly seasons, the dependence of man on the soil, on weather, on manual work, on good health, on domestic animals, on good and evil spirits. It speaks of the winter's cold, the summer's heat, of the village festival, of birth, marriage and death. Centering in the agricultural village, with its community life, it is group, not individual, art. The craftsman expresses himself, not by accurate images of men, or birds, or flowers, the result of his own observation, but by accepted models, handed down by his ancestors. There is no sense of plagiarism, since peasant art strives consciously to maintain old forms and old motifs. It is this which explains the crudeness and frequent incongruity of peasant art. The deer which the housewife weaves in her linen becomes geometric; the bird on the pie-plate is larger than the tree on which it perches; one has to guess whether the flower on the cupboard is a rose or a tulip or a forget-me-not.

The motifs of German peasant art have their origin in mythology, although endless variations and the passage of years often have altered or obscured the original meaning. One wonders whether the peasant knows the historical significance of the trefoil carving on the back of his chair, or the wheel in the panel of his chest, or the double peacock on his coverlet. He has an especial predilection for geometric forms, for the cross, the spiral, the circle, the star, the vortex, the quatrefoil, the sexfoil, the wheel, borrowed perhaps from Gothic ornamentation in the churches, but in his mind full of deep and mysterious meaning. To these he adds other symbols, taken from folklore or storybook or fable—the double horn, double birds, double animals, mermaids; fish, the heart. Religious motifs are especially frequent in Roman Catholic regions, where one finds images of Christ or the saints, or scenes from the Bible painted on wardrobes and beds, engraved on pottery, moulded on stove-plates, or woven in the linen. And on all sides are evidences of the peasant's love of flowers in the tulip or rose or forget-me-not found on dower chest and *Schrank*, stucco wall, chair and bedstead, pie plates, dishes and mugs, flatirons, glassware, stove plates and stove tiles, lace, woolens, birth certificates.[64]

This *Volkskunst* the south Germans and Swiss brought to Pennsylvania, where it persisted far into the nineteenth century. Since it had its foundations so deep in peasant life, traditions, superstitions, and religion, the immigrant could not cast it aside in his new home. He might imitate the architecture of the English as better suited to American conditions than his own, but he had no taste for English furniture, pottery, glassware, utensils. He was insensible to the beauties of the Philadelphia Chippendale chair or table, would have considered a Thomas Affleck highboy an intruder in his living-room. So he surrounded himself in Pennsylvania, as his ancestors had done in Germany, with useful objects carved or painted or moulded, when time or his means permitted, with the images and designs which to him were of such deep significance.

German peasant art was deeply influenced, of course, by the transit to the New World. Itself largely the creation of the old community life of the agricultural village, it suffered from the change to the isolated farm. The frontier period, with its emphasis upon the primitive needs of existence, tended to discourage artistic craftsmanship and to weaken the bond of tradition. The high cost of labor made it unprofitable to lavish time and thought upon intricate decorative details, upon carving and inlaying. So German peasant art in Pennsylvania became cruder, more primitive, the designs simpler, not so well executed.

But it remained from the first remarkably impervious to American influences. The pottery of Montgomery, or the dower chests of Berks or Lehigh reflected, not the new ideas, the new method of life in America, but the traditions of hundreds of years of existence on the soil of Germany or Switzerland. One finds the same geometric figures and symbols, the same doves,

[64]Konrad Hahm, *Deutsche Volkskunst;* Edwin Redslob, Ed., *Deutsche Volkskunst* (12 Vols.); F. Rudolf Uebe, *Deutsche Bauernmöbel;* Alexander Schöpp, *Alte deutsche Bauern stuben und Hausrat;* Adolf Spamer, *Die Deutsche Volkskunde* (2 Vols.). (Leipzig, 1934).

eagles and peacocks, the same constant reiteration of the tulip, while he looks in vain for an ear of Indian corn, or a canoe, or chipmunk, or a leaf of tobacco, or a view of the Susquehanna. Only in the later years, when Pennsylvania folk art was on the wane, do representations of George Washington, the American eagle and the American flag find their way into pottery or woven coverlets.

Since the Germans and Swiss who came to Pennsylvania were Protestants, many religious themes common in the homelands were lacking in their art. Just as the Protestant rejected the cruciform church building, the chalice and the altar, so he refused to paint his bedstead or his wardrobe with religious scenes which in his mind were associated with Catholicism. On the other hand, his art was full of religious symbolism, expressed in the holy heart, or the holy eagle, or the lily, while he covered the plates of his stove with scenes from both the Old and the New Testament.

The most beloved motif of German folk art in Pennsylvania is the tulip, the Persian symbol of love,[65] and accepted in Germany as a variation of the holy lily. Brought to western Europe in the sixteenth century, this flower created a furor of interest, the so-called tulipomania, which culminated in that strange phenomenon, the tulip "boom" of Holland. Since in south Germany the universal favor in which it is held is reflected in its constant use as a decorative theme, it was inevitable that the craftsmen who migrated to America should continue there to work it into almost every design. The cabinetmaker painted it on the dower chest, the clockmaker on his dial, the Dunker sister, in the seclusion of the cloister, wove it in endless patterns into psalm books and hymnals, the potter traced it on his dishes, the stovemaker cast it upon his plates.[66]

The German love of flowers was by no means confined to the tulip. We recognize on all sides the drooping fuchsia;[67] the rose;

[65]Albert Jacquemart, *History of the Ceramic Art* (London, 1877), p. 121.

[66]H. D. Eberlein and Abbot McClure, *The Practical Book of American Antiques*, pp. 229, 230; Edwin A. Barber, *Tulip Ware* (Phila., 1903), pp. 82–83; Cornelius Weygandt, *The Red Hills*, pp. 119–120.

[67]E. A. Barber, *Tulip Ware*, Figs. 49, 50, 51, 52, 55.

the sky-blue forget-me-not with its yellow center, the symbol of friendship; the flower of the pomegranate, denoting fertility and prosperity; and others. In addition are many designs in which it is impossible to identify the blossom, either because of the crudeness of the work or because it was intended to represent flowers in general rather than a particular species. Usually, however, the flower was chosen because of its symbolic appropriateness to the theme of decoration, whether love, friendship, piety, or duty.

In Pennsylvania, as in Germany, birds constitute an ever-recurring motif, especially the dove, the peacock, the parrot, the eagle. The dove, symbolic of love and conjugal happiness, rivals the tulip itself in popularity. The peacock, too, was a favorite motif, for the beauty of this bird, the habitant of every farmyard, could not escape the artistic craftsman. The eagle, king of birds and emblem of patriotism, is especially frequent in hand-woven coverlets, but we run across it also on pottery,[68] stoves, and elsewhere.

The unicorn, that mythological defender of purity, is seen frequently on the Pennsylvania dower chest, while the deer is a favorite with potters. The lion, so widely used by the craftsmen of Germany, in Pennsylvania becomes rare,[69] but the rabbit and the horse attain new popularity. Unabashed by their lack of skill as draftsmen, the potter or cabinetmaker frequently depicted human beings—perhaps a colonial trooper, perhaps a soldier, perhaps a bride and groom, perhaps a hunter, perhaps a fiddler and dancing couples.

The Pennsylvania German was not so fond of symbolic geometric figures as his south German or Swiss ancestor, yet one finds the star within the circle, the whirl, the quatrefoil, and similar decorations upon spoon racks,[70] stove plates, and especially on the front of barns. The barn decorations are frequently quite simple, a circle enclosing a four-pointed star, a quatrefoil, or a whirl, painted in two or more colors, but occasionally they take the form of complicated geometric rosettes, with a maze of

[68] E. A. Barber, *Tulip Ware*, Figs. 17, 59, 66. [69] *Ibid.*, Fig. 74.
[70] Wallace Nutting, "Carved Spoon Racks," *Antiques*, Vol. VII, p. 312.

wheels, stars, diamonds and circles. They can be matched not only by motifs on German and Swiss chairs, chests, utensils, but upon the fronts of highland peasant houses,[71] from which these barns developed (Fig. 25). Tucked away under the front gable end of one house alone in Upper Bavaria, we find no less than

FIGURE 25. (UPPER) DECORATIONS OF PENNSYLVANIA BARNS. (LOWER) DECORATIONS FROM UPPER BAVARIAN PEASANT HOUSE

eight of these circles with four of the designs frequently seen in the Pennsylvania barn.[72]

Some have questioned, then, the oft repeated assertion that these "symbols are supposed to keep lightning from striking the barn . . . and to prevent the animals housed in the barn from being bewitched or 'ferhexed.'"[73] It was a practice common enough among the Pennsylvania Germans to place hex marks or talismans on various articles in order to drive off witches—on cups, knives, dishes, butter-prints, and on door latches to prevent the witch from entering. But the hex marks consist usually of crosses—St. Andrew's cross or the Greek cross or the Maltese

[71] *Schweizerisches Archiv für Volkskunde,* Vol. XXIX, pp. 73–79.
[72] *Das Bauernhaus in Deutschland,* Vol. II.
[73] Cornelius Weygandt, *The Red Hills,* p. 126.

cross—or sometimes the so-called toad-foot, consisting of a W within a U. Moreover when one questions the farmer as to his barn decoration he will invariably deny that it has any occult significance. "Ne, verdamptsei net," said one old man. "An so sache glawe mir net."[74] On the other hand, I am informed by one of the most distinguished authorities on German folk art that the star and the sunburst are commonly employed by peasants in Germany to protect their houses from evil spirits. No doubt the barn decorations in Pennsylvania, like the paintings on dower chests and the designs on pottery, bore originally symbolic meanings now obscured by the passage of time and life in America.

It is impossible to trace Pennsylvania-German art back to any one district of Germany or Switzerland, either in the matter of motifs or methods of work. Like the Pennsylvania-German dialect, the local art was a mixture of south German influences, of the Hessian pottery, the Bavarian furniture, the Palatine stove casters. Nor was this mingling entirely a matter of the New World. The journeyman craftsmen of Germany, wandering from place to place in search of work, spread abroad the methods and designs which their masters had taught them. Consequently we find similar forms of decoration in furniture, pottery, glass and woven materials in widely separated districts.[75] It was only when some city or town became a center for this craft or that and developed methods and styles of its own, that we can detect marked individuality. Even then, to trace these styles to Pennsylvania is often a hazardous undertaking. Perhaps one might imagine, for instance that the geometric flowers of the Montgomery and Lehigh dower chests have a direct relation to those of the Hül's pottery, but until we discover the names of the cabinet-makers and the province from whence they or their fathers came, we are proceeding on nothing better than guesswork.

On the other hand, peasant art, once transferred to America, sometimes developed marked local characteristics. These differ-

[74]J. J. Stoudt, *The Historical Review of Berks County,* Oct., 1937, p. 7.

[75]Dr. Hans Lehmann, "The Painted Peasant Furniture of Switzerland," in *Antiques,* Vol. XIII, p. 282.

ences no doubt resulted in part from different traditions, in part from local tastes or local materials, in part from the individuality of the worker. We can recognize at a glance a David Spinner pie plate, or a Christian Selzer dower chest. At the same time, the American product as a unit gradually took on individuality of its own, an increasing crudeness, the repetition of certain themes, the neglect of others, the absence of symbols associated with Catholicism, the use of American clay or American wood.

Of especial interest in Pennsylvania-German craftsmanship is the painted dower chest. In Germany, it was customary for the groom to present to his bride a set of furniture—four-poster bed, cupboard, chairs, and chest—all often decorated with hearts, tulips and other figures symbolic of love and devotion.[76] These objects were sometimes the handiwork of the groom himself, and, though more often done by professional cabinet-makers, always reflected the groom's personal sentiments. In Pennsylvania, however, the chest was presented by the maiden's father long before she attained the marriageable age, so that the accumulation of the bride's linen to fill it was a matter of years. It was these chests which were chosen especially for decoration, and upon them were painted in artistic profusion tulips, hearts, unicorns, birds, geometric figures. Why the cupboard, bed, and wardrobe were neglected is not clear, since in Germany and Switzerland they came in for their full share of attention. Perhaps the fact that many German dower chests were brought to the province as trunks, thus providing the local craftsmen with models, may account for the preference shown them. At all events, scores of charming chests have been preserved in the families who inherited them, or in museums, or by collectors.

The typical Pennsylvania chest is about four feet long and two feet high, with hinged top, four supporting feet and often two or three drawers below. Unlike the German and Swiss chests, the designs are seldom carved in the wood, but are painted.[77] The background often is dark blue, or olive green, and the decorations in various colors—red, brown, green, or in black and

[76]Dr. Hans Lehmann, *Antiques,* Vol. XIII, p. 487.
[77]*Antiques,* Vol. XI, p. 453.

LATE 48. SISTERS HOUSE AND SAAL, EPHRATA

LATE 49. NAZARETH HALL, NAZARETH, PENNSYLVANIA

PLATE 50. *Top Left:* Berks County chest. *Top Right:* Lehigh County chest. *Bottom Left:* Lancaster County chest. *Bottom Right:* Dauphin County chest.

white. The front is divided into two or three panels, usually merely painted on, but in some cases a part of the structure of the chest. To these panels are devoted the chief decorative interest, for they abound with flowers growing from vases, birds, or unicorns, but other spaces—between the panels, at the two ends, on the top of the lid—are also decorated. Despite the obvious similarities between the chests made in south Germany and in Pennsylvania, there are certain general differences. The American chests never show the elaborate landscapes or human figures or views of cities which often adorn those of Germany; they are not so heavy, lack the elaborate mouldings and the floral decorations are different.

Not only did the Pennsylvania dower chests develop an individuality as a whole, but marked differences grew up between the various counties within the province, which no doubt were the result in part of tradition, in part of local influences, and in part of the predilections of the craftsmen. The Lancaster chests may be identified at a glance by their sunken panels with round or pointed arches supported by turned or fluted pilasters, the whole lending an architectural character lacking in the chests from other counties (Plate 50). Within the panels the floral designs of tulips, carnations and forget-me-nots are varied and graceful, while frequently parrots, doves, pheasants, and peacocks are prominent. It has been suggested that the Lancaster cabinet-makers were under the influence of the Mennonite Church, which attached peculiar significance to such natural forms as birds, animals, and flowers.[78]

In Montgomery and Lehigh counties the distinguishing feature of the chests was the geometric accuracy of the designs. Stars, interlaced circles, and bulging hearts abound, while even the flowers are laid out with a meticulous accuracy which suggests the aid of the compass[79] (Plate 50). The Lebanon County chests, like those of near-by Lancaster, tend to the architectural style, but the panels, set under arches supported by banisters, are painted on instead of being a structural part of the box. The design within the panel invariably presents a vase with laterally branch-

[78]Esther S. Fraser, in *Antiques,* Vol. VIII, pp. 82–84. [79]*Ibid.,* p. 82.

ing tulips and what appears to be an open tulip rising in the center.[80]

The Berks County chests are noted for the frequent appearance in their designs of unicorns and men on horseback, but they bear also other and more usual motifs, the tulip growing from a vase, the star within the circle, flowers growing from a heart (Plate 50). The Dauphin chests are of especial interest because some of the craftsmen were accustomed to sign their names. In this way the work of Johann Rank, John Peter Rank, and John Selzer have become known. Their designs are easily identified by the painted panels enclosing flowers growing from a vase, pitcher, or tumbler[81] (Plate 50).

Similar in purpose and in decoration to the dower chest, but not in size and form, are the little bride boxes. These boxes are usually oval in shape, made of thin pieces of pine, painted with a solid ground color and decorated with figures and designs in bright hues. They were filled with linen, laces, ribbons and other finery dear to the bride's heart. The decorative motifs are similar to those of the dower chests, save for the frequent recurrence on the cover of human figures representing the bride and groom, accompanied invariably by tulips, pinks, or fuchsias, and sometimes by doves or parrots. Running around the border of the top often appear sentimental inscriptions such as: "Over my heart will right be seen; will this loyalty remembered be?"[82] Similar boxes are found in various parts of Germany. The Saxon bride boxes, with their representations of bride and groom amid floral decorations, seem most closely affiliated with those of Pennsylvania, but those of the Palatinate and even of north Germany show many similarities both of form and of decorative motifs.[83]

The student of Pennsylvania-German folk art will find pottery perhaps even more interesting than the painted dower chests and

[80]Joseph Downs, *The House of the Miller,* Fig. 5.

[81]*Antiques,* Vol. XI, pp. 119–123, 253, 280–282. Joseph Downs, "The De Forest Collection," Metropolitan Museum of Art, *Bulletin,* Vol. XXIX, No. 10; *The House of the Miller at Millbach.*

[82]H. D. Eberlein and A. McClure, *Practical Book of American Antiques,* pp. 247, 248; *Antiques,* Vol. VIII, pp. 20–23; see examples in Metropolitan Museum of Art.

[83]*Deutsche Volkskunst,* Edwin Redslob, Ed., Vol. XII; *Die Pfalz,* by Theodor Zink, Figs. 118, 119; Konrad Hahn, *Deutsche Volkskunst,* Fig. 99.

bride boxes. Since it proved just as impractical to import German pottery as German furniture, the settlers early began to make their own pie plates, vegetable plates, vases, teapots and bowls. Among the immigrants were many who were familiar with the wheel and the slip cup, and they took up the work in Pennsylvania just where they had left off in Germany. So here and there one could stumble upon small establishments, where the kiln, the piles of clay, the batter, the rollers, the disc cutters, and other tools, together with rows of earthen pots and jars proclaimed the pottery. In Nockamixon Swamp, in the upper part of Bucks County, where the clay was especially good, there were no less than seven potteries within a radius of ten miles.[84]

The Pennsylvania potters brought with them almost unchanged the methods and tools of the Rhine valley—the preparation of the clay, the wheel, the smoothers, the glazing, the pounding, the rolling, the slip-cup, the etching. In America as in Germany they decorated their wares with slip designs. This they did in two ways—by slip-tracing or slip-painting, and by slip-engraving or sgraffito. In the first method the slip, or light clay mixed with water to the consistency of cream was traced over the surface of the ware by means of the quill cup, precisely as the housewife traces designs of icing upon the birthday cake. After the slip had dried sufficiently it was usually beaten with the batter to force it into the clay and make the surface smooth[85] (Plate 52). In the second process, the ware was entirely covered with a coating of slip through which the design was etched with a sharpened stick. Thus in the slip-traced ware the background was dark and the design light, in the sgraffito ware the background was light and the design dark (Plate 51).

Although Pennsylvania pottery is merely German pottery transplanted in America, it has in the decorative motifs a certain degree of individuality. There is a complete absence of the geometric treatment so striking in the famous Hüls plates and dishes; Roman Catholic themes are strictly avoided; the work is less complicated, less skillful; mottoes around the rim of dishes and plates appear far more frequently. But the beloved tulip is

[84] E. A. Barber, *Tulip Ware* (Phila., 1903), p. 59. [85] *Ibid.*, pp. 53–54.

ever present in Pennsylvania as in Germany, while other flowers, double birds, horses, deer, rabbits, human figures are as common in one country as in the other. One has only to compare the German with the Pennsylvania pottery displayed in adjacent cases in Memorial Hall, Philadelphia, to note the obvious similarities. There is an especially close affinity between the American ware and that of the Palatinate, Alsace and the Rhine province.[86]

So close is the parallel with Palatinate pottery that it seems certain that some of the Pennsylvania workers received their training in that province, or from "Palatine" immigrants. In describing the plates and dishes of the potteries at Dirmstein, Hassloch and Edenkoben, Theodor Zink says, "Humorous inscriptions and the date appear on the rim, while the center is decorated with a flower, often a bird or a geometric figure."[87] The same description would fit perfectly the dishes of the Pennsylvania potters. One is struck also by the similarity between the work of Johannes Neesz and a plate made in 1736, now in the Historic Museum at Speier, showing two mounted trumpeters. The affinity of Pennsylvania pottery with that of Alsace and Marburg is perhaps best explained by the fact that both exerted a powerful influence upon the potters of the Palatinate[88] (Plate 52).

As with the local cabinet-makers, potters often developed distinct characteristics, which makes it fairly easy to distinguish their wares. Thus the dishes of Georg Hübener usually have two circles of lettering on the rim instead of one, while he seems especially fond of the figure of a peacock preening his plumes.[89] David Spinner, of Bucks County, is known for his gay cavaliers on horseback, hunting scenes, and colonial troopers, his pictures occupying almost the entire space, so that room is left only for an occasional flower, tree or other decoration[90] (Plate 52). Johannes Neesz, of Montgomery County, was fond of the figure of a mounted Continental soldier, possibly representing George Wash-

[86]*Ibid.*, pp. 81–96; Eberlein and McClure, *American Antiques*, pp. 228–235; Konrad Hahm, *Deutsche Volkskunst*, Figs. 159–162; *Deutsche Volkskunst*, Vol. III, pp. 30–33; Vol. V, p. 32; Vol. VII, Figs. 155–158; Vol. XII, Figs. 146–150.

[87]*Deutsche Volkskunst, Die Pfalz*, p. 39.

[88]*Ibid.*, p. 38.

[89]E. A. Barber, *Tulip Ware*, pp. 112–117.

[90]*Ibid.*, pp. 127–136.

PLATE 51. SGRAFFITO POTTERY, PENNSYLVANIA-GERMAN

PLATE 52. *Upper Left:* Pennsylvania-German slipware plate. *Upper Right:* David Spinner–Sgraffito, 1800. *Lower:* Palatinate pottery

PLATE 53. STOVE PLATE—SAMSON AND DELILAH

PLATE 54. *Left:* Stove plate, later period. *Right:* Stove plate—David and Jonathan

ington, while his floral decorations invariably centered upon the fuchsia.[91] John Leidy usually made a large tulip his central theme, set off by a band of scroll work and the usual circular inscription.

While the Pennsylvania potters were turning their dishes, plates, teapots and mugs, in far-off North Carolina another group of Germans were doing work equally interesting and in some respects superior. Although many of the Carolina Germans came from or through Pennsylvania up the beaten path of the Shenandoah valley, the traditional influence which has shaped their pottery is European, not Pennsylvanian. However, since the potter's art in both provinces had a common origin, there are obvious similarities in motifs and methods of work. But the differences are also marked. One never finds sgraffito work in North Carolina, the potters working always with the slip cup; inscriptions are rare; the conventional designs of the borders are superior to those of Pennsylvania, the floral motifs inferior. But the clay is much the same, the tulip is in evidence, occasionally the familiar figure of a bird appears in the bottom of plate or dish.[92]

The art of the German-American potter, like the art of the cabinet-maker, gradually declined. By degrees the tulip and lotus patterns and the lively human figures disappeared, the German motifs with their quaint mottoes became rarer. The colors grew less varied. Finally there remained only the yellowish surface of the pie dish to remind us of the German tradition, and with the advent of cheap crockery the potter's art died out entirely.

In expressing himself through his homely *Volkskunst,* the German peasant did not neglect his stove. The iron *Ofen* seems to have come into use in Germany in the fifteenth century. It was a very simple device indeed, consisting of five plates fastened together to form top, bottom, front and two sides, while the rear, left open, was placed against an opening through the partition into a fireplace in the adjoining room. Thus one fire heated both rooms. When one wished more heat, he had only to go

[91] *Ibid.,* pp. 136–147.

[92] Joe Kindig, Jr., "A Note on Early North Carolina Pottery," *Antiques,* Vol. XXVII, pp. 14, 15.

into the next room and push into the stove a few hot embers from the fireplace. "The German stove is like a box, one side wanting," said Benjamin Franklin. "Tis composed of five iron plates scru'd together and fixed so that you may put the fuel into it from another room. . . . This invention certainly warms a room very speedily and very thoroughly with a little fuel. . . . Its inconveniences are that people . . . are obliged to breathe the same unchanged air continually."[93]

But whatever its merits or its faults, the stove in the humble homes of the Rhine valley or the Black Forest was so much the center of family life as to take on the sanctity of a shrine. To the peasant it was a thing enchanted, the dwelling place of kings, the prison of princesses, perhaps the symbol of the fiery nether world. Upon its iron plates he cast the images and symbols, especially religious images, which were most frequently in his mind. Here we have figures of the saints appearing upon a background of Gothic adornment, here Pharaoh at the Red Sea, here Justice holding the scales, here the death of Absalom, there Daniel in the Lion's Den.

When he came to Pennsylvania, if purse and cargo space permitted, the peasant took apart his stove and brought the plates with him. "If you should come bring with you an iron stove," wrote a recent immigrant to his brother in 1734. "The people of the Palatinate generally bring them with them, and I think they buy them in Rotterdam or they bring them with them out of their own country."[94] When the first stoves wore out, it became very difficult to secure a fresh supply from Germany, because of the barrier of the Navigation Acts, so that the colonists had to manufacture them for themselves.

The early iron furnaces in Pennsylvania were conducted, usually, by Englishmen, who did not concern themselves with the making of stoves. But when the Germans began calling upon them to repair broken stove plates, their attention was called to this new field of activity. So they took on German workmen, perhaps imported a few plate moulds, and began the manufacture

[93]"An Account of the New-Invented Pennsylvania Fireplaces," *Works of Benjamin Franklin,* John Bigelow, Ed., p. 500. [94]*Penna.-German.* Vol. IX, pp. 369–370.

of entire stoves.[95] The Redding and the Warwickshire furnaces, in Chester County, the Elizabeth and the Cornwall furnaces, in Lancaster County, the Colebrookdale furnace, near Pottstown, the Durham furnace, in Bucks County, no doubt all participated in this industry.

The earliest Pennsylvania plates seem to have been cast from German moulds, and so represented German rather than colonial art. But the inevitable step to making American moulds, showing the work of Pennsylvania designers, was not long delayed. Two patterns, one depicting Adam and Eve and the other Cain and Abel, both cast in 1741, and almost certainly the product of the Durham furnace, are unmistakably American in design and execution.[96] From this date until 1768, when artistic casting practically came to an end, new colonial designs were created almost every year. We find representations of David and Jonathan (Plate 54), the Molten Calf, the Temptation of Joseph, the Miracle of Cana, the Plow, David and Goliath, Samson and the Lion, Samson and Delilah (Plate 53), Elijah and the Ravens, the Scales, the Winged Head, and many others.

Although the smelters found many skilled iron workers among the Germans, they looked in vain for artists who could match the mould cutters of the mother country. In the American stove plates the carving of the figures, the details of the backgrounds, the canopies, and the lettering of the inscriptions, all show a crudeness unknown in the imported moulds or plates. "The designs become rude and primitive," says Doctor Henry C. Mercer, "as if the German workman, secluded in the American forest, had become more earnest, childlike and direct."[97] But the decorative spirit still prevailed in the balance of canopies and inscriptions, and the crude pictures never fail in the direct presentation of their thought.

In time the artists themselves seem to have become conscious of their lack of skill in making human figures, for the Biblical scenes were generally abandoned in favor of conventionalized floral patterns. There is an upper panel divided by two vaulted

[95]H. C. Mercer, *The Bible in Iron*, p. 35.

[96]*Ibid.*, pp. 43–44.

[97]*Ibid.*, p. 50.

canopies, enclosing set patterns, usually a flower-pot and tulip to the right and a fluted circlet around a heart from which spring three or more tulips to the left. Running through the center of the plate is a narrow band bearing an inscription in Latin, and beneath it a lower panel with the date enclosed in a medallion. The whole pattern is filled with lozenges, wheat sheaves, stars, and tulips (Plate 54).

The decay of this simple art was accelerated when the American smelters found that they could produce stove-pipes, which made possible the casting of six-plate stoves and later of ten-plate stoves. The former, standing clear of the wall on iron legs and fired through a fuel door, soon replaced the five-plate stoves, while the ten-plate stove in turn, equipped to bake meat, cakes, pies, and bread, in a very few years made the six-plate stoves also obsolete.[98] In both types the various doors and other openings interfered with decoration, while the usefulness of the new stoves was recognized beyond the limits of German America, where the designs were unfamiliar and the German inscriptions meaningless.[99] Artistic casting continued far into the nineteenth century, but the designs gradually became more mechanical, less imaginative and interesting, until they disappeared entirely.[100]

Forty years ago Doctor Henry C. Mercer, while making his interesting collection of early American implements, ran across a box about a foot long, six inches broad, with several compartments containing several little glass bottles. After considerable investigation he discovered that it was a color-box, used in the German schools a century ago in giving instruction in the art of fractur, or illuminative writing. The longest compartment was for goose-quill pens, and for brushes made of cat hairs. The caked colors in the bottles had been home-made inks and paints, and the glue-like substance the varnish made of cherry-tree gum mixed with water. It was with these crude materials that the

[98]*Ibid.*, p. 69. In Ludwig Miller's *Chronicle of York*, old Elizabeth Holl is shown hovering over a typical six-plate stove standing on four legs and with stove-pipe.

[99]H. C. Mercer, *The Bible in Iron*, p. 107.

[100]*Antiques*, Vol. XXV, pp. 60–63. Walter A. Dyer, "American Firebacks and Stove Plates"; B. F. Fackenthal, Jr., "Classification and Analysis of Stoveplates," Bucks Co. Hist. Soc. *Papers, Vol. IV*, pp. 55–61.

teacher at the log schoolhouse, perhaps by the light of his lard lamp, illuminated title pages, book marks, and song books.[101]

It was a long cry from the Pennsylvania forests of the eighteenth century to the European monastery of the Middle Ages. Yet the art of illuminating hymn books, book marks, title pages, birth-, baptismal-, and marriage-certificates among the Pennsylvania Germans was but a survival, perhaps the last survival in any part of the world, of medieval fractur. And there is an exact parallel between Sisters Anastasia and Iphigenia, bending over their hymnals, quill in hand, in their tiny cells in the Sisters' House at Ephrata, and the artist monk at Goslar or St. Gallen.[102]

The Ephrata illuminations occur on title pages, as single-page embellishments, as decorations at the end of hymns, or on double bars in the music, in the *Zionitischer Rosen Garten, Paradisisches Wunder-Spiel,* and other hymnals.[103] The colors are vivid and various—green, blue, carmine, brown, red. As for the pen-work, one wonders at the patience and care shown in every line. The close affinity between religious and secular art in Pennsylvania is illustrated by the constant recurrence on hymnals of many of the same motifs we have learned to know on furniture, pottery, and stoves—the tulip, the pomegranate, the dove. But the Ephrata sisters worked with a precision and formality which was lacking in the secular artists, while their designs have a predilection to the geometric almost as pronounced as those of the Hüls potters or the Montgomery cabinetmakers[104] (Fig. 26).

Of distinctly inferior quality was the *Taufschein* or baptismal certificate and *Trauschein* or wedding certificate, the work of schoolmasters or of wandering professional penmen. The decorations varied greatly, but the old familiar themes recur over and over again—the bulbous heart, tulips, birds, geometric figures, human figures, scroll-work. The text, which is usually in ornamented German script, not only gives the necessary names, but perhaps a motto. "I am baptised. Even should I die at once, how can that harm me?" we read on the birth and baptismal certificate of

[101] Henry C. Mercer, "The Survival of the Medieval Art of Illuminative Writing," etc., Amer. Philosophical Soc., *Proceedings,* Vol. XXXVI, p. 424.

[102] *Antiques,* Vol. V, p. 136.

[103] *Antiques,* Vol. VII, p. 263.

[104] Eberlein and McClure, *American Antiques,* pp. 252–253, 291–292.

Elizabeth Schupp, "born on the 29th day of October at half past seven in the morning" in the year 1807.[105]

Like other Pennsylvania-German arts, fractur work gradually deteriorated. The early decorations show a freshness in color, a sincerity in the motifs, a skill in execution which are lacking later. The beginning of the end was at hand when the figures were stamped on the paper by a printing-press, leaving to the artist only the task of filling in with colors. This was quickly followed by lithographs where all the quaint German art was

FIGURE 26. (LEFT) DISPLAY INITIAL "G" FROM THE KLOSTER FONT. (RIGHT) A DECORATION FOR CHAPTER ENDS

excluded, as well as all vestiges of the German language.[106] German-American fractur, like the decoration of dower chests, stoves, and pottery, by 1850 had fallen a victim to the mechanical age.[107]

The German love of symbolism and ornamentation found frequent expression in wrought iron—a picturesque weather-vane, a strap hinge, a foot-scraper, a trammel, a wagon-hook, a fork, a meat-hook. Here as elsewhere the heart and the tulip are favorite motifs, the workers hammering them out on the handle of a fork, or welding them to the head and tail of the cock of a weather-

[105]T. Kenneth Wood, in *Antiques,* Vol. VII, p. 263–266.
[106]*Antiques,* Vol. VII, p. 264–265.
[107]H. C. Mercer, in Amer. Philo. Soc. *Proceedings,* Vol. XXXVI, pp. 232–233.

vane, or stamping them on a rest for hot dishes. Of especial interest is the weather-vane of the Bell house, Bethlehem, still flying from its original shaft, after nearly two centuries of continuous service. It shows the figure of a lamb, the pascal lamb of St. John, with a banner perforated with the word "heyl," or salvation, thus symbolizing the carrying of salvation to the four points of the compass.[108]

In wood carving the Germans of Pennsylvania accomplished little to remind us of the elaborate chairs, chests, cupboards and household utensils of the mother country. That among the settlers there were some workers skilled with the knife we know from the wooden moulds for stove plates, from an occasional bit of furniture, and from a few beautifully carved small household accessories, especially spoon racks. In a rack found near Bethlehem, a fine example of the carver's skill, there are four panels divided horizontally by strips each with a handsome scroll, while in the panels themselves are the familiar geometric designs of the circle enclosing stars and whorls. Surmounting the whole is a fan-shaped figure probably intended to represent the rising sun.[109] Not less interesting is the weaving stool of Elizabeth Stauffer, decorated with stars and with tulips and other flowers, and inscribed with mottoes.[110] It is to be noted, however, that the most elaborately carved bits of furniture are usually quite small, such as might conveniently have been brought over from Germany, and so may be representative of German rather than Pennsylvania art.

Surveying Pennsylvania-German art as a whole, and giving full credit for the rather remarkable body of accomplishment, one is struck by its plainness, crudeness, and meager output as compared with the peasant art of Germany and northern Switzerland. The living-room of a Berks farmer might boast an inlaid grandfather clock, a painted chest, a few bits of slip ware, perhaps an illuminated birth certificate hung on the wall, but it lacked the richness of the German *Bauernstube* in which almost every object bore evidence of the decorator's art. This, of course, is ex-

108Albert H. Sonn, *Early American Wrought Iron,* Vol. III, Plate 248, Fig. 1.
109Wallace Nutting, in *Antiques,* Vol. VII, p. 313.
110Wallace Nutting, *Pennsylvania Beautiful,* p. 221.

plained by conditions in America. In the eager desire to conquer nature, to acquire wealth—to erect barns and residences, build up a stock of cattle, cultivate the wide fields—the time which could be spared for fancy metal work, wood carving, and the painting of furniture was limited indeed. True, the professional craftsmen showed by many fine examples that they were quite capable of imitating the most complicated decorations, but in America labor, especially skilled labor, was dear. One wonders whether this was not at the bottom of the quarrel between the York cabinetmaker George Adam Gosler and a certain Mr. Bailey for whom he made a grandfather clock case. Ludwig Miller tells us that when Bailey refused to pay the price charged by Gosler, the latter "took his hatchet and cut the case all in splinters."[111]

FIGURE 27. GOSLER SMASHES HIS CLOCK-CASE

It is not the crudeness nor the meagerness of the output of Pennsylvania-German art which occasions surprise, but its vigor and persistence. Despite frontier conditions, labor costs, isolation from Germany, contact with other nationalities, and the substitution of farm life for the community life of the agricultural community, it kept doggedly upon its own way. Nothing reveals more strikingly the virility of German peasant traditions, the deep imprint upon the soul of the German immigrant of many generations of ancestors who had spent their humble lives under the spell of the Rhine valley or the mountains of Switzerland. Inheriting their deep piety, their sense of kinship with nature, their superstitious fears, their homely virtues, their love of simple beauty, they continued for a century and a half to give expression to them through their peasant art.

Despite the gradual deterioration of this art, it died out in

[111]Ludwig Miller, *A Chronicle of York.*

America in many instances no earlier than in Germany, and it died out for the same reason—the killing competition of factory-made goods. The time came when the potter could no longer compete with cheap crockery, when the cabinet-maker yielded to machine-made furniture, when the simple five-plate stove was superseded by the oven and eventually the furnace. And with the production of the last Pennsylvania bit of fractur, the last slip pie plate, the last dower chest, the last decorated stove-plate, there snapped one strand in the rope which bound the German-American to his past, the valleys of the Susquehanna, the Lehigh and the Schuylkill with the middle Rhine and the mountains of Switzerland.

CONCLUSION

IT IS said that when a man is drowning the panorama of his entire life passes before him, and the experiences of many years are compressed into a few minutes. The transplanting of old cultures and their development in a new country give us a similarly telescoped view of the processes which create civilization. These forces are in operation in even the most static of societies. Although few would turn to England to illustrate the operation of the melting-pot, we know that the centuries have brought many foreign strains to the Anglo-Saxon stock, Danish, Norman, Scotch, Flemish, Huguenot. Local conditions, so important a factor in shaping new civilizations, have operated powerfully although much more slowly upon the old, perhaps through the depletion of forest areas, perhaps by the draining of marsh lands, perhaps because of the choking up of harbors with sand or river silt, perhaps by the discovery of mineral deposits. Just as the colony reshapes its life by contact with the mother country, so the cultures of the older nations are affected, although usually less profoundly, by contact with the civilizations of other countries. The architects everywhere acknowledge their debt to Italy, the writers of many lands to Shakespeare; American inventions are transforming the world.

But the founding of colonies, the uprooting of groups of people from their old soils and replanting them in entirely different environments, give us an especially favorable opportunity to study the forces which create and remould civilizations, for the processes which in Europe often cover centuries, unfold themselves before our eyes in a decade or two. The agricultural village of the Rhine valley, dating back to the early Middle Ages, vanished in German Pennsylvania like ice before the sun; the occasional shifting of populations in medieval and modern Europe, important though they were, created in all no greater cultural crosscurrents than the mingling of Dutch, Germans, English, New Englanders, Scotch, Swedes on the soil of colonial New Jersey;

the gradual rise in wages in England during the fourteenth and fifteenth centuries was more than matched by the mere migrating of the worker from Europe to America. In other words the study of the transit of civilizations is like viewing a motion picture of the growth of plant life, in which the changes are made obvious by the accelerated speed of the reel.

The principles illustrated by the founding and development of the Middle Colonies are applicable not only to New England and to the South, but to colonies in other parts of the world and in other ages. We can trace them in Mexico, in Peru, in New Zealand, in South Africa, even in the colonies of ancient Greece. But though the principles are always the same, their relative importance and the conditions under which they operate vary greatly. In the territory embraced within the present United States the melting-pot has rejected the aborigines, in certain countries of Latin America the blood is predominantly Indian; in one colony the life of the mother country may be largely duplicated, in another profoundly changed.

But nowhere can the founding of a civilization be studied to greater advantage than in the Middle Colonies. In New England the people were not only chiefly of English stock, but most of them came from the same part of England, from the same social class and were almost entirely of one religious belief. For this very reason New England offers unique problems in the transit of culture, but its early history does not illustrate so well as that of New York, or New Jersey, or of Pennsylvania some of the chief factors in the creation of American civilization. In the Chesapeake Bay region we have the opportunity to view the transformation of English life under the influence of the tobacco plantation, but the melting-pot was inactive there too until the eighteenth century when Germans and Scotch-Irish crossed over the Potomac from Maryland and pushed up the Shenandoah valley. On the other hand, in the Middle Colonies the heterodox character of the population, the diversity of economic conditions, the isolation of certain racial groups from their mother countries, create the perfect laboratory for observing a new civilization in the process of formation. We see the Dutchmen of Stuyvesant's time duplicating in the Hudson valley so far as they could the life of Holland, building their towns on the model of Amsterdam and Utrecht, establishing Dutch law, Dutch customs, the Dutch Reformed Church, absorbing into their population Flemings, Walloons, Germans, and English; then we see them under English rule struggling vainly to retain their language, their religion, their customs, the purity of their blood. We look on with interest as the Palatine tries to live on the banks of the Susquehanna and the Lehigh the life to which he had been accustomed in the Rhine valley. We see him gradually discard his peasant costume, his Frankish court with its characteristic farm buildings, his agricultural village, his peasant art; we see him clinging to his religion, his language, to some extent to his customs and his superstitions. We witness the first intersectional migration in British America, find that it is governed by the same laws as those which govern the transit of civilization from one country to another, and secure valuable light upon the vast movements of population within the United States in the eighteenth and nineteenth centuries. We look on as Penn makes his noble experiment upon the banks of the Delaware, and trace it through its vicissitudes to its end during the American Revolution.

Throughout we must bear in mind that what we are witnessing is no less than the founding of the United States. After all, the founders of the nation were the pioneers of the seventeenth century rather than the patriots who declared our independence and made it good upon the field of battle, or the framers of our Constitution or the men who put it into successful operation. However important was the work of Washington, Madison, Jefferson, Hamilton, in giving unity, strength and direction to America, they built on the foundations laid by their grandfathers and great grandfathers. In fact it is not too much to say that American civilization had taken on its definite form, the form in essentials that it has today, before these men were born. Isolation, the wealth of natural resources, the high value put upon labor, the melting-pot had been at work for a century and a half when Congress assembled in the old Pennsylvania State House to declare the Americans an independent people.

It was these forces which endowed the Americans with their love of freedom, their self-reliance, their optimism, their desire for democracy which in turn made political independence possible. After all, the first and most important declaration of independence was that expressed by the action of individual Englishmen in leaving England to settle in America. They made a further step towards independence when they reared their houses, produced their own food, made their own clothes, when they organized distinctly American churches, created regional architectural types, developed governments differing in many respects from that of England, devoted their fields in part to tobacco, Indian corn and other American crops, discarded intensive for extensive agriculture, mingled their blood with that of Germans, Dutch, Scotch-Irish, Swiss.

As we look back to the little colonies stretched out along the Atlantic coast or creeping timidly up the deeper river valleys, weak, disunited, dreading the Indian, the French and the Spaniard, lost as it were in the vast American forest, dependent on Europe for existence, it is difficult to realize that they constituted the foundation on which was built the United States. It would have been even more difficult for Sir William Berkeley or John Winthrop or William Penn to peer through the veil of the centuries to envisage the America of today with its teeming millions, its agricultural expanses, its great cities, its network of railways and concrete roads, its wealth, its power, its accomplishments in education, science, literature and art. Yet the America of today is in essentials merely colonial America grown large. Just as it is necessary in studying a great cathedral or temple to examine its foundation to ascertain its strength, its proportions, the materials of which it is made, so we cannot understand the United States without a knowledge of the principles which governed the founding of American civilization.

INDEX

INDEX

INDEX

INDEX

INDEX

INDEX

INDEX

INDEX

INDEX

INDEX